'This book is the best and most detailed thing ever written about the Freud brothers who emigrated to England, their businesses and families, and their important relationship with Sigmund Freud. Roger Willoughby has devoted more than a decade to researching the British branch of the Freud family. And he has uncovered things that Freud biographers have laboured in vain to research for decades. Highly recommended!'

Christfried Tögel, editor of the *Sigmund Freud Gesamtausgabe*, the first complete Freud edition in 23 volumes, and author of *Sigmund Freud 1856–1939: A Biographical Compendium*

'A fascinating, evocative, and enlightening portrayal and study of many aspects of Freud's history not clearly laid out before. The phrase in the title 'lost lives' touches both loss and gains in the vicissitudes of Freud's history and makeup. That he would die in England on Yom Kippur a year after seeking safety in England keeps the mystery of his life open and in this book lives and character of the Freud family sparkle in depth and richness'.

Michael Eigen, psychoanalyst, author of *The Psychotic Core*, *The Mystical Psychoanalyst*, *Feeling Matters*, and *Bits of Psyche*

'Willoughby has dug deep and brought us lost shadows behind Freud – and now, not so lost. No individual exists outside his context. This extensively researched history places Freud within forgotten elements of his family. His family was the setting from which the Oedipal world of early psychoanalysis sprang and which has demanded the willing and unwilling review of human nature in the twentieth century. In other words, no man is an island outside the spreading ocean of his original family. There could be no more relevant context in which to place Freud. And this book contributes a well-researched aim into the heart of psychoanalysis itself'.

R D Hinshelwood, Emeritus Professor of Psychoanalysis, University of Essex, Fellow of the British Psychoanalytical Society, founder of *Psychoanalysis & History*, and author of *A Dictionary of Kleinian Thought* amongst other books

'In this very interesting book, Roger Willoughby uses newly available archives to relate the history of Freud's "English" family in depth. Settling in Manchester, Emmanuel and Philipp Freud became importers of fancy goods – haberdashery, perfumes, trinkets, fabrics – and integrated perfectly, each in their own way, into the English Jewish bourgeoisie. Freud visited them twice, in 1875 and 1908. Willoughby hypothesizes that Freud's links with Britain materialized through his relationship with his brothers, giving rise to his Anglophilia and to his admiration for the constitutional monarchy. This attachment would partly explain why Freud chose, in 1938, to go into exile in London, city of the superego, symbol of a liberal regime conducive to the development of psychoanalysis. From a historiographical point of view, the author relies on modern principles of a study of 'minor lives' or anonymous existences, generally repressed by official history. Here is a work which testifies to the richness of studies devoted to Freud over the past twenty years'.

Élisabeth Roudinesco, Head of Research in History at the
Université de Paris VII-Diderot, psychoanalyst, and author of
Jacques Lacan & Co and Freud: In His Time and Ours

'This outstanding study of the "English" Freuds is long overdue. It provides detailed insight from *inside* Freud's family about the master's personal life as well as background to his own dreams. We encounter the great psychoanalyst in the heart of both his Austrian and English families. There is, as added bonus, a rich account of the distinguished visitors and patients seen during his last days in London'.

Ross M Skelton, Professor of Philosophy and Psychoanalysis (Emeritus),
Trinity College Dublin and Editor-in-Chief of The Edinburgh International
Encyclopaedia of Psychoanalysis

'Biography often creates protagonist-giants trampling their contemporaries. John Freud, Sigmund's infant playmate, vanished so mysteriously from the historical record that certain fantasists could even argue Freud had killed him. In a sense Freudian historiography has done just that. By dint of intense and wide-ranging research, Roger Willoughby has finally managed to sketch John's actual story – and thus restore him to life. On a wider scale Willoughby's book maps out the web of relationships between Freud and his Manchester relatives – his half-brothers, Emanuel and Philipp and their families. Willoughby has not only traced as much of their history as can be recuperated from the archival records, he also unearths their previously ignored influence on Freud's character and work throughout his life. What makes this research remarkable is its passion to reclaim for history neglected figures who have hitherto been treated as mute bystanders. Willoughby asserts their value and agency. The Freuds of Bloom Street, Manchester, bear comparison with Joyce's Leopold Bloom: in Willoughby's telling they are all accorded the respect due to the common man, the real 'hero' of our anti-heroic culture'.

Michael Molnar, ex-Director of the Freud Museum, London, author of Looking
Through Freud's Photos and editor of The Diary of Sigmund Freud 1929–1939

'Roger Willoughby has written a fascinating and absorbing narrative of Freud's 'British family', and its enduring presence in his life and work. *Freud's British Family* holds the promise of deepening our appreciation of how Freud's psychoanalytic thought reflected his lived experiences with the Freud "families" he came to know in Manchester, Vienna, and Freiberg. In focusing on Freud's British family, the author has made a genuinely new contribution to Freud biography and the historiography of psychoanalysis'.

Nellie L. Thompson, New York Psychoanalytic Society and Institute,
editor of 100 Years of the IPA: The Centenary History and
Play, Gender, Therapy: Selected Papers of Eleanor Galenson

Freud's British Family

Freud's British Family presents ground-breaking research into the lives of the British branch of the Freud family, their connections to the founder of psychoanalysis, and into Freud's relationship to Britain.

Documenting the complex relationships the elder Freud brothers had with their much younger brother Sigmund, *Freud's British Family* reveals the significant influence these hitherto largely forgotten Freuds had on the mental economy of the founder of psychoanalysis. Roger Willoughby shows how these key family relationships helped shape Freud's thinking, attitudes, and theorising, including emerging ideas on rivalry, the Oedipus complex, character, and art. In addition to considering their correspondence and meetings with Freud in continental Europe, the book carefully documents Freud's own visits to his brothers and to Britain in 1875 and again in 1908. *Freud's British Family* concludes with a discussion of Freud's final 15 months in London after he left Nazi Vienna as a refugee. *Freud's British Family* offers a rich, contextualised understanding of the sibling, familial, and socio-cultural ties that went into forming the tapestry of psychoanalysis.

Freud's British Family will be of great interest to psychoanalysts and psychotherapists in practice and in training, and to scholars of the history of psychoanalysis, twentieth century history, psychosocial studies, and Jewish studies.

Roger Willoughby is a clinical psychologist, historian, academic, and writer. He is a Fellow of the Royal Historical Society and holds doctorates in psychoanalytic studies from the University of Kent and University of Oxford. He is a founder and co-editor of historiesofpsychoanalysis.com.

History of Psychoanalysis
Series Editor Peter L. Rudnytsky

This series seeks to present outstanding new books that illuminate any aspect of the history of psychoanalysis from its earliest days to the present, and to reintroduce classic texts to contemporary readers.

Other titles in the series:

Theories and Practices of Psychoanalysis in Central Europe
Narrative Assemblages of Self Analysis, Life Writing, and Fiction
Agnieszka Sobolewska

Sigmund Freud and his Patient Margarethe Csonka
A Case of Homosexuality in a Woman in Modern Vienna
Michal Shapira

Sigmund Freud, 1856–1939
A Biographical Compendium
Christfried Toegel

The Marquis de Puysegur and Artificial Somnambulism
Memoirs to Contribute to the History and Establishment of Animal Magnetism
Edited and translated by Adam Crabtree and Sarah Osei-Bonsu

The Subversive Edge of Psychoanalysis
David James Fisher

Freud's British Family
Reclaiming Lost Lives in Manchester and London
Roger Willoughby

For further information about this series please visit https://www.routledge.com/The-History-of-Psychoanalysis-Series/book-series/KARNHIPSY

Freud's British Family

Reclaiming Lost Lives in Manchester
and London

Roger Willoughby

LONDON AND NEW YORK

Designed cover image: Front cover image design by Roger Willoughby and Robert J Scarlett

First published 2025
by Routledge
4 Park Square, Milton Park, Abingdon, Oxon OX14 4RN

and by Routledge
605 Third Avenue, New York, NY 10158

Routledge is an imprint of the Taylor & Francis Group, an informa business

© 2025 Roger Willoughby

The right of Roger Willoughby to be identified as author of this work has been asserted in accordance with sections 77 and 78 of the Copyright, Designs and Patents Act 1988.

All rights reserved. No part of this book may be reprinted or reproduced or utilised in any form or by any electronic, mechanical, or other means, now known or hereafter invented, including photocopying and recording, or in any information storage or retrieval system, without permission in writing from the publishers.

Trademark notice: Product or corporate names may be trademarks or registered trademarks, and are used only for identification and explanation without intent to infringe.

British Library Cataloguing-in-Publication Data
A catalogue record for this book is available from the British Library

ISBN: 978-1-032-65201-6 (hbk)
ISBN: 978-1-032-65198-9 (pbk)
ISBN: 978-1-032-65202-3 (ebk)

DOI: 10.4324/9781032652023

Typeset in Times New Roman
by Apex CoVantage, LLC

But the iniquity of oblivion blindely scattereth her poppy, and deals with the memory of men without distinction to merit of perpetuity . . . Who knows whether the best of men be known? Or whether there be not more remarkable persons forgot, then any that stand remembred in the known account of time, with the favour of the everlasting Register? The first man had been as unknown as the last, and Methuselah's long life had been his only Chronicle.
– Sir Thomas Browne, *Hybriotaphia, Urn Burial*

The tradition of all dead generations weighs like a nightmare on the brains of the living.
– Karl Marx, *The Eighteenth Brumaire of Louis Bonaparte*

Contents

List of Images   *xii*
List of Charts   *xiv*
Acknowledgements   *xv*
List of Abbreviations   *xvii*

Introduction   1

1   **The Freud family: sites of belonging, imagination, and diaspora**   7
     Introduction 7
     Freud and his family: composition, relationships, and revenants 7
     Farewell to Freiberg 16
     Reflections 21

2   **Settling in Britain: kinship, social networks, and material enterprise**   29
     Introduction 29
     Establishing lives in Britain 29
     A letter from Vienna 33
     A Scandal in Vienna: Uncle Josef and the counterfeit roubles 34
     Reflections 36

3   **Emanuel's trilogy of loss, pain, and relocation**   41
     Introduction 41
     From hopes to adversity and loss, 1865–1870 41
     Vienna and Die Räuber *43*
     Moving to the suburbs 45
     Reflections 47

4 'Talking, walking, eating and drinking': Freud's 1875 visit to Britain   50
Introduction 50
Freud in Manchester 51
From a seahorse on the seashore to the primal scene 55
Heading home with indelible impressions 59
Reflections 61

5 Emanuel in everyday life 1875–1907: identity, art, and pathology   65
Introduction 65
Naturalisation and the vicissitudes of life, 1877–1882 66
The Leipzig-Dresden meeting: freud, physiognomy, and art 67
The Vienna family conference and a 'neuropathological taint' 74
Tending sibling networks 76
Reflections 82

6 From an 'insignificant little man' to a Joycean hero: Philipp Freud's journeys   88
Introduction 88
Philipp's new start 89
Philipp's Freud & Co: making a go of it 92
The end of days 93
Reflections 99

7 Freud's 1908 visit to Britain   104
Introduction 104
Freudian meetings in Salzburg 104
A journey interrupted and a wish fulfilled 106
Freud at the seaside 108
Freud does London 111
Reflections 118

8 Savigny Platz to Platt's Siding: Emanuel's final journeys   123
Introduction 123
Savigny Platz, Berlin 123
Southport: the declining years 125
Death at Platt's Siding 132
Reflections 134

9 Freud's British nephews: Sam and John   138
Introduction 138
'I know so little about you': Sam and Freud 138
The (dis)appearance of John Freud 150
Reflections 155

10	**Berggasse in London, NW3, 1938–1939**	163

Introduction 163
A negotiated exit 164
Arrival at Victoria Station 169
39 Elsworthy Road 170
The Hotel Esplanade, 2 Warrington Crescent 177
20 Maresfield Gardens 179
Freud's last patients 188
Freud's last war 190
Reflections 199

11	**Epilogue**	211

Sources and References	*217*
Index	*229*

Images

1.1	Jacob and Amalia's children, including (left to right) Sigismund, Esther (Dolfi), Alexander, Anna, Paula, Marie (Mitzi), and Rosa, in a now lost contemporary oil painting, c.1868	9
1.2	Jacob Freud and Sigismund, c.1864	21
2.1	96 Shudehill, in 1925, the home of Freud & Co between c.1861–1884	30
3.1	Sigismund and Amalia Freud, c.1872, thus taken in between the *Die Räuber* performance and Freud's visit to Manchester	44
4.1	A recreation of 12 Green Street, Ardwick	51
5.1	The Hotel Stadt Freiberg, Leipzig, where Emanuel, Philipp, and Sigmund initially stayed in 1883	68
5.2	*The three eldest children of Charles I*, c.1635, by Anthony van Dyck	69
5.3	*The Meyer Madonna*, c.1526, by Hans Holbein the Younger	70
5.4	*The Sistine Madonna*, c.1513–14, by Raphael	71
5.5	*The Tribute Money*, c.1516, by Titian	72
5.6	61 Bloom Street, Manchester, the site of E Freud & Son, 1897–1941	78
5.7	Freud in 1906, two years before his second visit to England	79
6.1	Jacob Freud, with Morris and Pauline, in September 1883	91
6.2	Philipp Freud, March 1902, by Johannes Dobbel, Berlin	93
6.3	Philipp Freud's matzevah (gravestone), Philips Park Cemetery, Manchester	95
7.1	Max Oppenheimer's portrait of a beardless Freud, 1908	105
7.2	*The Night Watch*, c.1642, by Rembrandt van Rijn	107
7.3	The North Promenade, St Annes, c.1908 (author's collection)	108
7.4	The Raphael Tuck & Son postcard, as sent by Freud to his daughter Mathilde in 1908	109
7.5	Ford's Hotel, 13–16 Manchester Street, London, as it was at the time of Freud's 1908 stay	111
7.6	The Chandos portrait of William Shakespeare, c.1610, attributed to John Taylor	114
7.7	Charles Darwin, c.1883, by John Collier	115
7.8	The SS *Copenhagen*, on which Emanuel, Marie, Bertha, and Freud crossed to the Continent in September 1908	117

8.1	The Promenade, Southport	125
8.2	Bertha and Emanuel Freud, *c.*1910	127
8.3	Jean Martin Freud, *c.*1910, not long before his visit to England	128
8.4	Sophie Freud, *c.*1913, by Max Halberstadt	129
8.5	Anna Freud, *c.*1914, at the time of her visit to England	131
8.6	Emanuel and Marie Freud's matzevah, (gravestone), Manchester's Southern Cemetery	133
9.1	Freud with Heinz and Ernst, 1923	144
9.2	John Froud's grave marker, Highgate Cemetery, London	154
10.1	Mathilde Hollitscher, Sigmund Freud, and Ernest Jones, on the doorstep of 39 Elsworthy Road on 6 June 1938	171
10.2	Freud engaged with his manuscript of *Moses and Monotheism* at his desk in 39 Elsworthy Road in summer 1938	172
10.3	Freud and W Ernst Halberstadt at the Esplanade Hotel in September 1938	178
10.4	Freud's BBC recording at 20 Maresfield Gardens, 7 December 1938	184
10.5	Freud walking in the garden at 20 Maresfield Gardens, 1939	190
10.6	Freud's funerary urn in the columbarium at Golders Green Crematorium	196

Charts

1.1 The Freud family and key relatives   6
3.1 Emanuel Freud and his family   42
6.1 Philipp Freud and his family   88

Acknowledgements

A work such as this inevitably relies on the generous help of many individuals and institutions. Of the individuals who have assisted in one way or another, I wish to particularly single out four friends and colleagues, Alistair Ross, Philip Kuhn, Christfried Tögel, and Joanne Warren. Alistair travelled with me for a decade at the University of Oxford as this story was pieced together. His unflagging encouragement has been both essential and matchless. Philip has been an exemplary friend, generous, entertaining, and supportive, and our discussions on the history of psychoanalysis in Britain have stimulated my thinking considerably. Chris has been unfailingly generous in sharing ideas, as well as his own research and writings, in helping with German-English translations, and in his ongoing modelling of what Freud scholarship can be. For her part, Jo supported the research in myriad ways, as well as reading parts of the manuscript, and reminding me of gaps in the story, particularly of the too often silent or opaque presence of the Freud family women. I am very grateful to them all.

I wish to also thank the following individuals for their help and support in various ways large and small with the present research: Sally Alexander, Gordon Bates, Steve Brinksman, Lucas Bruijn, Tom Buchanan, Gabriele Cassullo, Sharon Colucci, Alexandra Cropper, Neil Cumming, Aleksandar Dimitrijevic, Alan Gall, Rivka Goldblatt, Mary Hitt, Jill Fear, Dean Kirby, Jane McAdam Freud, Vanessa Manley, Michael Molnar, Barbara Murken, Dany Nobus, Lucy Polkinghorne, Élisabeth Roudinesco, Carol Seigel, Nellie Thompson, and Neil Vickers.

Of the institutions and their staff, I want to acknowledge the help and support of Ken Robinson, Joanne Halford, Helene Martin, Saven Morris, and the other past and present staff at both the archives and library of the British Psychoanalytical Society, London. I want to also thank the various staff at the Bodleian Library, Oxford, the British Library, the Crosby Library, Manchester's Central Library, Manchester Jewish Museum, the Department of Special Collections at the John Ryland Library, Manchester, the Library of the National Railway Museum, York, and the Wellcome Library, London, the resources of which have been of immense value. Further thanks go to Patrick Kerwin and the staff of the Manuscript Division of the Library of Congress, Washington, DC, for access to the Sigmund Freud

Papers and allied collections, and to the staff at the Freud Museum, London, for their generous help with archival material.

Work on the project was facilitated in its formative stages by research time granted to me by Birmingham Newman University, where the support of Professor Dave Trotman was particularly important.

Finally, I wish to thank my children for their forbearance, love, and support during the too many years when I have been at times distracted from them by Freud and his family.

Abbreviations

BPAS	British Psycho-Analytical Society
Die Brautbriefe	Gerhard Fichtner, Ilse Grubrich-Simitis & Albrecht Hirschmüller (eds) *Die Brautbriefe, 1882–1886.* 5 volumes. Frankfurt am Main: S. Fischer, 2011–2021.
Freud-Abraham	E Falzeder (ed) *The Correspondence of Sigmund Freud and Karl Abraham*, London: Karnac, 2002.
Freud-Binswanger	Gerhard Fichtner (ed) *The Sigmund Freud-Ludwig Binswanger Correspondence 1908–1938*, New York: Other Press, 2003.
Freud-Eitingon	M Schröter (ed) *Sigmund Freud-Max Eitingon, Briefwechsel 1906–1939*, Tübingen: edition diskord, 2004.
Freud-Ferenczi	E Falzeder, E Brabant & P Giampiere-Deutsch (eds) *The Correspondence of Sigmund Freud and Sándor Ferenczi*, 3 volumes, Cambridge, Mass: Belknap Press, 1992–2000.
Freud-Fliess	J M Masson (ed) *The Complete Letters of Sigmund Freud to Wilhelm Fliess 1887–1904*, Cambridge, Mass: Belknap Press, 1985.
Freud-Freud	Ingeborg Meyer-Palmedo (ed) *Correspondence 1904–1938 Sigmund Freud and Anna Freud*, Cambridge: Polity Press, 2014.
Freud-Jones	R Andrew Paskauskas (ed) *The Complete Correspondence of Sigmund Freud and Ernest Jones 1908–1939*, Cambridge, Mass: Belknap Press, 1995.
Freud-Jung	William McGuire (ed) *The Freud/Jung Letters: The Correspondence between Sigmund Freud and CG Jung*, Princeton, NJ: Princeton University Press, 1974.
Freud-Lampl-de Groot	Gertie Bögels (ed) *The Letters of Sigmund Freud and Jeanne Lampl-de Groot, 1921–1939*, London: Routledge, 2023.

Freud Letters	Ernst L Freud (ed) *Letters of Sigmund Freud 1873–1939*, London: Hogarth, 1961.
Freud-Pfister	Heinrich Meng & Ernst L Freud (eds) *Psychoanalysis and Faith: The Letters of Sigmund Freud & Oskar Pfister*, New York: Basic Books, 1963.
Freud-Rank	E James Lieberman & Gregory C Richter (eds) *The Letters of Sigmund Freud and Otto Rank: Inside Psychoanalysis*, Baltimore: Johns Hopkins University Press, 2012.
Freud-Silberstein	W Boehlich (ed) *The Letters of Sigmund Freud to Eduard Silberstein 1871–1881*, Cambridge, MA: Belknap Press, 1990.
IJPA	*International Journal of Psycho-Analysis*
IRPA	*International Review of Psycho-Analysis*
Life & Work	E Jones *Sigmund Freud: Life and Work*, 3 volumes, London: Hogarth, 1953–1957.
P&H	*Psychoanalysis and History*
Reisebriefe	S Freud *Unser Herz zeigt nach dem Süden: Reisebriefe 1895–1923* [Our Heart Points to the South: Travel Letters 1895–1923], edited by Christfried Tögel in collaboration with Michael Molnar, Berlin: Aufbau-Verlag, 2002
Rundbriefe	Gerhard Wittenberger & Christfried Tögel (eds) *Die Rundbriefe des 'Geheimen Komitees'* [The Circular Letters of the Secret Committee], 4 volumes. Tübingen: Diskord, 1999–2006.
SE	J Strachey (ed) *The Standard Edition of the Complete Psychological Works of Sigmund Freud*, 24 volumes. London: Hogarth Press, 1953–1974.
UOR SC	University of Reading Special Collections

Introduction

What does it feel like to be marginalised, ignored, indeed forgotten? It is only now that the stories of many are being told for the first time. The lives of the majority have been conspicuous by their absence from traditional historical narratives. Omissions include such groups as women, people of colour, and the working classes. A century ago, Virginia Woolf notably highlighted the oblivion of the former, depicting women as 'all but absent from history'.[1] Similarly, although in a very different style, Frantz Fanon contrasted the unrecorded lives of people of colour, denuded of meaning in the colonial situation, with those of the settler, who ideologically became inscribed as the makers (and authors) of history.[2] And the broader point is made by Christopher Hill, amongst others, who commented that 'most of our history is written about, and from the point of view of, a tiny fragment of the population'.[3] It is with such omissions, such silences, such repressions, that the present work is concerned, at least as they are manifest within the early history of Freud and his hitherto unknown British family. With this concern, the aim here is to work towards a repopulation of the early British Freudian habitat and to thus enable a revised reading of that history.

It is rather ironic that such work is needed. Psychoanalysis as a practice is profoundly interested in silenced histories: the lives and stories of those people who have participated in the evolving process have fundamentally shaped its theories, techniques, and texts. Paradoxically however, psychoanalysts themselves, at least according to the eminent historian of psychoanalysis Alain de Mijolla, have tended to be less than interested in the history of their own discipline, a phenomenon which he suggested may be to do with a wish for priority.[4] Arguably, this was sponsored by the received histories of psychoanalysis, in texts such as Freud's own 1914 monograph *On the History of the Psycho-Analytic Movement* and Ernest Jones's three-volume authorised *Sigmund Freud: Life and Work*, which offered largely decontextualised and highly politicised accounts of the development of Freudian psychoanalysis.

One clear result of the so-called Freud wars[5] was that Freud's theories and praxis began to have recognisable antecedents: psychoanalysis did not spring from Freud's mind *ex nihilo*. Lancelot Whyte's *The Unconscious Before Freud*, for example, highlighted these within the European philosophical traditions between roughly 1680 and 1880.⁶ More substantively, Henri Ellenberger's landmark book *The Discovery of the Unconscious*, in contrast to much of the earlier received history of psychoanalysis, situated the emergence of dynamic psychiatry in a long arc of Western cultural processes, within which the Freudian unconscious exists not so much at a point of fundamental epistemological rupture but rather as part of a continuum.⁷ The volume is, as Mark Micale says, a massive contextualisation of Freud's work,⁸ albeit one that privileges a Continental perspective. More locally, Carl Schorske's influential work situated the origins of psychoanalysis in a particular historical and cultural context, *fin-de-siècle* Vienna.⁹ These are important and ground-breaking works.

However, Freud had another much more personal set of sources for his ideas: his own lived experience, his family life, his remembered-reconstructed early childhood and later relationships, his own subjectivity with its interiority of fantasies and dreams, and his family roots in Central European Judaism. Freud's reflections on his own biography, what is often referred to as his self-analysis which began in earnest following his father's death in 1896, substantially shaped his nascent psychoanalytic ideas. It is with part of this cast of characters, specifically Freud's British family – his older half-brothers Emanuel and Philipp and their close kin – that the present book is substantially concerned, into which Freud's three periods in Britain in 1875, in 1908, and finally in 1938–39 are then woven. The resultant story is thus a dual history, in which there is a shifting text and context between the Manchester Freuds and Freud and his family in Vienna, with each at times occupying one or other alternate position. In a more abstract psychoanalytic sense, with their history and emotional connectedness, they form a species of oscillating container-contained relationship,¹⁰ with each for example supporting, nurturing, influencing, cheering-on, stabilising, and changing the other.

The affection and complexities of feeling Freud maintained for his half-brothers and their families in Britain is here revealed for the first time in detail. These relationships influenced his imagination,¹¹ and his thinking and theorising on mental structure and psychodynamics. They would also – in many cases – act as templates for his own interpersonal relationships. Some of Freud's thinking about his British family is emblematic of a family romance.¹²

Elsewhere, Leonore Davidoff brilliantly explores the importance of sibling relationships in Freud's life, concentrating especially on his sisters in Vienna.¹³ However, she largely ignores the previously obscure stories of Freud's British family, an omission which is unfortunate as Freud's early relationships with them were particularly formative. His subsequent reflections on these core relationships became indispensable building blocks during his self-analysis and theorising. Some of these stories, in turn, were used illustratively in Freud's published correspondence and several individuals – notably his nephew John Freud – appear as key characters in *The Interpretation of Dreams* and other works. Through such inscription, Freud's early life has itself become the founding case history of psychoanalysis as a discipline.¹⁴ Its leading actors – notably Freud's British family – continue to exert an active influence on subsequent psychoanalytic generations,¹⁵ with even his more general readers being typically introduced to psychoanalysis through the medium of Freud's biography. And in the present context, Freud's hitherto obscure British family and his own life and times in Britain, has served as an unappreciated access point for a British and wider English-speaking audience to his thinking. One related derivative aspect of this, which is far better known, is Freud's engagement with English literature – a love built on his attachment to his English-speaking British family.[16]

Shifting away from a concentration on the well-trodden 'originary decade [1895–1905] of Freud's science', as Young-Bruehl terms it,[17] the present volume offers a more systemic, relational, and contextual perspective on Freud through its displaced focus onto his older half-brothers, Emanuel and Philipp, and their families, who migrated to Britain in 1859, and lived and worked predominantly in Manchester. This was Freud's forgotten British family, people whose very names have been marginalised and frankly excluded from received narratives about the origins of psychoanalysis.

The depiction of the British branch of the Freud family in the psychoanalytic and historical literature has previously been cursory and often misleading. Ronald Clark describes Freud's half-brothers Emanuel and Philipp as running 'prosperous businesses'.[18] By contrast, Ernest Jones (1879–1958) depicted Emanuel as having achieved 'some success',[19] though he later suggested he was 'never well off',[20] and that Philipp was an 'insignificant little man' who 'is said to have ended up as a pedlar'.[21] Leslie Adams suggested Emanuel Freud's Manchester-based business 'prospered',[22] though his brother Philipp eked out a living as pedlar (as did their father), and the Freud family's lack of cooperation with his research suggested there was 'some desperately disillusioning truth',[23] probably poverty. Such references to the British Freuds' wealth, or lack of it, may be a shorthand characterisation, unsurprising given the dearth of publicly available archival material touching on Freud's British family and the tantalising sense that this absence marks a repression of the history of this branch of the family. Ernst Freud even pointed to this when he noted that: 'Complete collections of letters, such as those to my father's half brother, Emanuel, and his nephew John, *have obstinately refused to come to light*'.[24]

The following chapters give voice to Freud's British family and address the lack of knowledge about them. They deserve to be heard, not only because they have been poorly served until now, but also because of their inherently interesting lives and the light they obliquely shine on Sigmund Freud. Their lives are discussed here comprehensively for the first time using original and often new source material. In the process, Freud too comes across in ways that are different, which is perhaps unsurprising as consideration of one side of a family inevitably highlights unseen or underappreciated aspects of the other. Freud's own time in Britain is revealed with much new detail.

Freud's British family and the differing qualities they represented, helped shape his thinking and their presence is woven through Freud's key texts in an understated way. These relationships subtly illuminated for Freud the importance of key phenomena, such as sibling and familial relationships, play, forms of belief, psychopathology, power and authority, and Oedipal dynamics. They also undoubtedly bolstered Freud's wider Anglophile attitude and values. England, for him, became a locale of imagined intellectual freedom, and fed his ambition to have his ideas disseminated in English and to see psychoanalysis established in Britain, his older brothers' home and what would become his final home as a refugee from Nazi persecution. But for now, let's go back to the beginning of the story.

Notes

1. V Woolf *A Room of One's Own*, edited by M Schiach, Oxford: Oxford University Press, 1998, p. 56.
2. F Fanon *The Wretched of the Earth*, London: Penguin, 2001, pp. 39–40.
3. Christopher Hill *The World Turned Upside Down: Radical Ideas during the English Revolution*, London: Maurice Temple Smith, 1972, p. 16.
4. Alain de Mijolla & Annick Ohayon 'De l'histoire personelle à l'historire de la psychanalyse: une trajectoire', *Nouvelle Revue de Psychosociologie*, 2015, 2, p. 255; see also Mark S Micale 'Henry F Ellenberger and the origins of European psychiatric historiography', in *Beyond the Unconscious: Essays of Henri F Ellenberger in the History of Psychiatry*, Princeton, NJ: Princeton University Press, 1993, p. 48.
5. John Forrester *Despatches from the Freud Wars: Psychoanalysis and Its Passions*, Cambridge, MA: Harvard University Press, 1997; Mikkel Borch-Jacobsen & Sonu Shamdasani *The Freud Files: An Inquiry into the History of Psychoanalysis*, Cambridge: Cambridge University Press, 2012.
6. Lancelot L Whyte *The Unconscious before Freud*, New York: Basic Books, 1960.
7. Henri F Ellenberger *The Discovery of the Unconscious: The History and Evolution of Dynamic Psychiatry*, New York: Basic Books, 1970; Alain de Mijolla & Annick Ohayon 'De l'histoire personelle à l'historire de la psychanalyse: une trajectoire', *Nouvelle Revue de Psychosociologie*, 2015, 2, p. 255.
8. Mark S Micale 'Henry F Ellenberger and the origins of European psychiatric historiography', in *Beyond the Unconscious: Essays of Henri F Ellenberger in the History of Psychiatry*, Princeton, NJ: Princeton University Press, 1993, p. 59.
9. For a useful discussion of this see Carl E Schorske *Fin-de-Siècle Vienna: Politics and Culture*, Cambridge: Cambridge University Press, 1981, especially pp. 181–207.
10. Wilfred R Bion *Attention and Interpretation: A Scientific Approach to Insight in Psycho-Analysis and Groups*, London: Tavistock, 1970.
11. *Life & Work*, 1, pp. 15 and 26; Jacques Szaluta 'Freud's ego ideals: A study of admired modern historical and political personages', *JAPA*, 1983, 31, pp. 161–162.
12. S Freud 'Family romances', *SE*, 1909, 9, pp. 235–242.
13. Leonore Davidoff *Thicker Than Water: Siblings and Their Relations 1780–1920*, Oxford: Oxford University Press, 2012.
14. It is worth emphasising that psychoanalysis as it is understood here incorporates three distinct, though interrelated, entities: it is a theory of the mind, a research activity, and a therapeutic practice. Psychoanalysis is thus not coextensive with a method of treating patients; that is merely one application of the overarching theory, albeit an important one. For a useful discussion on this, see David Bell *Psychoanalysis and Culture: A Kleinian Perspective*, London: Duckworth, 1999, pp. 1–7.
15. Elisabeth Young-Bruehl 'A history of Freud biographies', in Mark S Micale & Roy Porter (eds) *Discovering the History of Psychiatry*, Oxford: Oxford University Press, 1994, p. 158.
16. For a discussion of Freud's engagement with English texts, see S S Prawer *A Cultural Citizen of the World: Sigmund Freud's Knowledge and Use of British and American Writings*, London: Legenda, 2009.
17. Ibid., p. 170.

18 R W Clark *Freud: The Man and the Cause*, London: Jonathan Cape and Weidenfeld & Nicholson, 1980, p. 14.
19 *Life & Work*, 1, p. 15.
20 Ibid., p. 173.
21 *Life & Work*, 2, p. 483.
22 Leslie Adams to the British Library, 21 July 1951, Manchester Central Library archives.
23 Leslie Adams to Sidney Horrocks, 10 February 1952, Manchester Central Library archives.
24 Ernst L Freud 'Preface', in *Freud Letters*, p. vii; emphasis added.

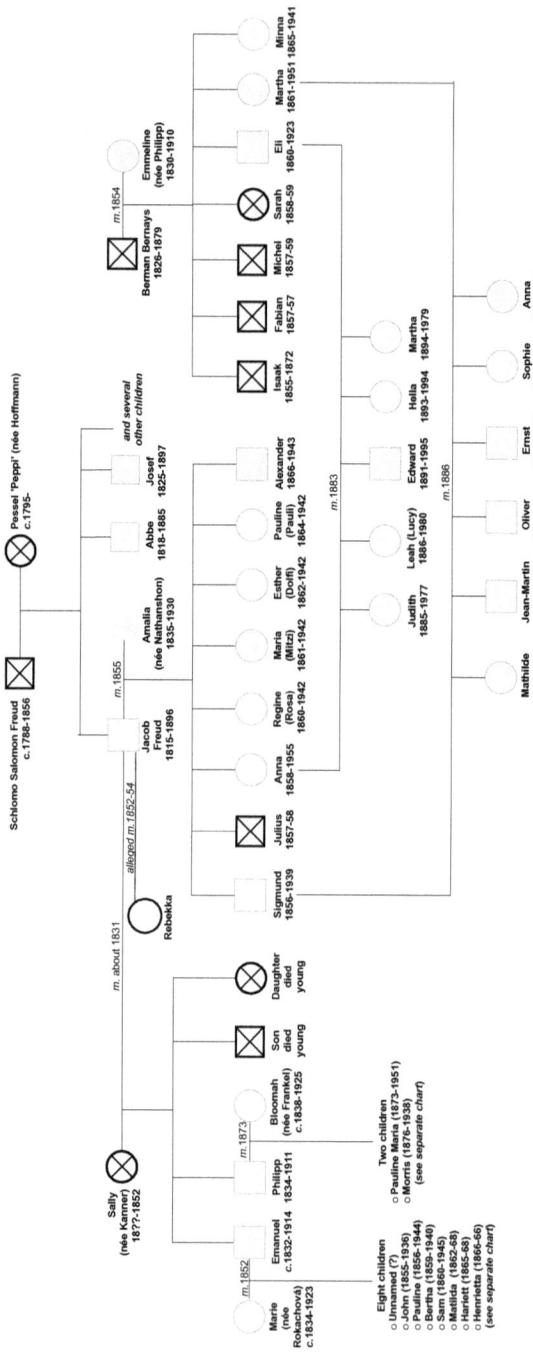

Chart 1.1 The Freud family and key relatives

Chapter 1

The Freud family
Sites of belonging, imagination, and diaspora

Introduction

Family relationships form the matrix from which identity, imagination, and cultural life emerge, the dung heap of stories from which psychoanalysis grew.[1] For his raw material, Freud drew on the narratives of his patients – mainly women – and from the dreams and stories that made up his own remembered life history, as rediscovered and reorganised in his self-analysis. Such accounts must inevitably carry caveats, given the plastic and constructional nature of memory, and Freud's own recollections from the 1890s of events 40 years previously are no exception to this. That said, the present chapter offers a close consideration of Freud's early family history, outlining the family's complex structure, and their various sites of cultural and domestic belonging. The family's life in Freiberg was but one instance of this, after which their dispersal in 1859 would take Freud and a reduced nuclear family ultimately to Vienna and his older half-brothers and their entourage to Britain.

Freud and his family: composition, relationships, and revenants

Born in the family home, a rented upstairs room at 117 Schlossergasse,[2] in Freiberg (Příbor) on 6 May 1856, Sigismund Schlomo Freud was the first child of a middle-aged father, Jacob Freud (1815–1896), and his considerably younger second (or *possibly* third) wife, Amalia (née Nathansohn: 1835–1930).[3] Freud already had two considerably older surviving half-brothers, Emanuel (1832–1914) and Philipp (1834–1911), from his father's first marriage to Sally (née Kanner: c.1815–1852), both of whom were old enough to be his father. As many have pointed out, including Freud himself, Emanuel functioned as an alternative benign, dynamic, and effective father figure in Freud's mental economy. He would also become, as will be emphasised here, an assimilated member of Anglo-Jewry and overtly secular for at least the second half of his life. More obscure in the historical records, Philipp served a shadow function to that of his older brother, being rather more traditional and seemingly forbidding, yet with a liking for jokes at the same time. In contrast to Emanuel, Philipp would retain his religious belonging,

DOI: 10.4324/9781032652023-2

something Freud as a self-declared 'godless Jew' eschewed,[4] yet to which he would nonetheless devote much study, the evolving fruits of which would appear firstly in 1913 in *Totem and Taboo*, followed by *The Future of an Illusion* in 1927, and *Civilization and Its Discontents* in 1930, before reaching their apogee in his final 1939 book *Moses and Monotheism*.

Jacob Freud was born in Tysmenitz, in Galicia, on the eastern fringe of the Austrian Empire (now Tysmenytsia, in western Ukraine), and initially worked in partnership with his maternal grandfather Siskind Hofmann (*c*.1768-*aft*.1848), primarily as a travelling wool and linen merchant, though he also traded in tallow, honey, furs, and other goods.[5] By the late 1840s or early 1850s (during which period Siskind probably died), Jacob must have established himself as a sole trader, being latterly assisted by Emanuel and then Philipp. Coming from an orthodox Hasidic Jewish tradition, Jacob apparently renounced this path in his early twenties,[6] his much later marriage to Amalia on 29 July 1855 being conducted by a Rabbi of the Reform movement.[7]

From the 1850s through to the 1880s at least, Jacob and his immediate family were solidly working class, albeit with more bourgeois aspirations, aspirations which – economically at least – never materialised for Jacob himself. While class status can be a slippery concept, the Freud family's hand-to-mouth economic existence, their inability to sustain a consistent home address, and Jacob's relatively unskilled and unsuccessful working life all point to this conclusion. So do Freud's own accounts of his life, from his childhood through to this early adulthood. Commenting, for example, on a somewhat clumsy and sentimentalised oil painting from about 1868 of Jacob and Amalia's children, Freud dryly noted that 'The painter . . . has graciously overlooked the holes in the soles of my shoes', which his son Martin linked to the family's early poverty.[8]

Freud would privately tell Wilhelm Fliess in September 1897 of the 'severe [financial] worries that robbed me of my youth', while two years later noted 'the helplessness of [my own early] poverty'.[9] In 1930, when more comfortably off, Freud would publicly declare in a footnote in *Civilization and Its Discontents* that: 'Anyone who has tasted the miseries of poverty in his own youth and has experienced the indifference and arrogance of the well-to-do, should . . .[understand and support] endeavours to fight against the inequality of wealth among men and all it leads to'.[10] In the same vein Freud would write in his evocative 1936 open letter to Romain Rolland (1866–1944), 'A disturbance of memory on the Acropolis', of the psychic struggle in going beyond his early paternal and class horizons, and the work of mourning that this triumph necessitated.[11]

Eva Laible had documented Freud's younger brother Alexander receiving a tuition waiver for his *Gymnasium* fees in 1879 and Freud himself receiving grants from two Jewish philanthropic foundations to help fund his medical training in 1878 and 1879, as well as financial support for his undergraduate research visits to Trieste and post-doctoral study in Paris with Jean-Martin Charcot.[12] Independently, Ernst Brücke supported Freud's candidature for a post as an assistant at the Physiological Institute in Graz, tellingly writing that: '*he is a very poor Jew*, who would

Image 1.1 Jacob and Amalia's children (left to right) Sigismund, Esther (Dolfi), Alexander, Anna, Paula, Marie (Mitzi), and Rosa, in a now lost contemporary oil painting, c.1868

Source: Chronicle/Alamy

have to live on his salary, which, incidentally, he would manage easily, given his simple and regular way of life'.[13]

Freud scholars readily acknowledge Jacob's lack of business success. Peter Gay, for example, depicted Jacob as 'generally impecunious', before proceeding to describe him as 'An incurable optimist at least on the surface, he was a small merchant with insufficient resources to cope with the industrializing world around him'.[14] However, in a disguised autobiographical fragment, Freud would later suggest that he 'was the child of people who were originally well-to-do and who, I fancy, lived comfortably enough in that little corner of the provinces'.[15] This family romance (wherein origins are more or less aggrandised), originally identified by Siegfried Bernfeld as pertaining to Freud's imagined early childhood,[16] depicts the Freuds in mid-nineteenth-century Freiberg as a middle-class bourgeois family. Writers have understandably and correctly tended to moderate this claim,[17] yet more often proceed to socially frame the family through the lens of the history of European Jewry and anti-Semitism to the neglect of intersectional factors such as social class and poverty.[18]

Characterologically, Jacob was not a stern forbidding man by any means. Surviving accounts depict him as gentle, discursive, relatively democratic, fond of Jewish aphorisms and jokes, thoughtful, and a committed reader amongst other qualities. His granddaughter, Judith Bernays Heller (1885–1977), lived with him and his family in 1892 to 1893 and later described him as dividing:

> his time between reading the Talmud (in the original) at home, sitting in a coffee house, and walking in the parks. . . . Tall and broad, with a long beard, he was very kind and gentle, and humorous in the bargain. . . . [He] lived somewhat aloof from the others in his family, reading a great deal – German and Hebrew (not Yiddish) – and seeing his own friends away from home. He would come home for meals, but took no real part in the general talk of the others. . . . But what I think struck me most about my maternal grandfather was how . . . he remained quiet and imperturbable, not indifferent, but not disturbed, never out of temper and never raising his voice.[19]

A regular visitor to Freud's apartment at Berggasse 19 during the 1890s, Jacob made a vivid impression on those he met. Freud's son Martin (1889–1967) described how:

> Every member of my family loved Jakob and treated him with great respect. . . . He was terribly nice with us children. He brought us small presents and he used to tell us stories, mostly with a twinkle in his great brown eyes, as if he wanted to say, 'Isn't everything we are doing and saying here a great joke?'.[20]

Freud too loved, admired, and identified with his father,[21] but his relationship with him was complex. From his pre-adolescence, Freud was also wont to construe Jacob as an occasional disappointment, as a less-than-heroic figure, and, as Daniel Boyarin notes, as a somewhat traditional, gentle, eastern European Jew rather than the 'tough' or 'muscle' Jew of western modernity.[22] A key event in that context for Freud came when he was 10 or 12 years old with Jacob's relating to him what we may here call the parable of the fur hat, a story seemingly rooted in his early religious orthodoxy. While walking as a young man one Saturday in Freiberg, Jacob was racially assaulted by a Christian, who, having knocked his new shtreimel off his head and into the mud, shouted 'Jew! Get off the pavement!' Jacob's response was to quietly retrieve his hat from the road. At the time, Freud thought this was 'unheroic conduct on the part of the big strong man',[23] this catalysing his interest in Hannibal and his father Hamilcar Barca as alternative stereotypically 'heroic' models of assertive Semitic masculinity.[24] The gentleness, containment, and equanimity Jacob embodied in the narrative, however, would in due course become better appreciated by Freud and would form an important counterbalance in both his thought and in psychoanalysis, helping to sustain a creative dialectic between dimensional constructs such as activity and passivity, radical and traditional, masculine and feminine. In its clinical practice, psychoanalysis would thus typically give pause to the tough men of action, the Hannibals and Hamilcar Barcas, instead fostering thought and reflection, qualities arguably embodied in the more schlemiel-like Jacob.

For her part, Amalia originated in Brody, in northeast Galicia, though grew up in Odessa and Vienna, the daughter of Jacob and Sara Nathansohn, a solidly middle-class Jewish family of some status in the provinces with a number of rabbis, merchants, and bankers in its ranks.[25] Notionally at least, her health was delicate, Freud noting in 1883 for instance that she was suffering yet again from 'a minor recurrence of her old protracted lung trouble'.[26] Later commentators speculated – not unreasonably – that she suffered from tuberculosis.[27] From 1857, she would thus spend many summers taking *cures* at various spa resorts, initially at Rožnau and subsequently at Baden near Vienna and at Aussee, stays which typically occupied two to three months at a time. During these sojourns, Amalia was often accompanied with an assortment of children and occasionally other relatives.[28] Lacking as we are any clear medical evidence about the actual state of Amalia's health, her spa visits may have been as much to do with her engagement in a fashionable bourgeois leisure activity that was marketed as having supposed health benefits. In this way, somatic complaints might have been a socially legitimised and strategic way of expressing resistance within a largely patriarchal society and securing a degree of privilege, position, and status. Certainly, the visits mostly separated her from Jacob, who as earlier noted came to have a certain marginality in the domestic cut and thrust of the largely female dominated household. They would also often reduce Amalia's childcare, with some of the children being left behind to pursue their own activities. In the Freud household, it was Amalia rather than Jacob who seems to have held centre stage.[29]

While traditional accounts of Amalia, such as that by Ernest Jones, depicted her often vaguely as having a 'lively personality' and as prone to refer to Freud as 'mein goldener Sigi',[30] subsequent authors offered more nuanced and focussed pictures. Peter Gay thus described her as 'a doting, energetic, and domineering mother', a 'formidable personage . . . [who, quoting Judith Bernays Heller] was a tyrant, and a selfish one'.[31] Joel Whitebook convincingly argues that the popular image of Amalia as adoring her first born son was a myth, a defensive idealisation. Most accounts, when examined carefully, paint her as 'a difficult woman: infantile, dependent, demanding, and self-centered'.[32] Moderating this somewhat, Martin Freud suggests Amalia's dominance was part of her distinctive gritty eastern Galician heritage, something which enabled that particular Jewish population to resist the Nazis during the Warsaw Ghetto Uprising and elsewhere during the Second World War.[33] It was a point that did not escape Krüll, Gay, Whitebook, and other commentators.[34]

When Freud was about eight to nine months old, Amalia became pregnant and gave birth to a second son, Julius, events which would have taken Amalia away, psychologically and physically, from Freud. This loss may have been offset by a string of local nursemaids who assisted with his care.[35] They, however, were a mixed blessing as notoriously one or other brought the infant Freud to local

Catholic church services, informed him of some of the workings of sexuality, and committed an alleged theft of Freud family items which reputedly led to one nursemaid's imprisonment following Philipp fetching the police.[36] The latter episode, depriving Freud of his desired nursemaid as it did, seems to have contributed to a developing wedge between himself and Philipp.

Unsurprisingly, Freud responded to his younger brother's arrival with mixed feelings. Writing to Wilhelm Fliess on 3 October 1897 (four decades later), Freud recalled: 'I greeted my one-year-younger brother (who died after a few months) with adverse wishes and genuine childhood jealousy'.[37] In March 1858, when Freud was nearly two years old and Julius nearly six months old, Amalia again became pregnant. The following month, on 15 April 1858, Julius died from a bowel infection.[38] He was buried in grave 417 in the Jewish Cemetery in Weisskirchen, some 35 kilometres west of Freiberg.[39] His passing would form, as Didier Anzieu points out, the 'primal scene' for Freud's own anxieties about death, the psychic pain of which bit with each subsequent loss, fuelling both his capacity to identify with victims and transcend his rivals, at least in phantasy.[40] Writing later to Fliess, Freud described the loss of his brother as having 'left the germ of [self-]reproaches in me'.[41] Freud's feelings of guilt and contrition were inevitably complicated with his mother's own parallel experience of loss. These, compounded by the fact that Amalia was pregnant at the time of Julius's death, further complicating and extending her own mourning,[42] would have rendered her less available to emotionally support Freud through this crucial period. It was, for Freud, a double catastrophe, the death of his brother magnified by his psychically dead mother, a situation insightfully discussed elsewhere by Joel Whitebook using André Green's work.[43] In this context, on 31 December 1858 Sigmund's sister, Anna, was born. Freud would later have no memory of the event and they would never be close.[44]

Freud's elder half-brother Emanuel, born in Tysmenitz on 25 December 1832,[45] probably worked initially with his father, principally as a wool and cloth merchant, operating out of Freiberg, branching out latterly on his own account.[46] As with Jacob, work entailed regular travel, with visits to Vienna for example being noted from February 1853.[47] He had married Marie Rozená (née Rokachová; 1835–1923), a daughter of Ferdinand Rokachov (c.1810–) and his wife Babeth (née Kanner), in about 1852.[48] The couple established their family home at 42 Marktplatz,[49] a few streets away from that of Emanuel's father and relations between the two households were, as Jones declared, 'so intimate that the two families might be regarded as almost one'.[50] They had eight children together, though only four survived to adulthood.[51] The identity of *one* of the children, most probably their first, who seemingly died in infancy, is unknown, its brief existence being only documented on the 1911 English census, which gathered more data than previous versions. The absence of this child (a) from earlier British census returns and (b) from UK birth or death registration indexes, suggests the child was born and died while the family were living in Freiberg or elsewhere in continental Europe, presumably sometime during 1852 to 1854 or just possibly in 1857.

By the time of Freud's birth, Emanuel and Marie had one surviving son, Johann, who had been born in Freiberg on 13 August 1855.[52] A daughter, Paulina, was also born there on 20 November 1856, when Freud was seven months old. Emanuel and Marie's third *known* (but more probably fourth) child, Bertha, was born on 22 February 1859 in Freiberg, the last member of the extended Freud family to be born there before their exodus and dispersal. Of these children, Johann, or John as he later became known, was Freud's closest companion for his first three years,[53] while Paulina occupied a slightly more distant though significant position.

In writing of John, Freud emphasised the importance of this early friendship, its alternating emotional tones, particularly of affection and aggression, providing him with an early iteration of a pattern that would endure throughout his life. In 1897, Freud thus told Fliess that:

> I have also long known the companion of my misdeeds between the ages of one and two years; it is my nephew, a year older than myself, who is now living in Manchester. . . . The two of us seem occasionally to have behaved cruelly to my niece, who was a year younger. The nephew and this younger brother [Julius] have determined, then, what is neurotic, but also what is intense, in all my friendships.[54]

Freud took up his involvement with John in more detail in *The Interpretation of Dreams*, especially in Chapter 6 in his discussion of the 'Non Vixit' dream, writing that:

> Until the end of my third year we had been inseparable. We had loved each other and fought with each other; and this childhood relationship, as I have already hinted above, had a determining influence on all my subsequent relations with contemporaries. Since that time my nephew John has had many re-incarnations, which revived now one side and now another of his personality, unalterably fixed as it was in my unconscious memory. There must have been times when he treated me very badly and I must have shown courage in the face of my tyrant.[55]

Generalising this pattern, Freud went on to write that:

> I have already shown how my warm friendships as well as my enmities with contemporaries went back to my relations in childhood with a nephew who was a year my senior; how he was my superior, how I early learned to defend myself against him, how we were inseparable friends, and how, according to the testimony of our elders, we sometimes fought with each other and – made complaints to them about each other. All my friends have in a certain sense been re-incarnations of this first figure . . .: they have been *revenants*. My nephew himself re-appeared in my boyhood [during 1870], and at that time we acted the parts of Caesar and Brutus together.[56] My emotional life has always insisted that I should have an intimate friend and a hated enemy. I have always been

able to provide myself afresh with both, and it has not infrequently happened that the ideal situation of childhood has been so closely reproduced that friend and enemy have come together in a single individual – though not, of course, both at once or with constant oscillations, as may have been the case in my early childhood.[57]

Freud saw in his early relationship with John the original developmental template, through which core dynamic features of subsequent relationships were shaped. With the latter as revenants of his relationship with John, Freud here articulates the importance of his own sustained transference or projection of his own dynamic memory of John onto others.

In his correspondence with Fliess, Freud alluded to his 'adverse wishes and genuine childhood jealousy' towards Julius (albeit without naming him to Fliess, a significant act in itself) and pairs him with John as the twin sources of both vitality and the neurotic in his friendships.[58] This coupling is undone in *The Interpretation of Dreams*, wherein Julius is erased from the public narrative and the developmentally later tales of John take centre stage. Not only are the encounters with John thus privileged, but they promote a preferred public narrative of Freud as the underdog with which heroic identifications assist him in coping with his 'tyrant'. With Julius by contrast, Freud was the older boy, the 'tyrant', feeling – if not acting on – cruel jealous thoughts towards him. Freud thus occupied both positions, victim and tyrant with John and Julius respectively.[59] However, with Julius silent in *The Interpretation of Dreams*, Freud symbolically occupies Julius's position as victim (although he, unlike Julius, survives). Some of Freud's very early feelings towards his dead younger brother thus may be manifest in John, while Freud himself incarnates the resurrected Julius.[60] History is thus layered for Freud, with the present on the past, relations being reversible, and fantasy suffusing reality.

With Paulina, Freud recalled her presence in a screen memory which also involved himself and John playing. This arose during the course of Freud's self-analysis and was reproduced in barely disguised form in his paper 'Screen Memories', completed in May 1899. In stark contrast with the earlier story of his relations with John, Freud occupies the role of tyrant towards his niece, who thus acts as a later iteration of the deceased Julius. The central memory ran as follows:

Three children are playing in the grass. One of them is myself . . .; the two others are my boy cousin, who is a year older than me, and his sister, who is almost exactly the same age as I am. We are picking the yellow flowers and each of us is holding a bunch of flowers. . . . The little girl has the best bunch; and, as though by mutual agreement, we – the two boys – fall on her and snatch away her flowers. She runs up the meadow in tears and as a consolation the peasant-woman gives her a big piece of black bread. . . . [W]e throw the flowers away, hurry to the cottage and ask to be given some bread too . . .; the peasant-woman cuts the loaf with a long knife. In my memory the bread tastes quite delicious.[61]

In discussion with the imagined reporter of this memory, Freud reveals its compound nature. He depicts it as incorporating an amalgam of memories of (a) an adolescent and unexpressed crush he had towards Gisela Fluss, the yellow-dress wearing daughter of family friends in his native Freiberg, and (b) the earlier joint predation on Paulina in the same place, expropriating her better flowers, symbolically deflowering her, and getting the reinforcing material gratification of the bread.

It is a scene that subsequent commentators, from Siegfried Bernfeld,[62] through Ernest Jones, to Barbara Rocah,[63] amongst others, have elaborated on in some detail. Jones's crude and much quoted exegesis took up just part of the scene when he suggested expropriating the flowers represented an 'unconscious phantasy of [Paulina] being raped by [Freud and] John' and that such a scenario pointed to a degree of bisexuality in Freud's gender identity, or – in the words of Jones – that 'Freud's sexual constitution was not exclusively masculine'.[64] David Lotto usefully expands on this, proposing that the trio's early relationship formed a template in which Freud's male (or what he calls 'homosexual') friendship with John was deepened through their combined attack on Paulina. Lotto suggests this dynamic would be later re-enacted by Freud in several triangulated relationships, notably those he had with Fliess and Emma Eckstein and later Jung and Sabina Spielrein. The guilt such sadism caused Freud assisted him in working through his problematic unruly homosexual attachments and making reparation.[65]

What is often missing from analyses of the screen memory is any mention of precursor events with Julius. The offered narrative similarly has Freud as the jealous persecutor, though here the outcome is very different. In contrast to Julius, Paulina survives, while responsibility for her predation is shared (and thus diffused) with Freud's older nephew John, the encounter is perhaps defensively sexualised, and all the key characters comfortably unite to enjoy the black bread, helped by the 'peasant-woman' who turns a blind-eye to the preceding events. As such, it is a more palatable narrative, a form of wish fulfilment or a happily-ever-after fairy tale.

In stark contrast to the 'big strong man' that was his father and the rival attractions of the charismatic Emanuel, for Freud his still-single brother Philipp occupied a very different position in his mental economy. For those two father figures, his actual father Jacob and his fantasised substitute father Emanuel, Freud partly sustained them as childhood ideals through displacing more negative and rivalrous affects onto Philipp. Thus, Philipp was depicted as not only responsible for the supposed removal and arrest of Freud's early childhood nursemaid, but he was also paired as the fantasy husband-lover of Amalia, stealing her affections, and causing her pregnancies.[66] Such displacement preserved both Freud's dependent relationship to his actual (ambivalently) loved father and his fantasy of Emanuel as a desired younger substitute father. Both were left untroubled by perceptions of exclusive and exclusionary relationships, adult sexuality, and ambiguity, phenomena that Philipp was left to carry. Why this should have been so remains a point of contention, though several features made Philipp vulnerable to such projections.

Firstly, he was very close at hand, both geographically and occupationally, to the core family while in Freiberg; Philipp conveniently lived there in a rented room at house 416, just opposite 117 Schlossergasse.[67] Relatedly, he worked closely with Jacob and Emanuel and like them would occasionally have to travel for work.[68] He thus satisfied the proximity criterion seen in what Freud would later call the 'narcissism of minor differences'.[69] Secondly, he was marked out by his personality, Freud later noting how Philipp habitually spoke in an 'elusive and punning fashion',[70] which left his comments prone to being misunderstood by his younger brother. And thirdly, Philipp had in some respects a rather odd physical appearance. Thus, in February 1860 when he was about 23, he was described as: 'approximately 5' tall, with a long face, a curved nose, black-brown hair and, as a particular feature, a wobbly gait. He speaks German and Moravian'.[71] It seems possible, especially given his documented short stature and unsteady gait, that Philipp had a then undiagnosed and unrecognised syndrome or disability.[72] All of this points, perhaps, to phenomena that may have rendered Philipp a target for projections and indeed stigmatisation. Following Freud's early childhood rivalry with him, he would become, for Freud, a marginal figure with whom he would have less connection. That said, although their relationship would lack warmth, it would not be without fraternal obligation or significance.

Farewell to Freiberg

By early 1859 the extended Freud family reached a turning-point in their life together in Freiberg and a decision was made that they would all have to move to live elsewhere, the hitherto close-knit extended family dispersing at the same time. Freud later suggested the move was precipitated by 'a catastrophe' in the local wool and textile market, as a result of which his father 'lost all his means and we were forced to leave'.[73] Previously, he had written in more muted tones that Emanuel and Philipp's move was similarly inspired, their business having experienced an 'unfavourable turn', which 'caused them to move to England'.[74] Adding to this, Jones noted the rise of Czech nationalism and associated anti-Semitism was another motivating factor,[75] and other commentators would propose additional or alternative theories. These included the collapse of an ostrich feather farm in South Africa that Emanuel and Philipp were supposedly involved in,[76] more prosaically helping them evade military service,[77] or more luridly a possible entanglement in a counterfeiting conspiracy. Such additional speculations have so far been without any real evidential support.

By contrast with such possible external reasons, Marianne Krüll puts forward various speculative internal drivers, including the idea that the move was provoked by the fantasy or reality of Amalia and Philipp having an affair, the family's dispersal and relocations being instigated by Jacob to put distance between them.[78] In her acclaimed biography of Freud, Élisabeth Roudinesco dismisses the latter as 'imagined, without . . . the slightest proof',[79] yet imagination is something to be taken more seriously.

Internal drivers were likely to have played a part in the family's action. The decision did simplify what is generally agreed to have been (at least for the three-year-old Freud) a complex and potentially confusing family structure. By sheering-off both Emanuel and his family and Philipp and relocating them at a considerable distance from Jacob's new family with Amalia, this latter family was privileged or reinforced as the core unit while the former were marginalised. Similarly, moving away from Freiberg shifted both groups away from their historical ties there, again reiterating the novelty and primacy of Jacob's now core family with Amalia. These actions would have offered certain compensations for the older brothers, Emanuel and Philipp, such as greater independence and engagement with progressive modernity and possibly capital incentives. The brothers thus stepped aside, with Emanuel in particular ceding his position as Jacob's eldest son in favour of the nascent Freud, the eldest child of Jacob's new family. Elsewhere, Michael Molnar hinted at the obligation this perhaps placed Freud under vis-à-vis his older brother: 'For Freud, it is as if . . . Emanuel, as the real eldest son of Jacob, had consented to transfer his birthright (the father's blessing) to the younger'.[80] With this perspective on the family action, a dynamic of duplication and then replacement (or marginalisation) occurs both within and between systems: the Jacob-Amalia family replace or marginalise that of Jacob-Sally and Freud replaces or marginalises Emanuel. Freud's frequently mentioned 'two mothers' (Amalia and his nursemaid) represents a variant of this,[81] as does his psychic relationship to Jacob and Emanuel. This pattern, as we will see later, would continue within Emanuel's family.

For Freud as a child the decision, though advantageous in certain ways, stacked still further losses on top of that of Julius and his various nurses: he would now lose both his familiar small town, being instead pitched into city life, and his complex extended family with its capacity for emotional containment, being left with a more nuclear family set-up with – as Suzanne Bernfeld describes – 'the inescapable Oedipus-situation'.[82] These further compound losses contributed to Freud's nostalgic view of Freiberg and later pleasure in country pursuits,[83] as well as further reinforcing his existing ties to his half-brothers and their families in Britain.[84] In *The Interpretation of Dreams* Freud would later liken this exodus to a departure from his beloved Rome and acknowledged his envy of his 'relatives who . . . had the opportunity of removing their children to another country'.[85]

Jacob began to collect what paperwork he could in February and March 1859 to help establish his and his immediate family's *bona fides* elsewhere.[86] He set his sights initially on settling in Leipzig in Saxony, despite local legislation there severely restricting Jewish immigration. Arriving there on 9 May 1859 at the start of the Leipzig Easter Fair, Jacob quickly petitioned the authorities for permission for permanent domicile.

Emanuel seems to have accompanied his father to Leipzig, however he soon moved on to Vienna, arriving there by 19 May and staying for a time at the Hotel National in Leopoldstadt.[87] The National had been built in 1848 and was one of the better hotels in Vienna, with central heating, an inner courtyard, a roof garden, and a café which offered a wide range of international newspapers. The next three weeks saw Philipp arrive in Vienna on 29 May and then Emanuel returned along with his family on 9 June, both again checking into the Hotel National.[88] Emanuel and his family were still noted in the hotel on 11 June.[89]

These sojourns in Vienna were a preamble to Emanuel and his family and Philipp's final departure from Freiberg. Whether they entertained settling in Leipzig, Vienna, or elsewhere in continental Europe is unknown. However, given the absence of surviving evidence of them making formal residence applications in such places or securing the types of references Jacob had obtained in Freiberg,[90] it seems less likely that these destinations featured in their thinking. Instead, Emanuel and Philipp were now largely surviving on credit and over the summer of 1859 they raised substantial funds primarily from within the Jewish community for a new start, which would prove to be in Britain. They did this by generating bills of exchange which – intentionally or otherwise – they would default on, with the National and similar hotels perhaps providing reassuring window dressing for such trades.

The brothers thus passed at least seven bills of exchange by the end of August 1859 at various places in the Austrian Empire and neighbouring German states, with a total face value equivalent to 8,096 Austrian florins.[91] This was made up of 4,646 Austrian florins and 2,300 vereinsthalers from the German states.[92] Reports about three of these bills (for 1,500, 500, and 593 florins), failed to note the dates they were originally transacted, though they were the first to result in court proceedings in Neutitschein, when the wool trading company Zeisler and Bretholz sought settlement from Emanuel.[93] At the hearing, on 31 October 1859, the court ordered that Emanuel (who was not present and whose whereabouts were not known) make payment arrangements and they placed a lien on linen, silk, and other goods he had supplied to Gebrüdern Wagschal in Husiatyn and Israel Leib Frisch in Skala-Podilska, small Galician towns some 120 kilometers east of Tysmenitz.[94] These bills of exchange were probably transacted early in the summer of 1859 and predated a bill transacted on 10 July for 2,300 vereinsthalers which Philipp drew in Freiberg and Emanuel passed on, which was due to be paid in Leipzig (hence the German currency) at the end of October. Jacob was also party to this particular bill, perhaps because of his plans to settle in Leipzig. Again, with Philipp and Emanuel defaulting on this bill's payment and their whereabouts still unknown, the Neutitschein court urged the brothers through press notices to arrange settlement.[95] This proved ineffective and in due course Philipp was declared a fugitive and was pursued by the court for fraud.[96] Emanuel drew three further bills of exchange (for 708 florins on 28 July to M Rokach in Freiberg, for 500 florins on 8 August to Constant Liewehr, and for 845 florins on 30 August to S Rokach),[97] which again went unsettled and the possessors sought recompense through the Neutitschein court.[98] With the exception of a portion of Zeisler and Bretholz's claim, none of these proceedings appear to have secured settlements, a failure probably due to the disappearance of the Freud brothers from the Austrian Empire.

Having passed his last bill of exchange on 30 August, Emanuel seems to have hurriedly and quietly moved to Britain, his family and Philipp probably travelling with him at the same time. He did so without terminating the lease on his Freiberg house, his hurried departure being evident in the furniture, linens, and clothing he abandoned there. His landlord, Franz Rjepa, filed a claim for 95 florins and 55 kreutzers back rent and fees with the Freiberg District Court, which was to be adjudicated on 16 April 1860.[99] News of this action seems to have reached Zeisler and Bretholz and they subsequently secured a court order for the sale of Emanuel's remaining possessions, valued at 236 florins 44 ½ kreutzers, to be set against 1,500 florins they were still owed. Emanuel's personal chattels were duly auctioned on 2 July 1860 in Freiberg, with 16 July being reserved for a second auction should any items remain unsold.[100] Whether Zeisler and Bretholz ever recovered any further money is unclear, though Sigmund Bretholz, along with his daughter Anna and a nephew from Czernowitz, visited Jacob in Vienna for several days in a row in mid-June 1873. Their visits, and particularly the 'wise' nephew's company, were pleasant enough, at least as the adolescent Freud would describe them to his friend Emil Fluss at the time.[101]

Meanwhile, back in Leipzig by 2 August, Jacob's initial residence application had been declined, the authorities concluding that his presence in the city 'would not be of such particular advantage for local trade'.[102] It was well over two months since Jacob had made this application and having done so he seems to have shuttled backwards and forwards between Leipzig and Freiberg to organise his immediate family's move to what he hoped would be their new home. Hearing the news of his failed application sometime in early August, Jacob lodged an appeal expanding on his original submission, claiming he was now involved in additional business ventures. On 11 August Amalia secured a passport from the authorities in Brünn/Brno for herself, her children Sigismund and Anna, and maidservant Anna Hrazek (c.1830–), to facilitate their travel to Leipzig, for what was declared would be a 'continuing [i.e., permanent] stay'.[103]

Finally departing from Freiberg, travelling initially by coach to Ostrau, the family caught the train from there to Leipzig, breaking the journey in Breslau for a night or more with Jacob's younger brother Abraham. Freud would later recall passing through the station, where he saw gas lighting for the first time, and the alarming flames 'reminded me of spirits burning in hell'.[104] It was an experience of some significance for the young Freud, being implicated he thought in his subsequent phobia of train travel. The family arrived in Leipzig sometime before 19 August, on which day Jacob received news that his appeal had also been declined. The following day, facing an order that he and his family should leave the city within three days, he lodged a further appeal with the city council, this time aided by a solicitor. In processing this latest application for the council, the city's trade deputation this time reported that Jacob Freud's business interests were not merely inconspicuous (as they had reported with respect to his first application) but ominously added that 'his past makes it seem advisable to protect our place from such a businessman'.[105] What exactly was being alluded to is unclear, but it spelled the end of Jacob's attempt to settle in Leipzig.

On 15 October, Jacob, Amalia, and their immediate family left Leipzig to begin their journey not back to Freiberg but to Vienna, where Amalia's parents lived. Many scholars would later situate this journey as the one during which, spending a night with his mother, his 'libido toward *matrem* was awakened . . . seeing her *nudam*'.[106] This is commonly seen as a root for Freud's theorising of the Oedipus complex,[107] while his descent into Latin for inscribing the maternal body echoes with his contemporaneous Rome neurosis. Freud thought he was two to two-and-a-half years old during this scene, which would have dated it a year prior to the present journey. While this is usually regarded as an error, it may not be so, just as its supposed location in a railway carriage may not be so either. Indeed, the railway carriage assumption appears *particularly* shaky and has led several commentators into extensive revisionist exegeses.[108] For his part, Freud only specifies it was 'on the occasion of a journey with her from Leipzig to Vienna', a report quite compatible with it eventuating during an overnight stop in a town en route.[109]

The present journey took several days and Jacob may have left the main party to conduct business before arriving in Vienna. On reaching the city, Amalia and the children stayed with her parents at their apartment at 726 Leopoldstadt (now 45 Untere Donaustrasse). Whether Jacob also lived there for a time is unclear, but he was noted staying in Vienna at the Hotel National on 10 December 1859, then the Hotel Schröder on 23 December,[110] and subsequently the budget Weissen Ross Gasthof (White Horse Guesthouse).[111] Jacob had raised 2,000 florins through four bills of exchange with Viennese businessman Benjamin Leisorowitz (1810–1889)[112] at some point in 1859 and must have been using this, savings and other credit to both fund his and the family's living expenses and sustain his business ambitions during this period. As 1859 drew to a close, hopes that the radical changes initiated earlier in the year would pay dividends dwindled, a downward trajectory crudely visible in the declining status of the hotels Jacob frequented.

In January 1860 what hopes remained crumbled as Jacob's creditors began to demand repayment. On 24 January 1860, Benjamin Leisorowitz filed a suit with the Commercial Court in Vienna for repayment of the four bills of exchange he held, Jacob's precise whereabout at that point being unknown to the court, he having left the Weissen Ross Gasthof sometime previously. A hearing was set for 23 February.[113] In advance of that, a second creditor, Leopold Hecks, a furrier from Losoncz, initiated bankruptcy proceedings against Jacob in Vienna and the Provincial Court there declared him bankrupt on 17 February 1860.[114] By the time these proceeding had commenced, Jacob had moved to stay with Amalia and the children at his in-laws' apartment. Further creditors were invited to lodge claims with the court by 30 April and a creditors meeting was set for 24 May.[115] What they received then, if anything, is unknown as further papers do not appear to have survived.

Straitened times followed for Jacob Freud and his family in Vienna. While they did manage to move out from the Nathansohns' by mid-March 1860 into an apartment across the Danube canal at 3 Weissgärberstrasse,[116] the family's economic and social situation in Vienna was and continued to be precarious. Jacob's bankruptcy was undoubtedly a major factor in this, being an indelible blot on his business reputation and a brake on future ventures. Nevertheless, as Georg Augusta points out, there were small signs that Jacob still managed to conduct some business and he certainly continued to style himself as a wool dealer into the 1860s. Court notices

Image 1.2 Jacob Freud and Sigismund, c.1864
Source: © Freud Museum, London

highlighted his involvement in purchasing a bill of exchange originally issued in May 1861 and concluding a 5,000 florin 'salt deal' with Theodor Külcher's son in April 1862, neither transaction going smoothly, while Freud commented he was doing business in Russia in 1883.[117] Regular financial assistance came from the Nathansohns,[118] and by the 1880s from Eli Bernays as well as remittances from Emanuel at least. It was clearly a hand-to-mouth existence, underlined by Jacob's name being omitted from Viennese registers of merchants and tax returns. The family's difficulties were undoubtedly compounded by the birth of five further children between 1860 and 1866[119] and the precarity of their situation underlined by their lack of a stable home: Jacob and his immediate family would live in 12 different apartments between 1860 and his death in 1896.[120]

Reflections

Not dissimilar from that of much of the Western working classes, the Freud family story in the nineteenth century is one in which economic adversity was common and sites of belonging were tenuous, their membership of European Jewry aggravating these hardships intersectionally. Restrictive practices and widespread anti-Semitism made basics – such as having a home fixed in one place or the right to work – something that could not be taken for granted for the Freuds. In the context of such precarity and oppression, the family's time in Freiberg may be regarded as an interlude of relative stability, particularly so for Freud and his real and quasi siblings given their then limited perspectives.

The next two decades and more in Vienna would be difficult ones for Freud and his family, marked by continuing struggle and poverty. In this context Freiberg was not the only lost ideal;[121] so too was his relationship with Emanuel, Philipp, and his extended family members. These were not absolute losses however and, with his half-brothers (and Emanuel particularly), Freud as we will see in the ensuing chapters would retain warm attachments which were sustained through correspondence and occasional visits, all of which allowed a sense that theirs might be a road he too could follow one day. Britain, in this context, became Freud's *other place*, a counterpoint to his early grim life in Vienna, somewhere that held out the prospect of acceptance and success, a New Jerusalem.

The watershed period for the family between Freiberg, Vienna, and Manchester was marked with economic failure, displacement, and dispersal, alongside desperate measures by the family to raise capital that in Philipp's case at least resulted in him being sought for alleged fraud. Emanuel was yet more deeply involved, and Jacob to a moderate extent, though both were fortunate to evade the stigma that Philipp acquired. Whether some or all of the bills of exchange the brothers transacted were entirely and intentionally fraudulent is unlikely; certainly, those associated with Zeisler and Bretholz related at least in part to linen, silk, and other actual goods that were being traded. Yet the pattern of defaulting on payment when it was due and of effectively skipping the country with the proceeds inevitably raises serious questions about the brothers' then probity and business integrity. What remains unknown are the real drivers of the brothers and the wider Freud family's actions at this point in time, actions which from a longer-term perspective appear aberrant. And what is equally unknown is whether efforts were made to repay the debts in the fullness of time.

For the Freuds and other Jews, belonging particularly rested on cultural and religious foundations, family and relational networks, investments which promoted survival in such inauspicious circumstances. They also promoted empathic, reflexive, and critical capacities for exegesis and hermeneutic endeavours that would in due course contribute so much to the foundations of psychoanalysis.[122] For Freud, reflecting during his self-analysis on his remembered early experiences with his extended family in Freiberg and later Vienna, was not only one of the key founding acts of psychoanalysis, but also instantiated this cast of characters into the rubrics of the discipline.

Notes

1 In this context, Freud would revealingly refer to his evolving and semi-autobiographical manuscript of *The Interpretation of Dreams* as 'so completely my own, my own dung

heap, my seedling and *nova species mihi* [a new species of myself] on top of it' (Freud to W Fliess, 28 May 1899, *Freud-Fliess*, p. 353).
2 Renamed Zamečnicka ulice since 1918, see R Gicklhorn 'The Freiberg period of the Freud family', *Journal of the History of Medicine*, 1969, 24, p. 42.
3 Jacob's alleged brief second marriage to Rebekka (1825–1854), if it indeed happened, was apparently without issue. For a discussion of this see M Krüll *Freud and his Father*, London: Hutchinson, 1987, pp. 96–97 and 135–137; see also Cesare Romano 'L'enigma di Rebekka Freud', *Psicoterapia e Scienze Umane*, 2018, 52, pp. 215–248.
4 Freud to Oskar Pfister, 9 October 1918, *Freud-Pfister*, p. 63.
5 M Krüll *Freud and his Father*, London: Hutchinson, 1987, p. 92.
6 Freud to A A Roback, 20 February 1930, in *Freud Letters*, p. 394.
7 M Krüll *Freud and his Father*, London: Hutchinson, 1987, pp. 98, 235 and 267.
8 Martin Freud *Glory Reflected: Sigmund Freud – Man and Father*, London: Angus & Robertson, 1957, p. 15.
9 Freud to W Fliess, 21 September 1897 and 21 September 1899, *Freud-Fliess*, pp. 266 and 374.
10 S Freud *Civilization and Its Discontents*, SE, 1930, 21, p. 113.
11 S Freud 'A disturbance of memory on the Acropolis', *SE*, 1936, 22, pp. 237–248.
12 E Laible 'Through privation to knowledge: Unknown documents from Freud's university years', *IJPA*, 1993, 74, pp. 775–790.
13 Ibid., p. 775; emphasis added.
14 P Gay *Freud: A Life for Our Times*, London: Max, 2006, pp. 4 and 10.
15 S Freud 'Screen memories', *SE*, 1899, 3, p. 312.
16 S Bernfeld 'An unknown autobiographical fragment by Freud', *American Imago*, 1946, 4, pp. 3–19.
17 See for example P Gay *Freud: A Life for Our Times*, London: Max, 2006, p. 8.
18 Augusta for example, in an otherwise admirable work, seeks to argue (partly on the basis of the family having a maid servant, which was not an exclusively bourgeois asset, and Freud's school fees, which were settled through unknown means) that Jacob's family enjoyed an at least modestly bourgeois life in Vienna (see Georg Augusta '"Dann kamen die langen, harten Jahre": Zur Situation der Familie Freud nach ihrer Ankunft in Wien im Jahr 1859' ["Long and difficult years followed": The situation of Freud's family after their arrival in Vienna in 1859'], *Luzifer-Amor*, 2015, 28, pp. 125 and 126). Other authors too tend to gloss over the family's substantively working-class life during the decades Freud was growing up, perhaps influenced in so doing by a preferred perception of psychoanalysis as a bourgeois and indeed elitist creation.
19 Judith Bernays Heller 'Freud's mother and father', *Commentary*, May 1956, 21, 5, p. 419.
20 Martin Freud *Glory Reflected: Sigmund Freud – Man and Father*, London: Angus and Robertson, 1957, p. 10.
21 M Krüll *Freud and his Father*, London: Hutchinson, 1987, pp. 109–110.
22 Daniel Boyarin *Unheroic Conduct: The Rise of Heterosexuality and the Invention of the Jewish Man*, Berkeley: University of California Press, 1997, p. 34; see also Paul Breines *Tough Jews: Political Fantasies and the Moral Dilemma of American Jewry*, New York: Basic Books, 1990, and Warren Rosenberg *Legacy of Rage, Violence, and Culture*, Amherst, MA: University of Massachusetts Press, 2001.
23 S Freud *The Interpretation of Dreams*, SE, 1900 [1899], 4, p. 197.
24 Ibid., pp. 197–198; Jacques Szaluta 'Freud's ego ideals: A study of admired modern historical and political personages', *JAPA*, 1983, 31, pp. 157–186.
25 For detailed discussion of Amalia's family background see Georg Augusta 'Die familie Nathansohn', *Zeitschrift für psychoanalytische Theorie und Praxis*, 2015, 30, 3–4, pp. 431–453.

26 Freud to Martha Bernays, 9 September 1883, *Freud Letters*, p. 72.
27 M Krüll *Freud and his Father*, London: Hutchinson, 1987, pp. 117, 148 and 262 note 52; H P Blum 'Reconstructing Freud's prototype reconstructions', *International Forum of Psychoanalysis*, 2015, 24, pp. 47–57; E Laible 'Through privation to knowledge: Unknown documents from Freud's university years', *IJPA*, 1993, 74, p. 775.
28 Josef Sajner documents 24 visits to Rožnau alone between 1857–1899; see J Sajner 'Die Beziehungen Sigmund Freuds und seiner Familie zu dem mährischen Kurort Rožnau', *Jahrbuch der Psychoanalyse*, 1989, 24, pp. 73–96.
29 D P Margolis 'Freud and his mother', *Modern Psychoanalysis*, 1989, 14, pp. 37–56.
30 *Life & Work*, 1, p. 3.
31 P Gay *Freud: A Life for Our Times*, London: Max, 2006, pp. 11 and 505
32 J Whitebook *Freud: An Intellectual Biography*, Cambridge: Cambridge University Press, 2017, p. 34; see also Judith Bernays Heller 'Freud's mother and father', *Commentary*, May 1956, 21, 5, pp. 419–421 and Martin Freud *Glory Reflected: Sigmund Freud – Man and Father*, London: Angus and Robertson, 1957, pp. 10–12.
33 Martin Freud *Glory Reflected: Sigmund Freud – Man and Father*, London: Angus and Robertson, 1957, p. 11.
34 M Krüll *Freud and his Father*, London: Hutchinson, 1987, pp. 116–117; P Gay *Freud: A Life for Our Times*, London: Max, 2006, pp. 504–505; J Whitebook *Freud: An Intellectual Biography*, Cambridge: Cambridge University Press, 2017, pp. 35–36.
35 Václav Buriánek suggests Terezie/Rezi Wittek looked after Freud from at latest 5 June 1857 when he was with his mother at the spa at Rožnov, whilst two other women, Magdaléna Kabátová and Monika Zajícová, are known to have also worked for the family. For a discussion on this and related matters see V Buriánek 'Paradise lost and trauma mastered: New findings on little Sigmund', *International Forum of Psychoanalysis*, 2015, 24, 1, pp. 22–28. A fourth woman, Anna Hrazek, was the only servant with the family when they moved from Freiberg in August 1859; see M Schröter & C Tögel 'The Leipzig episode in Freud's life (1859): A new narrative on the basis of recently discovered documents', *Psychoanalytic Quarterly*, 2007, 76, 1, p. 206.
36 For the received account of this supposed episode see M Krüll *Freud and his Father*, London: Hutchinson, 1987, pp. 59, 121–122, 124, 214, 259n; Buriánek, however, notes no trace of such a crime, trial or imprisonment could be found in local archives: see V Buriánek 'Paradise lost and trauma mastered: New findings on little Sigmund', *International Forum of Psychoanalysis*, 2015, 24, 1, p. 25.
37 Freud to W Fliess, 3 October 1897, *Freud-Fliess*, p. 268.
38 M Krüll *Freud and his Father*, London: Hutchinson, 1987, p. 135.
39 Ibid., p. 135; L Ginsburg & S Ginsburg 'Paradise in the life of Sigmund Freud: An understanding of its imagery and paradoxes', *IRPA*, 1992, 19, p. 298.
40 D Anzieu *Freud's Self-Analysis*, London: Hogarth, 1986, p. 385.
41 Freud to W Fliess, 3 October 1897, *Freud-Fliess*, p. 268.
42 See for example Emanuel Lewis & Patrick Casement 'The inhibition of mourning by pregnancy: A case study', *Psychoanalytic Psychotherapy*, 1986, 2, 1, pp. 45–52.
43 J Whitebook *Freud: An Intellectual Biography*, Cambridge: Cambridge University Press, 2017, pp. 34–42.
44 M Krüll *Freud and his Father*, London: Hutchinson, 1987, pp. 134–135; D Anzieu *Freud's Self-Analysis*, London: Hogarth, 1986, p. 18.
45 See his Naturalisation Papers, TNA ref: HO 45/9428/61301; Emanuel's correspondence with Freud, see Emanuel Freud to Freud, 18 March 1906 and 30 December 1909, LoC ref: mss39990, box 2; English census data; and Emanuel's gravestone inscription.
46 According to Renée Gicklhorn, Emanuel 'took over' his father's business in 1858, though she fails to cite the document that allegedly recorded this (see R Gicklhorn 'The Freiberg period of the Freud family', *Journal of the History of Medicine*, 1969, 24, p. 42). Other historians have failed to corroborate such a claim, which in any event

appears unlikely given the unfolding of the family's business history as revealed in the present chapter.
47 He is thus noted as a Freiberg merchant's son staying in the National Hotel, in Leopoldstadt, in the *Fremden-Blatt*, 9 February 1853, p. 5, being simply described as a merchant the following year (*Fremden-Blatt*, 12 December 1854, p. 6).
48 While the exact date of their wedding is currently unknown, the 2 April 1911 English census states they were married 58 years by that date. Marie was, according to at least one source, born on 6 May 1835 (Christfried Tögel, personal communication, October 2022). See also M Krüll *Freud and his Father*, London: Hutchinson, 1987, pp. 96, 235, and 268.
49 M Krüll *Freud and his Father*, London: Hutchinson, 1987, pp. 104, 105, and 131.
50 *Life & Work*, 1, p. 6.
51 The 1911 English census records Emanuel and Marie as having had eight children, of whom four died (see TNA ref: RG 14/22868).
52 Confirmation of Johann and Paulina's birth dates is reproduced in E Miller *Passion for Murder*, San Diego: Future Directions, 2008, p. 310.
53 John's significance has been widely noted by biographers, beginning with Fritz Wittels. See his *Sigmund Freud: His Personality, his Teaching, and his School*, London: Allen and Unwin, 1924, pp. 15, 19, 45 and 226.
54 Freud to W Fliess, 3 October 1897, *Freud-Fliess*, p. 268.
55 S Freud *The Interpretation of Dreams*, SE, 1900 [1899], 5, p. 424.
56 Jones notes that during this visit, in 1870, Freud and John performed the respective roles of Brutus and Caesar based on Schiller's *Die Räuber*: see *Life & Work*, 1, p. 26.
57 S Freud *The Interpretation of Dreams*, SE, 1900 [1899], 5, p. 483.
58 Freud to W Fliess, 3 October 1897, *Freud-Fliess*, p. 268.
59 These might be conceived as varieties of required and avoided relationships, the latter being kept out of consciousness in order to ward off a calamity; for a discussion of this trio of object relationships, see Henry Ezriel 'Psychoanalytic group therapy', in L R Wolberg & E K Schwartz (eds) *Group Therapy 1973: An Overview*, New York: International Medical Books, 1973, pp. 183–210, especially pp. 191–192.
60 See also Robert Lippman 'Freud's botanical monograph screen memory revisited', *Psychoanalytic Review*, August 2009, 96, 4, pp. 579–595.
61 S Freud 'Screen memories', *SE*, 1899, 3, p. 311; the possible site of this episode and the wider geography of Freiberg is usefully discussed in L Ginsburg & S Ginsburg 'Paradise in the life of Sigmund Freud: An understanding of its imagery and paradoxes', *IRPA*, 1992, 19, pp. 285–308.
62 For a discussion of their collaboration see Harry Trosman & Ernest S Wolf 'The Bernfeld collaboration in the Jones biography of Freud', *IJPA*, 1973, 54, pp. 227–233.
63 Barbara S Rocah 'The language of flowers: Freud's adolescent language of love, lust, and longing', *The Psychoanalytic Study of the Child*, 2002, 57, 1, pp. 377–399.
64 *Life & Work*, 1, p. 12.
65 D Lotto 'Freud's struggle with misogyny: Homosexuality and guilt in the dream of Irma's injection', *JAPA*, 2001, 49, pp. 1289–1313. My thanks to David Lotto for sharing the full unabridged version of this paper. See also C Bonomi *The Cut and the Building of Psychoanalysis, Volume 1: Sigmund Freud and Emma Eckstein*, Hove: Routledge, 2015.
66 S Freud *The Interpretation of Dreams*, SE, 1900 [1899], 4–5, pp. 247–248 and 583–584; S Freud *The Psychopathology of Everyday Life*, SE, 1901, 6, pp. 49–52; Freud to W Fliess, 15 October 1897, *Freud-Fliess*, pp. 27–273; *Life & Work*, 1, pp. 10–11; M Krüll *Freud and his Father*, London: Hutchinson, 1987, pp. 124–128; E Rice *Freud and Moses: The Long Journey Home*, Albany: SUNY Press, 1990, pp. 17–18; L Shengold *'The Boy Will Come to Nothing': Freud's Ego Ideal and Freud as Ego Ideal*, New Haven: Yale University Press, 1993, pp. 35–37.
67 M Krüll *Freud and his Father*, London: Hutchinson, 1987, pp. 104, 105 and 108.

68 Philipp was first noted as a Freiberg merchant staying in the National Hotel in Leopoldstadt in May 1853; see the *Wiener Zeitung*, 19 May 1853, p. 11.
69 S Freud *Civilization and Its Discontents*, SE, 1930, 21, p. 114.
70 S Freud *The Psychopathology of Everyday Life*, SE, 1901, 6, p. 51; see also Freud to W Fliess, 15 October 1897, *Freud-Fliess*, p. 272.
71 *Brünner Zeitung der k. k. priv. mährischen Lehenbank*, 26 February 1860, p. 379.
72 Various underlying conditions might restrict growth, produce unsteadiness, and/or language diversity, such as forms of arthritis, rickets, ataxia, and Silver-Russell syndrome among others.
73 S Freud 'Screen memories', *SE*, 1899, 3, p. 312.
74 Freud to E Silberstein, 9 September 1875, *Freud-Silberstein*, p. 126.
75 *Life & Work*, 1, pp. 13–14.
76 P Roazen *Meeting Freud's Family*, Amherst, MA: University of Massachusetts Press, 1993, p. 37; A Freud-Bernays *Eine Wienerin in New York. Die Schwester Sigmund Freud's erinnert sich*, Berlin: Aufbau-Verlag, 2004, p. 98; M Schröter & C Tögel 'The Leipzig episode in Freud's life (1859): A new narrative on the basis of recently discovered documents', *Psychoanalytic Quarterly*, 2007, 76, 1, pp. 195–196.
77 R Gicklhorn 'The Freiberg period of the Freud family', *Journal of the History of Medicine*, 1969, 24, pp. 37–43; M Krüll *Freud and his Father*, London: Hutchinson, 1986, pp. 140–147; M Schröter & C Tögel 'The Leipzig episode in Freud's life (1859): A new narrative on the basis of recently discovered documents', *Psychoanalytic Quarterly*, 2007, 76, 1, pp. 194–198. No records relating to military call-up have been found for either Emanuel or Philipp in the Czechoslovakian archives or the Oesterreichiches Staatsarchiv/Kriegsarchiv (Chris Tögel, email to the author, 13 May 2019).
78 M Krüll *Freud and his Father*, London: Hutchinson, 1986, pp. 60, 116, 124–128, and 140–147; this speculation is reiterated by various writers, including more recently by Joel Whitebook, see his *Freud: An Intellectual Biography*, Cambridge: Cambridge University Press, 2017, p. 34.
79 Élisabeth Roudinesco *Freud in His Time and Ours*, Cambridge, MA: Harvard University Press, 2016, p. 15.
80 Michael Molner *Looking Through Freud's Photos*, London: Karnac, 2015, p. 81.
81 Freud to W Fliess, 3 October 1897, *Freud-Fliess*, p. 268; J Swan 'Mater and Nannie: Freud's two mothers and the discovery of the Oedipus complex', *American Imago*, 1974, 31, 1, pp. 1–64; H P Blum 'Reconstructing Freud's prototype reconstructions', *International Forum of Psychoanalysis*, 2015, 24, pp. 47–57; V Buriánek 'Paradise lost and trauma mastered: New findings on little Sigmund', *International Forum of Psychoanalysis*, 2015, 24, 1, pp. 22–28; D Knafo 'The significance of the Oedipal in dreams of Sigmund Freud and C G Jung', *IRPA*, 1992, 19, pp. 351–358.
82 Suzanne C Bernfeld 'Freud and archeology', *American Imago*, 1951, 8, 2, p. 115.
83 Ibid., p. 113.
84 S Freud *The Interpretation of Dreams*, SE, 1900 [1899], 5, p. 444. See also R W Clark *Freud: The Man and the Cause*, London: Jonathan Cape and Weidenfeld & Nicholson, 1980, p. 14; J Whitebook *Freud: An Intellectual Biography*, Cambridge: Cambridge University Press, 2017, pp. 48–49.
85 Freud *The Interpretation of Dreams*, SE, 1900 [1899], 5, p. 444.
86 See Sigmund Freud Papers, LoC ref: mss39990, box 13; M Schröter & C Tögel 'The Leipzig episode in Freud's life (1859): A new narrative on the basis of recently discovered documents', *Psychoanalytic Quarterly*, 2007, 76, 1, pp. 196–197.
87 *Wiener Zeitung*, 19 May 1859, p. 12.
88 *Fremden-Blatt*, 29 May 1859, p. 7 and 9 June 1859, p. 6.
89 *Wiener Zeitung*, 11 June 1859, p. 11.
90 No such credentialing applications have been found in the Czechoslovakian archives or the Oesterreichiches Staatsarchiv/Kriegsarchiv for either of the brothers (Chris Tögel, email to the author 13 May 2019).

91 While conversion rates are imprecise, 8,096 Austrian florins are approximately the equivalent of €121,918 (as of 2022); see www.eurologisch.at/docroot/waehrungsrechner/#/.
92 These were imprecisely referred to as 'reichsthalers' in the press reports (see *Brünner Zeitung*, 10 February 1860, p. 268). At the time, one vereinsthaler was worth one-and-a-half florins.
93 Isak Zeisler and Sigmund Bretholz (who was originally from Tysmenitz) founded this company, which traded primarily in wool, in 1855 in Freiberg.
94 *Brünner Zeitung*, 6 November 1859, p. 2147; my thanks to Chris Tögel for bringing this source to my attention.
95 Ibid., 10 February 1860, p. 268.
96 Ibid., 26 February 1860, p. 379.
97 Whether either of these creditors was related to Emanuel's wife – Marie Rokach (Rokachová) – is unclear, though if it were so it would suggest the situation was very desperate indeed.
98 *Brünner Zeitung*, 29 December 1859, p. 254 and 25 February 1860, p. 372.
99 Ibid., 17 March 1860, p. 513.
100 Ibid., 23 June 1860, p. 1187.
101 Freud to Emil Fluss, 16 June 1873, in Ernst Freud (ed) 'Some early unpublished letters of Freud', *IJPA*, 1969, 50, p. 426.
102 M Schröter & C Tögel 'The Leipzig episode in Freud's life (1859): A new narrative on the basis of recently discovered documents', *Psychoanalytic Quarterly*, 2007, 76, 1, p. 202.
103 Ibid., p. 206.
104 Ibid., p. 207; Freud to W Fliess, 3 December 1897, *Freud-Fliess*, p. 285; Laura Marcus 'Oedipus express: Psychoanalysis and the railways', in *Dreams of Modernity: Psychoanalysis, Literature, Cinema*, Cambridge: Cambridge University Press, 2014, p. 45; Diane O'Donoghue *On Dangerous Ground: Freud's Visual Cultures of the Unconscious*, London: Bloomsbury Academic, 2019, pp. 134–135 and 143.
105 M Schröter & C Tögel 'The Leipzig episode in Freud's life (1859): A new narrative on the basis of recently discovered documents', *Psychoanalytic Quarterly*, 2007, 76, 1, p. 204.
106 Freud to W Fliess, 3 October 1897, *Freud-Fliess*, p. 268.
107 See for example Laura Marcus 'Oedipus express: Psychoanalysis and the railways', in *Dreams of Modernity: Psychoanalysis, Literature, Cinema*, Cambridge: Cambridge University Press, 2014, p. 45.
108 See for example Diane O'Donoghue *On Dangerous Ground: Freud's Visual Cultures of the Unconscious*, London: Bloomsbury Academic, 2019, pp. 121–173, which also includes discussion of various other authors reconstructions using this same material.
109 M Schröter & C Tögel 'The Leipzig episode in Freud's life (1859): A new narrative on the basis of recently discovered documents', *Psychoanalytic Quarterly*, 2007, 76, 1, p. 208; more recently, Tögel noted favouring an inn somewhere along the route as the more probable site of this primal scene of psychoanalysis (email to the author, 24 October 2023).
110 Jacob's younger brother Abraham Freud (1818–1885) checked into the hotel that same day.
111 *Wiener Zeitung*, 8 February 1860, p. 240.
112 For brief background detail on Leisorowitz see Georg Augusta '"Dann kamen die langen, harten Jahre": Zur Situation der Familie Freud nach ihrer Ankunft in Wien im Jahr 1859' ("Long and difficult years followed": The situation of Freud's family after their arrival in Vienna in 1859'), *Luzifer-Amor*, 2015, 28, p. 115.
113 *Wiener Zeitung*, 8 February 1860, p. 240.
114 *Gerichts Zeitung*, 3 March 1860, p. 108; *Wiener Zeitung*, 28 February 1860, p. 355; *Allgemeine Österreichische Gerichtszeitung*, 3 March 1860, p. 108.

115 For further discussion of this period see Georg Augusta '"Dann kamen die langen, harten Jahre": Zur Situation der Familie Freud nach ihrer Ankunft in Wien im Jahr 1859', *Luzifer-Amor*, 2015, 28, pp. 108–129, and Christfried Tögel 'Über Sigmund Freuds erste und über seine *beinahe* letzte Unterkunft in Wien', 2019, available online at: www.freud-biographik.de/kleine-texte-zur-freud-biographik/.
116 Freud's sister Regine ('Rosa') Deborah was born here on 21 March 1860 (see Georg Augusta '"Dann kamen die langen, harten Jahre": Zur Situation der Familie Freud nach ihrer Ankunft in Wien im Jahr 1859', *Luzifer-Amor*, 2015, 28, p. 118).
117 Georg Augusta '"Dann kamen die langen, harten Jahre": Zur Situation der Familie Freud nach ihrer Ankunft in Wien im Jahr 1859', *Luzifer-Amor*, 2015, 28, pp. 111 and 120; see also *Gerichtshalle*, 17 November 1864, p. 541
118 *Life & Work*, 1, pp. 19 and 67.
119 Rosa was born 21 March 1860, Marie (Mitzi) on 22 March 1861, Esther Adolfine (Dolfi) on 23 July 1862, Paula on 3 May 1864, and Alexander on 19 April 1866.
120 Over the next several years Jacob Freud and his family lived in a series of rented Vienna apartments, viz: 2 Dampfschiffstrasse (February 1860–February 1861), 114 Weissgärberstrasse (February 1861–Spring 1864), 5 Pillersdorfgasse (Spring 1864–early 1865), 1 Pfeffergasse (early 1865–Autumn 1868), 30 Glockengasse (Autumn 1868–Autumn 1870), 5 Pfeffergasse (Autumn 1870–1873); 19 Pazmanitengasse (1873–1874), 3 Kaiser-Josef-Strasse [now renamed Heinestrasse] (1874–1881), 33 Kaiser-Josef-Strasse (1881-August 1884), 32 Darwingasse (August 1884–November 1886), 30 Praterstrasse (November 1886–1890), and 14 Grüne Thorgasse (1890–1930). Freud himself moved out of the family home on 1 September 1882 into doctors' accommodation at the AKH General Hospital, following which he lived in Paris (1885–86), 7 Rathausstrasse (15 April-29 September 1886), 8 Maria-Theresien-Strasse (29 September 1886–14 September 1891), and then 19 Bergasse (14 September 1891–4 June 1938). My thanks to Chris Tögel for supplying most of these address details.
121 S Freud 'Screen memories', *SE*, 1899, 3, p. 312; L Ginsburg & S Ginsburg 'Paradise in the life of Sigmund Freud: An understanding of its imagery and paradoxes', *IRPA*, 1992, 19, pp. 285–308.
122 For detailed discussions see Peter Gay *A Godless Jew: Freud, Atheism and the Making of Psychoanalysis*, New Haven: Yale University Press, 1987, and alternative views by Emanuel Rice *Freud and Moses: The Long Journey Home*, Albany, NY: SUNY Press, 1990, and Moshe Gresser *Dual Allegiance: Freud as a Modern Jew*, Albany, NY: SUNY Press, 1994.

Chapter 2

Settling in Britain
Kinship, social networks, and material enterprise

Introduction

The present chapter traces the Freuds in Britain through a plethora of activities from their arrival in 1859 to 1865 as they find places to live, establish themselves in business, and negotiate community and family connexions. It may thus seem somewhat piecemeal, yet, as Leonore Davidoff makes clear, these aspects of people's lives were intimately connected. As she puts it, 'The heart of . . . kinship and social networks was the financial and material enterprise that supported families and households'.[1] Sibling bonds are especially important here at crucial periods for the Freuds and these networks extended to the family in Vienna. The role of religion in the family's life is considered also as part of such networks, with new light being thrown here on the type and level of the Freuds' religious engagement during this period. Freud's own connectedness to his relatives and their lives is briefly captured through his earliest surviving letter, while other now lost letters to Uncle Josef are noted which could have, unjustifiably I suggest, embroiled the Manchester Freuds in the counterfeit Russian roubles scandal.

Establishing lives in Britain

In or around September 1859 Emanuel quietly emigrated to Britain, with his wife Marie, their children John, Paulina, and six-month-old Bertha, and his younger brother Philipp probably accompanying him on the journey.[2] They took with them a minimum of baggage, Emanuel and his family seemingly abandoning clothes and other household effects in Freiberg as they made in effect a moonlight flit. Behind them, they left their rent unpaid in Freiberg and a considerable string of debts, with creditors beginning to pursue them for repayment through the Austrian courts from October.

The question of why they chose Britain, and specifically Manchester where they would ultimately settle, was probably influenced by at least three factors. Firstly, immigration into and settlement in Britain during this period of Victorian liberalism was relatively easy from a legal point of view, a particularly important consideration for European Jewry who elsewhere in Europe faced widespread legal

DOI: 10.4324/9781032652023-3

Image 2.1 96 Shudehill (centre), in 1925, the home of Freud & Co between c.1861–1884

Source: Manchester Libraries, Information & Archives

impediments on movement, settlement, and trade (as effectively illustrated through Jacob's struggles in Leipzig).[3] This is not to say that anti-Semitism was not present in Britain; it certainly was, it was widespread. However, in England the nineteenth century was marked legislatively with increasing Jewish emancipation, with the Jews Relief Act 1858 for example allowing Jews to enter the Westminster Parliament by taking a modified oath of office.[4] Secondly, it removed the brothers from the immediate jurisdiction of the Austrian courts and gave them some respite from their creditors. And thirdly, there were positive economic advantages to the Freuds basing their businesses in Britain. Manchester was undoubtedly Britain's second city at the time. As a rapidly growing industrial centre, it had a burgeoning cosmopolitan population, which by 1861 included 1,755 Jews.[5] It was socially, culturally and politically vibrant, a centre of radical thought, being a one-time Chartist stronghold, as well as a site of Irish nationalist politics, peaking notoriously in 1867 around the so-called Manchester Martyrs trial and public execution.[6] It was also for 22 years, on and off from 1842 through to 1870, the home of Friedrich Engels, who drew on his experiences there in the 1840s to write *The Condition of the Working-Class in England in 1844*, describing conditions for the working poor in Manchester's Angel Meadow slum as 'Hell upon Earth'.[7] The Manchester Jewish community too was diverse, containing radical and nonconformist elements, increasingly so as the long nineteenth century wore on.[8] However, most conspicuously, Manchester was the heart of the country's international linen trade.[9] It was this latter feature, at least, that made the city a good fit with the brothers' previous business experience. It was also, according to the sometimes-unreliable Anna Freud Bernays, supposedly a city in which Jacob had 'business interests',[10] although his only known visit to the city occurred in September 1883 (when he was about 67 years old), to see his eldest sons who were by then well-established there.[11]

Emanuel at least (and probably his family and very possibly Philipp) lived initially in London, in a rented property at 39 Greek Street, Soho.[12] Most if not all of the properties the Freuds lived and worked in over the ensuing 50 years were also occupied on a leasehold basis, reflecting a European cultural tradition towards renting property, their economic circumstances, and an ambivalence towards becoming too settled. One effect of this positioning, and the instability of rented property in Britain, is seen in the significant number of house moves the Freuds endured over the years ahead.

By the end of 1859, Emanuel and his family moved to Salford, near Manchester, where he established himself as a general merchant, running the business out of the family's home at 6 Wellington Terrace on Camp Street,[13] in the suburbs at Lower Broughton, an area with a significant Jewish immigrant community. Again, Philipp accompanied his elder brother and formed part of a slightly extended family. Here, they were less than a mile north-west of both the Great Synagogue (the Manchester home of Ashkenazim Jewry and the city's Old Hebrew Congregation) and the breakaway Manchester Synagogue of British Jews (the home of Reform Jewry), both recent constructions dating from 1858, built following the schism over Reform two years previously.[14] Both traditions would exert an influence on the Freuds in Manchester, with Philipp sustaining the closest affiliation, though neither brother nor their families were very conspicuous in synagogue life. Gravitating initially in the 1860s towards the Great Synagogue with its Orthodox tradition, its appeal was perhaps enhanced for the Freuds by its elite status among the established bourgeois Manchester (predominantly German) Jewry and its assimilationist anglicised ethos, hence its soubriquet of the *Englischer Schule*. It was, however, a difficult establishment to secure seatholder status in, and still more so to become a coveted free member of. Neither Emanuel nor Philipp appear in the synagogue's archives holding either status,[15] though their moderate affiliation to this and subsequently other synagogues probably aided the family in creating and sustaining roots and a certain status in the local community; such affiliations were also, as Davidoff points out, commonly regarded as good for business.[16]

Emanuel maintained some connections with the Continent, describing himself in 1860 as an 'importer of foreign small wares' and apparently had business interests and premises in Kamerniz Podolaki (what is now Kamianets-Podilskyi), on the Smotrych

River in Western Ukraine (then part of the Russian Empire). The extent to which this international trade leaned on any of Emanuel's or the wider family's pre-existing business networks (and may have thus inadvertently revealed his whereabouts to his creditors) is unknown. So too is whether Emanuel and Philipp were attempting during this period to straightforwardly service their debts on the Continent, which in the first few months of 1860 were coming before the Austrian courts. What is known is that on 4 May 1860 Emanuel was officially declared 'out of business', and that morning he appeared as an insolvent debtor at the Court House at Lancaster Castle, in Lancashire, over 50 miles north-north-west of Salford.[17]

Which creditors were party to these proceedings is unclear. Were they the same European creditors who were pursuing him through the Austrian courts who (a) had somehow tracked him down or (b) with whom he had failed to reach an amicable private agreement? Or were they other creditors, newly acquired in the first few months of his new business venture in Britain? Whoever they were, over the ensuing week Emanuel clearly came to some agreement with them to settle his debts and on Friday 11 May he was discharged and able to resume trading.[18] It would not be the last encounter the Freuds would have with bankruptcy courts.

On 28 June 1860, Emanuel and Marie's next child, Solomon, was born in the family home at Wellington Terrace.[19] The first of Emanuel's children to be born in Britain, he was probably – like Freud – originally named after his grandfather Schlomo (Solomon) Freud, who had died in Tysmenitz in February 1856. Emanuel registered his birth on 1 August and was still recording him as Solomon on 7 April 1861 when that year's census was conducted. Sometime over the next decade (and by 1871 at the latest), his given name would be replaced by the more Anglicised 'Samuel', often abbreviated to the diminutive Sam.[20] The change of his son's name reflects Emanuel's strong assimilationist tendencies, of which more later.[21] All three of Sam's British-born sisters would be given distinctively English names.

Following the ignominy of appearing in the debtor's court, Emanuel established a formal business partnership with Philipp, styling themselves as 'importers of French and German fancy goods', 'fancy goods warehousemen' and 'Birmingham and Sheffield warehousemen'. Operating under the banner of Freud & Co, which Philipp had utilised from at least April 1861, they ran the business initially from Wellington Terrace.[22] As a wholesale business, Freud & Co's stock of 'fancy goods', and the 'small wares' previously referred to, would have included predominantly small ornamental items suitable for presents, accessories and impulse purchases, which if functional would have had a decorative finish. Contemporary advertisements thus referred to items such as souvenirs, buckles, ribbons, buttons, fans, snuff boxes, scent bottles, trinket boxes, leather work, pin cushions, needlework, and other forms of haberdashery under these headings.[23] The Freuds would concentrate, for a time at least, on European imports, which perhaps offered a certain fashionable cachet to domestic British consumers as well as appealing to fellow migrants. Such stock was of course also significantly gendered, with women involved in some item manufacture but being more especially intended as the ultimate consumers. Such orientation towards the feminine, or at least a view of the feminine, would also characterise much of Freud's work and certainly his best-known cases.[24]

When the 1861 census was taken on 7 April that year, the Freud family were still living at Wellington Terrace.[25] At this stage they were employing 27-year-old Johannah Hehient (c.1834–) as a live-in domestic servant. Hehient was an Austrian national and may have migrated with the Freuds two years previously. Over the coming years, the employment of a female domestic servant to undertake the menial domestic chores was commonplace in the British Freud households and was broadly typical of middle-class practices. More intriguingly perhaps, 6 Wellington Terrace was also the temporary home of a wealthy assimilated Jewish Viennese mercantile family: Moses Hirsch ('Heinrich') Goldscheid (1826–1897), his wife Barbara ('Betty') (née Reitzes: 1832–1906), and their first child Siegfried (1858–1895), together with his nurse, a local Ardwick woman recorded as Mary (c.1847–) on the census.[26] Heinrich Goldscheid was working in Manchester as a 'foreign agent', presumably involved in the import-export trade. The Goldscheids had not been in Britain quite as long as the Freuds and it seems probable that they were involved together in business dealings, though whether these predated the Freud brothers' migration is less certain. The Goldscheids left Manchester before the end of the year, returning to Vienna.[27]

Later in 1861 or early 1862 the Freuds moved to 96 Shudehill, in the inner-city business district of Market Street in Manchester, just a few minutes walk from Angel Meadow. The building served as the trading address for Freud & Co, 'importers of French and German fancy goods',[28] and the home for both Emanuel, his family, and Philipp. Opening directly onto a busy commercial street, the Freuds business would have at least occupied the ground floor of this four-storey building, with stock probably taking up some of the space on the upper floors and the family living space on the higher floors also. The building would serve the Freuds, in various family and business configurations, for the next 23 years. The first domestic event of significance there occurred on 12 May 1862, when Emanuel and Marie's sixth child, Matilda, was born.[29]

On 9 March 1864 Emanuel and Philipp formally dissolved their partnership,[30] but it was not an explosive rupture. The brothers' business ventures began to diverge, but everyone stayed living where there were for the moment.

A letter from Vienna

Sometime during this period Emanuel received a letter from Freud, what is today the earliest surviving example of the latter's prodigious correspondence. The undated letter, written in German, was prompted by Freud's receipt of a now lost communication from one of Emanuel's sons, the contents of which letter Freud tells him he was unable to understand.[31] Whether this was on account of poor legibility, it being composed in English, or for some other reason is unknown. The 'your dear son' Freud referred to in his letter's opening line might have been either his early childhood companion, John, or his younger brother Samuel, though John seems the more likely original correspondent.[32] The body of the letter briefly declared that Freud and the family in Vienna were doing well and offered his greetings to Emanuel, his 'esteemed family' and 'brother Philipp', before signing off as 'Sigismund Freud'.[33]

The letter was, as Benjamin Goodnick commented, 'quite stilted' in parts, particularly in Freud's use of phrases such as 'esteemed family'.[34] Goodnick suggests Freud thus promoted relative *distance*, especially vis-à-vis Emanuel's children, in contrast to his narrative of *closeness* to his older half-brother (a strategy he would also deploy elsewhere vis-à-vis Philipp). What is more pressing in Freud's text is not any positioning within the family pecking order, but his overtly *reassuring* family narrative. It is a narrative of a warm fraternal relationship, of homage to Emanuel's immediate family and to Philipp, and dubious claims about the well-being of the Vienna branch of the family. The various intra-familial relationships were ruptured, most vividly when the family dispersed in 1859, and Freud would later depict his early years in Vienna to third parties as 'hard times and not worth remembering'.[35] The letter then may be read as a wish; a wish for that which has been lost and a wish for that which never was.

Ernst Freud suggested his father's letter might have been written in about 1863, making him about seven years old. Noting Freud's later good command of English, Jones stated that he began reading Shakespeare at the age of eight, adding without an obvious sense of hyperbole that Freud also told him that he read nothing but English books for a decade.[36] Be that as it may, the lost letter, presumably written in English by his former rival John, may have become a spur to this determination to also master the language.

A further spur to this probably came from Emanuel and Freud's occasional yet sustained and important correspondence over the ensuing decades. Most of this – significantly – Emanuel wrote in English,[37] with concerns about health and regular (typically vague) reports of ill-health among the female family members being prominent motifs. Emanuel's use of English as the medium for this correspondence underlines both his own assimilation into British culture and one of the principal means by which he propagated such culture and language as an ideal to his younger brother. The substantive continuation of this correspondence between the two branches of the family by Sam following his father's death continued in this pattern, albeit supplemented with increasing and more explicit reference to Freud's own developing health problems. The correspondence with Emanuel (and latterly with Sam) was something which – along with a few periods of time spent together – nourished their positive siblings and transferential relationships and by extension inscribed Britain as a warm place in Freud's mind. This in turn would impact positively on Freud's motivation to disseminate his ideas in Britain and the English-speaking world.

A Scandal in Vienna: Uncle Josef and the counterfeit roubles

One 'hard time' in Vienna concerned the brothers' uncle, Josef Freud (1826–1897), the shadow of whose involvement with a counterfeiting affair extended to Britain. Josef was arrested on 20 June 1865 for possession of 359 counterfeit 50 rouble notes and their attempted distribution, that is for 'uttering'.[38] Josef's son-in-law, Adolf Kornhauser, was also arrested,[39] as was another Jewish businessman Osias Weich. Kornhauser was soon released, the authorities not finding any incriminating evidence against him. Weich, by contrast, appeared to have been the source of the counterfeit notes, which he allegedly obtained in London, and he then supplied a quantity to Josef, doing so to guarantee a loan. The authorities noted Josef had also travelled three times to Britain since 1861, visiting London, Birmingham, and Manchester while there, as well as other European cities. No doubt he would have met with Emanuel and Philipp on at least some of these journeys. Correspondence apparently from Emanuel and Philipp to Josef attracted particular attention, the Austrian Minister-President, Richard Graf von Belcredi (1823–1902), citing two letters which he suggested had 'very questionable content', thus:

> One of these letters' states that they . . . have money like sand on the seashore, that since they were wise, clever, and very circumspect, fortune could not but smile on them. In another letter they enquire whether the lucky star of the House of Freud has risen for him as well, and ask the recipient to find a banking house for goods, one with larger, quicker, and more profitable outlets.[40]

Clearly highly circumstantial (as well as obviously discrepant with Emanuel and Philipp's then *precarious* economic circumstances), it was such fragments that influenced Belcredi's conclusion that the forgeries emanated from 'England'. That said, there was counterfeiting of primarily small denomination Russian rouble notes in Britain during the 1860s and a steady trickle of court cases were documented in the British press, most of the identified parties involved being described as German, Polish, and French Jews.[41] Such enterprises were largely centred in London according to press reports, none of which revealed any connections whatsoever to Manchester.

In Josef's trial, the prosecution subsequently argued that the culprits were immigrants, mostly Jews, and the enterprise was motivated by seditious nationalist intent, albeit without advancing evidence for the latter. It was a projective and anti-Semitic line that probably played well to the gallery. On 21 February 1866, Josef Freud and Osias Weich were sentenced to eight- and ten-years imprisonment with hard labour respectively, though Josef's case was referred to a higher court for possible mitigation of the sentence, his tariff being reduced to six years.[42]

The affair was clearly shocking for the wider Freud family, Freud famously noting in *The Interpretation of Dreams* that his own father's 'hair turned grey from grief in a few days', whilst adding that Jacob would reassuringly 'say that Uncle Josef was not a bad man but only a simpleton'.[43] Freud himself was less convinced and more direct, calling Josef a 'criminal'.[44]

This subject was one about which the Freud family, and Anna Freud in particular, were sensitive when earlier potential biographers made enquiries.[45] Jones, in his authorised biography, gave the story two opaque sentences.[46] Later writers have sometimes been far more expansive,[47] with some arguing that it had a profound structuring and in fact destabilising effect on Freud's thought.[48] It is a view that has convinced few, if any, sober commentators,[49] though it inevitably muddied the reputations of Emanuel and Philipp in the literature, both through frequent repetition and a tendency to elide speculation with established fact.[50] This seems ill-deserved, since there was no evidence advanced at the time or since that linked the brothers to the forgery or indeed any other criminal activity in Britain. Quite the reverse in fact. Both brothers would show strong records of social conformity, industriousness and Emanuel would, as we see in due course, pass his police vetting for naturalisation and be commended in the process as 'a respectable man', a highly unlikely result if there had been even rumours of past impropriety.

Reflections

During the six years reviewed here, the Freud brothers had managed to successfully relocate to Britain, living successively in London, Salford, and Manchester, where they began to establish themselves in business as wholesalers of fancy goods and small wares, which they imported from the Continent, as well as miscellaneous Birmingham and Sheffield wares. Despite struggles with debt, a period in partnership allowed the elder Freud brothers to reorient their work lives by 1864. From this point onwards they would sustain largely independent businesses trading in diverging product lines.

While collaboration between the Emanuel and Philipp was important during this period, and mutual support would be over the ensuing years, underscoring Leonore Davidoff's stress on such networks,[51] so too were their links to the family in Vienna and to Manchester Jewry. The Freuds were, the evidence suggests, relatively traditional in their religious views during much of the 1860s, albeit with strong assimilationist tendencies, particularly evident in Emanuel and his children during the following decades, which will be further taken up in the ensuing chapters.

With family networks extending to Vienna, the influence of the brothers' values, enterprise, and progressivism on Freud begins to peep through during this period in a fragment of surviving correspondence. Emanuel particularly, as the older progressive and assimilated brother, is seen as a key mentor and quasi father figure, with his children as siblings, missed since their departure from Freiberg. However, both older brothers also offered models of small businessmen's entrepreneurial drive to the younger Freud, contributory ingredients in his own future life as a small businessman in private practice.

The sustained links with Uncle Josef, incorporating entwined themes of family support and enterprise, however, threw a shadow of suspicion over Emanuel and Philipp, at least insofar as Belcredi was concerned during the 1865 investigations of Josef's involvement in passing counterfeit Russian roubles. A story widely dined out on by other Freud scholars, there seems no credible evidence of any involvement by Emanuel or Philipp in their uncle's criminality or indeed impropriety by them in other spheres since moving to Britain. More creatively, such experiences would fructify Freud's thinking in the years ahead about the place of relationships in psychic life.

Notes

1. Leonore Davidoff *Thicker Than Water: Siblings and Their Relations 1780–1920*, Oxford: Oxford University Press, 2012, p. 57.
2. Freud to E Silberstein, 9 September 1875, *Freud-Silberstein*, p. 126; TNA ref: HO 334/7/2149, Emanuel's naturalisation application dated 10 January 1877, noted he had lived for the past 17 years in Britain. The Freuds arrival in Britain does not appear to be recorded among the surviving Home Office 'Return of alien passengers, July 1836-December 1869' in the HO3 series at TNA.
3. William D Rubinstein *Antisemitism in the English-Speaking World*, New York: Oxford University Press, 2010, p. 459; see also Panikos Panayi *German Immigrants in Britain during the Nineteenth Century 1815–1914*, Oxford: Berg, 1995.
4. On 26 July 1858 Lionel de Rothschild (1808–1879) was the first Jew admitted to Parliament following this change, followed by David Salomons (1797–1873) the following year, both as members of Palmerston's Liberal Party.
5. With a population of some 70,000 at the start of the century, by 1861 the city's population had reached 319, 848 (*Manchester Courier*, 10 December 1868, p. 6); between 1841 and 1871 the Jewish population in Manchester rose from 625 to 3,444. See Bill Williams *The Making of Manchester Jewry 1740–1875*, Manchester: Manchester University Press, 1976, p. 356, with the subsequent pages detailing a breakdown of their occupations and settlement patterns.
6. The lead up to this incident involved two prominent Irish-American leaders of the failed 1867 Fenian Rising, Thomas Kelly and Timothy Deasy, being inadvertently arrested in the early hours of 11 September that year in Oak Street, near the Freuds then home in Shudehill. Later freed by armed accomplices, one policeman was killed in their rescue and a subsequent trail of 26 rounded up suspects resulted in three men being publicly executed outside Salford Gaol on 23 November (see P Rose *The Manchester Martyrs: The Story of a Fenian Tragedy*, London: Lawrence & Wishart, 1970). It seems likely that Manchester Jewry and other immigrant groups were also cowed by the establishment's racialised crackdown on the Irish community.
7. F Engels *The Condition of the Working-Class in England in 1844*, London: Swan Sonnenschein & Co, 1892, p. 53, the original German text having been published in Leipzig in 1845; see also D Kirby *Fredrich Engels and Angel Meadow: The Origin and Development of Victorian Manchester's 'Hell upon Earth' Slum*, PhD thesis, Manchester Metropolitan University, 2022; S Marcus *Engels, Manchester, and the Working Class*, Abingdon: Routledge, 2017; R Whitfield *Fredrich Engels in Manchester: The Search for a Shadow*, Salford: Working Class Movement Library, 1988.
8. Rosalyn D Livshin *Nonconformity in the Manchester Jewish Community: The Case of Political Radicalism, 1889–1939*, PhD thesis, University of Manchester, 2015.
9. Stuart Hylton *A History of Manchester*, Stroud: Phillimore, 2016; Alan Kidd *Manchester*, Keele: Keele University Press, 1996; Simon Taylor *et al Manchester: The Warehouse Legacy*, London: English Heritage, 2002; Liliane Weissberg 'Ariadne's Thread', *MLN*, 2010, 125, 3, pp. 671–673; *Life and Work*, 1, p. 15.
10. Anna Freud Bernays 'My brother, Sigmund Freud', *The American Mercury*, 51, November 1940, p. 336.
11. Freud to Martha Bernays, 23 September 1883, LoC ref: mss39990, box 4, reel 2.
12. *The Manchester Courier and Lancashire General Advertiser*, 21 April 1860, p. 2.
13. 1861 English census, TNA ref: RG 9/2908/22/17; 6 Wellington Terrace was three houses before the junction with Lord Street. See also *Slater's Directory of Manchester and Salford*, Manchester: Isaac Slater, 1863, street directory section, p. 25, and the 1886 edition, street directory section, p. 45. Following extensive redevelopment in the area, the property no longer exists.

14 For details of the history of the Jewish community in Manchester at this period (albeit without *any* mention of the Freud family) see P Selvin Goldberg *The Manchester Congregation of British Jews 1857–1957*, Manchester: MCBJ, 1957, Bill Williams *The Making of Manchester Jewry 1740–1875*, Manchester: Manchester University Press, 1976, and his *Jewish Manchester: An Illustrated History*, Derby: Breedon Books, 2008.
15 Surviving archives of the Great Synagogue note the Freud name just twice, on 1 August 1875 and 27 January 1907. On the first occasion a seatholder recorded as 'A Freud' attended a general meeting, while 26-years later this apparently same seatholder was contacted due to non-payment of his seat fees. This was most probably Abraham Freud, a tailor based in the Strangeways district during the 1870s and 1880s. He does not appear to have been related to Emanuel and Philipp. See Manchester Central Archives ref: GB127.M139/1–4, Great Synagogue General Meetings Minute Book, 1856–1880 and Accounts Book, 1907 (box 42796); for other mentions of this Abraham Freud see *Manchester Evening News*, 26 June 1875, p. 1 and *Slater's Manchester Directory*, 1883, part 2, p. 230.
16 Leonore Davidoff *Thicker Than Water: Siblings and Their Relations 1780–1920*, Oxford: Oxford University Press, 2012, p. 53.
17 *The Manchester Courier and Lancashire General Advertiser*, 21 April 1860, p. 2. Like most other bankruptcy cases, no official records of these or subsequent proceedings involving the Freuds survive in The National Archives in London or the local Lancaster and Manchester archives.
18 Ibid., 12 May 1860, p. 7; see also *The Preston Guardian*, 12 May 1860, p. 1; *Ulverston Mirror and Furness Reflector*, 12 May 1860, p. 8.
19 GRO birth record: Salford Registrar's District, July–September 1860, vol. 8d, p. 32; the certificate gives the more general area as 'Camp Street'.
20 Noting his first meeting with Samuel in 1875, Freud remarked that his first name (i.e., Samuel) 'has been fashionable in England ever since Pickwick' (Freud to E Silberstein, 9 September 1875, *Freud-Silberstein*, p. 127), indicating perhaps that this name was not only fashionable, but was also literary (and we know Emanuel admired Charles Dickens).
21 Martin Freud *Glory Reflected: Sigmund Freud – Man and Father*, London: Angus and Robertson, 1957, pp. 12–13.
22 *Slater's Directory of Manchester and Liverpool*, Manchester: Isaac Slater, 1861, p. 165 (Slater dates the book's preface as 'April 1861'). The business *may* have also operated during this period from 26 Market Street (see Sidney Horrocks, Manchester Central Library, to Leslie Adams, 6 March 1952, Manchester Central Library archives).
23 See also for example the *Official Catalogue of the Great Exhibition of the Works of Industry of All Nations*, London: Spricers Brothers and W Clowes & Sons, 1851, and George A Sala *Notes and Sketches of the Paris Exhibition*, London: Tinsley Brothers, 1868, pp. 307–318. No specific product advertisements or sales catalogues by Freud & Co have been located.
24 See L Appignanesi & J Forrester *Freud's Women*, London: Weidenfeld & Nicholson, 1992.
25 1861 English census, TNA ref: RG 9/2908/22/17; see also *Slater's Directory of Manchester and Salford*, Manchester: Isaac Slater, 1863, street directory section, p. 25, and the 1886 edition, street directory section, p. 45. Following extensive redevelopment in the area, the property no longer exists.
26 1861 English census, TNA ref: RG 9/2908/22/17; the family do not appear again on other British census records; personal information from Randy Schoenberg, email to the author, 29 September 2018.
27 See *Deutsche Biographie*, available online at: www.deutsche-biographie.de/sfz21586.html.
28 *Slater's Directory of Manchester and Salford*, Manchester: Isaac Slater, 1863, p. 172.

29 GRO birth record: Manchester Registrar's District, April-June 1862, vol. 8d, p. 261.
30 *The London Gazette*, 18 March 1864, p. 1627; *Liverpool Mercury*, 21 March 1864; *Blackburn Standard*, 23 March 1864.
31 Freud to Emanuel Freud, undated [*c*.1860s], University of Manchester Library ref: GB 133 SSF/1/6/1. The letter is reproduced in E Freud, L Freud, & I Grubrich-Simitis (eds) *Sigmund Freud: His Life in Pictures and Words*, London: W W Norton, 1985, pp. 56–57, and tentatively dated 'about 1863'.
32 Michael Molnar also suggests John was the original correspondent (see M Molnar *Looking Through Freud's Photos*, London: Karnac, 2015, p. 76), while Benjamin Goodnick assumes it was Samuel (see B Goodnick 'A childhood letter of Sigmund Freud', *Psychoanalytic Psychology*, 1994, 11, 4, p. 540) and that the letter dates from 1867–8. The present attribution is based on the relative ages of the candidates and the immaturity of Freud's text when compared to his letters from the early 1870s to Silberstein and Emil Fluss.
33 Freud gradually abandoned this form of his name in favour of the more Germanic 'Sigmund' during the early to mid-1870s: see for example *Freud-Silberstein*, 11 April 1875, p. 112.
34 Benjamin Goodnick 'A childhood letter of Sigmund Freud', *Psychoanalytic Psychology*, 1994, 11, 4, p. 542.
35 *Life & Work*, 1, p. 17; S Freud 'Screen memories', *SE*, 1899, 3, p. 312 quotes this as: 'Long and difficult years followed, of which, as it seems to me, nothing was worth remembering'.
36 *Life & Work*, 1, p. 24.
37 All the surviving correspondence from Emanuel to Freud from 1886 to 1914 in the Library of Congress (LoC ref: mss39990, box 2) is in English, his sole other piece of correspondence there – to Eli Bernays, written in 1892 – being in German (LoC ref: mss39990, box 12). Surviving correspondence is cited later. For reference to now lost (earlier) correspondence see for example Freud to E Silberstein, 2 October 1875 and 22 July 1879, *Freud-Silberstein*, pp. 131 and 173 respectively.
38 The total, 17,950 roubles, if they had been genuine, represented a considerable sum. Though direct comparisons are difficult, in 1879 (the first year for which systematic data is available), the average annual salary for workers in Moscow was just 189 roubles (see: www.opoccuu.com/rab1913.htm). Grinstein suggests the total value of the roubles equated to about US$13,821 at the time (A Grinstein *Freud at the Crossroads*, Madison, CT: International Universities Press, 1990, p. 68).
39 *Neue Freie Presse*, 18 February 1866, p. 7.
40 M Krüll *Freud and his Father*, London: Hutchinson, 1987, p. 165, based on originals reproduced in Renée Gicklhorn *Sigmund Freud und der Onkeltraum: Dichtung und Wahrheit*, Horn, NÖ: Ferdinand Berger & Söhne, 1976, p. 40. Neither letter was cited in the newspaper reports of the trial and were presumably not entered as evidence, probably being regarded as ambiguous and unhelpful to the prosecution.
41 See for example the trials reported in the *Morning Chronicle*, 14 January 1862, p. 3, which stated it was 'well known for a long time past that persons, both in this country and abroad, had been trading in forged rouble notes, which, after being manufactured, are transmitted to Russia where they get into circulation'; *Daily News*, 20 January 1862, p. 7, which noted 'nearly the whole of the persons so convicted were Jews, and mostly from Poland'; *The Times*, 1 April 1865, p. 27; *Reynolds's Newspaper*, 13 August 1865, p. 8; *The Morning Post*, 1 September 1865, p. 7, regarding six 'well dressed Germans' and 500 forged five roubles notes; *Aberdeen Journal*, 6 September 1865, p. 8, regarding Poles, Russians and Germans, who had 'long practiced the forging of Russian paper notes, chiefly five rouble notes'; *The Leeds Mercury*, 14 January 1867, p. 4, regarding 107 forged five rouble notes; *The Times*, 28 November 1867, p. 9; *Illustrated Police News*, 30 May 1868, p. 5, regarding five Jews and 1,512 five rouble notes and other

denominations; *Daily News*, 29 October 1868, p. 6, which stated 'the fabrication of forged Russian rouble notes was carried on to an enormous extent in this country by German Jews'; and the *Morning Post*, 2 April 1869, p. 5, which reported there was 'a thriving trade' in St Petersburg in forged 50 rouble notes, which apparently came from Paris.

42 *Morgen-Post*, 7 April 1866, p. 3.
43 S Freud *The Interpretation of Dreams*, SE, 1900 [1899], 4, p. 138.
44 Ibid., p. 139.
45 Mikkel Borch-Jacobsen & Sonu Shamdasani *The Freud Files: An Inquiry into the History of Psychoanalysis*, Cambridge: Cambridge University Press, 2012, p. 262.
46 *Life & Work*, 1, p. 4.
47 See for example Alain de Mijolla 'Freud, Joseph (1826–1897)', in A de Mijolla (ed) *International Dictionary of Psychoanalysis*, Farmington Hills, MI: Thomson Gale, 2005, p. 627, and his earlier 'Mein Onkel Josef à la une', *Études Freudiennes*, April 1979, 15–16, pp. 183–192; M Krüll *Freud and his Father*, London: Hutchinson, 1987, pp. 164–166; David Cohen *The Escape of Sigmund Freud*, New York: Overlook Press, 2012, pp. 28–31.
48 Renée Gicklhorn *Sigmund Freud und der Onkeltraum: Dichtung und Wahrheit*, Horn, NÖ: Ferdinand Berger & Söhne, 1976; N T Rand & M Torok *Questions for Freud: The Secret History of Psychoanalysis*, Cambridge, MA: Harvard University Press, 1997.
49 Élisabeth Roudinesco *Freud in his Time and Ours*, Cambridge, MA: Harvard University Press, 2016, pp. 18–19; Paul Roazen *The Historiography of Psychoanalysis*, New Brunswick, NJ: Transaction Publishers, 2001, p. 248; and Kim Larsen '[Review of] *Questions for Freud: The Secret History of Psychoanalysis*', *Scandinavian Psychoanalytic Review*, 22, 2, pp. 311–314.
50 Such slippage is evident even in the work of some of the most careful Freud scholars, see for example Diane O'Donoghue *On Dangerous Ground: Freud's Visual Cultures of the Unconscious*, London: Bloomsbury Academic, 2019, pp. 287–289.
51 Leonore Davidoff *Thicker Than Water: Siblings and Their Relations 1780–1920*, Oxford: Oxford University Press, 2012, especially pp. 49–77.

Chapter 3

Emanuel's trilogy of loss, pain, and relocation

Introduction

The present chapter continues the story of the Manchester Freuds' relationships, examining here Emanuel and his family's life during the watershed decade from 1865 to 1875. While economic concerns were no doubt important, with further struggles with debt evident at the start of this period, it would be the sudden deaths of three of Emanuel's daughters in the 1860s that would exercise a defining effect on the family, impacting particularly on their private and observant lives.

A visit to Vienna in 1870, where John and Freud would perform a duologue from *Die Räuber*, would carry shadows of these losses. More conspicuous perhaps among the sequelae was the family's move to Manchester's rapidly growing southern suburbs. It was a move common for members of the aspiring middle classes in search of a healthier environment, a better quality of life, and to sustain their habitus and social standing.[1] For Emanuel's family, it was probably also an attempt to get away from the ghosts of the recent past and to make a fresh start. Included within this would be the beginnings of a reorientation to Judaism.

From hopes to adversity and loss, 1865–1870

Following the dissolution of the brothers' partnership in March 1864, Emanuel briefly took over Freud & Co as a business name, focussing on trade in so-called 'fancy goods'. However, within 18 months the company was in serious financial difficulties and on 17 October 1865 Emanuel signed a deed of composition with his creditors, agreeing to pay three shillings in the pound to be released from his debts.[2]

Despite the business difficulties, Emanuel and Marie's family continued to expand. On 11 August 1865 their seventh child, Harriet Emily, was born at 96 Shudehill.[3] Almost precisely one year later, on 12 August 1866, their eighth and final child, Henrietta, was born, again in the family home.[4]

While the lives of Freud's brothers and their families have been sparsely documented, several aspects of their stories have suffered particular neglect. One such area relates to their financial struggles, which mirror – albeit to a lesser extent – the day-to-day poverty with which Freud and the family in Vienna had to contend. This

DOI: 10.4324/9781032652023-4

42 Emanuel's trilogy

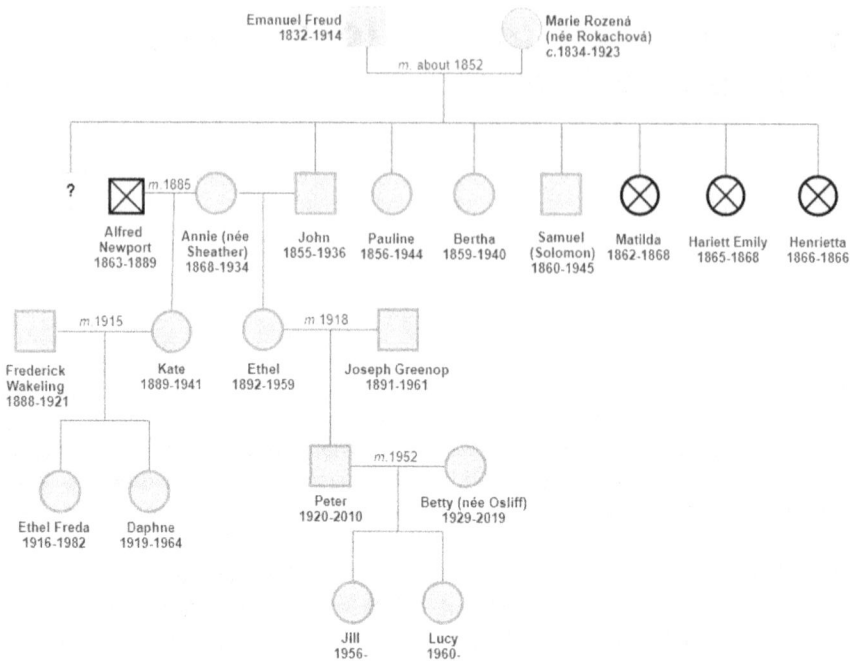

Chart 3.1 Emanuel Freud and his family

was, as David Cohen and others have argued, probably humiliating later for Freud and the wider family, particularly Amalia and the middle class Nathansohns.[5] In Emanuel's family another specific lacuna relates to the multiple bereavements they suffered, losses compounded if not at least partially caused by the family's economic situation and the squalid conditions of the inner city. In Manchester, the newest addition to the family, Henrietta, was unwell from birth, living just 18 days and died at home from marasmus, a severe form of malnutrition, on 31 August 1866.[6] That same day, Emanuel registered her birth and death *and* – in line with Orthodox tradition – Henrietta was buried in the Great Synagogue's cemetery at Queens Road, Miles Platting.[7] Used predominantly for burials of children from poor Jewish families until 1872, Henrietta's interment here probably exacerbated the emotional pain of her loss.

Two years later, this wound was compounded when Emily (as Harriet was by then referred to) and Matilda both contracted scarlet fever. It was a very serious condition and one of the commonest causes of child mortality in Manchester at that time. Some 3,360 children up to the age of ten died from its effects in the city between 1851 and 1861, and the severe shortfall in hospital accommodation for it and allied febrile infectious diseases (particularly among what was then referred to as the 'independent poor') was the subject of an inquiry in 1868.[8] Scarlet fever and typhus were particularly prevalent in the Shudehill area of Market Street, as well as the neighbouring districts of Deansgate, Ancoats, and St George, and there was a further spike in cases in the autumn of 1868, with 46 mostly children dying from it during the week ending 28 November.[9] Emily and Matilda both succumbed to the disease then, Emily dying at home on 27 November 1868 and Matilda dying two days later, on the twenty-ninth.[10] They were just three-and-a-half and six-and-a-half years old respectively. Both girls were buried on 29 November, this time in the Great Synagogue's main cemetery at Bury New Road, Prestwich.[11] Whether the multiply bereaved and financially straitened family ever managed to erect matzevahs (or gravestones) to commemorate Henrietta, Emily, or Matilda is unclear, though no such stones marking their brief lives survive today.

Despite a high rate of childhood mortality at the time,[12] the loss of four children would have been very painful for most families. For Emanuel and his family, it seems to have been particularly so. The cumulative losses of Henrietta, Emily, and Matilda between 1866 and 1868, left the family emotionally fragile, hypervigilant about their health, and largely unable to separate as will be seen. Unsurprisingly, given this *huis clos*,[13] the girls' lives would pass unmentioned in the surviving family correspondence, a traumatised silence disappointingly reiterated by most Freud scholars with respect to the children and their deaths in particular.

Sometime after this compound of losses, Emanuel and his family veered away from the Old Hebrew Congregation, affiliating instead with Reform Jewry and the Manchester Synagogue of British Jews, though their day-to-day lives seem to have been increasingly secular. Though speculative, it seems likely that the girls' deaths were influential in catalysing this change. Establishing a detailed chronology for the transition has not been possible. Most of the Manchester Synagogue of British Jews' own records were destroyed by German bombing in June 1941 and Emanuel and his family were conspicuous by their absence from external press reports about synagogue life. However, surviving cemetery records reveal that almost all of Emanuel's family would opt to be cremated (a practice Orthodox Jews opposed) and Reform Rabbis would officiate over their burials, as we will see later.

Emanuel also began to separate himself and his family from 96 Shudehill, doing so initially by renting nearby 9 Thomas Street as additional living and business space in late 1868 or early 1869.[14] For the next year or so they would straddle both addresses.

Vienna and *Die Räuber*

In 1870 Emanuel and John visited their kin in Vienna. During the trip, Freud and John performed scenes from Schiller's play *Die Räuber* (The Robbers).[15] This, at one level, was a story of sibling and Oedipal rivalry. In the play, the aged Count Maximilian of Franconia banishes his eldest son Charles because of his debts and puerile behaviour, having been nudged to do so by his younger physically deformed ambitious son Francis. Charles becomes the leader of the eponymous band of robbers in the forests of Bohemia and in one quasi dream scene there retells in verse a dialogue between Caesar's ghost and his supposed son Brutus. It was this act, a play within a play, that Freud and John performed, where they took the roles of Brutus and Caesar respectively, for an audience of other children. *Die Räuber* itself would end with a crescendo of violence and contrition. Charles and his band of robbers stormed Maximillian's castle, leading to Francis committing suicide and their father dying. Having forsworn a life with his beloved Amelia, Charles kills her and finally – in a moral ending – surrenders to justice.[16]

It was a play that gripped Freud's adolescent imagination and by 1874 he had been to two or perhaps three performances,[17] aside from his own earlier recital. Freud recalled the latter performance in his discussion of the 'Non Vixit' dream in *The Interpretation of Dreams*, noting that: '. . . he [John], too, was a *revenant*, for it was the playmate of my earliest years who had returned in him'.[18] (In *Die Räuber* characters turning up who had been thought dead, i.e., revenants, was a frequent plot device). With their early childhood roles thus reversed, John is here symbolically reduced to a revenant, a haunting animated corpse, his incarnation of this signifier no doubt promoted by his status as the dead Henrietta, Emily, and Matilda's surviving brother. It was a position that foreshadowed his fading in the history of the Freud family.

Image 3.1 Sigismund and Amalia Freud, c.1872, thus taken in between the *Die Räuber* performance and Freud's visit to Manchester

Source: Chronicle/Alamy

Freud did not delve further in *The Interpretation of Dreams* into *Die Räuber*, though it re-emerged shortly afterwards in a discussion of rivalry with his younger brother Alexander in *The Psychopathology of Everyday Life*. There, on one occasion Freud likens Alexander to a female patient's brother, wondering: 'Would my brother in the same circumstances have behaved in a similar way, or would he have done the opposite?' Importing this into the framework of *Die Räuber*, the anxious thought become whether Alexander would wish to depose Freud as Francis had done to Charles. Later, misreading a newspaper prompts Freud to recognise his own preference to retreat into art and antiquity (focussing on art in the age of Alexander of Macedon) rather than his closer at hand rivalry with Alexander over their respective prospects of gaining a professorship.[19]

The shadow to this, however, was as usual deposited with Philipp and went unmentioned by Freud in these cases. Aspects of this peak through at three points. Firstly, in the opening plot of *Die Räuber*, with its issues of rivalry, banishment, and a younger brother's physical problems, these characteristics are resonant with the family's situation in 1859 and the older brothers' emigration to Britain. Secondly, Anzieu points out that in the historical background to Shakespeare's *Julius Caesar*, Mark Antony had raised the populace against the conspirators who were defeated at the battle of Philippi, with Cassius and Brutus both dying effectively by their own hands.[20] And thirdly, several commentators have suggested that the convenient narrative of Philipp as the fantasy lover of Amalia remerged with Alexander's birth, pointing to both his eponymous namesake Alexander the Great being the son of Philip II of Macedon and Freud's bird-beaked figures anxiety dream prompting associations to another Philipp, as evidence for this idea.[21] It would take Freud decades to digest these complex fantasies and transform them in his writings into a praxis, liberating himself a little in the process from their grip. For Philipp, John and the other family members, their working through of their own experiences of these events would take different paths.

Moving to the suburbs

With Philipp Freud continuing to live and run his own business from 96 Shudehill close to the centre of Manchester Jewry, by 1871 Emanuel and his family had moved out from the noise, unhealthy conditions, the perceived miasmatic environment, and general pollution of the city centre, to live in the southern suburb of Ardwick, at 12 Green Street, off Ardwick Green North.[22] The census taken on 2 April 1871 shows Emanuel, Marie, John, Pauline, Bertha, and Samuel in their new home, along with an Irish maid, 50-year-old Margaret Crofton.[23] She was one of a series of such domestic servants employed to assist the family, a common practice at the time, especially among the middle classes. All the children were in school apart from John, who was noted as then working as an office boy. Sam attended the Chorlton High School. The move also offered the family a potential new start, away from the ghosts of Matilda, Emily, and Henrietta.

Emanuel's family's move reflected a wider trend among the city's middle class to relocate there during this period. It was a better environment, with fresher air, away from the squalor and unhealthy conditions of the industrial city centre.[24] It was also, as Bill Williams makes clear, a move away for a number of established Jewish families from their traditional haunts of Strangeways and the southern parts of Cheetham Hill, which were facing a decline in their social standing due to an influx of poor Polish and Eastern European Jewish migrants, to more fashionable environs.[25] The growing Jewish population in the south led to the establishment of the South Manchester Synagogue in 1872, nominally a branch of the Great Synagogue, though in effect a break-away group. The group secured permanent premises in Sidney Street, Chorlton-on-Medlock, the new synagogue being consecrated on 17 September 1873. This represented the growing social bonds and aspirations of the local Jewish community, who (while accepting the Chief Rabbi and thus restricting the synagogue's primary constituency to Ashkenazi Jewry) opted for the then novel use of English for prayer, something that no doubt appealed to its more Anglicised congregation.[26]

For Emanuel and his family, and in due course for Philipp and his family, the South Manchester Synagogue was their nearest synagogue. Drawing on a personal communication with Bill Williams, Marianne Krüll asserts Emanuel and Philipp were among the synagogue's founding members.[27] In turn, Emanuel Rice used these sources to claim Emanuel and Philipp remained part of the Orthodox Jewish community, while Möshe Gresser cited Rice to support a similar assertion, as did Joseph Berke.[28] Certainly, the lineaments of Orthodoxy were discernible in Emanuel's family in the 1860s, and may be inferred in that of Philipp. However, in Emanuel's branch of the family at least, this allegiance was waning and in its place the Reform tradition would take hold. Emanuel's move south to Green Street was something of a new start (and it would be this house that Freud resided in during his 1875 visit, which will be considered in the next chapter). The location of their house certainly brought them into the synagogue's orbit, yet the Freuds' choices of their domestic neighbourhoods were arguably more related to wider social trends, cultural and economic matters. By contrast, the family's association with Reform Jewry was by no means based on geographical convenience, the Manchester Synagogue of British Jews being well over two miles from their new neighbourhood. Williams did not, in fact, include the brothers in his published list of the South Manchester Synagogue's founder members.[29] Nor has other material emerged so far linking Emanuel and his family to it.

In his business life Emanuel was also making a new start, re-establishing himself as a fent dealer (a textile merchant specialising in remnants and ends of rolls of cloth) in new premises further up Thomas Street at number 69, operating under the trading name 'E Freud'. Although close by, his business association with 96 Shudehill now ceased. This re-orientation and re-branding of his business was also substantially complete by 1872.[30]

Reflections

For Emanuel, care for the family overlapped with degrees of control, which traded on traditional notions of seniority, gender roles, and capital. However, the family's difficult financial circumstances in the mid-1860s and their home in Shudehill, in the congested heart of inner-city Manchester, steps away from the Angel Meadow slum, exposed them to particularly unhealthy environmental conditions. The deaths of three of Emanuel and Marie's children here between 1866 and 1868 must have been a hammer blow for the family. Their short lives were subsequently passed over in silence, at least insofar as is revealed in the surviving correspondence. While such silence can be common in unprocessed painful trauma, Henrietta, Emily, and Matilda's deaths compounded with earlier losses would materially shape the family's going-on-being. Caregiving would be sustained, including to Freud and the wider family, but somatic concerns – particularly among the surviving females – and degrees of rigidity would become increasingly manifest in Emanuel's immediate family, crippling its fuller development, while at the same time symptomatically expressing their understandable vulnerability.

Externally however, the family was not conspicuously broken. Emanuel was able to rebuild his business and he was able to travel with John, maintaining ties with the family in Vienna. At home in Manchester, they moved from Shudehill to the city's healthier and socially more desirable developing southern suburbs. And they would rework their filiation with Judaism, reorienting towards the Reform movement.

The next chapter takes up a key episode, Freud's 1875 summer in Manchester, mostly with Emanuel and his family in their new home in Green Street, Ardwick. For Freud, his sojourn in Manchester would crucially help clarify his career and intellectual ambitions.

Notes

1 Bill Williams *The Making of Manchester Jewry 1740–1875*, Manchester: Manchester University Press, 1976, pp. 310–311.
2 *The London Gazette*, 3 November 1865, p. 5160; *Perry's Bankrupt Weekly Gazette*, 4 November 1865, p. 868. No relevant records survive from the Manchester County Court or the District Court of Bankruptcy for this period.
3 GRO birth record: Manchester Registrar's District, July–September 1865, vol. 8d, p. 223.
4 GRO birth record: Manchester Registrar's District, July–September 1866, vol. 8d, p. 223.
5 D Cohen *The Escape of Sigmund Freud*, New York: Overlook Press, 2012, p. 31.
6 GRO death record: Manchester Registrar's District, July–September 1866, vol. 8d, p. 201.
7 Manchester Hebrew Burial Ground Register, 1841–1872, Manchester Central Library, ref: GB127.M139/7/6/1. In the 20th Century, the cemetery (situated off what now is Knightley Walk, between Queens Road and Thornton Street North, and sometimes referred to as Collyhurst cemetery) fell into disrepair, was vandalised, and was finally

redesigned as a small green space in 1986; no matzevahs (gravestones) remain visible and no transcriptions of any details thereon survive.
8 *Manchester Courier*, 10 December 1868, p. 6; 1861.
9 *Manchester Times*, 31 October 1868, p. 5; *Manchester Courier*, 30 September 1868, p. 6, 1 December 1868, p. 7 and 15 December 1868, p. 6.
10 GRO death records: Manchester Registrar's District, October–December 1868, vol. 8d, p. 213 (both children being recorded on the same page).
11 Manchester Hebrew Burial Ground Register, 1841–1872, Manchester Central Library, ref: GB127.M139/7/6/1; Emily's date of death is here recorded as 28 November 1868. The cemetery today is overgrown, with some stones badly weathered, broken and/or toppled. Despite a careful search in November 2021, matzevahs relating to the girls could not be found.
12 In this widely debated area, Vallin suggests that in Britain during this period the probability that a child would die before reaching its fifth birthday stood at 25 per cent: see Jacques Vallin 'Mortality in Europe from 1720 to 1914: Long-term trends and changes in the patterns by age and sex', in Roger S Schofield, David S Reher, & Alain Bideau (eds) *The Decline of Mortality in Europe*, Oxford: Clarendon Press, 2002, pp. 38–67.
13 The notion of *huis clos*, referring figuratively here to an enclosed or restrictive space, within which one is trapped facing the tormenting being of oneself and others, here partly leans on Jean-Paul Sartre's 1944 existentialist play of the same name. See Jean-Paul Sartre *Huis Clos – Piece en un Acte*, London: Horizon, 1945.
14 Manchester Electoral Register, Citizens' Roll, 1868–69.
15 *Life & Work*, 1, p. 26.
16 For a fuller summary of the play see A Grinstein *Sigmund Freud's Dreams*, New York: International Universities Press, 1980, pp. 297–305.
17 Freud to E Silberstein, 2 August 1873, *Freud-Silberstein*, pp. 29–31; Freud to Emil Fluss, 6 March 1874, in E Freud (ed) 'Some early unpublished letters of Freud', *IJPA*, 1969, 50, p. 427.
18 S Freud *The Interpretation of Dreams*, *SE*, 1900 [1899], 5, p. 424.
19 S Freud *The Psychopathology of Everyday Life*, *SE*, 1901, 6, pp. 23–24 and 107–109.
20 D Anzieu *Freud's Self-Analysis*, London: Hogarth, 1986, pp. 384–386.
21 Ibid., pp. 304–305 and 517–518; S Freud *The Interpretation of Dreams*, *SE*, 1900 [1899], 5, p. 583–584; M Krüll *Freud and his Father*, London: Hutchinson, 1987, pp. 166–167; E Rice *Freud and Moses: The Long Journey Home*, Albany, NY: SUNY Press, 1990, pp. 17–18.
22 In the mid-1950s the street was substantially redeveloped, 12 Green Street being demolished in the process, and the street itself then renamed Durling Street in about 1955. See also Sergey V Aleinikov's useful though not wholly accurate '12 Green street', available online at: freudproject.ru/?p=7948 (accessed 4 April 2020).
23 1871 English census, TNA ref: RG 10/3975/135/21. A move elsewhere seems to have been contemplated in June 1871, as the house was then advertised to let (*The Guardian*, 20 June 1871, p. 7), though this move was then evidently abandoned for the time being.
24 The death rate measured over the first three quarters of 1868 for Deansgate was 38.3 per 1,000, while that for Ardwick was 28.6 and nearby Chorlton-on-Medlock, where the family would subsequently move, was 18.6 (*Manchester Times*, 31 October 1868, p. 5).
25 Bill Williams *The Making of Manchester Jewry 1740–1875*, Manchester: Manchester University Press, 1976, pp. 310–311; see also Bill Williams 'East and West: Class and culture in Manchester Jewry, 1850–1920', *Studia Rosenthaliana*, 1989, 23, pp. 88–106.
26 Ibid., pp. 312–319.
27 M Krüll *Freud and his Father*, London: Hutchinson, 1987, p. 175.
28 E Rice *Freud and Moses: The Long Journey Home*, Albany, NY: SUNY Press, 1990, pp. 57–58; M Gresser *Dual Allegiance: Freud as a Modern Jew*, Albany, NY: SUNY

Press, 1994, p. 33; J H Berke *The Hidden Freud: His Hassidic Roots*, London: Karnac, 2015, p. 94.
29 Bill Williams *The Making of Manchester Jewry 1740–1875*, Manchester: Manchester University Press, 1976, pp. 352–353.
30 Manchester Electoral Register, 1872–73.

Chapter 4

'Talking, walking, eating and drinking'

Freud's 1875 visit to Britain

Introduction

Freud's first visit to Britain in the summer of 1875 offers a useful commentary on the lives of the Manchester Freuds, their characters and social standing. More importantly, it highlights and undoubtedly reinforced the place of Freud's family there in his own mental economy, with Emanuel as the lead actor and his nephew John – who was still living with them at the time – continuing to feature prominently.

It was a trip that had been previously mooted in early 1873 and seems to have been provisionally scheduled for that summer, between Freud's final school exams, the *Matura*, and his commencing university. Some have suggested the visit was a reward for his success in that exam,[2] and while it *might* have been held out at some point by Jacob as an inducement to his son, it was clear even by the spring of 1873 (well before his exams) that hopes of the trip happening that year were ebbing away. Slim possibilities of it occurring seemed to remain in the balance until that summer, when in August Freud finally declared it was off,[3] probably due to a lack of parental support in view of the costs involved. The latter extended beyond the simple monetary to the emotional costs he anticipated his mother might exact, Freud having been keen earlier in the year she should not learn of his ambitions to travel to Manchester until it was a fait accompli.[4] In this context, his thirst for things English was almost unquenchable. 'If this were to go on', Freud wrote at the time, 'I shall get the "English disease" rather late in life. I read English history, write English letters, declaim English verse, listen to English descriptions, and thirst for English glances'.[5] Britain thus represented both a contagion and a liberation, a new compromise formation that provided him some independence from Jacob and Amalia, whilst at the same time offering closer contact with two of his alternative parental imagos, Emanuel and Philipp,[6] as well as alternative cultural referents.

When the trip eventually came about two years later, the Manchester Freuds were clearly enamoured with Freud and lost few opportunities of singing his praises to anyone who might listen, including to Freud himself, as well as confidently anticipating his future potential achievements. They thus exercised an important

DOI: 10.4324/9781032652023-5

Image 4.1 A recreation of 12 Green Street, Ardwick
Source: Manchester Libraries, Information & Archives[1]

cheerleading function, something which contributed to Freud's self-confidence, though there were other subtler feelings too.

The visit to Britain also exposed the young Freud to his brothers as men of business, engaged in practical activities, and apparently able to be self-supporting, rather different middle-class role models to the more working-class Jacob Freud. Extending from all this, Freud would seek out a series of British scientific and other texts during this visit, which would influence his emerging intellectual orientation more towards empiricism and reinforce his own Anglophile leanings and appreciation of what he took to be British cultural values. Freud's memories of this trip would exert a long-lasting influence on him and in due course on the dissemination of psychoanalytic ideas.

Freud in Manchester

In 1875 Sigmund made his first trip to visit his brothers and their families in Manchester, leaving Vienna on Friday 16 July. In total, it would be seven-and-a-half weeks before he would return home. Breaking his journey in Leipzig to see his teenage friend Eduard Silberstein (1856–1925), Freud then took the evening sailing from Hamburg to Grimsby, on the SS *Huddersfield*, part of the Manchester, Sheffield & Lincolnshire Railway Co, on Tuesday 20 July, and went on to Manchester by train.[7]

Staying with Emanuel and his family at 12 Green Street, the 19-year-old Freud spent his time 'talking, walking, eating and drinking'.[8] Freud was, as usual during his youth, short of money and was getting by on the small amount of cash he had brought with him, supplemented with money loaned to him by Silberstein, an allowance from Emanuel (totalling 11 shillings by 3 August), the belief that some funds would arrive from Vienna, and the further expectation of cash gifts on his departure.

Such impecuniousness was only too familiar to Freud and its legacy haunted him in the years to come, fuelling a powerful work-ethic. He told Fliess on 21 September 1899: 'My mood also depends very strongly on my earnings. Money is laughing gas for me. I know from my youth . . . the helplessness of poverty and continually fear it'.[9] A decade later he wrote to Carl Jung about coaching himself to 'give up wanting to cure . . ., [just] learn and make money, those are the most plausible conscious aims'.[10] These reveal the impact of economic poverty on Freud's sensibilities and his determination to meet his obligations through his own efforts, whilst acknowledging his history. These were not wholly hidden matters for Freud as he reflected on and discussed his own motivations and surviving correspondence suggests neither were they for his half-brothers. However, Freud's childhood and early adult working-class impecuniousness existed in the context of the extended family's financial crisis in 1859–1860 and the desperate lengths to which they went attempting to surmount this. On that topic he is largely silent with his own children at least,[11] and it appears likely that those earlier events formed a traumatic real-world substructure to the remembered poverty and his later industriousness, which had a clearly driven quality.

Describing his brothers and their circumstances during his 1875 visit, Freud wrote in qualified terms:

> I can say that they now hold a generally respected position, not because of their wealth, for they are not rich, but because of their personal character. They are shopkeepers [in English in the original], i.e., merchants who have a shop, the elder selling cloth and the younger jewellery [in English in the original], in the sense that word seems to have in England. My two sisters-in-law are good and jolly women, one of them [Bloomah Freud] an Englishwoman, which made my conversations with her extremely agreeable.[12]

It is clear Freud admired both brothers, with a certain hesitation about their modest means, their bourgeois occupations, and the apparently common-or-garden jewellery that Philipp sold. This dual aspect is underlined in his depiction of his older brothers as 'shopkeepers', his rendering of this in English reinforcing this and echoing the sometimes-derisive depiction of England as a nation of shopkeepers, a quote commonly though perhaps apocryphally attributed to Napoleon, with whom Freud had partly identified during his youth. Yet, Freud appears to be suggesting that his brothers' status as men of 'personal character', *menschen*, is epitomised precisely through their capacity to do such unglamorous work.

With regards to his nephew John, Freud emphasised to Silberstein that he 'is an Englishman in every respect, with a knowledge of languages and technical matters well beyond the usual business education',[13] having earlier noted that he 'speaks and understands a little Spanish' too,[14] a titbit linking John to Freud's correspondence with Silberstein in that language. John's younger brother, Sam, had sat the Oxford Local Examinations in May 1875 and the results of these were released on Saturday 21 August. Sam passed as a junior candidate in the third division,[15] no doubt a cause for some small celebration, though it went unmentioned in Freud's surviving correspondence. Whether the Manchester Freuds' girls were formally educated to the same level is unclear and probably unlikely. Their names do not appear in published results lists.

The opportunity to practice his English with Philipp's wife Bloomah, who he had married just two years previously (and who will be properly introduced in Chapter 6), was clearly welcome. She was, as Freud told Silberstein, 'an intelligent and lovable wife'.[16] Freud's enjoyment of his conversations with her highlighted not only his affection for her but also his growing Anglophile attitude, which was further catalysed by this visit. He was explicit about the latter with Silberstein, writing:

> As for England itself, I . . . can say straight out that I would sooner live there than here, rain, fog, drunkenness, and conservatism notwithstanding. Many peculiarities of the English character and country that other Continentals might find intolerable agree very well with my own makeup. Who knows, dear friend, but that after I have completed my studies a favourable wind might not blow me across to England for practical work.[17]

Though Freud here fails to precisely specify the agreeable 'peculiarities of . . . character and country', the idea of 'practical work' may be related and this marked something of a turning point for him. He elaborates on this in the same letter, thus:

> I now have more than one ideal, a practical one having been added to the theoretical one of earlier years. Had I been asked last year what was my dearest wish, I would have replied: a laboratory and free time, or a ship on the ocean with all the instruments a scientist needs; now I waver about whether I should not rather say: a large hospital and plenty of money in order to reduce or wipe out some of the ills that afflict our body. That is to say, if I wished to influence a large number of people instead of a small number of readers or fellow scientists, England would be just the place for that purpose. A respected man, supported by the press and the rich, could do wonders in alleviating physical ills, if only he were enough of an explorer to strike out on new therapeutic paths.[18]

After a brief digression, Freud reveals his reading while in Britain and further clarifies his position, thus:

> [T]he acquaintance with English scientific books I made over there will always ensure that in my own studies I shall always be on the side of the Englishmen in whose favour I am now highly prejudiced: Tyndall, Huxley, Lyell, Darwin, Thomson, Lockyer, et al.[19]

Freud here associates himself with British empiricism. Beyond that, his thinking was here emerging in the context of his relationship with Emanuel in particular, but also Philipp, their retail and wholesale trade and their entrepreneurship. Theirs was 'practical work'.

Certainly, Emanuel (who functioned as an alternative father figure for Freud) offered a 'practical' model for his adolescent younger brother; he was a man who was managing to economically sustain himself and his family, in contrast to Freud's experience of their actual father. It was in this sense that Freud would later discuss a parapraxis in the first edition of *The Interpretation of Dreams* where a brother's name was substituted for a father's (Hasdrubal for Hamilcar Barca, Hannibal's brother and father respectively).[20] In the course of analysing this slip, Freud noted both his adolescent dissatisfaction with his own father over his lack of overt protest in the face of anti-Semitism and his turning instead towards Emanuel, wondering 'how different things would have been if I had been born the son not of my father but of my brother'.[21] These phantasies seem to have strengthened during Freud's 1875 stay with Emanuel, alongside an unstated 'change' in his relationship with Jacob. In this context, Emanuel evidently 'admonished' his younger brother several times and on one memorable occasion cryptically told him that: 'One thing . . . that you must not forget is that as far as the conduct of your life is concerned you really belong not to the second but to the third generation in relation to your father'.[22] What if anything provoked this admonishment is unclear, but Freud certainly remembered Emanuel's injunction with respect to 'filial piety',[23] which repositioned him not one but two generations from his father, *as if* situating him as Emanuel's son and John's brother. While this may represent Emanuel's rivalrous usurpation of paternal authority and the concomitant marginalisation of Jacob into a grandfather role,[24] if the earlier characterisation of Jacob as a gentle schlemiel Jew holds water then this may also be a manifestation an early modernist quest for an assertive Semitic masculinity.

Freud also played with the aetiology of his turn to the practical that was catalysed during his visit to Manchester. In his 'Screen memories' paper, Freud suggested his father and Emanuel engineered the visit to lure him towards more lucrative and practical yet prosaic pursuits, through settling in Manchester and marrying Emanuel's daughter, his own childhood occasional playmate Paulina (now 'Pauline').[25] She did not excite Freud's imagination – erotic or otherwise – during his visit. However, England certainly had and Freud in turn made a considerable impression on his older brother. Emanuel and the Manchester Freuds would become Freud's first British followers and cheerleaders. Over half a century later, Anna Freud Bernays thus recalled Emanuel's enthusiastic letters about her brother which her father shared with the family. 'You have', one such letter apparently went:

> given us great pleasure by sending us Sigmund. He is a splendid specimen of a fine human being, and if I had a pen of a Dickens, I could well make a hero of him. . . . All your descriptions of him have been worthless; only now, since he is with us, do we see him as he really is.[26]

Emanuel depicts Freud's visit as his father's gift and Freud as a hero in the making, his potentiality inadequately drawn by his father. Declining to directly compete with Jacob, Emanuel instead signals his relative assimilation into British culture through his reference to Dickens as the epitome of literary style. This was Emanuel's cultural capital. It was, arguably, a curious choice given Dickens's anti-Semitism, although turning a blind eye to the latter and identifying with him was perhaps an instance of the price of entry into British society, a form of what Anna Freud later called identification with the aggressor.[27] Indeed, Bill Williams has argued more broadly in this vein that anglicisation promoted a degree of conditional acceptance as well as status for Jews in Manchester society and this typically involved approximating to native bourgeois ideals.[28] The extent to which Emanuel achieved this was particularly noteworthy as we shall see later.

From a seahorse on the seashore to the primal scene

While Freud was in Britain for about 46 days on this first visit, no day-to-day chronology of his activities survives. Instead, he offered Silberstein a broad-brush picture of his time with his British relatives, his impressions of the culture, and the influence this and British scientists were having on his thinking. One small exception to this condensed account was the more specific remark to his friend, and particularly his poetic sensibilities, that: 'I have seen the sea, sacred thalatta [The Sea!],[29] following the waves of the high tide as they retreated thunderously from the shore, and have caught crab and starfish on the beach'.[30]

It is an iconic scene that Freud here paints, evocative of Rabindranath Tagore's line: 'On the seashore of endless worlds children meet'.[31] Creatively misquoting Tagore, Donald Winnicott would later cite the line as: 'On the seashore of endless worlds, children play',[32] before offering three successive psychoanalytic perspectives on its meaning. In the first of these the shore and sea represent an endless intercourse between man and woman, from which the child emerged to repeat the cycle of its life course. The second interpretation suggested that the sea is the mother birthing babies onto the shore, which in turn represents her body over which she and baby begin to relate. Winnicott's third, and favoured, interpretation proposes that play at its most intense is located in a potential space between the subjective object and the object objectively perceived, and where every object (play-thing) is a 'found' object. Cultural experience in its many forms is the sequelae of such play.³³ For Winnicott such intermediate space exists between primary narcissism and object relations, with activities therein imbued with aspects of both poles. For his part, Freud was clearly struck with his experience that day on the beach on the Lancashire coast, poetically engaged in exploratory play between the sea and the land, and in catching or finding crab and starfish from the seabed.

Underscoring the personal significance of this day, Freud expanded on his memory of it in *The Interpretation of Dreams*, recalling how he had:

> spent a whole day on the shore of the Irish Sea. I naturally revelled in the opportunity of collecting the marine animals left behind by the tide and I was occupied with a starfish – the words '*Hollthurn*' and '*holothurians* [sea-slugs]' occurred at the beginning of the dream – when a charming little girl came up to me and said: 'Is it a starfish? Is it alive?' 'Yes', I replied, 'he is alive', and at once, embarrassed at my mistake, repeated the sentence correctly.³⁴

Freud's recollections had been sparked by his analysis of a dream he had on 18–19 July 1898 during a train journey. Going into his first-class train compartment, an elderly aristocratic couple appeared annoyed at his entrance, the woman placing her umbrella on the seat opposite them to prevent Freud sitting there, and both were unresponsive to Freud's initial greeting. The couple further discouraged Freud from opening the window, despite the heat, and when the ticket collector arrived the woman declared (as if emphasising their status) that her husband has a free pass. Silently angry over the encounter, Freud went to sleep and had what has since become known as the Hollthurn dream. This began with:

> 'Hollthurn, ten minutes' being called out. I at once thought of holothurians [sea-slugs], of a natural history museum, that this was the spot at which valiant men had fought in vain against the superior power of the ruler of their country, yes, the Counter-Reformation in Austria, it was as though it were a place in Styria or the Tyrol. I then saw indistinctly a small museum, in which the relics or belongings of these men were preserved. I should have liked to get out, but hesitated to do so. There were women with fruit on the platform. They were crouching on the ground and holding up their baskets invitingly. I hesitated because I was not sure whether there was time, but we were still not moving. I was suddenly in another compartment, in which the upholstery and seats were so narrow that one's back pressed directly against the back of the carriage. I was surprised by this, but I reflected that I might have changed carriages while I was in a sleeping state. There were several people, including an English brother and sister; a row of books were distinctly visible on a shelf on the wall. I saw *The Wealth of Nations* and *Matter and Motion* (by Clerk-Maxwell), a thick volume and bound in brown cloth. The man asked his sister about a book by Schiller, whether she had forgotten it. It seemed as though the books were sometimes mine and sometimes theirs. I felt inclined at that point to intervene in the conversation in a confirmatory or substantiating sense.³⁵

Freud woke at that point, perspiring in the hot sealed compartment, the train having stopped in Marburg station.[36] Writing the dream down subsequently, Freud was only then able to recover another element of it, namely that: 'I said [in English] to the brother and sister, referring to a particular work [by Schiller]: "It is from . . .", but corrected myself: "It is by . . ." "Yes", the man commented to his sister, "he said it right" '.[37] This concluded the manifest dream content.

Freud went on to detail a number of associations, although he regarded the final recovered element – and hence the story of the starfish – as the best key to the dream. That 'part of a dream that has been rescued from oblivion in this way' he thus wrote, 'is invariably the most important part; it always lies on the shortest road to the dream's solution and has for that reason been exposed to resistance more than any other part'.[38] Of the two other main reported associations, Freud termed the first 'a somewhat extravagant phantasy', that the elderly aristocratic couple were annoyed at his entrance as it prevented their planned 'affectionate exchanges' that night, while the second related to the change of compartments, supposedly while asleep and in a '*automatisme ambulatoire*' state, in the dream. This, he associated to a man he had successfully treated for an obsession that he might murder people in an unconscious state, thoughts that were displacements, Freud suggested, from hostile impulses directed in childhood against his rather overbearing father. This latter scenario Freud said mirrored an early memory of his own, in which he had entered his parents' bedroom, perhaps out of sexual curiosity, only to be ordered out by his father.[39] However, aside from saying that the 'broken fragments' of the early part of the dream report concealed the 'fearful vengeance . . . insults and humiliations' he had in phantasy heaped upon the aged aristocratic couple, he left the dream otherwise uninterpreted due to 'its gross indecency'.[40]

It was only after an intervening 60 pages (in the *Standard Edition* text) that Freud again took up the story, focussing this time on the recovered coda to the dream, noting that '*Das Buch ist von Schiller*' should be translated into English not with 'from' but with 'by', a grammatical mistake that had its autobiographical precursor in the starfish episode. There, in response to the little girl's questions, 'Is it a starfish? Is it alive?', Freud fumbles his English reply saying 'Yes, *he* is alive', before correcting himself, 'Yes, *it* is alive'. In German of course all nouns are gendered, *der Seestern* (the starfish) being masculine, unlike its gender-neutral English language equivalent. The story is framed as particularly innocuous in this context to bolster its effective disguise, its claim of innocence being writ loud in what Freud saw as a 'magnificent piece of condensation' in a homophone that traded on the acoustic identity of 'the English "from" and the German adjective "fromm" [meaning "pious"]' in the dream's soundscape.[41] Yet in this *pious* memory Freud was 'using a word indicating gender or sex in the wrong place', he was impiously 'bringing in sex (the word "he") where it did not belong'.[42] This was one of the keys to solving this particular dream and when taken in combination with a final clue, an associative link between the book title *Matter and Motion* and faeces, Freud thought the gaps in the dream's interpretation were easy enough to fill in.

What then might be the dream interpretation that Freud still declined to give his readers? Elements in the dream have been widely discussed in the psychoanalytic literature, with Alexander Grinstein and Didier Anzieu offering particularly detailed analyses.[43] With those exegeses in mind, the dream may at one level be interpreted as exemplifying the erotic and murderous unconscious phantasies that constitute a very early stage of the Oedipus complex, which Freud was beginning to articulate during this period of his theory building. This would be further developed later through the work of Melanie Klein. Such an interpretation might run something like this. Freud's arrival in the train compartment housing the aristocratic parental couple disturbs their supposedly sexual plans (the primal scene) and he is cold-shouldered. He may have a first-class ticket, but he does not have a free pass to access either the parental bedroom or the mother as much as he might wish. Enraged at his exclusion, Freud launches a silent vituperative attack on the woman (the active gatekeeper to the scene in the dream), and especially her feminine identity, noting she is 'haughty', 'discontented', and more bitingly that she is 'not far from the time of the decay of feminine beauty'.[44] The 'dreadful vengeance' he exacted is reflected in the 'broken fragments' of the first half of the dream text, Freud's account hinting at a murderous sexual anal-sadistic attack on the couple, using excrement as a weapon and anal penetration as a means of hostile control.[45] Holothurians are molluscs or 'sea-slugs', shaped like a penis or piece of excrement, and are used in the dream as an anal phallic symbol as Anzieu points out.[46] Eventually satiated by his excesses, Freud leaves the scene of the crime by changing compartments, his new berth being in a more benign, intellectual bookish and inclusive atmosphere, with an English brother and sister who accept his 'grammatical' lapse and its correction with equanimity. The now remembered starfish episode reconnects Freud with an appreciation both of the potentially murderous violence ('Is it alive?') and the sexual/anal assault ('sex in the wrong place'), with concern about the damage done being aroused by the 'charming little girl', a tender more empathic part of Freud's mind. By responding 'He is alive', Freud can comfort himself that his aggression was not fatal and his father is alive.[47]

As Anzieu and others have highlighted, much more may be said about this dream. Freud is clear, for example, in pointing to the aristocratic couple being among other things revenants of Jacob and Amalia. For the present purposes, however, we may conclude this discussion by underlining its connections to Freud's British family and to Britain. In the manifest dream content, the English siblings and famous English books create and inhabit an intellectual and accepting space, where Freud can find his voice and participate. The English brother and sister appear as revenants of Freud's British kin, possibly quasi-siblings such as John and Pauline or substitute parental figures such as Emanuel and Marie. Here, he is not excluded or provoked by pressing sexuality.

The key starfish association situates England as a place of wonder and exploration, where male and female elements may combine, where he might make discoveries and could have an audience that would listen to him. More than this, Freud's books too might be on the shelf, side by side with the index volumes of Adam

Smith and James Clerk-Maxwell. He had, in fact, copies of both volumes among his books, having obtained them not long after his first visit to Manchester.[48] It is works in English by British scientific writers that are thus given prominence in the dream, with ownership and access to these being both possible and uncontested. There is a freer exchange of knowledge. In Freud's associations to the dream, particularly its recovered coda, the prominence of the memory of his 1875 visit, and specifically his time on the beach collecting 'marine animals', the starfish, and the chance conversation with the little girl, testifies to the substantial influence of Britain as an idea on his thinking, instantiated through his ongoing relationships with Emanuel, Philipp, and their families. However, while his Manchester family would invite him back and Emanuel would offer to sponsor him in the future should he wish to emigrate and pursue his career in Britain, Freud was hesitant about the wish or necessity to make such a step. Just as Freud would struggle to visit Rome,[49] so too would he struggle to come back to Manchester, as will be discussed later. Some of this is superficially evident of course in the Hollthurn dream: there, his English billet is in a train compartment, a temporary accommodation rather than a permanent home.

Heading home with indelible impressions

With the Manchester, Sheffield, & Lincolnshire Railway steamships departing for the Continent on Wednesdays and Saturdays only, Freud's stay in Manchester probably came to an end on Saturday 4 September. Taking the connecting boat train that left Manchester at 3.00 pm, Freud would have arrived at Grimsby at about 6.15 pm and been able to catch that evening's steamer.[50] Getting back to Vienna on Tuesday 7 September 1875, Freud lamented having not been able to visit 'London, Sheffield, Birmingham, Oxford, and so on, all of which someone who travels for pleasure is expected to visit'. Freud's untraveled itinerary highlights his brothers' influence (deriving from their commercial links with Sheffield and Birmingham) as much as it does popular centres of cultural tourism. Freud expressed the hope that he would be able to return to Britain within the next year or two.[51]

It would be over three decades before he would next step foot in the country, though its impact on his imagination continued in the interim. This was stoked by a sustained narrative of support for and expressed belief in Freud and his potentiality by the Manchester Freuds and cemented in place by mutually affectionate bonds of kinship, with tokens passed in both directions. Some expressions of this were superficially small. For example, Freud was momentarily expecting photographs of his Manchester nieces in October 1875.[52] He would send Philipp a portrait photograph the following year, significantly signing a dedication on it with 'Sigismund', a style which he was by then abandoning in other spheres of correspondence, yet here used perhaps to underline their familiarity and common Jewish identity.[53] As a name, 'Sigismund' had a once popular cachet among European Jewry, particularly following kings Sigismund I and II of Poland and Sigismund of Luxembourg who were relatively tolerant of Jews, though Ronald Clark and others suggest the name became a common target in Viennese anti-Semitic jokes, perhaps prompting Freud's public abandonment of it in favour of the Germanic 'Sigmund'.[54] Nevertheless, in private family conversation, 'Sigismund' would endure in Philipp's lexicon into the twentieth century,[55] revealing a certain continued doubling of his younger brother's identity, both secular and Jewish. Another token of filiation was evident in 1891 when Freud would name his third son 'Oliver', ostensibly after Oliver Cromwell whom he greatly admired, though the choice of such an English name was undoubtedly also a way of curating his ties to his British family.[56]

All this was a form of mutual celebration and others were expected to join in. When Bertha wrote to Freud in 1882, he thus forwarded her letter to Martha Bernays (1861–1951) early in their courtship, instructing her to: 'not be shocked by the family vanity expressed in it; *I am a good part of the hope of mine*, and I expect that once you see her you will come to love Bertha very much'.[57] And, as previously emphasised, Freud extended his own warm reciprocal feelings to his older brothers' adopted country. One month later, in August 1882, Freud for example told Martha how:

> England reappears before me, with its sober hustle and bustle, its generous devotion to general purposes, the stubbornness and sensitive sentiment of its inhabitants ... all the indelible impressions that have been influencing me since the life-defining journey seven years ago.[58]

It was, he thought in September 1882, a place where he could successfully practice as a doctor, should recognition in Vienna be slow in coming.[59] Indeed, Emanuel had encouraged him to move to Manchester when he had completed his hospital residency and had agreed to accommodate him while he established a practice.[60] It was a pleasant offer and echoes of this persisted in their correspondence, Emanuel for example years later giving Freud a biography of Julius Dreschfeld (1845–1907), a Jewish Bavarian émigré who had settled in Manchester where he became a distinguished professor of medicine and a neurologist.[61] Yet Freud consciously saw Emanuel's daughters (his would-be siblings) as without adequate dowries to find husbands,[62] a shortcoming that must inevitably rest with his would-be benefactor, Emanuel. It was a narrative he probably realised was something of a rationalisation for a more general failure to launch in a rather enmeshed nervous family and consequently sustained a working distance from them.

With such mixed feelings about entrusting his future to provincial Manchester and his kin there, Freud in 1882 also entertained notions of emigrating to the USA or Australia and the available evidence suggests he continued to consider the USA as an option into at least March 1886 and probably beyond.[63] This is particularly interesting in view of his subsequently expressed ambivalence towards that country.[64] Hearing of Freud's return from studying with Charcot in Paris at the end of February 1886 (events relating to which period will be further discussed in the next chapter), Emanuel was jubilant. Writing to Rosa, he fondly imagined that 'Father must be in his glory about him. I feel very happy to think how you must have all rejoiced to see the dear fellow come back among you'.⁶⁵ Freud however was less sanguine about his prospects in Vienna and evidently reiterated thoughts of emigrating to the USA in a now lost letter to Emanuel on 19 March 1886. Emanuel was characteristically encouraging in his reply, urging his younger brother to persevere with his career in Vienna, adding 'I entrust you for goodness sake don't talk now of going to America. That would be taking away the sunshine from a dear house in Navarre Street'.⁶⁶ Emanuel's powerful plea here to his younger brother is telling. Drawing on ancient imagery of the sun, the centre of the universe, the giver of life, and an enduring symbol of abundance and divinity, its imagery most notably deployed in modern history by Louis XIV,⁶⁷ Emanuel situates his younger brother in distinguished company. This impression is further reinforced by Emanuel's reference to Navarre Street, the family home at the time in Vienna being an apartment at Novaragasse 29 (i.e., 29 Novara Street).⁶⁸ Perhaps Emanuel also had in mind the kingdom of Navarre and to Shakespeare's *Love's Labour's Lost*, which was set there. Be that as it may, Emanuel figuratively bound Freud to his family and Europe, which – without directly deprecating the United States – inserted an emotional wedge between the old and new worlds.

Reflections

Freud's experience of his siblings and their families in Manchester over the long summer holiday of 1875 exerted a strong influence on him. Their love and support were very real and so too was Freud's reciprocation and his shift towards the practical, the empirical, an appreciation of British sensibilities, and the English language. Yet given all this, why did it take Freud 33 years to return to Britain? One possible reason relates to the earlier discussed dynamic of replacement wherein Emanuel surrendered his position as Jacob's first-born son in favour of Freud. Emanuel and his family, as may be seen in their eulogising correspondence, seemed to regard Freud as the family's messiah, the chosen one who would transform the family's fortunes, who would make Emanuel's abdication justified, and on the back of whose achievements they may derive some vicarious satisfaction. Perhaps he was also seen as a returning lost child. Perhaps a reincarnation of Henrietta, Emily, or Matilda. Yet for Freud, this weight of responsibility must have been a burden to carry and maybe entailed painful feelings of guilt over his having replaced (or, symbolically, killed off) Emanuel. It was a scenario that Freud would himself discuss in relation to the Oedipus complex and to religious beliefs in both *Totem and Taboo* and *Moses and Monotheism*, discussions no doubt informed by these family relationships and his self-analysis.⁶⁹ Hints of such feelings may be discerned in Freud's later attitudes towards Emanuel and his ambivalence in taking up Emanuel's invitations to again visit Britain.

Notes

1 The original of this photograph depicts 14 Green Street, a mirror image of its neighbour 12 Green Street. The present photograph is reversed to recreate a semblance of what 12

Green Street, on the junction with Leigh Avenue, looked like as you go towards Ardwick Green.
2 *Life & Work*, 1, p. 22; Anna Freud Bernays 'My brother, Sigmund Freud', *The American Mercury*, 51, November 1940, p. 339.
3 Freud to Emil Fluss, 1 May 1873, in E Freud (ed) 'Some early unpublished letters of Freud', *IJPA*, 1969, 50, p. 424; Freud to E Silberstein, 10 July 1873, 11 July 1873, and 6 August 1873, *Freud-Silberstein*, pp. 20, 21, and 32.
4 Freud to E Silberstein, 11 July 1873, *Freud-Silberstein*, p. 21.
5 Freud to E Silberstein, 6 August 1873, *Freud-Silberstein*, p. 32.
6 Walter Boehlich suggests Freud's reference to the 'English disease' (*englische Krankheit*) refers both to rickets and his Anglophilia (*Freud-Silberstein*, p. 34n). In its former usage, Freud may have been obliquely referring to his brother Philipp, whose stature and gait – as discussed earlier – might have been related to rickets.
7 The long ferry crossing probably took over 30 hours, with the subsequent Grimsby-Manchester train journey taking a further 3 hours 25 minutes on average (e.g., the 1875 MSL Railway timetable suggests the 6.15 am train from Grimsby would reach Manchester at 10.40 am); information courtesy of Emily Brunell of the National Railway Museum archives, York.
8 Freud to E Silberstein, 3 August 1875, *Freud-Silberstein*, p. 123.
9 Freud to W Fliess, 21 September 1899, *Freud-Fliess*, p. 374.
10 Freud to C Jung, 25 January 1909, *Freud-Jung*, pp. 202–203.
11 E Laible 'Through privation to knowledge: Unknown documents from Freud's university years', *IJPA*, 1993, 74, p. 787.
12 Freud to E Silberstein, 9 September 1875, *Freud-Silberstein*, pp. 126–127.
13 Ibid., p. 127.
14 Freud to E Silberstein, 3 August 1875, *Freud-Silberstein*, p. 124.
15 *The Guardian*, 23 August 1875, p. 8.
16 Freud to E Silberstein, 3 August 1875, *Freud-Silberstein*, p. 123.
17 Freud to E Silberstein, 9 September 1875, *Freud-Silberstein*, p. 127.
18 Ibid.
19 Ibid., p. 128.
20 S Freud *The Interpretation of Dreams*, *SE*, 1900 [1899], 4, p. 197.
21 S Freud *The Psychopathology of Everyday Life*, *SE*, 1901, 6, pp. 219–220.
22 Ibid., p. 220.
23 Freud's later reuse this term in 1936 in discussing his experience of derealisation when visiting the Acropolis (which he understood as a defence against the recognition of having gone beyond his father's and early familial horizons) silently harks back to this; see S Freud 'A disturbance of memory on the Acropolis', *SE*, 1936, 22, p. 248.
24 R Bowlby 'The Cronus complex: Psychoanalytic myths of the future for boys and girls', in V Zajko & M Leonard (eds) *Laughing with Medusa: Classical Myth and Feminist Thought*, Oxford: Oxford University Press, 2006, pp. 32–34; D Meghnagi 'From the dreams of a generation to the theory of dreams: Freud's Roman dreams', *IJPA*, 2011, 92, p. 684.
25 S Freud 'Screen memories', *SE*, 1899, 3, pp. 314–315; *Life & Work*, 1, pp. 28–29.
26 Anna Freud Bernays 'My brother, Sigmund Freud', *The American Mercury*, 51, November 1940, p. 340; see also *Life & Work*, 1, pp. 26–27.
27 Anna Freud *The Ego and the Mechanisms of Defence*, London: Hogarth, 1968, pp. 109–121.
28 Bill Williams 'East and West: Class and culture in Manchester Jewry, 1850–1920', *Studia Rosenthaliana*, 23, 1989, pp. 92–93.
29 Walter Boehlich suggests this was a reference to Xenophon's *Anabasis*, 4.7, where the roaming 10,000 Greeks delightedly catch sight of the Black Sea from Mount Theches

following their participation in the failed campaign against the Persian Empire, and/or to Heinrich Heine's 1826 poem cycle *Die Nordsee* (The North Sea); see *Freud-Silberstein*, p. 128, note 6.
30 Freud to E Silberstein, 9 September 1875, *Freud-Silberstein*, pp. 127–128; see also S Freud 'A disturbance of memory on the Acropolis', *SE*, 1936, 22, p. 247.
31 R Tagore '60 [On the seashore]', in *Gitanjali*, with an introduction by W B Yeats, London: The India Society, 1912, pp. 34–35.
32 D W Winnicott 'The Location of cultural experience', 1967, in *Playing and Reality*, Harmondsworth: Penguin, 1985, p. 112.
33 Ibid., pp. 112 and 118–119.
34 S Freud *The Interpretation of Dreams*, *SE*, 1900 [1899], 5, p. 519.
35 Ibid., pp. 455–456. James Strachey here translates 'dem Leder' as 'the upholstery' rather than 'the leather', which would have been more precise and perhaps evocative. It is rendered as 'leather' in A A Brill's 1913 translation.
36 Freud suggested he must have subconsciously heard 'Marburg' being called out, initially supporting this contention by pointing to Schiller's appearance in the dream and that he was born in a town of the same name. Only later did Freud recognise this was an error (that Schiller was born in Marbach) and that Marburg perhaps related to a 'business friend' of his father's (*SE*, 5, p. 456 and *SE*, 6, pp. 217 and 219), the dream characters thus being proxies of Freud's family rather than more remote strangers on a train. Christfried Tögel suggests Herr Marburg may have been Salomon Marburg (1835–1913), a sheep wool trader ('*Schafwollagent*') who lived near Jacob (personal communication, 27 January 2023).
37 S Freud *The Interpretation of Dreams*, *SE*, 1900 [1899], 5, p. 456.
38 Ibid., pp. 518–519.
39 Ibid., pp. 457–459; Freud had related this scene at greater length earlier, noting how at age seven or eight: 'before going to sleep I disregarded the rules which modesty lays down and obeyed the calls of nature in my parents' bedroom while they were present. In the course of his reprimand, my father let fall the words: "The boy will come to nothing". This must have been a frightful blow to my ambition, for references to this scene are still constantly recurring in my dreams and are always linked with an enumeration of my achievements and successes, as though I wanted to say: 'You see, I *have* come to something' (*SE*, 4, p. 216). See also *Life & Work*, 1, p. 7; L Shengold *'The Boy Will Come to Nothing': Freud's Ego Ideal and Freud as Ego Ideal*, New Haven: Yale University Press, 1993, pp. 13–17.
40 S Freud *The Interpretation of Dreams*, *SE*, 1900 [1899], 5, pp. 457 and 519.
41 Ibid., p. 519.
42 Ibid., pp. 519–520.
43 A Grinstein *Sigmund Freud's Dreams*, New York: International Universities Press, 1980, pp. 334–353 and D Anzieu *Freud's Self-Analysis*, London: Hogarth, 1986, pp. 324–332.
44 S Freud *The Interpretation of Dreams*, *SE*, 1900 [1899], 5, p. 457.
45 Such phantasies of primitive infantile excremental attacks were later theorised by Melanie Klein. See her book *The Psychoanalysis of Children*, London: Hogarth, 1980, pp. 144–147; see also D Meltzer *The Claustrum*, Perthshire: Clunie Press, 1992, who develops Klein's views on projective identification, intrusive states and the precarity of subsequent existence in the compartmentalised internal object.
46 D Anzieu *Freud's Self-Analysis*, London: Hogarth, 1986, p. 328.
47 A Grinstein *Sigmund Freud's Dreams*, New York: International Universities Press, 1980, p. 352.
48 Freud dated the Maxwell and Smith volumes 31 July 1877 and 7 August 1879 respectively. See J K Davies & G Fichtner *Freud's Library: A Comprehensive Catalogue*, London & Tübingen: Freud Museum and Edition Diskord, 2006, catalogue numbers 2381

and 3296. He further noted his acquisition of *The Wealth of Nations* in his correspondence with Silberstein; see Freud to E Silberstein, 10 August 1879, *Freud-Silberstein*, p. 175.
49 S Freud *The Interpretation of Dreams*, *SE*, 1900 [1899], 4, pp. 193–194; Freud also connected Rome with his childhood Freiberg (see *SE*, 5, pp. 441–444).
50 I am grateful to Emily Brunell, of the National Railway Museum archives, York, who uncovered the Manchester, Sheffield, & Lincolnshire Railways advertisement of this service.
51 Freud to E Silberstein, 9 September 1875, *Freud-Silberstein*, p. 127.
52 Freud to E Silberstein, 2 October 1875, *Freud-Silberstein*, p. 131.
53 Lilly Freud-Marlé *Mein Onkel Sigmund Freud: Erinnerungen an eine grosse Familie*, edited by Christfried Tögel & Magdalena Frank, Berlin: Aufbau-Verlag, 2006, pp. 273–274.
54 Ronald W Clark *Freud: The Man and the Cause*, London: Jonathan Cape and Weidenfield & Nicholson, 1980, p. 36; see also D Anzieu *Freud's Self-Analysis*, London: Hogarth, 1986, p. 7 and Ian S Miller 'Spinoza: Multiple identities at the origins of psychoanalytic psychology', *International Forum of Psychoanalysis*, 2020, 29, pp. 209–210.
55 Philipp Freud to Marie Freud, 12 March 1902, LoC ref: mss39990, box 13, folder 44.
56 P Roazen *Meeting Freud's Family*, Amherst, MA: University of Massachusetts Press, 1993, p. 168.
57 Freud to Martha Bernays, 4 July 1882, LoC ref: mss39990, box 3, reel 1; *Die Brautbriefe*, 1, p. 150; emphasis added.
58 Freud to Martha Bernays, 16 August 1882, LoC ref: mss39990, box 3, reel 1.
59 Freud to Martha Bernays, 25 September 1882, LoC ref: mss39990, box 3, reel 1.
60 Freud to Martha Bernays, 20–21 December 1883, LoC ref: mss39990, box 5, reel 2.
61 Emanuel Freud to Freud, 23 June 1907, LoC ref: mss39990, box 2; for details on Dreschfeld see *The Guardian*, 15 June 1907, p. 7 and 8; *BMJ*, 22 June 1907, pp. 1,519–1,520; *Oxford DNB*, 2004; E M Brockbank *Dreschfeld Memorial Volume*, Manchester: University of Manchester Press, 1899/1908. A nephew of Dreschfeld's, Dr Felix Gattel (1870–1904), was Freud's first pupil in 1897, though he proved disappointing; see *Freud-Fliess*, especially pp. 244–245, 266 and 275–276 and Michael Schröter & Ludger M Hermanns 'Felix Gattel (1870–1904): Freud's first pupil', *IRPA*, 1992, 19, pp. 91–104 and 197–208.
62 Freud to Martha Bernays, 1 November 1883, LoC ref: mss39990, box 5, reel 2; *Die Brautbriefe*, 2, p. 390.
63 For a brief discussion see *Life & Work*, 1, pp. 196–197; see also Anna Freud Bernays 'My brother, Sigmund Freud', *The American Mercury*, 51, November 1940, p. 339.
64 For a discussion of this see Ernst Falzeder ' "A fat wad of dirty pieces of paper": Freud on America, Freud in America, Freud and America', in John Burnham (ed) *After Freud Left: A Century of Psychoanalysis in America*, Chicago: University of Chicago Press, 2012, pp. 85–109.
65 Emanuel Freud to Rosa Freud, no date but probably *c*.March 1886, LoC ref: mss81404, box 1.
66 Emanuel Freud to Sigmund Freud, 28 March 1886, LoC ref: mss39990, box 2.
67 For an accessible and fascinating consideration of the sun in art, see Marianne Mathieu & Michael Philipp (eds) *Face au Soleil: Un Astre dans les Arts*, Vanves: Éditions Hazan, 2022.
68 C Tögel *Freud Diarium*, Giessen: Psychosozial-Verlag, 2023, p. 237.
69 For a wider discussion of Jewish guilt see Simon Dein 'The origins of Jewish guilt: Psychological, theological, and cultural perspectives', *Journal of Spirituality in Mental Health*, 2013, 15, pp. 123–137.

Chapter 5

Emanuel in everyday life 1875–1907

Identity, art, and pathology

Introduction

Continuing the story of Emanuel Freud and his family's life, the present chapter follows their stories from the period after Freud's extended stay with them in 1875 through to 1907. After the emotional watershed period of the later 1860s on through the early 1870s, marked as it was with repeated painful bereavements and losses, business concerns will dominate much of Emanuel's public life during this period, while he would attempt to refashion his personal life into an English mould. Tending to his and the family's identity, would also emerge in Emanuel's application for naturalisation and in his ongoing emotional and material support and control of the wider Freud family networks. Such masculine caregiving was clearly important for Emanuel, but came at some emotional cost, with travels to the Continent for 'refreshment', the opportunity to just kick back, being rather furtively obtained under the guise of 'business trips'.

The women in the family by contrast lived far more restricted lives, within which non-specific somatic ailments seemed common, yet details of the precise nature of the complaints were generally conspicuous by their omission. Among the female members of Freud's own family in Vienna, similar symptoms were common. They too would follow and sometimes accompany Amalia in her long-term pursuit of spa cures, trips framed not too dissimilarly from those of the Freud men. Paul Roazen noted the prevalence of migraine headaches and vomiting among 'the ladies' there, symptoms that occurred in the context of an otherwise unusually peaceful household.[1] Though these complaints within the extended family were not dissimilar from the complaints of several of his female patients, which Freud helped to better articulate, the woes of his British female family members went unbroached in the surviving correspondence during this period and the decades ahead. What Freud may have made of them in private is perhaps quite something else.

Emanuel's parallel trips offered, among other things, opportunities to reconnect with Freud and other members of the extended family (both part of the needed 'refreshment') and one such trip is considered here in some detail, the cultural encounters in Leipzig and Dresden in 1883. This would contrast with the less than relaxing 1884 trip to Vienna, which was intended to help re-establish the family

DOI: 10.4324/9781032652023-6

there on a more realistic financial footing. Caretaking efforts with the family network are noted right up the end of this period, with Emanuel slowly – and with some apparent reluctance – transferring more control of the family business to his second son Sam. Sam's story and that of John will be taken up in Chapter 9.

Naturalisation and the vicissitudes of life, 1877–1882

The pain of Emanuel's life, and that of his family, in the 1860s and their subsequent reorganisation was consolidated during the later 1870s and onwards in his increasing assimilation into Anglo-Jewry, an identification with British cultural values and mores, and a surrender of his Austrian allegiance. In this context, he sought to apply to become a naturalised British subject, a procedure then governed by the Naturalisation Act of 1870, which allowed so-called aliens to acquire citizenship after five years residence if they satisfactorily passed police and other checks. As part of this process, Emanuel was able, by 1877, to state that his business was on a sound footing in the fent textile market. And when the Chief Constable of Manchester reported on his application on 19 January that year, he explicitly declared that Emanuel was 'a respectable man'. In his application, Emanuel was able to apply for naturalisation for himself, his wife Maria and their children, Pauline, Bertha, and Samuel, who were eligible as they were still under 21 years old. The application was successful, with a certificate of naturalisation being granted on 24 January 1877. Emanuel swore the oath of allegiance on 29 January and the documents were registered by the Home Office on 6 February 1877.[2] It marked a significant step in Emanuel and his family's assimilation into British civil society.

By contrast with his older brother, the more traditional Philipp never obtained British citizenship, sustaining his Austrian affiliations. Whether he ever sought such is unknown, although Victorian liberalism meant that its absence would not have hampered his day-to-day business possibilities, rights of domicile, or freedom of travel. Neither did John apparently, whom Freud saw in 1875 as thoroughly Anglicised anyway.[3] As a legal adult, he was ineligible by a mere five months for inclusion on Emanuel's application at the time he submitted it.

In 1878, as a now naturalised British subject, Emanuel applied for his first British passport, which was duly issued to him on 23 August and armed with this he briefly visited the family in Vienna.[4] Later that year or in early 1879 he and his family moved to the middle-class Manchester suburb of Chorlton-on-Medlock, where they settled at 59 Shakespeare Street, a neighbourhood with a moderate Jewish community, close to the South Manchester Synagogue. During this period (1877–1880) Emanuel relocated his business premises successively to a fent and patchwork warehouse at 4 Green Street (plus a store at nearby 10 Carpenter's Lane) and then to 47 George Street, in central Manchester.[5]

Around this time, John – now in his early to mid-twenties – moved out of home into his own lodgings, the only one of Emanuel's children ever to make and sustain such a move. This marked the beginning of a turning point and souring in relations between the family and John, who would over the course of the next decade largely disappear off the scene, which will be taken up later. In John's stead, Sam would increasingly come to the fore, another iteration of a younger son replacing the first born. By 1881 Sam was working as a clerk in the family business alongside John, two of eight people Emanuel employed (six women and two men) at this stage.[6]

The George Street warehouse caught fire on the evening of 21 March 1882, which caused extensive damage to the back of the building and to fents and other stock on the ground floor.[7] An announcement in the *Manchester Courier* of an auction of items salvaged from the fire gives an insight into the extent of Emanuel's losses and the type of goods he traded. Of supposed interest to fent merchants, rag dealers, paper makers and others, the lots included:

> 10 tons of fancy and coloured velveteens, print, Silesia and white fents, indigo blue dabs, canvas, twine, etc; also about 3 . . . [hundredweight of] horsehair, a quantity of brass, iron bedsteads, carpets, oilcloths, timber, and other etceteras.[8]

How much the sale held on Tuesday 28 March 1882 by William Mitchell Auctioneers raised is unclear, as is whether Emanuel held any fire insurance that might further compensate him for the loss sustained. What was clear, as Emanuel would later tell Freud, was that business was not proving lucrative.[9]

The Leipzig-Dresden meeting: Freud, physiognomy, and art

Over the following three years Emanuel met Freud at least once a year. The first meeting, in 1883, followed a visit Jacob paid to Manchester in September that year,[10] one motivation for which may have been to solicit financial support for the family in Vienna. Three months later, Emanuel and Philipp travelled to the Continent, nominally in relation to business in Reichenberg and elsewhere. However, for both brothers the trip was essentially a holiday, a respite from Manchester and their immediate families, and no doubt an opportunity to celebrate Emanuel's upcoming fifty-first birthday. They wanted 'refreshment' on the Continent.[11] The brothers thus spent time socialising with Freud in Leipzig and Dresden from 16 to 19 December.[12] Freud reserved hotel rooms for them in the Hotel Stadt Freiberg in Leipzig, a twin room for Emanuel and himself and a separate room for Philipp, or 'Mr Robinson' as Emanuel had styled him ahead of their arrival.[13] That Philipp was accompanying Emanuel was evidently intended as (and was) a surprise for Freud, yet the bedroom arrangements physically separated Philipp off and Emanuel's ruse deprived him of his shared family name. Unaware of the subterfuge, Freud paired himself with Emanuel, noting the association between the hotel's name and his birthplace, 'where Emanuel and I met for the first time'.[14] When *both* brothers arrived, it was Emanuel who still took centre stage in Freud's imagination. Writing later to Martha, Freud remarked that Emanuel: 'is just the same old man, a little destroyed in his facial features, a little emaciated, a bit more nervous since I saw

Image 5.1 The Hotel Stadt Freiberg, Leipzig, where Emanuel, Philipp, and Sigmund initially stayed in 1883
Source: author's collection

him five years ago [in 1878], but just as good, so deliberate, joyful, so intimate and understanding'.¹⁵

Their time together passed quickly in Leipzig and then Dresden from 17 December, socialising, eating, drinking, and sightseeing. Both brothers were 'nervous',

Image 5.2 The three eldest children of Charles I, c.1635, by Anthony van Dyck

Freud thought, and in one restaurant complained to a waitress about poor table service, for which Freud excused them to Martha. At the Residenz Theatre in Dresden they saw Grillparzer's *Esther* and Molière's *The Imaginary Invalid*, Emanuel insisting on them having premium seats.[16] Money however was an issue, particularly vis-à-vis supporting the family in Vienna. Freud broached the subject with Emanuel, though the discussion ended inconclusively and with a little rancour.[17]

During the final day of their reunion, the three brothers visited the Gemäldegalerie Alte Meister, part of the Zwinger, in Dresden. Freud reunites Emanuel and Philipp there as the 'old boys' who need to rest and as 'two Englishmen', while he announces to Martha a newfound capacity for art appreciation. The works he particularly singled out to her were revealing: a *c.*1635 portrait by Van Dyck of *The three eldest children of Charles I*, the 1526 *Meyer Madonna* by Holbein, the 1513–14 *Sistine Madonna* by Raphael and finally Titian's 1516 painting *The Tribute Money*.[18] While some scholarly attention has been paid to the Christian subjects of the latter three works as markers of the role of such beliefs in Freud's infantile history and later personality,[19] the overall transferential context of the encounter with these four paintings has been largely neglected. Beginning with the Van Dyck, the three Freud brothers were able to view three other siblings, the eldest children

Image 5.3 The Meyer Madonna, c.1526, by Hans Holbein the Younger

of Charles I, a soon to be deposed and decapitated monarch. The painting thus offers a mirror to the brothers, temporarily physically reunited, and facing a crisis in which their king-father, Jacob, had failed economically and was needing support. The siblings were here moving to assume economic responsibility for the family, Jacob being not quite dethroned but certainly marginalised in the process.

With the Holbein and Raphael works, Freud notes the Madonna's gaze in both cases, mirroring those of a rapt public in the gallery. Not so for Freud, his thoughts went to Martha, wishing she was there with him. While the lack of idealisation, 'the ordinary ugly human faces', in the Holbein initially annoyed Freud, it was the facial features of both depictions of the Madonna that gripped him and from which aesthetic he sought to read something of their characters.[20] Holbein's Madonna having a 'holy expression' and being 'neither a woman nor a girl', her exaltation, Freud thought, precluded questions about her status, sexual or otherwise. Raphael's Madonna on the other hand, he suggested had a 'fresh and innocent expression', reminiscent of a this-worldly 'charming, sympathetic nursemaid'. It was a view Freud's unnamed Viennese – presumably Christian – friends disputed as heretical, an unsurprising verdict given Freud's outsider status as a Jew perusing Christian art.

Image 5.4 The Sistine Madonna, c.1513–14, by Raphael

Of all the paintings, it was Titian's *The Tribute Money* that made the deepest impression on Freud. As with his discussion of the Holbein and the Raphael, Freud here seeks to read something of the personality or psychology of the central figure of Jesus from his facial features. Thus, he writes to Martha:

> This head of Christ, my darling, is the only one that enables *even people like ourselves* to imagine that such a person did exist. Indeed, it seemed that I was compelled to believe in the eminence of this man because the figure is so convincingly presented. And nothing divine about it, just a noble human countenance, far from beautiful yet full of seriousness, intensity, profound thought, and deep inner passion; if these qualities do not exist in this picture, then there is no such thing as physiognomy.[21]

The painting made such an impression on Freud that he fantasised he might have walked off with it had it not been for a surfeit of 'English ladies' sketching, gazing, and whispering in the vicinity.[22] The English here are thus positioned as an ideal, an externalised aspect of the super-ego, holding darker acquisitive impulses in check.

Image 5.5 The Tribute Money, c.1516, by Titian

Freud omits mention of the second character in the painting, the Pharisee holding a coin in his extended hand. A stereotyped Jew, hook nosed, with dark skin and over-valuing money, as Nicholas Weber notes,[23] the anti-Semitic tropes are clear, as is the implied essentialist narrative of difference between the two figures. While Freud may have identified with Jesus in the painting, the culturally acceptable Jew in Western Europe, he had told Martha at some length of his resistance to anti-Semitic jibes he had faced on the train journey to meet his brothers several days before. Relatedly, Freud would later reclaim several culturally denigrated Jewish tropes, thus declaring himself both a 'Mediterranean man' and as having a 'money-making complex', of which more later.[24]

More immediately, in 1883 the Titian – in its content, its symbolism, and Freud's fantasy of purloining it – raises the spectre of money, something Freud was in pressing need of at this time; he was looking to Emanuel to cover much of the expenses of the present trip and to both brothers to assist with the wider financial straits of the family in Vienna. The questions of tribute money or taxation and the uncomfortable engagement with these earthly matters, as symbolised in the beautiful (and expensive) Titian, could not be put off for much longer.

Before turning to that, Freud's emphasis on physiognomy needs some comment, particularly as it strikes an apparently discordant note with later popular characterisations of him as championing the mind and subjectivity. Reaching that point for Freud, however, was an intellectual journey. The idea that facial appearance might reveal character (or intelligence or other psychological attributes) has had a long history, stemming back to the Ancient Greeks, before being revived by Johann Lavater (1741–1801) in his *Physiognomische Fragmente*,[25] which in turn influenced the rise of phrenology. Though now largely discredited, such ideas evoked widespread popular interest and manifested themselves in psychology, for example in the oeuvre of Francis Galton (1822–1911), especially in his 1869 volume *Hereditary Genius*, Hugh Welch Diamond (1809–1886), in his photographic efforts to classify physiognomies of mental illness, Charles Darwin (1809–1882), in his 1872 work on emotional expression, and Jean-Martin Charcot (1825–1893), especially in his employment of photography and visual 'demonstrations', the concept lingering on into the twentieth century in the works of Cyril Burt (1883–1971) and others.[26] Freud was clearly familiar with elements of this contested tradition, particularly so as a young medical doctor, where explanatory models typically sought to ground themselves in the material body, and from which scientific treatments would follow.

Arguably, the key influences on Freud's early ideas on the subject stemmed from Darwin, Meynert, and Charcot. From his gymnasium days, Darwin's theories attracted Freud, as he saw they 'held out hopes of an extraordinary advance in our understanding of the world'.[27] His views on emotional expression in particular seem to have influenced Freud's early thinking,[28] ideas which Darwin articulated in his 1872 book *The Expression of the Emotions in Man and Animals*, which (despite Darwin's criticisms of it) shared much in common with theories of physiognomy.[29] Freud owned a German translation of this volume.[30] By contrast, Freud's influential university lecturer, Theodor Meynert (1833–1892), under whom he had completed a five-month psychiatric residency at his clinic that summer, regarded Darwinian physiognomical theory as having limited evidential support, to which subject he would devote a lecture in 1887.[31] Charcot completes this trio and he would offer Freud another spectacle on the hysterical body, again reminiscent of theories of physiognomy, which Freud would view when he attended his lectures in the Salpêtrière in 1885. All three, Darwin, Meynert, and Charcot, represented in their own ways contemporary nineteenth century preoccupations with classification and identity, trends which extended beyond the sciences, into the humanities and art.

Through such influences, Freud evidently entertained a theory of physiognomy from the 1880s if not before through to at least 1908. In art, this is clear through Freud's efforts to discern a sitter's character through the painted representations of their physiognomy. In the clinic by contrast, psychoanalysis would come to challenge the sufficiency of biological explanations, largely replacing these with psychical ones.[32] In his practice, Freud would move from visual to narrative modes of representation (from drugs, through hypnosis and the pressure technique, to free association), a shift that was becoming evident by 1893–95 in Breuer and Freud's

Studies on Hysteria,³³ the interplay of internal and external landscapes becoming a key focus of the emerging psychoanalytic gaze.

Nevertheless, Freud would also employ Galton's physiognomically inspired production of 'composite photographs' as a metaphor for aspects of dream work in *The Interpretation of Dreams* in 1900 and elsewhere.³⁴ And in 1908 he would again lean on physiognomy in his approach to art when visiting London. Other early analysts, notably Karl Abraham (1877–1925), also discussed the possibility of reading character through physiognomy.³⁵ In such respects, Freud and psychoanalysis, like the hysteric, bear the marks of their histories.³⁶

The Vienna family conference and a 'neuropathological taint'

A month after returning from Dresden, a chance encounter with his father on a Vienna street, drove home to Freud the 68-year-old Jacob's lack of commercial realism and ineffectiveness as a provider: Jacob appeared 'still full of projects, still hoping' as Freud told Martha with clear irony on 10 January 1884. As a result, Freud solicited Emanuel and Philipp's help in bailing their father out, writing Emanuel 'a very sharp letter' on the subject.³⁷ The brothers agreed to meet and that summer Emanuel applied for a new passport, which was issued to him on 30 June, for the journey to Vienna.³⁸ Three months later, between 4 and 21 October 1884, Emanuel and Freud orchestrated a family crisis conference in Vienna to address their father's – and thus the family's – finances. Among other proposals, Emanuel suggested that Mitzi (1861–1942) and Rosa (1860–1942) get jobs, that their cousin Moritz (aka Maurice/Morris) Freud (1857–1920) – who had become engaged to Mitzi the previous December – should contribute funds, that they take in a lodger, and that they consider downsizing to a smaller apartment.³⁹ Freud saw his older brother as 'exceedingly good, . . . just and wise . . . Emanuel's influence was an invigorating and admonishing one'.⁴⁰ It seems clear that Emanuel, more so than the younger Freud,⁴¹ was able to find his voice with Jacob in such situations. It is thus little wonder Freud looked up to his 'strict eldest brother', as he would later describe him.⁴² Despite Emanuel's clearly pragmatic proposals, he and Freud accepted their obligations towards their father and the family, agreeing to assist by further regular financial contributions: Emanuel gave £50 annually to be channelled through his brother-in-law Eli Bernays,⁴³ while Freud contributed 10 gulden each month.⁴⁴ Emanuel also suggested that he might be able to find Rosa work in Manchester and that if Philipp relocated to London then he (Philipp) might also be able to sponsor his youngest brother, Alexander (nicknamed 'Shani'), in the capital as well.⁴⁵

Rosa accepted the offer and travelled to Britain a circuitous route through Hamburg and Queensborough in Kent, where Emanuel met her on 10 December, and they travelled on together to Manchester.⁴⁶ Staying with Emanuel until August 1885, Rosa shared some of the ups and downs of her stay with Freud, including Emanuel's temper. Freud wrote back to her in March 1885 that 'I can easily understand that he is often annoyed, especially when Pauline's health leaves so much to be desired. But it will certainly pass soon'.[47] As well as reassuring Rosa, Freud acts here again as an apologist for his admired eldest brother, reluctant – at this point – to see his rigidity and controlling behaviour. With regard to Pauline's fragile health, a later letter of Emanuel's to Rosa depicted her as having been prone to weeping, as inactive, remaining in bed when others got up in the mornings, and finding company difficult during this period.[48] Whatever else may have troubled Pauline, her father's account here could be taken to suggest a degree of melancholia.

In similar vein, when sharing his anxiety with Martha Bernays that there was a 'neuropathological taint' in his extended family, Freud would acknowledge that:

> of us 7 brothers and sisters there are very few symptoms of this kind to report except that we, Rosa and I (I don't count Emanuel), have a nicely developed tendency towards neurasthenia.[49]

Freud focuses on Jacob and Amalia's seven surviving children and while willing to recognise his own and Rosa's psychological issues, specifically brackets off Emanuel, who is not part of that branch of the family. Emanuel is excluded from those with neurasthenic tendencies and is at the same time brought into close proximity with the classification, an example of what Freud would later describe as negation. Marianne Krüll curiously interprets (or rather misinterprets) this as Freud's then conscious recognition of all three siblings having these 'nicely developed' tendencies.[50]

Emanuel had his own share of stresses that year in addition to concerns over 30-year-old Pauline's health and acting as host to Rosa. He had relocated his business to a four-storey warehouse at 6 Leamington Place, Princess Street,[51] and at about midnight on Saturday 30 May 1885, a fire broke out here in the basement, which caused considerable damage.[52] It must have been difficult for Emanuel to weather the impact, financial and otherwise, of two destructive fires on his business in just three years.

By August 1885, Rosa's eight-month stay in Manchester was drawing to a close. She had improved her spoken English, was cheerful, and (as Freud told Martha) her time there had been 'very satisfying and she has been treated brilliantly'.[53] On 25 August Freud met her and Emanuel, in Baden, on her return journey to the Continent.[54] The brothers had little time together on this occasion. As noted in the previous chapter, Freud was soon to depart for Paris, where he was to famously study under Charcot between 13 October 1885 and 26 February 1886. As a result of this he had to forego a subsequent invitation from Emanuel to visit them in Manchester in early 1886.[55]

Following her stay in England, Rosa maintained a correspondence with the Manchester Freuds in English, her command of the language attracting considerable praise from Emanuel. In a reply to her on 24 September 1885, Emanuel revealed that business was in a 'wretched condition', so much so that any expenditure that could be was being deferred.⁵⁶ Plans for Bertha fell explicitly into this category, though what they were went unstated. Two years previously, Freud told Martha that Pauline and Bertha were 'quite gloomy and beginning to wither. Poor things . . . they have too little money to find a husband in Manchester'.⁵⁷ This is less likely to have been a topic of correspondence between Rosa and Emanuel in the present instance. Possible travel plans, such as Bertha visiting her in Vienna, were a more likely subject of discussion. This became more explicit six months later, in March of 1886. With no upturn in the business, John found another job and Emanuel and Sam were apparently working alone in the warehouse, without much to do. In Emanuel's eyes, Sam was 'always ready for any work and service [and] makes himself busy'.⁵⁸ In those quieter times, Emanuel added, Sam occupied himself scanning advertisements in the German press, looking for a possible post as an English teacher abroad that might suit Bertha and allow her to visit the family in Vienna. Whether he ever found such a job for his sister and whether Bertha ever got to visit Vienna is unknown, and probably unlikely.

Tending sibling networks

On the domestic front, Emanuel's remittances to the family in Vienna (following the family conference in October 1884) were, as earlier noted, initially channelled through Eli Bernays. By April 1886, Eli had not acknowledged any of Emanuel's contributions. Although he sought to deny it, Eli's neglect clearly hurt or at least offended Emanuel, this perhaps being heightened due to his own then straitened financial position.⁵⁹ Emanuel switched to sending his remittances through Freud and additionally asked him to smooth the matter over with Eli.⁶⁰ It could precipitate, Freud thought, 'a nice disaster'.⁶¹

These circumstances overtly contributed to Emanuel's inability to attend Freud's wedding to Martha Bernays in Hamburg on 14 September 1886. However, having witnessed his younger brother's struggle with time, waiting for example for career success and for his bride, Emanuel now offered him a present heavy with symbolism: his own gold pocket watch. It was, Freud declared, an item that Emanuel reserved for 'solemn occasions'.⁶² As an intensely personal gift on his wedding, it further underlined Emanuel's commitment to his younger brother. At least this was the message Freud wanted to convey to Martha, downplaying the declined wedding invitation and what might be considered the sop of a second-hand gift.

Emanuel did, however, try to sustain both friendly and working relations with most in the family. Samuel had been taken into partnership in the business by 1891,⁶³ confirming his favoured position as John's successor. Emanuel, however, hung on to control, with Sam occupying the position of a junior partner, as reflected in the modified business trading name of 'E Freud & Son'.⁶⁴ By 1895 they moved their trading operations to Whitworth Street in central Manchester.⁶⁵ Further from home, Eli Bernays, having gone into bankruptcy, emigrated with Anna and their youngest son Edward in November 1892, leaving their daughters Judith (1885–1977) and Leah (1886–1980) in the care of Freud's elderly parents and Freud and Martha respectively in Vienna for a year while they established themselves. The members of the Bernays and Freud families clubbed together to raise funds to support them make a new start.[66] Despite his earlier frustrations with Eli, Emanuel (and Bertha) went to Liverpool to meet them in transit to New York.[67]

Emanuel's visits to see the family in Vienna continued. Travelling alone, he next stayed with them from 23 to 30 May 1896,[68] repeating the trip this time with Samuel four years later, from 2 to 6 June 1900. Jacob had died on 23 October 1896 and it may have been during his 1900 trip that Emanuel went to view the gravestone the family had erected in his memory in the Central Cemetery. Be that as it may, on one such visit Emanuel took it on himself to have a gardener severely prune a weeping willow that was overhanging the grave, so much so that the branches apparently grew up rather than hanging down. The results were not to everyone's taste and Alexander at least was really offended over Emanuel's unilateral actions; it would remain a 'constant thorn in his side' vis-à-vis Emanuel.[69] After their stay in Vienna, Emanuel and Samuel then went on with Dolfi to Berlin, which Freud somewhat enigmatically remarked was 'now the family headquarters'.[70] Whether Emanuel was thinking at this stage of establishing his family there on a more substantive basis is unclear, though this would come to pass later in the decade, when Berlin would indeed become Emanuel's family's headquarters.

In anticipation of his brother and nephew's stay in Vienna over that Whitsun period, Freud used it to postpone Wilhelm Fliess possibly visiting. It was a telling strategy. Writing to Fliess later about his brother's visit, Freud declared that Emanuel 'brought with him a real air of refreshment because he is a marvellous man, vigorous and mentally indefatigable despite his sixty-eight or sixty-nine years, who has always meant a great deal to me'.[71] In the context of Freud's relationship with Fliess, this characteristic feeling towards Emanuel may be seen as a harbinger of the contrasting disillusionment Freud was increasingly feeling towards Fliess. With the dissolution of the positive transference, Fliess was no longer 'a marvellous man' in Freud's mind.[72] Emanuel and Sam's visit itself was a clear punctuation point in this process, giving Freud legitimised psychic space ('head'-quarters) from and accelerating the decline of Fliess as a transferential object for Freud, as Didier Anzieu elsewhere suggests.[73] While the visit itself was a no doubt a convenient pretext, Emanuel's emotional specificity not only as Freud's much admired older brother but also as a father figure was clearly influential in promoting this change in Freud's outlook. Two years later, Freud's once crucial correspondence with Fliess ceased.

In about 1897 E Freud & Son made its penultimate business relocation in Manchester, taking over premises at 61 Bloom Street, close to Princess Street.[74] The firm would trade from here for the next 44 years. In contrast to the stability of their business address, Emanuel and his family's domestic accommodation continued to be marked with uncertainty. Thus, they moved to 3 Edensor Place in about September 1894 and to 6 Buckingham Crescent, Daisy Bank Road, near Victoria Park, by 1900, next door to the house Emmeline Pankhurst had lived in until recently.[75] Having recurrently asked Freud to visit Manchester, Emanuel issued

Image 5.6 61 Bloom Street, Manchester, the site of E Freud & Son, 1897–1941
Source: Budby, Flickr

a renewed invitation to his brother to visit them during August 1903, when their sister Rosa's husband, Heinrich Graf (*c*.1852–1908), who she had married in 1896, was due to visit. Emanuel added with some ambiguity that it might be the last opportunity to see them there.[76] It was not an invitation Freud took up.

This 'last opportunity', whilst perhaps playing on his sense of his own dwindling years, was more immediately because Emanuel was planning to retire from business. In that context, he entertained the idea of moving to the south coast of England early in 1904, though he was also exploring the idea of emigrating back to the Continent, the recent visits to Vienna and more particularly Berlin being perhaps a forerunner of this thought.[77] This period saw Marie unwell again during 1903 and she spent an extended time in the popular Lancashire resort town of St Annes (now Lytham St Annes), where she made a good recovery from her unspecified condition. With Emanuel's idea of retirement taking firmer hold, he and Marie began to take extended summer breaks together, probably along with Pauline and Bertha, while Sam took increasing responsibility for the business. Although visits from Freud remained elusive, other family members came calling, including Mitzi's husband Maurice Freud (1857–1920) and their daughter Lilly (1888–1970), during the

Image 5.7 Freud in 1906, two years before his second visit to England
Source: Chronicle/Alamy

mid-1900s.[78] Lilly would later recall enjoying a sunny day on the beach at Southport with the family during that visit.[79] While Southport had been one of their popular vacation destinations during this decade, the summer of 1904 saw Emanuel and Marie temporarily move to St Annes.[80]

Emanuel deferred his plans for permanent retirement and by August 1905 he was again in St Annes and commuting daily to work in Bloom Street.[81] In 1906, following a solo trip to Berlin and Wiesbaden at the beginning of June (or 'Whitweek' as the substantially assimilated Emanuel described it), he and Marie spent part of the subsequent summer in Wiesbaden. Pauline and Bertha may have accompanied them. Freud paid them a surprise visit one day, meeting them at Leberberg 7. It was the first occasion Freud had met Marie in person since 1875 and it was, as Emanuel said, 'a most pleasurable' day they spent together.[82] Wiesbaden was likely entertained as a retirement location, though by the end of the trip decisions about the future were again postponed until after the winter.

Returning to Victoria Park, Manchester, on 15 October that year, Emanuel was soon back in correspondence with his younger brother. Both of them appear to have been reading Upton Sinclair's recent novel *The Jungle* and to have formed a shared – though tantalisingly unstated – opinion about it. The ground-breaking book documented the largely downward trajectory of an émigré Lithuanian family amid the corruption and terrible conditions prevailing in various meatpacking plants in the Chicago stockyards and the demi-monde.[83] As holiday fiction goes, it was a bleak novel for the brothers to engage with and one that must have held echoes for them of their earlier lives. By contrast with the novel's protagonists (and 12 million other immigrants who came to the US between 1870 and 1900 alone), America was not the escape route from adversity they had pursued. *The Jungle's* portrayal of American life was unflattering, chiming with prevalent European stereotypes, and arguably contributed to Freud's own emerging negative sentiments about the country.

Closer to home, Emanuel closed his letter to Freud with the comment that he had the 'fortune or misfortune' to have heard George Bernard Shaw (1856–1950) give two speeches, reports of which he enclosed.[84] Shaw had been to Manchester over the weekend of 20–21 October and had given talks to the Manchester Fabian Society in Deansgate and later to the Ancoats Brotherhood at the New Islington Hall, Ancoats.[85] Shaw's comments were often deliberately provocative and his Manchester performances proved no exception. He thus remarked ironically to the local Fabian Society talk that Manchester might be better if it was burned down and its mayor hung. Later, in Ancoats, he satirically reworked the Ten Commandments, highlighting their restrictiveness and inconsistencies. During this, Shaw characteristically invoked the trope of the Jew as a very keen businessman who only reserved the one day, Shabbat, for religious observances. Well before his later support for dictators, this was not untypical of Shaw's passive-aggressive attitudes towards Jews,[86] such anti-Semitic prejudice being prevalent – and far more strongly voiced by some – in British culture at the time. Large audiences of the Manchester elite attended both events and responded with reported amusement and approval to Shaw's delivery. Others were less amused. The new Dean of Manchester, Bishop James Welldon (1854–1937), was critical of Shaw's comments on religion. Some of the newspaper coverage was critical too, bolstered by a flurry of letters in the Manchester press which condemned the talks as being potentially damaging to public morality. While Emanuel's letter to his brother unsurprisingly suggested he had a somewhat ambivalent response too, Freud – despite declaring to Havelock Ellis that he was 'not very fond' of Shaw[87] – would nevertheless cite him on at least 13 occasions.[88]

Pauline was unwell from the end of November 1906 through to at least July 1907. Beyond suggesting that there was 'nothing serious' the matter with her and that the doctor had been reassuring, Emanuel confessed that there had been 'a feeling of depression in the house' over the Christmas period, which impacted particularly on Marie.[89] Later, in March 1907, Freud invited Emanuel to meet him on his journey to Görlitz, in what was then Prussia (now Saxony), where Freud had arranged to see a patient and the psychiatrist Siegfried Kahlbaum on 31 March and 1 April. Emanuel declined the meeting, claiming that Pauline, though much better, was still not fully recovered from her unspecified 'ailment'.[90] The lure of the seaside however, perhaps as a tonic, drew Emanuel and the family back to St Annes, where they stayed on the North Promenade, during the latter part of July through to the end of August, following which they planned to visit Scarborough until the end of the summer season.[91]

In contrast to her sister, Bertha was in good health and was apparently pleased to receive a copy of Freud's *Der Wahn und die Träume in W. Jensens 'Gradiva'* directly from him, following its German publication on 8 May 1907.[92] Her two-line postcard from Harrogate (where the family were in May) thanking her uncle for the book however, seemed to leave Freud wondering what she actually made of the volume. Responding to his brother's authorial anxiety, Emanuel – having asked Bertha – reassured Freud that Bertha greatly admired the book, though felt 'too timid to speak up' amidst what she imagined was a chorus of congratulations he would be receiving from colleagues and disciples.[93]

Freud's gift to Bertha of the German edition of his *Delusions and Dreams in Jensen's Gradiva*, Bertha's brief response, and Emanuel's magnification of this, highlighted once more the close admiring reciprocal relations within the extended family. Among the Manchester Freuds, it was Emanuel, typically, who was most vocal in his support of his younger brother and his work, positive reviews which Freud for his part both sought and valued. Emanuel had, as we have seen earlier, been glowing about Freud when he visited Manchester in 1875. He had later warmly applauded Freud on his work with Charcot in Paris in 1886, sharing several of his brother's papers with his friend and physician Martin Heckscher (1824–1898), a Russian born émigré, with MDs from Berlin and St Andrews, who had an extensive practice among German speakers in Manchester.[94] In August 1905, while relishing the fine summer weather and afterglow of Edward VII and Queen Alexandra's recent royal visit to Manchester, Emanuel was convinced, so he wrote, that Freud's recent books had been favourably received and wanted Freud to share such reviews with him.[95] And eight months later he was requesting Freud send him an unnamed paper he had supposedly published in an American journal, which, 'being . . . your first literary attempt in English . . . would give me special pleasure to read'.[96]

What Freud may or may not have said to Emanuel to prompt this latter request is unclear. While he had written three pieces in English 22 years previously, back in 1884, two of which appeared in US journals,[97] no other papers by Freud would appear in English language publications anywhere until 1909 when a collection entitled *Selected Papers on Hysteria, and Other Psychoneuroses* came out. These were not written by Freud in English but were the first translations of his works by A A Brill.[98] Whether, as seems unlikely, Emanuel was referring to the earlier 1884 papers or was more possibly muddled about one of his brother's current works is uncertain.

What is perhaps clearer is something of the politico-emotional context. Emanuel's notion of his younger brother's American publishing success, which he wished to celebrate with him, thus emerged in the course of his own euphoria over the landslide victory by the Liberal Party, under Henry Campbell-Bannerman, in the General Election held during January and February 1906. It was a victory that many hoped would herald in an era of considerable social reform. It was a 'glorious result' as far as Emanuel was concerned, harking back to the Whig election victory following the passage of the Great Reform Bill in 1832. That was the year he had been born, as he reminded Freud, though he suspected English politics held little interest for his younger brother.[99] Whether Emanuel's supposition here is correct is open to doubt, more especially so with respect to the general trajectory of Freud's politics. While his political engagement has been less studied,[100] Freud's sentiments tended towards reform, greater liberalisation, and left-leaning politics. His voting record, as Tögel has pointed out, was always with the social democrats and he would regularly offer *pro bono* treatment, as well as financial support to students, and donate books to student libraries.[101] The brothers may be thus regarded as in broad political alignment.

Reflections

During the last quarter of the nineteenth century Emanuel's life was outwardly that of a respectable and reasonably successful middle-class Anglo-Jewish businessman. Yet earlier losses and on-going health issues, particularly among the women in the family, not to mention business concerns and two serious fires in his warehouses, all took their toll. It is perhaps little wonder that, even by 1883, Emanuel's 50-year-old face struck Freud as being 'a little destroyed' and he 'a little emaciated', depleted and nervous. These were observations that alternately reflected and fed Freud's aesthetic appreciation of art and his interest in surfaces and physiognomy.

At home, life was rather conventional and Emanuel could be rigid in his efforts to care for, protect, and direct the family. He was of course, by the end of this period, the oldest male with a claim to be the patriarch in the extended family. This somewhat claustrophobic atmosphere may have contributed not only to the increasingly pervasive somatic complaints in the family but also to John moving out to live more independently, and his subsequent drifting from the scene. While the women went to the English coast or to spa towns like Harrogate for restorative treatments, Emanuel took himself separately to the Continent for 'refreshment'. Somewhat in tension with his increasingly Anglicised persona, these trips brought Emanuel back into direct contact with and helped nourish his European roots. Reconnecting with friends and family there, and with Freud in particular, was an essential part of this.

For Emanuel and indeed much of the rest of the family Freud became an object of hope, not only that he would make-good but that he might also be an agent for their transformation. Beset with such a skein of hopes, it was probably unsurprising that Freud thought there was a streak of neuropathology in the family in Vienna and Britain. For the brothers, caring for the family, as well as ongoing network maintenance, or relational care, was clearly a felt necessity. Commercial and financial matters were at the forefront of the recorded encounters between the Manchester and Vienna branches of the family, but enduring bonds of love, affection and concern were equally evident.

Notes

1 P Roazen *Meeting Freud's Family*, Amherst, MA: University of Massachusetts Press, 1993, p. 131.
2 TNA ref: HO 334/7/2149 and HO 45/9428/61301.
3 Freud to E Silberstein, 9 September 1875, *Freud-Silberstein*, p. 127.
4 TNA ref: FO 611/13 ('Index of names of passport holders, 1877–1881'); *Life & Work*, 1, p. 172.
5 Manchester Rate Book, June 1877, Manchester Central Library (MCL) ref: M 9/40/2/348; *Slater's Directory of Manchester and Salford*, 1879, part 2, p. 85, and 1883, part 2, p. 91. The Manchester Electoral Registers, Citizens' Roll for 1880–81, p. 485, notes Emanuel having a shop at 69 High Street that year; if correct, it must have been for a short period.
6 1881 English census, TNA ref: RG 11/3919/40/3.
7 *Manchester Evening News*, 22 March 1882, p. 2; *Manchester Courier and Lancashire General Advertiser*, 22 March 1882, p. 6; *Manchester Times*, 25 March 1882, p. 6.
8 *Manchester Courier and Lancashire General Advertiser*, 25 March 1882, p. 8.
9 Freud to Martha Bernays, 23 October 1884, in *Die Brautbriefe*, 4, p. 69.
10 Freud to Martha Bernays, 23 September 1883, LoC ref: mss39990, box 4, reel 2. A photograph of Jacob taken on this trip with Philipp's children Morris and Pauline, appears as plate 135 in E Freud, L Freud, & I Grubrich-Simitis (eds) *Sigmund Freud: His Life in Pictures and Words*, London: W W Norton, 1985, p. 149 (where the children are misidentified as Jean Martin and Oliver; Michael Molnar also misidentifies them as Bertha and Sam, see his *Looking Through Freud's Photos*, London: Karnac, 2015, p. 80; by contrast, Lilly Freud-Marlé notes one of them as Pauline ('Polly'), see her *Mein Onkel Sigmund Freud: Erinnerungen an eine grosse Familie*, edited by Christfried Tögel & Magdalena Frank, Berlin: Aufbau-Verlag, 2006, p. 271).
11 Freud to Martha Bernays, 26 December 1883, *Die Brautbriefe*, 2, p. 514.
12 Freud to Martha Bernays, 16 and 20 [26] December 1883, in *Freud Letters*, pp. 92, 94 and 96–98; C Tögel *Freud Diarium*, Giessen: Psychosozial-Verlag, 2023, pp. 145–146; for further detail on the Leipzig and Dresden episode see Christfried Tögel *et al* 'Sigmund Freud in Dresden: Anmerkungen zu einem Besuch und zu Freuds ästherischer Auffasang', *Werkblatt Zeitschrift für Psychoanalyse und Gessellschaftskritik*, 2018, 80, pp. 1–21.
13 Freud to Martha Bernays, 12 December 1883, in *Die Brautbriefe*, 2, p. 494. We may wonder whether Philipp was actually travelling incognito at this point and more generally in Europe following the 1860 bills of exchange defaulting episode.
14 Freud to Martha Bernays, 16 December 1883, in *Freud Letters*, p. 94.
15 Freud to Martha Bernays, 20 [26] December 1883, in *Die Brautbriefe*, 2, p. 490; this passage was omitted from the Ernst Freud 1961 English translation and the letter misdated.
16 Christfried Tögel *et al* 'Sigmund Freud in Dresden', *Werkblatt Zeitschrift für Psychoanalyse und Gessellschaftskritik*, 2018, 80, pp. 1–21.
17 Freud to Martha Bernays, 5 October 1884 and 23 October 1884, in *Die Brautbriefe*, 4, pp. 39 and 69.
18 See also E Freud, L Freud, & I Grubrich-Simitis (eds) *Sigmund Freud: His Life in Pictures and Words*, London: W W Norton, 1985, p. 100.
19 Paul C Vitz Sigmund *Freud's Christian Unconscious*, Leominster: Gracewing, 1993, pp. 65–69; Nicholas Fox Weber *Freud's Trip to Orvieto*, New York: Bellevue Literary Press, 2017, pp. 239–272.
20 It was a strategy Freud was habitually using at the time. In his first few hours in Leipzig, for example, he described to Martha people-watching as he dined: 'I don't see so many grotesque and animal-like faces, so many deformed skulls and potato noses here. On

the contrary, if I were in Vienna I would think I was in the company of men of letters, professors and architects. However, not much seems to lie behind these finer, sharper features' (Freud to M Bernays, 16 December 1883, in *Freud Letters*, p. 94).
21 Freud to Martha Bernays, 20 [26] December 1883, in *Freud Letters*, p. 97; the title of the painting here is mistranslated and Anglicised as 'Maundy Money', Freud having used its standard German title, 'Zinsgroschen'; emphasis added.
22 Freud to Martha Bernays, 20 [26] December 1883, in *Freud Letters*, p. 98.
23 Nicholas Fox Weber *Freud's Trip to Orvieto*, New York: Bellevue Literary Press, 2017, p. 264.
24 Freud to C Jung, 18 July 1908 and 22 January 1911, *Freud-Jung*, pp. 164 and 231.
25 J K Lavater *Physiognomische Fragmente zur Beförderung der Menschenkenntnis und Menschenliebe*, Leipzig: Winterthur, 1775–78.
26 See, for example, Christopher G Goetz 'Visual art in the neurologic career of Jean-Martin Charcot', *Archives of Neurology*, April 1991, 48, pp. 421–425; Sharrona Pearl 'Through a mediated mirror: The photographic physiognomy of Dr Hugh Welch Diamond', *History of Photography*, 2009, 33, pp. 288–305; Cyril L Burt *The Young Delinquent*, London: University of London Press, 1925; Graeme Tytler *Physiognomy in the European Novel: Faces and Fortunes*, Princeton, NJ: Princeton University Press, 1982; Alan F Collins 'The enduring appeal of physiognomy: Physical appearance as a sign of temperament, character, and intelligence', *History of Psychology*, 1999, 2, pp. 251–276; Lucy Hartley *Physiognomy and the Meaning of Expression in Nineteenth-Century Culture*, Cambridge: Cambridge University Press, 2001.
27 Sigmund Freud 'An autobiographical study', *SE*, 1925, 20, p. 8.
28 James Strachey 'Editor's introduction', in Sigmund Freud *Inhibitions, Symptoms and Anxiety*, *SE*, 1926, 20, p. 84.
29 Rosemary Jann 'Evolutionary physiognomy and Darwin's *Expression of the Emotions*', *Victorian Review*, 1992, 18, pp. 1–27.
30 Charles Darwin *Der Ausdruck der Gemüthsbewegungen bei dem Menschen und den Thieren*, translated by Victor Carus, Stuttgart: E Schweizerbart'sche Verlag, 1872.
31 Theodor Meynert *Mechanik der Physiognomik*, Vienna: Wilhelm Braumüller, 1888, a copy of which Freud had in his library; see also Tom Dalzell 'What Freud learned in Theodor Meynert's clinic', *The Letter: Irish Journal for Lacanian Psychoanalysis*, 2011, 49, pp. 65–72.
32 See for example, Roy Porter 'The body and the mind, the doctor and the patient: Negotiating hysteria', in Sander L Gilman, Helen King, Roy Porter, G S Rousseau, & Elaine Showalter (eds) *Hysteria Beyond Freud*, Berkeley: University of California Press, 1993, pp. 236–242.
33 Ibid., pp. 236–237; Anne G Hoffman 'Archival bodies', *American Imago*, 2009, 66, pp. 5–40.
34 S Freud *The Interpretation of Dreams*, *SE*, 1900 [1899], 4, pp. 139, 293 and *SE*, 5, p. 494; see also Andreas Mayer 'Thinking in cases: On the afterlife of Galton's composite photographs in psychoanalysis', *Annual of Psychoanalysis*, 2015, 38, pp. 71–86.
35 Karl Abraham 'Contributions to the theory of the anal character', *IJPA*, 1923, 4, p. 417.
36 Josef Breuer & Sigmund Freud 'Studies on hysteria', *SE*, 1895, 2, p. 7; G Kohon *The British School of Psychoanalysis: The Independent Tradition*. London: Free Association, 1986, pp. 77–78. The history of physiognomy in Freud's thinking remains somewhat elusive and under-researched, with apparently just one paper on the topic: Peter Swales 'Physiognomy, phrenology, craniometry, and questions of character: pondering Freud's cognitive style' (2002). Frustratingly, no surviving copies of this have been traced.
37 Freud to M Bernays, 10 January 1884, in *Freud Letters*, p. 101.
38 TNA ref: FO 611/14 ('Index of names of passport holders, 1881–1885').
39 Freud to M Bernays, 23 October 1884, in *Die Brautbriefe*, 4, pp. 69–70.
40 Ibid.

41 Freud's inhibition here may be seen in an alleged anecdote Fritz Wittels (1880–1950) reported in which Jacob during the 1870s proudly declared 'My Sigmund's little toe is cleverer than my head, but he would never dare to contradict me!' See Fritz Wittels *Sigmund Freud: His Personality, his Teaching, and his School*, London: Allen and Unwin, 1924, p. 60.
42 S Freud *The Psychopathology of Everyday Life*, SE, 1901, 6, p. 227.
43 See for example Emanuel Freud to Sigmund Freud, 15 April 1886, LoC ref: mss39990, box 2, folder 21 and Freud to M Bernays, 23 October 1884, in *Die Brautbriefe*, 4, pp. 69–70.
44 It was a sum that, according to Jones, Freud tried to exceed wherever possible: see *Life & Work*, 1, pp. 173–174.
45 S Freud to Martha Bernays, 15 October 1884 and 23 October 1884, LoC ref: mss39990, box 6, reel 4.
46 S Freud to Martha Bernays, 5 December 1884 and 11–12 December 1884, LoC ref: mss39990, box 6, reel 4.
47 S Freud to Rosa Freud, 18 March 1885, LoC ref: mss39990, box 11.
48 Emanuel had actually described Pauline's *recovered* state, thus writing: 'Her tearful fountain has dried up like a well that never had any water (Irish Bull). I am happy to say that she is now . . . active and moving about in everything that comes to hand in the shape of either duty or pleasure. Gets up in the mornings like a [brisk?] and we all breakfast together a little before 8, and if you saw her now on or off duty at home or in company you would hardly know her again, so completely has she changed for the better, though to us it looks not so much of a change but rather a return to what she was before'. See Emanuel Freud to Rosa Freud, no date but probably *c*.March 1886, LoC ref: mss81404, box 1.
49 Freud to Martha Bernays, 10 February 1886, in *Freud Letters*, p. 223.
50 M Krüll *Freud and his Father*, London: Hutchinson, 1986, p. 15.
51 *Slater's Directory of Lancashire, Manchester & Salford*, 1886, p. 142.
52 *Manchester Courier and Lancashire General Advertiser*, 1 June 1885, p. 7 and 6 June 1885, p. 14.
53 Freud to Martha Bernays, 17 August 1885, LoC ref: mss39990, box 7, reel 5.
54 Freud to Martha Bernays, 26 August 1885, LoC ref: mss39990, box 7, reel 5.
55 Freud to M Bernays, 12 November 1885 and 21 February 1886, in *Die Brautbriefe*, 5, forthcoming.
56 Emanuel Freud to Rosa Freud, 24 September 1885, LoC ref: mss81404, box 1.
57 Freud to Martha Bernays, 1 November 1883, LoC ref: mss39990, box 5, reel 2; *Die Brautbriefe*, 2, p. 390.
58 Emanuel Freud to Rosa Freud, no date but probably *c*.March 1886, LoC ref: mss81404, box 1.
59 Freud to Martha Bernays, 3 May 1886, LoC ref: mss39990, box 7, reel 5.
60 Emanuel Freud to Sigmund Freud, 15 April 1886, LoC ref: mss39990, box 2, folder 21.
61 Freud to Martha Bernays, 18 April 1886, LoC ref: mss39990, box 7, reel 5.
62 Freud to Martha Bernays, 4 September 1886, LoC ref: mss39990, box 8, reel 5.
63 1891 English census, TNA ref: RG 12/3186/88/3; subsequently, on the 1901 census, Sam and Emanuel were again classified as 'employers', though by 1911 (while Emanuel retains this status) Sam is there described as a 'worker'.
64 The business is listed as such in the *Guardian*, 20 August 1892, p. 1, among subscribers to the St John's Fire Relief Fund.
65 *Slater's Manchester & Salford Directory*, 1895, part 2, p. 104.
66 See Freud to W Fliess, 31 October 1892, *Freud-Fliess*, p. 35, and Christfried Tögel 'Freuds Berliner Schwester Maria (Mitzi) und ihre Familie', *Luzifer-Amor: Zeitschrift zur Geschichte der Psychoanalyse*, 2004, 17, 33, p. 45.
67 Emanuel Freud to Eli Bernays, 2 November 1892. LoC ref: mss39990, box 12. After another decade, in July 1903, Emanuel did break off relations with Eli Bernays (see Emanuel Freud to Sigmund Freud, 27 July 1903, LoC ref: mss39990, box 2, folder 21.).

68 Freud to W Fliess, 30 May 1896, in *Freud-Fliess*, p. 190.
69 Harry Freud in interview with Kurt Eissler, 5 September 1952, LoC ref: 39990, box 115, ff. 18–19.
70 Freud to W Fliess, 12 June 1900, in *Freud-Fliess*, p. 417.
71 Ibid.
72 *Life & Work*, 1, pp. 344–345.
73 D Anzieu *Freud's Self-Analysis*, London: Hogarth, 1986, p. 525.
74 Manchester Electoral Register, Citizens Rolls, 1896–97; *Slater's Manchester & Salford Directory*, 1903, part 1, p. 52.
75 The family thus appear at 3 Edensor Place, 278 Dickenson Road, in about September 1894 (Manchester Rate Book, April 1894, MCL ref: M 10/23/5/68); Whitehall, 6 Buckingham Crescent, Daisy Bank Road, Victoria Park, Ardwick, by 1900 (1901 English census, TNA ref: RG 13/3683/33/4; along with Pauline, Bertha, and Samuel, Emanuel and Marie had one live-in domestic servant, Alice Adams (27) living with them at this point); and 6 Daisy Bank Road, Victoria Park, by 1903 (*Slater's Manchester & Salford Directory*, 1903, part 1, p. 160). The last two addresses appear alternative names for the same property. Pankhurst had occupied 4 Buckingham Crescent until 1898.
76 Emanuel Freud to Sigmund Freud, 27 July 1903, LoC ref: mss39990, box 2, folder 21.
77 Emanuel Freud to Sigmund Freud, 6 December 1904, LoC ref: mss39990, box 2, folder 21.
78 Christfried Tögel suggested this visit may have been around 1908 (email to the author, 6 November 2022).
79 Lilly Freud-Marlé *Mein Onkel Sigmund Freud: Erinnerungen an eine grosse Familie*, edited by Christfried Tögel & Magdalena Frank, Berlin: Aufbau-Verlag, 2006, p. 278.
80 Emanuel Freud to Sigmund Freud, 6 December 1904, LoC ref: mss39990, box 2, folder 21.
81 Emanuel Freud to Sigmund Freud, 2 August 1905, LoC ref: mss39990, box 2, folder 21.
82 Emanuel Freud to Sigmund Freud, 28 October 1906, LoC ref: mss39990, box 2, folder 21.
83 Upton Sinclair *The Jungle*, New York: Doubleday, Page & Co, 1906; Freud's teenage friend Eduard Silberstein also had a fondness for Sinclair's writing (see Rosita Braunstein Vieyra 'Biographical notes on Dr Eduard Silberstein', in *Freud-Silberstein*, p. 193); for a critical discussion of the novel see Harold Bloom (ed) *Upton Sinclair's The Jungle*, New York: Chelsea House, 2010.
84 Emanuel Freud to Sigmund Freud, 28 October 1906, LoC ref: mss39990, box 2, folder 21.; the reports are missing.
85 One of the lengthier reports of Shaw's talks appears in the *Manchester Courier*, 26 October 1906, p. 18.
86 David Nathan 'Failure of an elderly gentleman: Shaw and the Jews', *Shaw*, 1991, 11, pp. 219–238.
87 Freud to Havelock Ellis, 12 September 1926, *Freud Letters*, p. 372.
88 See also George S Viereck's comments to Kurt Eissler on 6 February 1952 on Shaw and Freud, LoC ref: mss39990, box 122, pp. 3–5.
89 Emanuel Freud to Sigmund Freud, 3 January 1907, LoC ref: mss39990, box 2.
90 Emanuel Freud to Sigmund Freud, 31 May 1907, LoC ref: mss39990, box 2.
91 Emanuel Freud to Sigmund Freud, 7 August 1907, LoC ref: mss39990, box 2.
92 The text, published in Leipzig and Vienna by Heller, was the opening volume of a new series, *Schriften zur angewandten Seelenkunde* [*Writings on Applied Psychology*], which was intended to include volumes advancing divergent opinions. Taken over by Franz Deuticke in 1908, the series ran to 20 volumes before ceasing publication in 1925 (*SE*, 9, p. 248).
93 Emanuel Freud to Sigmund Freud, 23 June 1907, LoC ref: mss39990, box 2.

94 Emanuel Freud to Sigmund Freud, 28 March 1886, LoC ref: mss39990, box 2; for details of Dr Heckscher see the *Manchester Courier*, 3 June 1898, p. 8 and *BMJ*, 4 June 1898, p. 1,494.
95 Emanuel Freud to Sigmund Freud, 2 August 1905, LoC ref: mss39990, box 2.
96 Emanuel Freud to Sigmund Freud, 18 March 1906, LoC ref: mss39990, box 2.
97 The three papers were 'A new histological method for the study of nerve-tracts in the brain and spinal chord' (*Brain*, 1884, 7, p. 86–88), 'Cocaine' (*Medical News*, Philadelphia, 1884, 45, p. 502), and a review 'The Bacillus of Syphilis' (*Medical News*, Philadelphia, 1884, 45, p. 673).
98 S Freud *Selected Papers on Hysteria and Other Psychoneuroses*, translated by A A Brill, New York: The Journal of Nervous and Mental Disease Publishing Company, 1909. A second, enlarged, edition was published in 1912.
99 Emanuel Freud to Sigmund Freud, 18 March 1906, LoC ref: mss39990, box 2.
100 The classical studies in this area are those by Philip Rieff 'The origins of Freud's political psychology', *Journal of the History of Ideas*, 1956, 17, 2, pp. 235–249, Thomas E Johnston *Freud and Political Thought*, New York: Citadel Press, 1965, and Paul Roazen *Freud: Political and Social Thought*, London: Hogarth Press, 1969.
101 Christfried Tögel, email to the author, 24 August 2023; cf. Christfried Tögel 'Freud als Unterzeichner von Aufrufen', 2019, available online at: www.freud-biographik.de; see also *Life & Work*, 2, p. 57.

Chapter 6

From an 'insignificant little man' to a Joycean hero
Philipp Freud's journeys

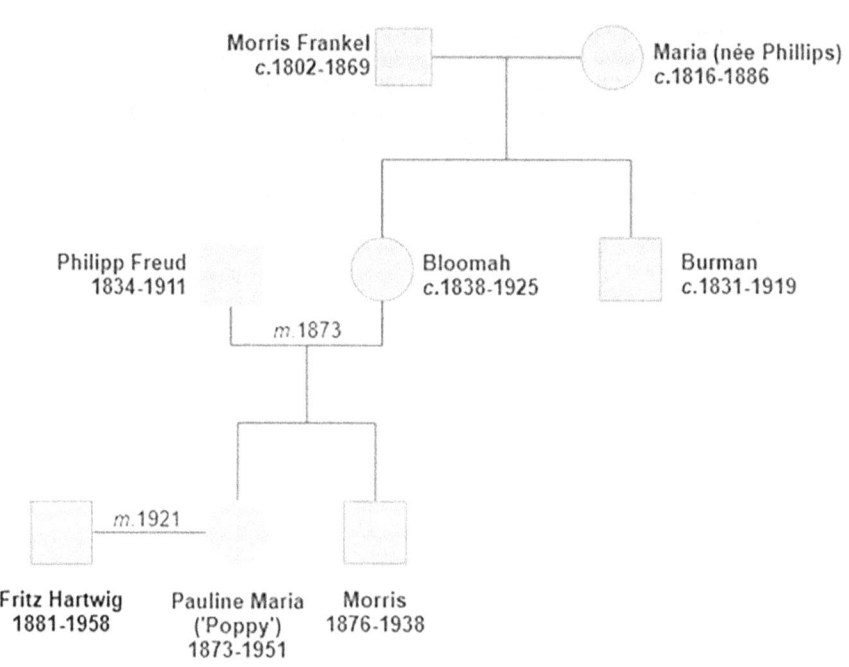

Chart 6.1 Philipp Freud and his family

Introduction

Ernest Jones's dismissal of Philipp Freud as an 'insignificant little man',[1] though typical of Jones's arrogantly superior and elitist attitudes, may be one that others might share, perhaps in more nuanced language. Certainly, less is known of Philipp's life in Britain and what details are available are unremarkable at first sight. Yet Philipp, as Emanuel's younger brother, appears to have been rather harshly judged by Jones and others.

DOI: 10.4324/9781032652023-7

Philipp's life may be better commended using a Joycean view of everyday heroism, which James Joyce best exemplified through his character Leopold Bloom in *Ulysses*. Joyce emphasises Bloom's mental qualities, his indomitable mind, his 'prudence, intelligence, sensitivity and good will'.[2] Bloom's individuality and ordinariness subvert easy identifications that rest on traditional views of the literary hero.[3] It is this ordinariness, this capacity to continue doing the necessary, simple, often dreary activities of everyday life with constancy year after year, doing his best in the face of structural adversity and limited resources that in Philipp's case, as in Bloom's, deserves far greater recognition and respect. As noted earlier, Freud made a similar claim about Philipp (and Emanuel) in 1875, that they were *menschen* very much because of their capacities for sustained ordinary work.[4] More generally, Freud took up this inverted perspective professionally, most conspicuously in *The Psychopathology of Everyday Life*, highlighting that which is special or notable in common or everyday mental and behavioural phenomena. Psychoanalysis expanded on this in the relating of case histories and elsewhere it became a key technique for sociologists in exploring the sociological imagination.[5] Philipp, as the present chapter will show, epitomised the Joycean ordinary heroism of everyday life, persevering in his business over decades despite few rewards, forming and maintaining a family of his own, and sustaining connections with his culture and wider family in Europe.

Philipp's new start

When Emanuel moved his business around the corner to 69 Thomas Street and his family to suburban Ardwick at the beginning of the 1870s, Philipp was left in sole possession of 96 Shudehill. This not only gave him untrammelled scope to run his business there, and sustained his life close to the heart of traditional Jewish Manchester, but it also allowed Philipp more freedom to develop a love relationship. In contrast to both his father and his older brother, Philipp was in solid middle age before he found a bride.

Bloomah Frankel (*c*.1838–1925), an Ashkenazi Orthodox Jew, was the third of apparently six children of Prussian born Moses (Morris) Frankel (*c*.1802–1869) and his wife Maria (née Phillips: *c*.1816–1886).[6] Her father was successively described as a gilt toy maker, a general dealer, and finally as a hawker, a downward social trajectory alongside which the family itself seemed to fragment. For her part, Bloomah grew up living for much of the time with her better off uncle, Myer Myers (*c*.1798–1873), and his British wife Rebecca (née Frankel: *c*.1799–1872),[7] to whom she was latterly described as a companion, and she was no doubt further supported by the Birmingham Hebrew Congregation Synagogue, where she was a seatholder.[8]

Myers was a successful Jewish Prussian émigré jeweller and steel pen manufacturer in Birmingham, operating in partnership with his son, Maurice Myers (*c*.1827–1895), as Myers & Son.[9] Bloomah probably met Philipp through her uncle, as Myer and Philipp traded in similar commodities. When exactly they became betrothed is unclear, but on 15 January 1873 Bloomah and Philipp were married in an Orthodox Jewish ceremony, officiated over by Moses Berlyn (1843–1914), the

Secretary of the Birmingham Hebrew Congregation, at Maurice Myers' substantial home, Bedford House, 5 Highfield Road, in Edgbaston.[10] Bloomah's maternal uncle, the prominent one-time Hong Kong businessman and now philanthropist Jacob Phillips (1803–1903),[11] and her paternal cousin, the fancy goods merchant and jewellers' supplier Leopold Louis Cohen (c.1827–1890), acted as witnesses. While both were prominent in Birmingham Jewry and business circles, they, the Myers, and the Frankels would now (if not before) also form part of Philipp's kinship network, this intertwining inevitably with new business opportunities.

It was a relatively late marriage for Philipp at about 37 and 'Bloome' (as she now styled herself) at 34, although their marriage certificate represents them as 34 and 28 years old respectively.[12] Perhaps each of them was modestly trying to enhance their appeal through this apparent under-reporting of their age.

The couple carved out their living space initially at 96 Shudehill, an area that was becoming increasingly commercial, with fewer mixed-use buildings and a somewhat run-down atmosphere. For whatever reason, nobody was recorded actually living at 96 or the neighbouring buildings on the 1871 or 1881 census returns, though it clearly remained Philipp's business and domestic address. It was here thus, on 21 October 1873, just 40 weeks after their marriage, that Philipp and Bloomah's first child arrived.[13] A daughter, Pauline Maria, she was perhaps named after Emanuel's eldest daughter and Bloomah's mother. Years later, Freud would recall carrying her about in his arms with enjoyment during his visit in 1875.[14] Not long afterwards, on 2 April 1876, Philipp and Bloomah's second and last child, Morris Herbert Walter, was born, again in the family home at 96 Shudehill.[15]

When Freud heard the news of Morris's arrival, he was on a month-long paid research visit to the University of Vienna's Zoological Experimental Station in Trieste, where he was involved in an anatomical study of eels, looking to discover the male's obscure sexual organs. It was his first scientific study. Over the course of this and a subsequent visit to Trieste in September, Freud would dissect some 400 eels, without arriving at what were for him satisfyingly definitive conclusions.[16] Writing to Silberstein about his experiences in Trieste and a daytrip to neighbouring Muggia, Freud remarked on the preponderance of attractive women and children in the latter fishing village (in contrast to those in Trieste, whom he described as 'bruta, bruta [ugly]'.[17] On the return ferry to Trieste, in the company of a 'beautiful woman with a lovely boy who had been visiting his uncle in Muggia', Freud was careful to note his own newly acquired status as a 'zio', or uncle. Having been once again on the seashore (an analogue to his earlier time by the Irish Sea), this time collecting shells, he gifted some of these to the 'lovely boy', a stand in for the newly arrived Morris.[18] It was also perhaps an oblique approach to the 'beautiful woman', Freud's letters from this period clearly revealing his ambivalent feelings towards women. While such relations would improve with time, Freud's relationship with Morris failed to flourish; they would never meet in person and rarely in correspondence.[19]

After Morris's birth, Philipp and Bloomah decided to look for a home in the more salubrious suburbs and by early 1879 had moved south to Ardwick, where they initially rented a large five-bedroom house at 36 Hyde Road,[20] before moving

From an 'insignificant little man' 91

to 12 Shakespeare Street by 1882.[21] This move made Philipp and Emanuel very close neighbours once more, Emanuel having lived at 59 Shakespeare Street since the late 1870s.[22]

It was, as noted earlier, an area with a growing Jewish population, as reflected in the establishment of the nearby South Manchester Synagogue in Sidney Street. An émigré Russian Jew, Isidore Simon (c.1849–1922), was elected Rabbi there in December 1883 and brought with him some moderately progressive practices, including preaching in English.[23] Philipp developed a quiet affiliation with the South Manchester Synagogue and Simon, which he would sustain up to his death.[24]

A relatively bourgeois area, Philipp's neighbours included occasional small businessmen like himself, clerks, schoolteachers, a chemist, salespeople and the like. At home, here and elsewhere, Philipp Freud employed a series of solo live-in female domestic servants to assist with the household between at least 1881 and 1911. Unsurprisingly, there was no continuity with these across the years and Philipp largely took the lead in recruiting replacements.[25]

In September 1883 Jacob Freud visited his sons in Manchester and was able to meet Bloomah and his new grandchildren, Pauline and Morris. The event was captured by the photographer Marcus Guttenberg (1828–1891), probably at his 361 Oxford Street studio in Chorlton-on-Medlock, in a rather touching picture, Jacob seated with Morris and Pauline standing at either side of him, holding an arm each, their heads inclining in towards this grandfather they had never previously met.[26]

Image 6.1 Jacob Freud (67), with Morris (seven), left, and Pauline (nine), right, in September 1883

Source: Alamy

Both children are well dressed for the occasion, though both look hesitant and uncertain. It is the only known occasion that Jacob visited his children and grandchildren in Britain and the only time Pauline and Morris ever met him.

Not unlike Emanuel, Philipp too seems to have occasionally travelled to the Continent on both business and for recreation. Few traces of these journeys survive, though we know of his previously discussed December 1883 trip with Emanuel to Leipzig and Dresden and Freud subsequently noted he was in Paris in June 1884, where he met Mitzi several times.[27] Sustaining sibling relationships was thus an integral part of these trips, though Freud makes it clear that for Philipp the December 1883 trip was substantively taken for 'refreshment'.[28] With two journeys is such close proximity to each other, it seems probable that Philipp was no stranger to such travelling, though no other details have come to light.

Back in Manchester, details of Philipp are again sparse. By 1893 he and his family moved further west to 187 Denmark Road,[29] before moving around the corner to 58 Carter Street, Chorlton-on-Medlock, in south Manchester, around 1894,[30] closer still to the South Manchester Synagogue. This would be Philipp's home for the final 15 years of his life.

Philipp's Freud & Co: making a go of it

Despite its inauspicious fate under his brother's management, Freud & Co was resurrected by Philipp by 1868 at the latest as his own business name.[31] The company, continuing at 96 Shudehill, in central Manchester, now traded in a somewhat eclectic range of products, principally to the wholesale market. It thus variously advertised itself as wholesale silversmiths and jewellers, as importers of London, Birmingham, and Sheffield fancy goods, and as an importer of foreign fancy goods.

From 1876 to 1896, Philipp developed Freud & Co's product lines, particularly in wholesale jewellery and imported fancy goods. Despite his efforts, the company struggled to make profits and at times faced serious financial crises. The latter came to a crescendo in October 1879, when the company's debts reached £1,645. Filing for liquidation in the Manchester County Court,[32] Philipp was able to reach an agreement with his creditors, although details of any composition deal have not been located.[33] Freud & Co thus continued to trade. Subsequently, Philipp diversified into manufacturing and fabricating European beaded fancy goods, employing several in-house staff and a number of homeworkers undertaking crochet and bead work. Securing and retaining such skilled staff in Manchester was not easy and Philipp advertised regular vacancies for both experienced and trainee workers in the *Manchester Evening News*.[34]

In around 1884, the company relocated to 71 Lever Street,[35] where it remained in operation until 1897. A further financial crisis that year involved Philipp agreeing a deed of assignment with creditors on 5 January and, with further claims being accepted until 27 March, a dividend was then declared.[36] Unlike earlier crises, this proved fatal for the business. Philipp, now in his early 60s, and after three decades of entrepreneurial effort, was unable to revive the firm, references to which abruptly cease at this point in Manchester.

A separate incarnation of the company, styled Freud & Co Ltd, would appear in London 13 years later. Incorporated in March 1910, with a capital of 3,000 one-pound shares and offices at Bush Lane House, Cannon Street, this shop fittings company was the creation of Mitzi's husband, Maurice. Operating internationally, Maurice Freud's principal offices were in Berlin at 20–22 Alte Jacobstrasse. Its London office was a short-lived enterprise, being struck off the register of companies in November 1915 due to the non-receipt of the previous year's annual returns, no doubt a result of the First World War.[37]

The end of days

At the time of the 1901 census, Philipp and Bloomah were renting out rooms in their home at 58 Carter Street to German and other lodgers, presumably to supplement their income. Of their children, Pauline remained living at home and had secured a job as an assistant in a rubber works, while Morris had left home and if he hadn't already would soon emigrate to South Africa,[38] sponsored by his maternal uncle Burman Frankel (c.1831–1919), who was settled in Port Elizabeth.[39] Whether Morris kept in regular touch with his family is unknown, but he certainly remained incommunicado vis-à-vis his uncle Sigmund until shortly before his own death.[40]

Retirement did not stop Philipp travelling. He was in Berlin in March 1902 where Mitzi told him about Freud's recent appointment as professor extraordinarius. Using an American art photography portrait postcard he had bought earlier, Philipp wrote to her from Magdeburg railway station on his way home, thanking

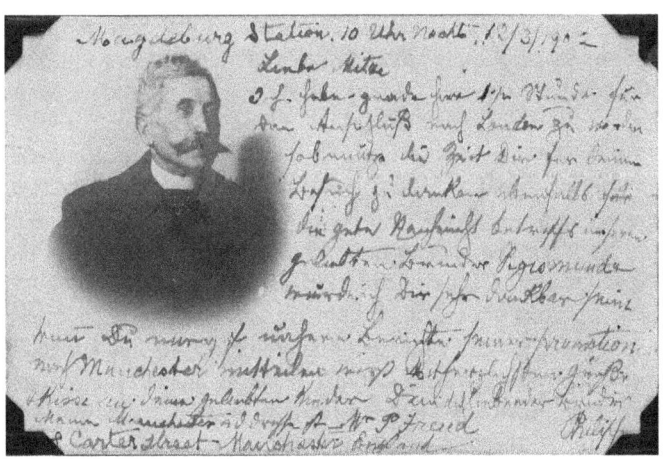

Image 6.2 Philipp Freud, March 1902, by Johannes Dobbel, Berlin
Source: © Freud Museum, London

Mitzi for the 'good news regarding our beloved brother Sigismund', adding he would be very grateful for more detailed reports of the event to share with the family in Manchester.[41] This, Philipp's single surviving postcard, reveals him as a follower of good-news stories about Freud like others in the Manchester family, yet his family-insider's use of 'Sigismund' (almost three decades after Freud had generally abandoned it) suggests a dissonant note. So too does the brevity of his contact with Freud during the latter's 1908 visit, which will be discussed in the next chapter. This further emerged in December 1909, when he wrote to Freud in now lost correspondence. Freud was thrown by the letter insofar as he forwarded it to Emanuel on 22 December for his advice on how best to respond. Clearly reluctant to be drawn into the matter, Emanuel simply proffered 'you had best act on your own good feelings'.[42] Without knowing the content of Philipp's letter or Freud's eventual response, we are left wondering about its nature: was it a challenge of some sort? A rebuke perhaps? A confession? A joke? Or a plea for some form of support? Emanuel's response seems to suggest that the matter did not directly touch on *his* own fraternal relationship with or obligations towards Philipp and was thus more likely a personal issue. The total lack of surviving correspondence between Philipp and his younger half-brother here further problematises any reliable exegesis, aside from underscoring the ambivalence in their relationship.

Philipp died at home at 58 Carter Street on 29 August 1911 from the effects of bowel cancer and collapse.[43] The funeral took place three days later, leaving Carter Street at 11.00 am on Friday 1 September for the South Manchester Synagogue's burial ground some distance away at Philips Park Cemetery in Miles Platting.[44] Rabbi Isidore Simon conducted the obsequies. Pauline, still living at home, registered his death and Emanuel informed Freud about it, who seemed relatively unmoved by his loss, referring to his death on just a single occasion, in a letter to Ludwig Binswanger (1881–1966).[45]

Nonetheless, in that same letter, having intimated that Emanuel was desperate to see him in the wake of their brother's death, a meeting he would keep, Freud's subsequent seemingly unrelated remarks deserve some scrutiny. Commenting on Binswanger's aspiration to write a paper on Freud's significance for clinical psychiatry, to parallel another which had outlined Carl Wernicke's (1848–1905) significance to the subject, Freud suggested: 'you must surely bear in mind that Wernicke has a far greater right to recognition, being already dead'.[46] Did Freud here have his very recently deceased brother in mind also as having a right to recognition? In concluding the letter, Freud mentioned his intention to write a new study on the psychology of religion (what would become *Totem and Taboo*), claiming his recent experiences seeing crucifixes while on holiday in the Tyrol had nudged him in this direction. While he was thinking about this in the run up to Philipp's death, Freud's noting it here must inevitably have resonated with what he knew of his brother's religious sensibility, as well as with the obsequies or ceremonials connected with his passing. Similarly, in the year after his death, Freud came to an increasing engagement with Moses, initially during September 1912 in Italy in the form of Michelangelo's statue, which would result in his initially anonymously published

1914 paper 'The Moses of Michelangelo'. This awakened interest seeded in the 1930s into Freud's controversial last major book, *Moses and Monotheism*. More generally, Philipp's passing must have also resurrected a wave of thoughts about his life and perhaps particularly about the early and at times traumatic years Freud shared with him. Touching on the latter, Barbro Sylwan has suggested in this context that childhood memories re-emerged of Freud's missing mother and nanny, and (here following Rand and Torok) of Uncle Josef and the counterfeit Russian roubles.[47]

The matzevah, or headstone, subsequently erected on Philipp's grave, with texts in Hebrew and then English, reveal his Hebrew name as Shraga, with the traditional acronym 'ת.נ.צ.ב.ה', referring to the eulogy in the first book of Samuel, 25:29, 'May his soul be bound up in the bond of eternal life', completing the Hebrew part of the inscription, the same text as appeared on his father Jacob's gravestone in Vienna.[48] For its part, the English inscription concludes with a quotation from Proverbs 3:24, 'Thou shalt lie down and thy sleep shall be sweet', a

Image 6.3 Philipp's matzevah (gravestone), in the Jewish section of Philips Park Cemetery, Manchester, damaged along with other stones when the section was desecrated c.2003

Source: author's collection

passage proclaiming the benefit of religious belief. All of this identifies Philipp as an observant Jew, secure in his faith and free from troubling dreams. Philipp died intestate, though – contrary to Jones's and others' aspersions – he appears to have had some capital, economic as well as cultural, to bequeath to his family.

Less than a month after the funeral, on 29 September 1911, Bloomah and Pauline vacated Carter Street.[49] Unlike Philipp, neither woman was bound to the South Manchester Synagogue. Where they subsequently lived and how they fared in the lead up to and during the difficult years of the Great War is unknown. Though born in Britain, Bloomah would have acquired her husband's nationality on marriage and does not appear to have renounced this afterwards.[50] With the outbreak of the First World War in August 1914, she would have been thus classified as an enemy alien and subject as such to police registration at the very minimum under the Aliens Restriction Act 1914 and subsequent legislation. Whether she was thus identified however is uncertain, as is how she and Pauline negotiated their way through the anti-Central Powers, anti-German, and at times anti-Semitic ferment of the war years that peaked in riots in London, Liverpool, Manchester, and other metropolitan centres. Such events, as Panikos Panayi argues, 'meant the disappearance of . . . German Manchester',[51] with Austrian communities suffering similarly. Given these circumstances (and assuming they avoided internment and/or repatriation), Bloomah and Pauline's obscurity during the war years may indicate they downplayed any Austrian affiliations and deliberately maintained a low profile.

By the war's end, what was clear was that Pauline (or 'Poppy' as Freud and others in the family referred to her) had managed to navigate her way through this socio-political turmoil sufficiently to establish herself in business as a wholesale milliner and costumier. She was perhaps partly following her father in this trade, Philipp having reputedly been a hat manufacturer very briefly in the mid-1880s.[52] Operating by January 1919 from premises at 51 Piccadilly, in Manchester, initially under the trading name Miss Pauline Freud,[53] Pauline successfully recast the business as Miss Freud Limited in September 1925, and relocated it at least four times over its initial two decades of operations.[54]

Pauline and Bloomah settled at 20 St Hilda's Road by 1920. That same year, Pauline purchased a house, 1 Hough Road, Withington, for £625. Hough Road had a sitting tenant in it, local bank manager Frank Barlow Cocker (1875–1944), and Pauline opened repossession negotiations with him in January 1921. As part of this, she offered Cocker tenancy of St Hilda's Road if he would surrender the Hough Road house. With Cocker declining the exchange, the matter was decided in Pauline's favour in court on 31 January 1921. Cocker's lawyer caused a stir however during the proceedings by suggesting Pauline had purchased the property with money loaned to her by a 'German national', which would be in contravention of the Aliens Act. Pauline responded that it was in fact Bloomah who had given her £300 as a deposit for Hough Road, silently letting her mother's married nationality pass in the process. This went unchallenged and Cocker's legal argument was dismissed, though its irregularity did attract some press attention.[55] Cocker's legal argument undoubtedly reflected ongoing post-war public anti-German sentiment.

The German national was in fact her fiancé, Fritz Franz Oswald Hartwig (1881–1958). Just over four months later, on 9 June 1921, Pauline and Fritz were married in Chorlton Register Office.[56] Whether he had been the source of the £300, as Cocker claimed, or it had come from Bloomah, as Pauline told the court, remains a moot point. Unlike Bloomah however, there was no hiding Fritz's nationality. Originally from Stutzerback, in Sax Weimer, Germany, Fritz came to Britain in September 1905. A glassblower by profession, he specialised in the manufacture of scientific glass instruments. Described as 'the most expert glass blower in England', he had been interned twice as an enemy alien between September 1914 and August 1915, for a total period of almost eight months, following which he was exempted on account of his skills which were in much demand during the First World War.[57] After the wedding, Fritz came to live with Pauline and her mother at 1 Hough Road. Unsurprisingly, given their age, Pauline and Fritz had no children.

Bloomah died at home on 21 February 1925 from the effects of cardiac syncope and old age, having survived Philipp by 13 years.[58] She was 89. Three days later, Bloomah was buried, not with Philipp in Philips Park Cemetery, but in the Jewish section of Manchester's Southern Cemetery, Rabbi Jacob Phillips of the Manchester Reform Synagogue conducting the burial service.[59] No matzevah was subsequently erected, leaving Bloomah's existence in death, as in life, lightly inscribed, a feature common to Freud women and indeed most women in history. Bloomah's estate in England and Wales was subsequently valued at £394 for probate purposes, with a further £208 of assets in South Africa.[60] It was clearly not a fortune, but (alongside the claimed Hough Road deposit and probable drawings following Philipp's demise) it supports the earlier view of Philipp as having the means to sustain himself and his family during his latter years.

The 1920s saw widespread economic hardship in Britain and Pauline's business suffered. It was subject to a receiving order in October 1926. With £1,861 in debts being written off, Pauline agreed a settlement with her creditors of 14 shillings in the pound on the residual liabilities in October the following year, before Miss Freud Limited went into voluntary liquidation on 25 March 1929.[61] Pauline continued to operate as a wholesale milliner, despite such setbacks, for the rest of her life.[62] She even managed to navigate her business successfully through the Second World War when her premises in St Ann's Square were bombed and she had to relocate the business to 1 Police Street.

During the war she met Mitzi and Maurice Freud's daughter Lilly in Manchester in October 1944. She was, Lilly noted in a rare pen-portrait:

> a capable person running her own business with taste and a very practical sense. . . . Completely at home in England, [Pauline and Fritz] have house, garden, cat, and their own car takes the aging couple into town every morning to work and back home in the evening. They are hospitable, loved by friends, and their love of nature takes them out into the English countryside on all their holidays.[63]

Though clearly idealised in some respects, Lilly's depiction of her cousin broadly tallies with the known details of Pauline's life, supporting a view of her as creative and successful in both her career and her personal life.

With Freud, Pauline maintained an irregular correspondence, a mere five pieces surviving, all of which date from the 1930s.[64] Freud told her of regretting his not having visited England more often and the story of the only time he spent with her, during his 1875 visit, when he liked to carry her about in his arms.[65] For her part, Pauline sent Freud fond wishes on his eightieth birthday, assuring him – as her cousin Sam would – that they often talk about him and follow the praise he gets in the press. At the same time, she regretted her inability to travel to see him, excusing herself through reference to an illness she had over Christmas 1935, which had left her with a weak lung.[66] This was, probably, the most specific symptom any of the family in Manchester disclosed to Freud in their surviving correspondence and points to Pauline at least suffering from a possible respiratory disease. Tuberculosis, pneumonia, COPD, and toxins from smoking and air pollution would have been prevalent causes of ill-health and premature death during this period,[67] and industrial Manchester suffered from considerable pollution.

Pauline later sent a parcel of 'delicacies' to Freud at Maresfield Gardens as a present over the 1938 Christmas period. Freud was 'highly appreciative', addressing her by the diminutive 'Poppy' for the first time in the process.[68] Six months later, Freud despatched his own gift to Poppy: a signed copy of the Alfred Knopf edition of *Moses and Monotheism*.[69]

One of the surviving letters from this period relates to the death of Poppy's brother, Morris, in South Africa. Morris worked as a bookkeeper for Singer & Co, a wholesaler in Port Elizabeth. With Freud, Morris had virtually no correspondence up until 1938 when he wrote to his uncle out of the blue. Freud replied but his next news of Morris was about his sudden death. On 21 November 1938, Morris was killed by a car on Russell Road in Port Elizabeth, the driver being charged with culpable homicide.[70] He was 62 years old and had never married. Freud wrote to Pauline – who had broken the news of her brother's death to him – speculating that Morris had 'enjoyed life in his own peculiar way',[71] an idea mooted to Freud by his nephew Sam, who had presumably also written to him with news of the death.

During their latter years, Pauline and Fritz settled in Timperley, at The Bend, 40 Thorley Lane. She continued to maintain contact with others in the Freud's family, including Ernst, and last visited Martha in London at 20 Maresfield Gardens in June 1951.[72] The last of the Manchester Freuds (bar John's descendants), Pauline became the custodian of the surviving family correspondence with Freud and was responsible for its preservation and accessibility. Her end was sudden. Coming home from work as usual on Monday 23 July 1951, she told Fritz she was feeling tired. When he next came into the room, Pauline was dead, having suffered a coronary occlusion. She was 76 years old.[73] Three days later, she was buried close to Bloomah in the Jewish section of Manchester's Southern Cemetery, the Reform Rabbi Percy Selvin Goldberg conducting the burial service.[74] She left an estate valued at £7,112.[75]

Reflections

While Philipp's life and that of his family are rather sparsely documented, its lineaments show him as a man of some ability, grit, and resilience, who was able to create and sustain both business as a wholesaler in tough economic conditions for over 30 years and his family life in relatively bourgeois circumstances. The family's various addresses during these decades and their capacity to continuously employ domestic staff, in addition to Philipp's track record as a small businessman, all support such a conclusion.

In contrast to Jacob, Emanuel, Freud and other family members, Philipp sustained a more traditional Jewish religious identity, as exemplified through his affiliation with the South Manchester Synagogue and concretely encapsulated in his funeral arrangements. Similar stability and grit may be discerned in his retention of Austrian citizenship, resisting common xenophobic and anti-Semitic pressures within British society to assimilate. Like his older brother, he sustained a network of sibling relationships, although with Freud he was clearly cooler and was less possessed by Emanuel's view of him as a somewhat messianic character. Philipp, as an observant Jew, had less need for a new messiah. Indeed, his reference to his younger brother in 1902 as 'Sigismund' arguably also revealed this and his relative orthodoxy, just as much as it expressed something of his better-known fondness for jokes, a characteristic of Jewish identity; that although Freud was now publicly professor extraordinarius, within certain strata of the family he was still the younger brother too. Philipp, in this respect, seemed less willing than Emanuel to cede his senior status, *his* birthright, to Freud and submit to the dynamic of replacement previously discussed.

For his part, Freud saw Philipp very irregularly and then only briefly during his adult years. Philipp's more traditional Jewish religious identity would not have sat easily with Freud's relative secularism (the latter's antipathy to Martha's religious belief and observance being well known) and this, in all likelihood, contributed to their restricted relationship. That said, Philipp's Judaism is likely to have been emblematic in Freud's thinking and his reckoning with his own Jewish past, contributing for example to his motivation to write *Moses and Monotheism*.

Philipp's reluctance to bend the knee, arguably contributed to some of the posthumous disparagement he suffered, most conspicuously in Jones's unwarranted mocking characterisation of him as an 'insignificant little man'. By contrast, such grit, I contend, made Philipp into something of a Joycean hero, who exhibited considerable psychological strength and endurance across his life, characteristics the young Freud also endorsed in 1875.

Many of these qualities were also manifest in other members of Philipp's family, most notably Poppy, who was able to pursue her own independent path and to sustain a capacity to love and work creatively across many years.[76] Though Philipp's family line ceased, that fact of life makes their achievements and influence no less real and no less significant.

Notes

1. *Life & Work*, 2, p. 483.
2. Richard Ellmann *James Joyce*, Oxford: Oxford University Press, 1983, p. 360.
3. See for example Morton P Levitt 'A hero for our time: Leopold Bloom and the myth of Ulysses', *James Joyce Quarterly*, 10, 1, pp. 132–146; Morton P Levitt '"The greatest Jew of all": James Joyce, Leopold Bloom and the Modernist archetype', *Papers on Joyce* 10, 11, 2004–2005, pp. 143–162; Luca Crispi *Joyce's Creative Process and the Construction of Characters in Ulysses: Becoming the Blooms*, Oxford: Oxford University Press, 2015.
4. Freud to E Silberstein, 9 September 1875, *Freud-Silberstein*, pp. 126–127.
5. C Wright Mills *The Sociological Imagination*, New York: Oxford University Press, 1959.
6. Bloomah (also referred to as Blooma and Bloome) does not appear to have had her birth formally registered, a not uncommon situation following the introduction of state registration of births in England in September 1837. She appears with her parents on the 6 June 1841 English census, aged 3, alongside her younger sister Matilda, aged 2. Matilda's birth was registered as occurring on 22 June 1839 and we can thus assume Bloomah was born in about 1838. Her mother, Maria, was noted on the 1841 English census as having been born in 'Foreign parts', though subsequent census returns describe her as born in Birmingham.
7. Bloomah thus appears on the 1851, 1861, and 1871 census returns living with the Myers family in Birmingham.
8. Birmingham Hebrew Congregation Finance Committee minutes, 1861–1881, Wolfson Centre for Archival Research, Library of Birmingham ref: JA/1/3/1/1, minutes for 8 January 1873.
9. See also Zoe Josephs *Birmingham Jewry 1749 to 1914*, Birmingham: BJHRG, 1980, pp. 7 and 98 regarding Myers' patent for 'an improved pen and pen-holder'.
10. Birmingham Hebrew Congregation Marriage Register, 1860–1873, Wolfson Centre for Archival Research, Library of Birmingham, ref: JA/2/C/1/3; GRO marriage record: Birmingham Registrar's District, January–March 1873, vol. 6d, p. 272.
11. See Zoe Josephs *Birmingham Jewry 1749 to 1914*, Birmingham: BJHRG, 1980, pp. 109–119.
12. The ages recorded on the wedding certificate *may* have been uncorrected clerical errors, though Bloomah's age was also under-reported on the previous 1871 English census.
13. GRO birth record: Manchester Registrar's District, October–December 1873, vol. 8d, p. 246.
14. Freud to Pauline Hartwig, 23 September 1937, Rylands Library ref: SSF/1/5/2.
15. GRO birth record: Manchester Registrar's District, April–June 1876, vol. 8d, p. 284.
16. Laura Gandolfi 'Freud in Trieste: Journey to an ambiguous city', *P&H*, 2010, 12, 2, pp. 129–151; Laurence Simmons *Freud's Italian Journey*, Amsterdam: Rodopi, 2006, pp. 51–78; *Life & Work*, 2, pp. 41–42.
17. Freud to E Silberstein, 23 April 1876, *Freud-Silberstein*, p. 153.
18. Ibid., p. 155.
19. Freud to Pauline Hartwig, 28 November 1938, LoC ref: mss39990, box 12, folder 4.
20. *Slater's Directory of Manchester and Salford*, 1879, part 1, p. 134; for a brief advertisement of the house see the *Manchester Evening News*, 24 January 1883, p. 4.
21. Manchester Electoral Register, 1882–83; *Slater's Directory of Manchester & Salford*, 1883, part 1, p. 135.
22. Shakespeare Street crossed the boundary between Chorlton-on-Medlock and Ardwick, with Emanuel and Philipp living in those respective parishes.
23. *Hampshire Independent*, 12 December 1883, p. 3; born Isidore Weischeiski, though adopting the Anglicised 'Simon', he became a naturalised British citizen in 1897, see TNA ref: HO 334/26.

24 Philipp does not appear in any of the examined newspaper reports documenting the life of the South Manchester Synagogue, though he entrusted his funeral and burial arrangements to Rabbi Simon.
25 See his advertisements in the *Manchester Evening News*, 12 February 1887, p. 1 and 7 May 1887, p. 1.
26 Freud to Martha Bernays, 23 September 1883, LoC ref: mss39990, box 4, reel 2. A photograph of Jacob taken on this trip with Philipp's children, Morris and Pauline, appears as plate 135 in E Freud, L Freud, & I Grubrich-Simitis (eds) *Sigmund Freud: His Life in Pictures and Words*, London: W W Norton, 1985, p. 149 (where the children are misidentified as Jean Martin and Oliver; Michael Molnar also misidentifies them as Emanuel's by then adult children, Bertha and Sam, see his *Looking Through Freud's Photos*, London: Karnac, 2015, p. 80).
27 Freud to Martha Bernays, 17 June 1884, in *Die Brautbriefe*, 4, p. 410.
28 Freud to Martha Bernays, 26 December 1883, *Die Brautbriefe*, 2, p. 514.
29 Manchester Electoral Register, 1893–94; *Slater's Directory of Manchester & Salford*, 1895, part 1, p. 218.
30 Manchester Electoral Register, 1894–95.
31 *Slater's Directory of Manchester & Salford*, 1869, p. 199.
32 *The Manchester Courier and Lancashire General Advertiser*, 18 October 1879, p. 4; *The London Gazette*, 17 October 1879, p. 6003; the first general meeting with his creditors under the 1869 Bankruptcy Act took place on 3 November 1879.
33 *The London Gazette*, 11 November 1879, p. 6399; the second formal meeting with creditors took place on 17 November 1879 at the offices of Edward Heath and Sons, Solicitors, at 41 Swan Street, Manchester. No relevant records survive from the Manchester County Court or the District Court of Bankruptcy for this period.
34 See for example the firm's advertisements in the *Manchester Evening News*, 30 June 1881, p. 3, 11 March 1882, p. 1 and 11 August 1883, p. 1 at Shudehill and 17 March 1887, p. 1 at Lever Street.
35 The previous occupier of 71 Lever Street, William Shackleton, a fancy goods manufacturer, had gone into liquidation in June 1883 (*Manchester Courier*, 23 June 1883, p. 7). By March 1885, Philipp was firmly in situ there and recruiting new staff (*Manchester Evening News*, 18 March 1885, p. 1). See also *Slater's Directory of Lancashire, Manchester & Salford*, 1886, p. 142.
36 *The Guardian*, 13 March 1897, p. 4; no court or legal records survive of these proceedings.
37 TNA ref: BT 31/13111/107894, company number 107894.
38 Fritz Franz Oswald Hartwig recollections of the Freud family in Manchester, undated (post 1951), LoC ref: mss39990, box 2.
39 Burman Frankel died in Port Elizabeth on 29 March 1919; see *The Guardian*, 11 April 1919, p. 12.
40 Freud to Pauline Hartwig, 28 November 1938, LoC ref: mss39990, box 12, folder 4.
41 Philipp Freud to Marie Freud, 12 March 1902, LoC ref: mss39990, box 13, folder 44. The portrait postcard, produced by Johannes Dobbel of the American Art Photography studio in Berlin, appears to be the only surviving image of Philipp (see also Harry Freud in interview with Kurt Eissler, 5 September 1952, LoC ref: 39990, box 115, f. 17). Other images in the Freud Museum London archives (refs: IN/0249; IN/0974; IN/1343; IN/1345) purportedly of Philipp appear to have been misidentified. See also *Freud-Fliess*, pp. 455–457, and Ronald W Clark *Freud: The Man and the Cause*, London: Jonathan Cape and Weidenfeld & Nicholson, 1980, pp. 208–210.
42 Emanuel Freud to Sigmund Freud, 30 December 1909, LoC ref: mss39990, box 2, folder 21.
43 GRO death record: Chorlton Registrar's District, July–September 1911, vol. 8c, p. 1250; *The Guardian*, 31 August 1911, p. 12.

44 *The Guardian*, 31 August 1911, p. 12; Section E, Grave 171, Manchester Corporation Register of Burials, Philips Park Cemetery, 1911, p. 499.
45 Freud to Ludwig Binswanger, 10 September 1911, in *Freud-Binswanger*, p. 73.
46 Ibid., p. 74.
47 Barbro Sylwan 'Freud & Co, marchands de Manchester: À propos de la mort de Philipp Freud et ses effets', in B Sylwan & P Réfabert (eds) *Freud, Fliess, Ferenczi: Des Fantômes qui Hantent la Psychanalyse*, Paris: Herman, 2010, pp. 225–245; see also N T Rand & M Torok *Questions for Freud: The Secret History of Psychoanalysis*, Cambridge, MA: Harvard University Press, 1997.
48 See Ernst Freud, Lucie Freud, & Ilse Grubrich-Simitis *Sigmund Freud: His Life in Pictures and Words*, New York: Norton, 1985, p. 161.
49 Rate Book (All Saints Ward), 1911, Manchester Central Library & Archives.
50 The British Nationality and Status of Aliens Act 1914 stipulated that widows who had been former British subjects did not resume their citizenship automatically on the death of their husbands (see www.legislation.gov.uk/ukpga/Geo5/4-5/17/enacted). While Bloomah might have sought a certificate of naturalisation to regain her citizenship, she does not appear to have formally done this.
51 Panikos Panayi *The Enemy in Our Midst: Germans in Britain during the First World War*, London: Bloomsbury, 2014, p. 283; see also J C Bird *Control of Enemy Alien Civilians in Great Britain 1914–1918*, Abingdon: Routledge, 2015.
52 Barbro Sylwan 'Freud & Co, marchands de Manchester: À propos de la mort de Philipp Freud et ses effets', in B Sylwan & P Réfabert *Freud, Fliess, Ferenczi: Des Fantômes qui Hantent la Psychanalyse*, Paris: Herman, 2010, p. 234.
53 *The Guardian*, 7 January 1919, p. 2; no listings for the company appear in the annual *Slater's Manchester Directory* before 1919, suggesting the business was first established during 1918.
54 The business subsequently operated from 21 New Brown Street in 1922, Albany Chambers, 20 St Ann's Square by 1924, 13 St Ann's Square by 1930 through to 1940 (the premises being severely damaged in the blitz; *Manchester Evening News*, 25 July 1951, p. 7) and 1 Police Street by 1941 (*Manchester Street Directory*, various dates).
55 *Manchester Evening News*, 31 January 1921, p. 4; *The Guardian*, 1 February 1921, p. 14.
56 GRO marriage record: Chorlton Registrar's District, April–June 1921, vol. 8c, p. 1666.
57 TNA ref: HO 144/11720, f. 210. See also his 1932 Naturalisation application, see TNA ref: HO 144/15676 and HO 334/130/2418.
58 GRO death record: Manchester South Registrar's District, January–March 1925, vol. 8d, p. 59; *The Guardian*, 23 February 1925, p. 16.
59 Plot B, Grave 100, Southern Cemetery, Manchester Reform Synagogue, Register of Deaths 1857–1959, Manchester Central Library, ref: GB127.M779/Box 76.
60 National Probate Register, 1925, p. 357; Western Cape Archives, South Africa, ref: Bloomah Freud estate papers, MOOC 13/1/5551, no. 800 and MOOC 6/9/2804, no. 8124. The South African investments were perhaps the residue of a bequest left to her by her brother, Berman, on his death in 1919. The Bank of England inflation calculator suggests that the total figure (£602) is the equivalent of £29,022 in November 2022, though using labour value and other algorithms would suggest considerably higher multipliers (see e.g., www.measuringworth.com/ukcompare).
61 *The London Gazette*, 8 October 1926, p. 6519, 7 October 1927, p. 6388, 20 December 1927, p. 8204, 10 January 1928, p. 285, 5 April 1929, p. 2321 and 2,323; 3 January 1930, p. 96. During this period Miss Freud Ltd had various shareholders, beginning with Hartwig, Mabel Sirett, and David Abercrombie in 1925. Hartwig disposed of her shares in the business the following year, while maintaining her directorship of the company (see TNA ref: BT 31/29221/208206 and BT 34/5048/208206).

62 *Manchester Evening News*, 4 March 1941, p. 4 and 25 July 1951, p. 7.
63 Lilly Freud-Marlé *Mein Onkel Sigmund Freud: Erinnerungen an eine grosse Familie*, edited by Christfried Tögel & Magdalena Frank, Berlin: Aufbau-Verlag, 2006, pp. 271–272.
64 This correspondence forms part of the Freud collection in the John Rylands Library, University of Manchester (ref: GB 133 SSF), with copies in the Freud Collection at the Library of Congress (see mss39990, box 12, folder 4); it has been published in French in Claude Vincent (ed) *Lettres de Famille de Sigmund Freud et des Freud de Manchester 1911–1938*, Paris: PUF, 1996 and Spanish in Tom Roberts (ed) *Viena y Manchester: Correspondencia entre Sigmund Freud y su sobrino Sam Freud (1911–1938)*, translated by Pedro Navarro Serrano, Madrid: Síntesis, 2000.
65 Freud to Pauline Hartwig, 23 September 1937, Rylands Library ref: SSF/1/5/2.
66 Pauline Hartwig to Freud, 4 May 1936, in Claude Vincent (ed) *Lettres de Famille de Sigmund Freud et des Freud de Manchester 1911–1938*, Paris: PUF, 1996, p. 109.
67 See for example Peter Burney 'Respiratory disease', *Epidemologic Reviews*, 2000, 22, 1, pp. 107–111.
68 Freud to Pauline Hartwig, Xmas 1938 [postmarked 26 December 1938], Rylands Library ref: SSF/1/5/4.
69 This volume was offered for sale by Raptis Rare Books, Palm Beach, Florida, in April 2021, see: www.raptisrarebooks.com/product-tag/pauline-freud/ (accessed 6 April 2021).
70 Morris Freud's death certificate, Port Elizabeth, Cape Province, South Africa, 1939; database on Ancestry.co.uk; Western Cape Archives, South Africa, ref: Morris Freud estate papers, MOOC 6/9/5195, no. 62062.
71 Freud to Pauline Hartwig, 28 November 1938, LoC ref: mss39990, box 12, folder 4. In an earlier letter, on 23 September 1937, Freud had lamented to Pauline that 'I don't even know what happened to [Morris]', a comment which she perhaps passed on to her brother and nudged his own letter.
72 Harry Freud in interview with Kurt Eissler, 5 September 1952, LoC ref: 39990, box 115, f. 18; *Manchester Evening News*, 25 July 1951, p. 7.
73 *Manchester Evening News*, 25 July 1951, p. 7; GRO death certificate ref: Bucklow Registrar's District, July–September 1951, vol. 10a, p. 83.
74 *Manchester Evening News*, 25 July 1951, p. 11; Manchester Corporation Register of Burials, Southern Cemetery, 1951, p. 499.
75 National Probate Register, 1952, p. 192. The Bank of England inflation calculator suggests this figure is the equivalent of £178,176 in November 2022. On his death, on 18 January 1958, Fritz Hartwig would leave an estate valued at £16,492 for probate purposes (National Probate Register, 1958, p. 262), the equivalent of £307,985 in November 2022 using the same metrics.
76 The suggestion that Freud claimed that the ability to love and to work ('Lieben und arbeiten') characterises normal positive functioning was first reported by Erik Erikson in *Childhood and Society*, 2nd edition, New York: Norton, 1963, pp. 264–265.

Chapter 7

Freud's 1908 visit to Britain

Introduction

Freud's 1908 visit to Britain was superficially a trip in two halves, the first a festival of talking, dining, and sightseeing with an aged Emanuel and his family at St Annes, tailed off with something of a token visit to Philipp in Manchester, with the second half of the holiday being passed in solitary sightseeing in London, with Freud feeling lonely much of the time there. The patterns of relating while in St Annes followed their now established course, with generally strong reciprocal sibling support warmly expressed. Yet the shadow of loss haunted the trip, the now undeniable signs of age evident in the geriatric Emanuel sitting inevitably alongside Freud's own sense of being at 53 well into his own midlife.

Shaving his iconic beard, while it was at one level a rather radical way of managing a disappointing visit to an unfamiliar barber, offered an opportunity to experiment with his appearance and identity. It was one that proved relatively short lived. In London, meeting John seems to have at one time been an idea, though he was out of town, and other soon-to-be professional friends and colleagues had not quite come into Freud's personal orbit. In their place, Freud would peruse museums and galleries, parks and monuments, his gaze seeking to divine the psychology he still thought lay beneath (and was expressed through) the physiognomy, as he had in Dresden 25 years previously. Art, which framed this trip, would thus provide a degree of containment and solace in the face of aging and incipient loss.

Freudian meetings in Salzburg

Since Freud's first trip to Manchester in 1875, Emanuel had regularly encouraged his younger brother to visit the family there. Despite such overtures, it would be 33 years before Freud next set foot in Britain and much had changed for him during the intervening period. Notably, his developing work on a theory of mind was beginning to take shape and by 1908 he and that theory – psychoanalysis – were beginning to garner growing international attention.

One of the small landmarks that year in this recognition was the *Zusammenkunft für Freud'sche Psychologie* (or *Meeting for Freudian Psychology*),[1] an event

Image 7.1 Max Oppenheimer's portrait of a beardless Freud, November 1908
Source: New York Psychoanalytic Society and Institute Archive

retrospectively and grandly rebranded as the First International Psychoanalytic Congress, which was held at the English sounding Hotel Bristol in Salzburg over the weekend of 26–27 April 1908. Among the attendees were just two from Britain, Ernest Jones and his friend, the London surgeon (and *later* distinguished neurosurgeon, author on the Herd Instinct, and Fellow of the Royal Society) Wilfred Trotter (1872–1939).[2] Although Jones suggests Trotter did not actually attend the opening session of the meeting when Freud gave his paper and left after a couple of days feeling antipathetic to both the subject and the Continent,[3] Trotter had in fact met Freud there, something Freud would remind him of three decades later.[4] In contrast to the sceptical Trotter, Jones was at the point of becoming increasingly committed to Freudian ideas and would go on to have a lifetime career in psychoanalysis. However, he was also on the eve of emigrating to Canada, following several allegations of unprofessional conduct that left him with limited employment prospects in London.[5]

Unknown to Freud, another British citizen and genuine supporter of Freud's ideas, was also at the hotel, not to attend the meeting but to happily ambush its eponymous main speaker: Freud's older brother Emanuel. The surprise may not quite have gone to plan however, as during the final banquet on the Sunday evening Freud spotted his older brother in the dining hall first.[6] Perhaps that was itself the plan. Spending time together that evening and the following day, it was, by Freud's own report, a good meeting, filled with talking, drinking beer, and sightseeing. However, while he suggested Emanuel still appeared 'amazingly vigorous' for a 75-year-old, Freud observed that 'for the first time he showed definite signs of having aged'.[7] Perhaps prompted by the sense of time for future get-togethers ebbing away, Freud agreed to visit Emanuel and the family in Britain, where they might devote part of their time taking a later summer seaside holiday.[8] By 30 June it had been decided that the visit to his 'aged brother' (as he told the 32-year-old Carl Jung) would take place in early to mid-September, following a family holiday in Berchtesgaden, where he was to be joined by Sándor Ferenczi (1873–1933).[9]

A journey interrupted and a wish fulfilled

Having cancelled plans to tour various towns and cities in Holland with Ferenczi before his trip to Britain,[10] Freud left Berchtesgaden on Tuesday 1 September, intending to travel directly to his brother in Lancashire via a midnight sailing from the Hook of Holland to Harwich. A missed train connection in Cologne, however, prevented him catching his scheduled ferry and allowed him to spend Wednesday in The Hague and the Rijksmuseum in Amsterdam viewing various works by Rembrandt, which he thought were magnificent, most particularly *The Night Watch*.[11] In a private notebook entry, Freud expanded a little, writing that: 'Rembrandt was certainly a scopophiliac and thus came upon the problem how someone looks different according to lighting. His darkness is that of infantile observation of parents. Infantile emphasis of the drawn contours'.[12] The infantile pleasure in looking at the other from the darkness, the gloom of Dutch seventeenth-century interiors, and the artist's use of chiaroscuro and allied techniques, clearly appealed to Freud's developing aesthetic. So too, in all likelihood, did their often-relational content, with *The Night Watch*, for example, depicting a captain and his lieutenant, together with their company, setting off on an enterprise. In comparison to the Freud brothers own current enterprise, Rembrandt's painting offered an enduring and heroic precursor.

Freud had wanted to visit these galleries originally but had promised his 'strict elder brother' Emanuel that he would travel over post-haste. It was only after he had caught a later steamer and was finally on the train to Manchester that he recalled seeing signs in Cologne for the connecting train he had managed to miss. It was, he thought, an unconscious contrivance, an error, that had allowed him to both consciously submit to Emanuel's request and yet get to spend the day guiltlessly touring galleries as he wanted. And it was something he could recycle, adding it in 1910 to the third edition of *Zur Psychopathologie des Alltagsleben*.[13]

While Freud's report of his supposed motivated error in Cologne emphasised his socially valued cultural and emotional engagement with art, Marianne Krüll suggested the account revealed his enduring respect for Emanuel and a corresponding inability to ignore his 'extremely authoritarian' brother's wishes.[14] Although Freud

Image 7.2 The Night Watch, c.1642, by Rembrandt van Rijn

wrote that he had 'promised [his] strict eldest brother' to take the shortest route and to do so without tarrying,[15] this falls a long way short of Krüll's interpretations that Freud was in thrall to Emanuel and that the latter was highly authoritarian. What was more apparent in Freud's preceding responses to Emanuel was his sense of his older brother's advancing years and by extension mortality, which reflexively bore on Freud's own aging. The conflict thus, seems to have related to Freud's strong wish to see his older brother, while at the same time wishing to forestall presentiments of death. Such wishes partly recapitulated the complex feelings Freud experienced at the time of Jacob's death in 1896, which he acknowledged in the preface to the second edition of *The Interpretation of Dreams* penned very shortly before this trip while on holiday in Berchtesgaden.[16] As an alternate father figure (and one who represented a stricter, more authoritative, and in some ways more effective paternal imago than Jacob's traditional gentle Jewish masculinity), Emanuel's evident advancing years no doubt reawakened Freud's paternal bereavement complex with some acuity, including thoughts of or wishes about his death.

In this context, Rembrandt and art more generally provided Freud with a refuge against object loss, a type of compromise formation suggesting ways in which memory might be preserved beyond bodily death. Furthermore, many of the Rembrandt paintings, as David Meghnagi points out, incorporated early biblical scenes of Jews prior to their political subjugation, a subject which allowed Freud to restore his earlier paternal image of Jacob whilst resisting Emanuel's demands.[17] Indeed, Freud's stay with Emanuel was not just prefaced with what might be regarded as symptomatic visits to galleries, it would also be concluded by a hefty round of such tours in London.

Freud at the seaside

Taking a 7.35 am train from Harwich on Thursday 3 September, Freud would have probably travelled via London to get to Manchester, there being no direct trainline at that point.[18] He was met in Manchester by Emanuel, who – despite his 75 years – impressively dragged Freud's heavy suitcase up the railway station stairs, with the wry comment that 'There is still life in the old dog'. It was an experience that Freud was reminded of three years later when challenged by Emma Jung (1882–1955) about what she perceived as the lukewarm state of his relationship with her husband. By contrast, Freud argued he was allowing Jung untrammelled space for his research and in doing so was drawing on and distinguishing himself from Emanuel who still felt the need to assert his strength and authority.[19]

Image 7.3 The North Promenade, St Annes, c.1908
Source: author's collection

Image 7.4 The Raphael Tuck & Son postcard, as sent by Freud to his daughter Mathilde in 1908

Source: author's collection

Over the next week Freud stayed with Emanuel and his family in St Annes. By his own account, Freud spent a lot of his time there:

> chatting and walking by the sea . . . I am talking and debating here all day in English. Everything is oral . . . [and we] eat very well. I have not enjoyed such a feeling of well-being for a long time; I have also changed in another way, I shall not say how.[20]

It was a narrative essentially similar to his declaration to Silberstein 33 years earlier about passing his 1875 visit 'talking, walking, eating and drinking'.[21]

The 'change' Freud hinted at above related to his beard. He had visited a barber, presumably in St Annes, and – unhappy with how his beard had been trimmed – had it shaved off on Saturday 5 September, leaving a moustache and sideburns.[22] This was a very unusual practice for Freud as an adult and the decision to fix a botched trim by shaving off his remaining beard appears disproportionate. In this context, Freud's awareness of Emanuel's aging perhaps points to his own shaving as an attempt to better curate his own appearance, to create a more manicured and youthful self-presentation, and to stave off the inevitability of aging and death.[23] The previous year, Freud had in fact noted his reluctance to sit for photographs since the early 1890s, telling Jung that this was 'because I am too vain to countenance my physical deterioration'.[24]

Some further support for this idea comes from a comic postcard Freud sent to his eldest daughter Mathilde that Saturday evening. The card, depicting Father Time, complete with scythe and long white beard, playing diabolo with his hour glass and two sticks, declares that '"Time" [is] fully occupied'.[25] Other cards in this series (which were apparently sold in sets of six) amplify this reference as relating to Act 5 Scene 1 of Shakespeare's *A Midsummer Night's Dream*, where Theseus asks: 'How shall we beguile the lazy time, if not with some delight?' Those cards actually misquote the line, substituting '*loss of*' for 'lazy'. Whether Freud saw any of the other cards in the series with this quotation is unknown, though he was very familiar with Shakespeare's works and the imagery on the card itself is at one level transparent in depicting precariously playing against dwindling time. Of course, the image in the present context also plays on the large scythe as a nightmarish barber's razor in the background while Father Time, unlike Freud, still manages to sport his long beard. In his message in German to Mathilde, Freud wrote: 'Greetings from Southport, where Uncle E[manuel] lived so long. Very nice. Pa'. Immediately after 'Pa' is a lilac ink postscript in English, in what appears to be another hand (probably Emanuel's), which declares: 'who looks much younger since since [*sic*] he came here'.[26]

The postscript applied to 'Pa' seems to suggest that his new shave gave Freud a rejuvenated appearance. For his part, while faces and physiognomy would feature in his reflections later in this trip, at this point Freud simply wrote 'shave – too late' in English in his pocketbook.[27] Whether 'too late' here indicates disliking his new look and consequent regret for his action, that he might have explored a clean-shaven look earlier, or other possibilities remains uncertain. He did however retain his practice of shaving over the next few months. Thus, when he met Jung in Zürich on 18 September the latter did not immediately recognise Freud.[28] And when he initially met the Italian physician and later psychoanalyst Edoardo Weiss (1889–1970) on 7 October, Weiss was struck by Freud's clean-shaven appearance and his 'English trimmed mustache'.[29] Later still that year, Freud sat for a portrait by the Jewish avant-garde Expressionist painter Max Oppenheimer (1885–1954), the resultant moustached but beardless image of Freud being rejected as a wedding present by its intended recipient, Freud's eldest daughter Mathilde. When Freud subsequently reverted to wearing a beard, it never grew back quite as prolifically as before.[30]

Aside from the time ensconced with the family in St Annes, Freud went on a series of day trips to some of the local tourist spots. He thus visited nearby Lytham and later Blackpool, from whence he wrote a brief postcard to his daughter Anna on a rather sunny Friday 4 September, with Emanuel and Bertha adding their own greetings to it.[31] The following day, with the weather cooler and conditions blustery, Freud abandoned a chance of crossing to the Isle of Man and instead visited

Southport.³² It was however St Annes that he preferred, it being 'deliciously quiet and distinguished'.³³ Spending the Saturday and Sunday there, Freud went to the 'seaside',³⁴ socialised with Emanuel and the family, ate at theirs and at restaurants in neighbouring towns, smoked fine cigars, and took in the sights on offer, whilst relaying the news back to the family in Vienna in a series of letters and postcards.

On Wednesday morning, 9 September, Freud and Emanuel went into Manchester where Freud spent some time with Philipp. It was the last day of Freud's stay with the family in Lancashire. Whether he had also seen Philipp earlier in the week is unclear. If he had, the event went unmentioned in his correspondence and pocketbook. Freud also appears not to have seen Philipp's children Pauline and Morris. In 1931 Freud would remind Pauline that they had last met when she was just two years old (i.e., on his 1875 visit).³⁵ Morris had left home and was probably in South Africa by this time. The brevity of the brothers contact clearly underscores their emotional distance from one another.

Freud does London

That same day, 9 September 1908, Freud went to London, taking the 4.10 pm London & North Western Railway corridor dining express from Manchester London Road (now Manchester Piccadilly) station, with a single stop at Stockport, arriving at Euston station at 7.40 pm.³⁶ Freud stayed for the next week at Ford's

Image 7.5 Ford's Hotel, 13–16 Manchester Street, London, as it was at the time of Freud's stay

Source: author's collection

Hotel, 13–16 Manchester Street, in Marylebone. Ford's was, according to its own publicity, a high-class family hotel, equipped with electric light and a lift, being convenient for Oxford Street, Regent Street, and the Wallace Collection, its daily rate tariff for single rooms starting at 5s 6d for bed and breakfast or 10s 6d for full board.[37] Its telegram address, 'Illusion, London', may have also caught Freud's attention. He had three other hotels listed in his notebook – the Manchester Hotel, the Hotel Russell, and Bueckers Hotel – presumably alternatives should Ford's illusion not work out.[38]

The contrast between this week and his sociable time in Lancashire was stark. Emanuel was unable to accompany him as he was preparing to move to Berlin for several months, whilst John – Freud noted to his family – was away travelling,[39] the implication being that he would have otherwise been found in London (of which, more later). John's family were unmentioned and perhaps unknown. The one other relative Freud might have *possibly* sought out for company in the city was Oscar Isaac Philipp (1887–1965), Martha's first cousin who moved to London from Hamburg sometime during this year. However, Freud had never previously met him, their first encounter being in Vienna in 1912.[40] Aside from relatives, Freud might conceivably have taken the opportunity to meet some of the people who had taken serious notice of his work. Of these, Wilfred Trotter (1872–1939) was based in London and had met Freud when he attended the Salzburg Congress with Ernest Jones in April 1908.[41] Havelock Ellis (1859–1939), who had both written positively about Freud's work for at least a decade by this time and had been in occasional correspondence with him,[42] lived mostly in Cornwall during this period, but a journey would not have been impossible. Freud reached out to neither man. For others, such as David Eder (1865–1936) and Bernard Hart (1879–1966),[43] their interest in psychoanalysis was just then budding and Freud was as yet unaware of them. Had his visit been timed just two or three years later, Freud might have had a very different social and professional experience in London. Similarly, had circumstances been otherwise, Ernest Jones might have been someone Freud could have met with during this time. However, Jones was a very recent acquaintance and had still more recently emigrated under a cloud to Toronto, whence he sailed on 22 August that year.[44] In the absence of such professional networking and on-hand family engagement, Freud's isolation was unabated by live company in London. With his thoughts turning to John, Freud absolved the city of concern for the fact that 'the only one I could meet here is travelling'.[45] Instead of flesh-and-blood companionship, Freud would occupy himself chiefly with the museums, galleries, monuments, and historical sights of the city. In these, as Michael Molnar remarked with respect to the National Portrait Gallery, Freud 'could at least encounter a number of intellectual acquaintances and redefine himself against the reality of their existence'.[46]

On his first full day in the city, Thursday 10 September, Freud visited the British Museum between 10.00 am and noon and again from 3.00 pm onwards. That day it was the Egyptian and Assyrian galleries that particularly drew his attention, with just two exhibits – the Rosetta Stone and a Neo-Assyrian clay tablet narrating the legend of Sargon's birth – leaving their marks in Freud's notebook. They were unsurprising choices given Freud's deep interests in archaeology, language and translation, his ongoing preoccupation with Oedipus, and his future work on Moses (the legend of Sargon's birth prefiguring that of both those characters in certain respects).

Freud made the mile-and-a-half journey between the hotel and the museum on foot in 30 minutes, though he also squeezed into this first day a hansom cab tour of the city's major sights. Freud seems to have taken his meals at the hotel, using his time to also read his correspondence, reply, and read up on activities for the next visits. Favouring walking in an effort to experience the city at close quarters, Freud thought the metropolis splendid, clean and elegant, the English 'a good-natured, generous people', but the prospect of Oxford Street put him off shopping with its crowds: 'one is crushed and confused'.[47] Nevertheless, he did manage to purchase cigars and a small Calabash pipe for himself that day.[48] While Freud had smoked a pipe since at least October 1880 and a Meerschaum from 1882, this London purchase was perhaps the start of what Wilhelm Stekel would later recall as Freud's habit of smoking an 'English' pipe.[49] Calabash pipes were manufactured from South African grown gourds, typically curved, the bowl often fitted with a meerschaum insert.

The melee in and around Oxford Street seemed to exacerbate Freud's sense of isolation and home-sickness for the first few days, prompting thoughts of cutting short his stay.[50] Perhaps similar withdrawal motivated Freud giving up evening plans to visit the theatre and exhibitions in favour of further solitary preparatory reading on the museums during these first few days.[51] Smoking the cigars, which he thought were 'excellent', and his new pipe probably acted as further small palliatives.

More expeditions to the British Museum followed, amid briefer visits to other landmarks, such as Westminster Abbey, where the monument to Queen Elizabeth I particularly drew his attention. Drawing on this experience, he later suggested Elizabeth formed the prototype for both Lady Macbeth and Macbeth himself.[52] Freud's notebook mentions 'Thames' and later 'Tower London Bridge' on his itinerary that Friday, the latter perhaps a conflation of Tower Bridge and the nearby Tower of London. The following day's itinerary cursorily notes 'Arch Greek, Roman, Bronzes': whether 'arch' here referred to Marble Arch, just 15 minutes' walk from Ford's Hotel, the slightly further away Wellington Arch, or was a contraction of 'archaeology' and thus pointed to another day in the British Museum is unclear, though the rest of the entry, 'Greek, Roman, Bronzes', suggests the latter.

On Sunday 13 September Freud walked in nearby Hyde Park and Kensington Gardens. He returned extolling its size and beauty, its deckchairs, the Serpentine, the relatively plain yet self-confident women, the freedom of speech especially around Speakers' Corner, and – reaching a height of caricature – the 'fabulously beautiful English babies and their often equally fabulously ugly nurses'.[53] In his letter home his reflections on the Albert Memorial, occupied the most space. The 187 carved portraits on its frieze of writers, musicians, artists, and others clearly interested Freud, with the series incompleteness striking him as 'strange'.

114 Freud's 1908 visit to Britain

That afternoon he visited the National Portrait Gallery, scribbling one- or two-word impressions in his pocket notebook of 19 men (and only men) whose portraits he had seen.[54] Freud later elaborated his thoughts on the visit in two-pages of notes entitled 'Bemerkungen über Gesichter u Männer, National Portrait Gallery [Remarks about faces and men, National Portrait Gallery]'.[55] Here, Freud attempts to offer a typology of the faces of people clustered in the gallery, as they were, according to occupational groups, artists, monarchs, politicians, soldiers, writers and so on. Reflecting on the depicted physiognomy, as he had back in 1883, Freud now plays with the idea that supposedly common traits derived from varying degrees of sublimation.[56] With a couple of exceptions, Freud's observations at the gallery failed to detect any such tally, noting close to the start of his 'Remarks' that 'In general, people's appearance does not show that they are *anything*, even less *what* they are' (emphasis added).[57] Nevertheless, alongside this, Freud jotted down categories he distilled from his viewing experience. Some appeared ironic in relation to their subjects, while the categories in general seemed rather elastic. Thus, heroes like Nelson and Wolfe have children's faces, though Freud thought born-writers fell into the same category, while he suggested truly heroic expressions manifested themselves in artists and literary figures, like Lord Frederic

Image 7.6 The Chandos portrait of William Shakespeare, c.1610, attributed to John Taylor

Image 7.7 Charles Darwin, c.1883, by John Collier

Leighton and Alfred, Lord Tennyson. Women here appeared as a single line: 'Famous women plain on principle'. Echoing his opening verdict, Freud went on to suggest what Michael Molnar described as 'his own working principles in the gallery', namely, that 'Face is race, family, and constitutional predisposition, of which only the last [more psychological] factor is interesting, actually mostly raw material, there is too little in it of experience, least of all of choice of career'.[58] We might add here that Freud clearly implies that what was to him the interesting factor in the triumvirate of 'race, family, and constitutional predisposition' failed to yield any worthwhile results.

The two exceptions to this somewhat lacklustre array of physiognomies were those of Shakespeare (in the so-called Chandos portrait, which is reputedly by John Taylor) and Charles Darwin (in the portrait by John Collier). Freud remarked that Shakespeare 'looks completely exceptional, completely unenglish – Jacques-Pierre', while Darwin 'has a gloriously idiosyncratic physiognomy, but not that of a research scientist'.[59] Taken as he was by both pictures of characters that were for him great intellectual and cultural heroes, Freud was still not claiming to be able to type their faces into occupational classifications. His comments on Shakespeare are perhaps the most interesting, distinguishing him from traditional English 'types' and locating him instead within a European – and specifically French – typology. Thus, Freud uses 'Jacques-Pierre' as a speculation, offered to him by a Professor Gentilli of Nervi, that these paired French forenames might form a root from which the name Shakespeare was derived.[60] This move repatriated Shakespeare to Europe, thus identifying him closely with Freud's traditional domestic pantheon of literary greats.[61] This reattribution of Shakespeare's origins to continental Europe prefigured Freud's later Oxfordian thesis from the 1920s and 30s, influenced by John Thomas Looney's book *Shakespeare Identified*, that posited the works of Shakespeare in fact originated from the pen of Edward de Vere, the Seventeenth Earl of Oxford.[62] Leaving that aside, these ideas from his visit to the National Portrait Gallery were not ones Freud took further in his writings, presumably in large part due to the evident weakness of typology and the lack of common ground among occupationally clustered subjects.

What deserves a little more reflection here is how the process Freud was engaged in might be understood transferentially. Freud was playing with his own self-presentation a few days earlier in St Annes when he shaved off his beard. The visit to the National Portrait Gallery allowed these issues to be reapproached now through external figures, through paintings of the great and the good, in relation to whom Freud might now measure himself. This year, 1908, was after all the year in which he and psychoanalysis began to gain increased international recognition. The portraits thus may have served a mirror function for Freud, seeing himself in them, comparing himself to them, and imagining his own portrait one day displayed there.[63] Though Freud did not note having such thoughts at the time, they would not have been foreign to him. In 1906, for example, when Freud was presented with a bronze portrait medal, sculpted by Carl Schwerdtner (1874–1916), by several colleagues as a birthday present, he recalled himself as a student imagining his bust alongside those of famous professors at the University of Vienna.[64] Freud gifted examples of this medal to colleagues, including Jung and Havelock Ellis, and had sent one to Emanuel in July 1906. While the portrait on the medal was not the best likeness of Freud that Emanuel claimed to have seen, he nevertheless found 'a peculiar pleasure in seeing your face in bronze', adding that there was 'an additional value in this medal being a token of the esteem and affection entertained for you by your many friends and disciples'.[65] While Emanuel clearly recognised the bronze portrait medal in 1906 as a marker of growing collegial recognition of his brother, it and other forms of iconographic representation would also serve as vehicles for disseminating the twin brands of Freud and psychoanalysis.[66] The paintings in the National Portrait Gallery may thus be seen as exercising a further mirroring function with respect to the scientific and intellectual establishment and with respect to common ways in which reputations were bolstered through their inscription in art.

Freud's penultimate day in London, Monday 14 September (his 22nd wedding anniversary), marked a turning point vis-à-vis his sense of isolation: as he told Martha, he felt at home again with his departure in sight. He seems to have visited the Thomas Cook & Son branch at 82 Oxford Street that day, most probably to secure his tickets for the following day's journey. Further up that street, at number 381, Freud noted an exhibition – which he probably visited – at the premises of print seller Joseph Wilson.[67] Freud's major excursion that day was to the National Gallery, where he would simply record 'Gainsborough, Reynolds, Hogarth, etc' as artists whose work he had seen.[68]

On Tuesday 15 September, Freud went for a last walk before beginning his return journey to the Continent. In his pocket notebook he laconically wrote 'Vasen – Letzter Spaziergang' (Vases – last walk) to signify his final activities in London. What and where these vases were is unstated, though the fine collection of Greek and other vases at the British Museum would in all likelihood have been on Freud's itinerary, tallying as they did with his antiquarian, cultural, and aesthetic tastes.[69] That evening, Freud took the 8.30 pm express train from Liverpool Street Station to Harwich to catch the connecting Royal Mail steamer *Copenhagen* for the night crossing to Hook, meeting Emanuel, Marie, and Bertha on the boat.[70] Together, they went on by train to Berlin where they meet Freud's sister Mitzi at the recently opened Excelsior Hotel, opposite the Anhalter Bahnhof.[71] She had been living in Berlin since early 1898, with her husband Moritz Freud and their four children, Margarethe (1887–1981), Lilly (1888–1970), Martha (aka Tom, 1892–1930), and Teddy (1904–1923).

Like Freud, Moritz was also rather an Anglophile who conducted extensive business as a dealer in furs and oriental carpets in Britain and encouraged all his children to learn English (helped by a live-in tutor from Leeds). Moritz was probably on close terms with the Manchester branch of the family and is likely to have

Image 7.8 The SS *Copenhagen*, on which Emanuel, Marie, Bertha, and Freud crossed to the Continent in September 1908

Source: author's collection

had business dealings with Emanuel and Philipp. Of his and Mitzi's children, Martha (better known as the brilliant avant-garde children's author and book illustrator Tom Seidmann-Freud) accompanied him to Britain on several occasions and spent six months in London in 1910–1911 studying art, during which period she wrote *Das Wölkchen* (*The Small Cloud*, 1910) and *Die Gärten des Leides* (*The Garden of Suffering*, 1911).[72]

In sharp contrast to his solitary sojourn in London, Freud's present stay in Berlin was anything but lonely. Caught 'between two camps of fond relatives [Emanuel's and Mitzi's families]',[73] as Freud later related, he was unable to explore the city or meet his Berlin colleague Karl Abraham.

Reflections

Freud's 1908 visit to Britain maintained the trajectory of his relations with Emanuel and his family, warm, friendly, and supportive, solidly reinforcing his affinities with his family and the country. His contact with Philipp was brief, though was not apparently fraught, and supports a view of Philipp and his Judaism being taken both seriously and respectfully. In London, without their support, Freud entertained himself most prominently in sightseeing and visiting museums and galleries, perusing objects from the past and exploring something of the psychology of art, trying to gaze beneath appearances. He eschewed the livelier opportunities of the theatres, music halls, and dance venues, along with that summer's other popular London attractions, the Franco-British Exhibition and the 1908 Olympics, both of which were drawing large crowds to White City.

In all of this, issues of aging and identity were close to the surface. Emanuel had visibly aged and Freud took the opportunity of being with him (and an unsatisfactory barber's appointment) to shave off his own beard, a very uncharacteristic practice for him. Whether this was a response to Emanuel's appearance, reminding him of the inevitably of aging and death, against which shaving offered some respite with a slightly more youthful countenance, Freud gives us no clue. Just as he gazed at the physiognomy of those depicted in gallery works, Freud seems to have been engaged in a parallel exploration of not merely his own physiognomy, but his own identity. He was at this point on the cusp of international recognition and standing alone in London looking at images of the great and the good intersected no doubt with questions of mortality, his own status, and that of his work, in such a lineage.

Notes

1. For Jung's initial letter of invitation to potential attendees, printed 18–20 January 1908 see *Freud-Jung*, pp. 110–111.
2. *Life & Work*, 2, p. 45. Here, Jones lists 42 attendees at Salzburg (up from just 22 in his reported remarks in 1924; see 'Bulletin of the IPA', *IJPA*, July 1924, p. 403). By contrast, the list maintained by Rank (which was published in H Nunberg & E Federn *Minutes of the Vienna Psychoanalytic Society*, vol. 1 (1906–1908), New York: International Universities Press, 1962, pp. 390–391) notes 38 attendees, two of whom are

not on Jones's list. Philip Kuhn is currently unconvinced of Trotter's attendance at the Salzburg meeting (personal communication, March 2024).
3   E Jones *Free Associations: Memories of a Psycho-Analyst*, London: Hogarth, 1959, pp. 167–168; E Jones '[Obituary] Wilfred Trotter', *IJPA*, 1940, 21, p. 114.
4   Freud to W Trotter, 21 August 1938, LoC ref: mss39990, box 42.
5   See for example P Kuhn ' "Romancing with a wealth of detail": Narratives of Ernest Jones's 1906 trial for indecent assault', *Studies in Gender and Sexuality*, 2002, 3, pp. 344–378 and P Kuhn 'In "The dark regions of the mind" – a reading for the indecent assault in Ernest Jones's 1908 dismissal from the West End Hospital for Nervous Diseases', *P&H*, 2015, 17, 1, pp. 7–57.
6   *Life & Work*, 2, p. 49.
7   Freud to Martha Freud, 29 April 1908, in *Freud Letters*, p. 282.
8   S Freud *The Psychopathology of Everyday Life, SE*, 1901, 6, p. 227.
9   Freud to C G Jung, 30 June 1908, *Freud-Jung*, p. 161.
10 Freud to S Ferenczi, 4 August 1908, *Freud-Ferenczi*, 1, p. 17.
11 S Freud *The Psychopathology of Everyday Life, SE*, 1901, 6, p. 227; *Life & Work*, 2, p. 57,
12 Freud pocket notebook, July 1908–March 1909, LoC ref: mss39990, box 50A with the translation from M Molnar 'Freud in the National Portrait Gallery', *American Imago*, Spring 2012, 69, 1, pp. 120–121.
13 S Freud *The Psychopathology of Everyday Life, SE*, 1901, 6, pp. 227–228.
14 M Krüll *Freud and his Father*, London: Hutchinson, 1987, pp. 123 and 258 (where, in support of her view, Krüll refers to an apparently unpublished conclusion Peter Swales reached after reading Emanuel's correspondence).
15 S Freud *The Psychopathology of Everyday Life, SE*, 1901, 6, p. 227.
16 The role of death wishes towards fathers and the subject of dead fathers more generally as Freud reflected on it in his self-analysis and as reported in *The Interpretation of Dreams*, is accessibly discussed in Stanley E Hyman 'On *The Interpretation of Dreams*', in Perry Meisel (ed) *Freud: A Collection of Critical Essays*, Englewood Cliffs, NJ: Prentice-Hall, 1981, pp. 131–136.
17 D Meghnagi 'From the dreams of a generation to the theory of dreams: Freud's Roman dreams', *IJPA*, 2011, 92, p. 684.
18 The probable route would have taken Freud on the Great Eastern Railway from Harwich to Liverpool Street and then the GNR from King's Cross to either Manchester Central or Manchester London Road. Information courtesy of Emily Brunell of the National Railway Museum archives, York.
19 Freud to Emma Jung, 2 November 1911, in Thomas Fischer and Christfried Tögel 'Der Briefwechsel zwischen Emma Jung und Sigmund Freud', *Luzifer-Amor*, 2024, 73, p. 192; see also Emma Jung to Freud, 30 October 1911, *Freud-Jung*, pp. 452–453 *et seq*.
20 Freud to the Freud family in Vienna, 7 September 1908, *Reisebriefe*, pp. 241–242.
21 Freud to E Silberstein, 3 August 1875, *Freud-Silberstein*, p. 123.
22 Oliver Freud to Anna Freud, 26 November 1955, Freud Museum London archives; P Roazen *Meeting Freud's Family*, Amherst, MA: University of Massachusetts Press, 1993, p. 130.
23 For some discussion on this point see M Molnar *Looking Through Freud's Photos*, London: Karnac, 2015, pp. 82–83.
24 Freud to C Jung, 19 September 1907, *Freud-Jung*, p. 88.
25 The card, coded as 'Diabolo 9564', was published by Royal Warrant holders Raphael Tuck & Sons in the Oilette series. For another card is this series see: tuckdbpostcards.org/items/63974.
26 Freud to Mathilde Freud, 5 September 1908, LoC ref: mss39990, box 12, and available online at: http://hdl.loc.gov/loc.mss/ms004017.mss39990.00221; see also *Reisebriefe*,

p. 239; Ronald Clark (*Freud: The Man and the Cause*, London: Jonathan Cape and Weidenfeld & Nicholson, 1980, p. 253) misattributes the postscript to Freud, suggesting he is referring to Emanuel. The present attribution of the postscript to Emanuel is based on the contemporaneous sample of his writing on the 4 September 1908 postcard Freud sent to Anna (LoC ref: mss39990, box 2, and available online at: http://hdl.loc.gov/loc.mss/ms004017.mss39990.00027) and his letters to Freud of 4 January and 13 February 1909, both of which use a similar purple pencil and script (see loc.gov/item/mss3999000045).

27 Freud pocket notebook, July 1908-March 1909, LoC ref: mss39990, box 50A.
28 M Molnar 'Freud in the National Portrait Gallery', *American Imago*, Spring 2012, 69, 1, pp. 130–131; Freud pocket notebook, July 1908–March 1909, LoC ref: mss39990, box 50A.
29 P Roazen *Edoardo Weiss: The House That Freud Built*, Abingdon: Routledge, 2005, pp. 66–67; see also Edoardo Weiss *Sigmund Freud as a Consultant: Recollections of a Pioneer in Psychoanalysis*, London: Routledge, 1991, p. 2 and Edoardo Weiss *The Structure and Dynamics of the Human Mind*, New York: Grune & Stratton, 1960, pp. x and xvii.
30 M Molnar 'Freud in the National Portrait Gallery', *American Imago*, Spring 2012, 69, 1, p. 131; Mathilde married a Viennese businessman Robert Hollitscher (1875–1959) on 7 February 1909. See also P Roazen *Meeting Freud's Family*, Amherst, MA: University of Massachusetts Press, 1993, pp. 130–131; P Roazen *Edoardo Weiss: The House that Freud Built*, Abingdon: Routledge, 2005, pp. 66–67; J-M Rabaté *James Joyce and the Politics of Egoism*, Cambridge: Cambridge University Press, 2001, p. 138. The Oppenheimer portrait of Freud, commissioned by Paul Federn, was donated after his suicide in May 1950 to the New York Psychoanalytic Society, where it remains (Nellie Thompson email to the author, 1 July 2019).
31 Freud to Anna Freud, 4 September 1908, *Freud-Freud*, p. 26; it was in fact a set of views, titled *Blackpool Pictorial Letters*, containing six local scenes in the resort.
32 Freud to the Freud family, 5 September 1908, *Reisebriefe*, p. 240; Freud to Mathilde Freud, 5 September 1908, *Reisebriefe*, p. 239.
33 Freud to the Freud family, 5 September 1908, *Reisebriefe*, p. 240.
34 Freud pocket notebook, July 1908-March 1909, LoC ref: mss39990, box 50A.
35 Freud to Pauline Hartwig, 1 January 1931, LoC ref: mss39990, box 12, folder 4.
36 Freud pocket notebook, July 1908-March 1909, LoC ref: mss39990, box 50A; LNWR timetables, 1908, National Railway Museum archives, York.
37 *Morning Post*, 29 June 1908, p. 14 and 21 September 1908, p. 1.
38 Freud pocket notebook, July 1908-March 1909, LoC ref: mss39990, box 50A; *Post Office London Directory, 1908*, London: Kelly's Directories, 1908. The Manchester and Buecker's were both mid-range hotels, popular meeting places for provincial business people visiting the city, perhaps thus recommended to Freud by Emanuel or Philipp. Buecker's was managed at the time by a German national, Gustave Ludwig Hohly (1843–1911), from Württemberg.
39 Freud to the Freud family, 5 September 1908, *Reisebriefe*, p. 240.
40 In London, Oscar established a branch of the international commodities firm, Philbro, at 118 Leadenhall Street, with his brother Julius (1878–1944). Oscar met Freud several times in Vienna from 1912 onward and again when Freud moved to London in 1938. His wife, Clarisse (née Weil: 1888–1971), who he had married in Paris in June 1914), suffered from epilepsy and consulted Ernest Jones about this sometime between late 1919 and early 1921, as a result of which he suggested she come into analysis with him. When Oscar then sought corroboration of this recommendation from Freud, his response was 'I am *surprised* that Jones wants to analyse her because this is not a case for analysis', before confirming the existing medical treatment with bromides as appropriate given existing knowledge. The matter does not appear to have been raised in

the surviving correspondence between Freud and Jones. Born in Hamburg, Oscar's brother Julius Jechiel Philipp was deported from Westerbork Camp in the Netherlands on 12 January 1944 to Bergen-Belsen Concentration Camp where he was killed on 15 March 1944 (yadvashem.org ref: 11607153). See also Oscar Philipp in interview with Kurt Eissler, 12 June 1958, LoC ref: mss39990, box 131, folder 12, f.17.
41 Freud to W Trotter, 21 August 1938, LoC ref: mss39990, box 42.
42 P Kuhn *Psychoanalysis in Britain 1893–1913: Histories and Historiography*, Lanham, MD: Lexington Books, 2017, pp. 262–264.
43 Ibid., pp. 235–242 and 264–266; M Thomson 'The solution to his own enigma: Connecting the life of Montague David Eder (1865–1936), socialist, psychoanalyst, Zionist and modern saint', *Medical History*, 2011, 55, pp. 69–71.
44 Jones sailed first class aboard the SS *Empress of Britain* from Liverpool on 22 August 1908, arriving in Quebec at 9.30 pm on 27 August and disembarking early the following morning (ref: Ottawa Archives, ref: RG 76-C; roll: T-4759 and online on ancestry.co.uk).
45 Freud to the Freud family, 12 September 1908, *Reisebriefe*, p. 245.
46 M Molnar 'Freud in the national portrait gallery', *American Imago*, Spring 2012, 69, 1, p. 124.
47 Freud to the Freud family, 10 September 1908, *Reisebriefe*, p. 244.
48 Ibid.
49 Wilhelm Stekel 'On the history of the analytical movement' (1926), *P&H*, 2005, 7, 1, p. 103.
50 Freud to the Freud family, 10, 12, and 13 September 1908, *Reisebriefe*, pp. 243, 245, and 247 respectively.
51 Freud to the Freud family, 12 September 1908, *Reisebriefe*, p. 245.
52 Michael Molnar 'Freud in the National Portrait Gallery', *American Imago*, Spring 2012, 69, 1, p. 126.
53 Freud to the Freud family, 13 September 1908, *Reisebriefe*, pp. 247–248.
54 LoC ref: mss39990, box 50A.
55 See Michael Molnar's 'Sigmund Freud's notes on faces and men: National Portrait Gallery, September 13, 1908', in M S Roth (ed) *Freud: Conflict and Culture*, New York: Knopf, 1998, pp. 41–50 and his 'Freud in the national portrait gallery', *American Imago*, Spring 2012, 69, 1, pp. 107–133. Molnar gave a lecture on this topic on 26 March 2011 at the Freud Museum, London, available as a podcast: www.freud.org.uk/2011/03/26/freud-at-the-national-portrait-gallery-michael-molnar; see also *Reisebriefe*, pp. 250–259.
56 See also Karl Abraham 'Contributions to the theory of the anal character', *IJPA*, 1923, 4, p. 417.
57 M Molnar 'Sigmund Freud's notes on faces and men: National Portrait Gallery, September 13, 1908', in M S Roth (ed) *Freud. Conflict and Culture*, New York: Knopf, 1998, p. 41.
58 Ibid., pp. 42 and 47; M Molnar 'Freud in the national portrait gallery', *American Imago*, Spring 2012, 69, 1, pp. 123–124.
59 M Molnar 'Sigmund Freud's notes on faces and men: National Portrait Gallery, September 13, 1908', in M S Roth (ed) *Freud: Conflict and Culture*, New York: Knopf, 1998, p. 41.
60 Freud to E Jones, 31 October 1909, *Freud-Jones*, p. 32; *Life & Work*, 3, p. 460. The actual identity of Gentilli (or Gentili) remains elusive, though Freud knew both Nervi, near Genoa (*SE*, 6, p. 22), and Dr Gustav Ortenau (1864–1950) who lived there for some time.
61 M Molnar 'Sigmund Freud's notes on faces and men: National Portrait Gallery, September 13, 1908', in M S Roth (ed) *Freud: Conflict and Culture*, New York: Knopf, 1998, pp. 45–46.

62 In addition to Molnar's papers that clearly address this topic, for an older reading see also Norman N Holland 'Freud on Shakespeare', *PMLA*, June 1960, 75, 3, pp. 163–173, while the extensive works of Richard M Waugman offer contemporary Oxfordian approaches to the topic.
63 See also M Molnar 'Freud in the national portrait gallery', *American Imago*, Spring 2012, 69, 1, pp. 124.
64 *Life & Work*, 2, p. 15.
65 Emanuel Freud to Sigmund Freud, 17 July 1906, LoC ref: mss39990, box 2.
66 Roger Willoughby 'Freud's use of iconography in curating his public profile', forthcoming.
67 *Post Office London Directory, 1908*, London: Kelly's Directories, 1908, p. 652.
68 Freud to Martha Freud, 14 September 1908, *Reisebriefe*, pp. 260–261.
69 Freud's library included three volumes of British Museum catalogues and would soon include a copy of Fritz Hoeber's *Griechische Vases*, Munich & Leipzig: R Piper & Co, 1909, his collection of antiquities would feature several and ultimately his ashes would be deposited in one.
70 Freud to Martha Freud, 14 September 1908, *Reisebriefe*, p. 260; Freud here says he was going to leave London on the afternoon of 15 September, though his pocket notebook twice records a time of 8.30 [pm] that day. The latter corresponds to the main daily London-Harwich-Hook ferry service, the Royal Mail route (*Lloyd's List*, 5 September 1908, p. 8; *Yorkshire Post*, 25 September 1908, p. 1).
71 Freud pocket notebook, July 1908-March 1909, LoC ref: mss39990, box 50A.
72 Lilly Freud-Marlé *Mein Onkel Sigmund Freud: Erinnerungen an eine grosse Familie*, edited by Christfried Tögel & Magdalena Frank, Berlin: Aufbau-Verlag, 2006, pp. 276–278; Barbara Murken 'Tom Seidmann-Freud: Leben und Werk', *Die Schiefertafel*, December 1981, 4, 3, pp. 165, 163–201; Barbara Murken '". . . die Welt ist so uneben . . ." Tom Seidmann-Freud (1892–1930): Leben und Werk einer grossen Bilderbuch-Künstlerin', *Luzifer-Amor*, 2004, 17, 33, p. 81, available online at: www.documenta14.de/en/artists/22765/tom-seidmann-freud; www.tomseidmannfreud.com/
73 Freud to K Abraham, 29 September 1908, in H C Abraham & E L Freud (eds) *A Psycho-Analytic Dialogue: The Letters of Sigmund Freud and Karl Abraham 1907–1926*, London: Hogarth, 1965, p. 52.

Chapter 8

Savigny Platz to Platt's Siding
Emanuel's final journeys

Introduction

While 1908 was an important year for Freud, it was of some significance for Emanuel too. It saw him return to the Continent, where he lived in Berlin for over a year with Marie and his two daughters Bertha and Pauline. Part of the purpose of the stay was to allow Marie to consult various German medical specialists, though Bertha and Pauline were also reportedly in varying states of ill health. For Emanuel, the extended time in Berlin probably held out the prospect of greater 'refreshment' than his brief earlier trips to the Continent had yielded, though whether this materialised for him being *en famille* is unknown. Certainly, his hope that being in Berlin would result in him seeing Freud more often was frustrated, with just one meeting being squeezed in.

The brothers met again in Hanover in 1911 following Philipp's death, through subsequently Freud seemed increasingly reluctant to take time out of his schedule to meet Emanuel. Something in Freud's perception of Emanuel had changed, making seeing him unsettling if not aversive. They would see each other just once more, in May 1913, in Vienna. That trip aside, when Freud's children Martin and Anna visited Britain in 1912 and 1914 respectively, Freud strongly encouraged them to meet Emanuel, perhaps as a guilty substitute for him not being there. He was also more explicit with Anna than before just what a difficult character Emanuel could be. Her visit ended prematurely due to the outbreak of war, without her getting to see her uncle. Three months later Emanuel would be killed in a fall from a train.

Savigny Platz, Berlin

Emanuel, Marie, and Bertha would now stay in Berlin, at 5 Savigny Platz, in the Charlottenburg district, for the next year. Freud left them on 17 September to return to Vienna, saying he would 'look [them] up occasionally',[1] a promise Emanuel would later remind him of. Pauline joined them in the third week of October.[2]

During their time in Berlin, Marie saw various doctors in an effort to treat her recurrent health problems. Emanuel was explicit about his reluctance to discuss Marie's condition – or indeed that of others in his immediate family – in his correspondence with Freud,[3] aside from on *one* occasion when he reported that a new doctor 'assured us it is only bad digestion, [for which he] prescribed . . . some medicin[e], a suitable diet including a table spoonful of cognac mixed with water twice daily at meals and going out when the weather permits'.[4] Such gastrointestinal maladies were, as will be seen later, something of a shared culture within the family. Though Pauline's health problems were also regularly alluded to, and to a lesser extend those of Bertha, neither woman's conditions were clarified even to this extent.

While in Berlin, Emanuel and his family would most probably have had ample opportunities to socialise with Mitzi and hers, who lived nearby at Bamberger Strasse 5. However, aside from one known meeting with Amalia and Dolfi in 1909,[5] being in Berlin failed to produce much contact with the wider Freud family in Vienna or with Freud. This was clearly disappointing for Emanuel.

He and his entourage had planned to return to St Annes during the second week of June 1909, though this was ultimately delayed until 6 October.[6] This was fortuitous insofar as it enabled Emanuel and Freud to meet once in Berlin, on 1 October. It was a rushed visit however, squeezed in during Freud's return journey from his Clark lectures in the USA. Travelling with Ferenczi, seeing Emanuel and the family was fitted around several professional activities in the city. Freud was thus able to meet Karl Abraham and Ferenczi – in an attempt to investigate thought transference – attended a private séance, with Freud's blessing and in his possible company. After such a long wait to see his brother, it must have been frustrating for Emanuel to be displaced by such activities. Whether Emanuel knew of these rival events, however, is debatable. Freud had actually alerted Abraham back in May that he would carve out the time to see him by concealing his own arrival in Berlin for half a day from Emanuel, who he described as his 'very jealous and incredibly youthful and energetic 75-year-old brother'.[7] Several days later Emanuel and the family returned to Britain (travelling via Cologne, Liege, Calais, Dover, and London).

The medium Ferenczi visited reputedly with Freud, Frau Lina Seidler (*c.*1869–1933), known as the Pythia of Berlin, would in due course become famous for her earlier prediction to General Helmuth von Moltke's wife of the date of the outbreak of World War I and was further rumoured to have been involved in intelligence activities during that war.[8] When Ferenczi met her, he requested a reading, while Freud – if in fact he was there – posed merely as his companion, his identity veiled under the pseudonym 'Professor Philipp'. While blindfolded, Seidler supposedly divined somethings of the contents of a letter from Freud, enough anyway to initially impress Ferenczi. Though more sceptical towards occult explanations, Freud tentatively suggested Seidler may indeed have a 'physiological gift' that gave her some insight into others' thoughts.[9] By 1912 however, Ferenczi would abandon these particular investigations as a 'complete failure',[10] Frau Seidler having declined to further assist him. Both men nevertheless retained an interest in telepathy and related phenomena. The adoption of 'Professor Philipp' as a mask for Freud's actual identity in this case, a name seemingly proposed by Freud himself, was tentatively associated with Martha's cousin, the painter John

Philipp (1872–1938), by Eva Brabant and her colleagues.[11] Unmentioned is the far more direct and proximate possibility of 'Philipp' relating to Freud's own older half-brother. This seems a more familiar object for the creation of this alter-ego, with Philipp's active Judaism perhaps providing a further fit in the context of exploring spiritism.

Southport: the declining years

Settling back in Southport (rather than St Annes as had been mooted earlier in the summer), Emanuel and his family were able to enjoy the thrills of Blackpool Aviation Week (18–22 October), Britain's first official air show, during which Henri Farman (1874–1958) set a new British distance record, flying 47 miles in one hour 32 minutes.[12] Emanuel would now occupy a succession of rented properties between 1909 and 1914 in Southport, including a three-bedroom house at 72 Promenade (by April 1911),[13] then 45A Promenade, and finally 21 Albert Road.

During the summers they took holiday accommodation slightly further down the Lancashire coast in St Annes. Sam, however, having taken more substantive charge of the business and its sole management during the rest of the family's stay in Berlin and having lived independently for the first time in his life (in Brookside, Marple Bridge, and then 40 Wellington Road, Heaton Chapel between 1908 and 1910), sustained this following Emanuel's return to Southport in October 1909.

Image 8.1 The Promenade, Southport
Source: author's collection

During the Christmas period that year, he visited the family in Southport from 24 to 28 December and would stay with them there periodically.[14] However, eschewing the long daily commute from Southport into their premises in central Manchester, Sam continued to reside in the city's southern suburbs. Relocating to 31 Elm Road, Heaton Moor, in 1910, he maintained this address until the winter of 1914.[15]

That Christmas of 1909, the country was in the midst of a constitutional crisis following the rejection by the House of Lords of the radical People's Budget, which was intended by the Liberals to fund their proposed social welfare reforms. In an effort to secure a stronger mandate, the Liberals called a general election, to be held during January and February 1910. Emanuel was furious over the Conservative's opposition, and that of their peers in the House of Lords in particular, and saw their electioneering as a crude attempt by the rich to buy the votes of the poor. Emanuel was particularly sorry to see his co-religionist Nathan Rothschild (1840–1915), a Baron in both the United Kingdom and the Austrian Empire, supporting this campaign and hoped that the election would result in 'the Lords get[ting] the sound thrashing they deserve'.[16] At the same time, he feared elements in the British working classes would be peculiarly susceptible to pressure from social elites. 'There is [here] among the lower classes', he wrote to Freud, 'a large number of people blessed with an amount of ignorance & stupidity coupled with adoration of rich nobles [that is] unknown in Germany'.[17]

While Freud's specific response to his older brother's political analysis is unknown, Emanuel was forthright about his views across three pages of his letter to him, suggesting he felt in the company of an ally. And indeed, that appears so. A self-critical liberal, Freud was sympathetic to the poor and working classes from which he had emerged, while at the same time seeing them as mostly needing the leadership of an enlightened elite with whom they might identify.[18] Freud would go on to explore these ideas in several works including *Totem und Tabu* (*Totem and Taboo*) in 1913 and *Massenpsychologie und Ich-Analyse* (*Group Psychology and the Analysis of the Ego*) in 1921.

In the more immediate context of the January 1910 British general election, both brothers' wariness over the susceptibility of the masses to populism and the influence of self-interested elites was partly validated. With a hung parliament, the Liberals only managed to retain power with the support of Labour and the Irish Parliamentary Party, but did then get the budget passed, and the power of the Lords was subsequently curtailed with the passing of the Parliament Act 1911.

Some 20 months later, writing to Freud with news of Philipp's death in August 1911, Emanuel expressed his hope that he could see Freud that autumn. Thinking of Emanuel's age and related issues of mortality,[19] Freud saw his brother's hope as 'very understandable' and deciding 'to go to England, Holland, Belgium or wherever he would like to meet me, after the [Weimar] Congress [on 21–22 September]',[20] he began clearing space in his diary to accommodate this. They soon agreed to meet in Hanover, which Freud described as 'surprisingly convenient', and Oliver Freud suggested a good train itinerary for his father.[21] Freud reached Hanover on 25 September, though no details of his meeting with Emanuel or their mourning survive.[22]

Image 8.2 Bertha and Emanuel Freud, c.1910
Source: © Freud Museum, London

The following year, the brothers planned to meet in Britain close to the anniversary of the Hanover meeting to celebrate Emanuel's 80th birthday. In anticipation of this visit, Freud suggested to Ernest Jones at the end of April 1912 that, as he had no other holiday plans and there would be no International Congress, 'it could be made possible to see more of you and of England than I had first thought of'.[23] Jones replied that he looked forward to the visit and to many others in the future, though could not offer Freud accommodation. By the end of July 1912, the trip was scheduled from 10 to 18 September, with Freud accompanied by Ferenczi and Rank, whom Jones, David Eder and Bernard Hart were looking forward to meeting.[24] This promised to be a rather different experience – more social and collegial – than the solitary experience he had in London in 1908. Brill and Karl Abraham were also invited by Freud,[25] the group now having as part of their agenda the establishment of a secret committee to coordinate the development of psychoanalysis.[26] Jones arranged for lodgings at 13 Princes Street, near Cavendish Square, where he was staying at the time.[27] Freud and Ferenczi initially anticipated spending the week after their London meetings together in Scotland, though (with Ferenczi thinking it might be rather cold there) Freud proposed they could 'certainly do anything else that occurs to us, maybe Stonehenge, Stratford-upon-Avon, or something else romantic or idyllic. There will be no lack of stimulation with both Joneses'.[28] A week before the trip, Freud cancelled his plans as his married eldest daughter, Mathilde Hollitscher (1887–1978), was taken seriously ill. She had been pregnant and with an already irritated appendicitis wound from previous surgery, she developed a fever. This necessitated a termination, following which she began to improve. It was a worrying time for the Freud family, though Freud regretted not having been able to make the journey and told Ferenczi that he 'could . . . have reproached himself'.[29]

The year did see one meeting between branches of the family come to fruition: in July 1912, Freud's eldest son Martin spent a short holiday in England, at least partly with Emanuel and his family in Southport. He recalled his uncle living in 'a large and comfortable house . . . that seemed so typically English' and that Emanuel himself 'had become in every possible detail a dignified English gentleman . . . and this applies to his dress, his manner and his hospitality'.[30] The extent of Emanuel's assimilation (or 'metamorphosis' as Martin saw it) particularly surprised him, though he was equally struck by his uncle's controlling behaviour. 'Life with him was not easy', Martin remembered, in illustration of which he recalled how:

Image 8.3 Jean Martin Freud, c.1910, not long before his visit to England
Source: © Freud Museum, London

at Southport one day I wanted to go out in a rowing-boat when uncle decided that I should ride on a merry-go-round, something I disliked. The result of the long argument was that I did neither.[31]

Martin was 22 years old at the time and was far from needing such direction with his holiday pursuits. The situation was probably not helped by Martin running short of cash during the visit, just as his father had in 1875. Freud telegrammed Emanuel immediately on hearing of Martin's position, asking him to give Martin four pounds, though Martin seems to have decamped by the time his father's message got through.[32] Whether Emanuel had become more rigid with age is unclear, though Martin's observations would tally with comments his father would make to Anna Freud in 1914. If it were a character trait, it may help our understanding of the nature of and tensions within Emanuel's family, particularly in relation to the inertia therein. It may also shed some light on the remarkable extent to which he was able to metamorphose into an English gentleman, a feature John and Sam would both share.

Emanuel and Freud planned to meet in Britain over Easter 1913, with Freud scheduling in a visit to his recently married daughter Sophie Halberstadt in Hamburg on his return journey. Freud seemed ambivalent about seeing Emanuel, although

Image 8.4 Sophie Freud, c.1913, by Max Halberstadt
Source: © Freud Museum, London

he wrote to Anna, who was staying in Merano, on 2 February that he could 'hardly postpone visiting Uncle Emanuel, who is now eighty'.[33] Writing to Ferenczi the following week, Freud alluded rather more directly to his reluctance when he declared 'I don't like to think about it, even though it will cost me only a few days beyond the obligatory vacation days'.[34] What communication passed between Freud and Emanuel over the next few weeks is unknown, but by 10 March the trip to Britain was cancelled. Instead, Freud met Anna, his youngest daughter, at Bolzano on Good Friday, 21 March, and they travelled on by train to Verona and Venice for a holiday.[35] Emanuel, however, was not to be put off and seven weeks later, on 10 May 1913, he made a surprise trip to Vienna. It would be the last time he and Freud would meet. Sam, himself in his 50s, accompanied his elderly father on this trip and would remind Freud years later how active Amalia had seemed to him during the visit.[36] Later still, Alexander's son Harry Freud (1909–1968) recalled Emanuel on this visit forbidding Sam from speaking German, as he was not fully fluent, and it would not be done for an Englishman to be laughed at. While Sam complied, Harry consequently thought Emanuel was 'a strange man'.[37]

Nineteen fourteen began in traditional fashion, with a telegram from Emanuel to Freud wishing him and the family a happy new year.[38] It was probably the following month that Emanuel saw in the press a book review of a volume which apparently contained 'a laudatory chapter on Professor Freud's psychology'.[39] Getting the book, he devoured the chapter and posted the volume to Freud without any covering note. Suspecting the surprise gift may have come from Emanuel (presumably on the basis of the handwriting and postmark on the package), Freud wrote to him twice, on 15 and 19 March. In response to his brother's enquiries, Emanuel 'plead[ed] guilty', before going on to explain the circumstances the present, adding that he had: '. . . read it all through, over and over again, and am glad to say I have been amply rewarded for my effort, as I have now gained a clearer conception, than ever I had before, of the grand work you are engaged in'.[40] Emanuel asked Freud for what he took to be three books, *Alltagsleben*, *Totem*, and *Taboo* before closing the same letter.

The surprising book was the sixth edition of Charles Lloyd Tuckey's *Psycho-Therapeutics: Treatment by Hypnotism and Suggestion*, which had been released in October 1913 by Baillière, Tindall and Cox. Chapter 11 of this volume was titled 'Introduction to the study of psycho-analysis' and was the work of Constance Long (1867–1923), a creative original member of the London Psycho-Analytic Society who was at this point being cold-shouldered by Ernest Jones due to her developing interest in Jung.[41] Writing to Jones on 19 March also, Freud (who perhaps initially wondered if the book was sent by him rather than Emanuel) welcomed Long's chapter, noting that it did not show signs of Jungian leanings. In response, Jones – never one to easily give ground – suggested Constance Long had only met Jung after the chapter was written and in any event it incorporated material supplied to her by M D Eder and Douglas Bryan (1878–1955).[42]

Emanuel spent a couple of days in St Annes at the beginning of April looking for a rental property for that summer and on his return found Freud had sent him the *two* books he had requested earlier, *Zur Psychopathologie des Alltagsleben* and *Totem und Tabu*. Expressing some apprehension about his ability to grasp all of his brother's scientific arguments, Emanuel nevertheless declared it was a task he was entering into with pleasure.[43] Two months later, Emanuel also received the English translation of *The Psychopathology of Everyday Life*, which Freud had asked its English publisher, T Fisher Unwin, to send him on its release. As he told his younger brother, it was a 'very agreeable surprise' and it would be 'a new pleasure to read the book again in English'.[44] This is the last of Emanuel's surviving letters to Freud, though evidently not the last he wrote.

That same summer Anna Freud came to Britain on holiday and Freud arranged to transfer money to her through his nephew Sam. On 16 July 1914 Freud wrote advising her to 'visit Uncle Emanuel, Marie and the old cousins and be very friendly to them, even if you cannot spend as long with them as they will demand'.[45] With an increased sense of urgency, he followed this up on 22 July,

Image 8.5 Anna Freud, c.1914, at the time of her visit to England
Source: © Freud Museum, London

writing that she should contact Emanuel '*as soon as possible*', before taking the opportunity to remind Anna that Emanuel was 'very sensitive, as you know, very stubborn and strange, but is full of gentleness'.[46] It was rather a different picture of Emanuel than that which Freud had previously articulated, but matched Martin's recent experience. While Anna did write to Emanuel as instructed that July, the outbreak of the First World War intervened. Anna was forced to return to Vienna by a circuitous route, so she did not get to visit Emanuel and her other British relatives on this occasion.

Death at Platt's Siding

The train journey between Southport and Manchester was very familiar to Emanuel by 1914 as he made his way between 21 Albert Road and 61 Bloom Street. On Saturday afternoon 17 October 1914 however, the familiar journey ended prematurely for Emanuel as the train ended his life. He was travelling on the Manchester to Southport express. Alone in his compartment, Emanuel was seen (by a passenger – housewife Mrs Janet Brennell [1856–1941] – in an adjacent compartment) fall from the train at 2.30 pm, it having just passed Parbold station. He was found dead by the tracks, near Platt's Siding, both legs badly crushed and the back of his head severely lacerated. When the train was stopped Emanuel's compartment door was found shut but the handle not turned. The inquest, held on 19 October, returned a unanimous verdict of accidental death.[47]

Emanuel's funeral service was conducted at 12.30 pm the following day at Manchester Crematorium, without flowers as was customary at Jewish funerals.[48] Cremation, by contrast, was a very uncommon practice for Jews at the time[49] and Emanuel's funerary arrangements situate him clearly as a very liberal member of the community in the Reform tradition. Indeed, cremation at the time was still an uncommon arrangement within wider British and European society, although it was somewhat more prevalent among progressive social and cultural elites. Its modern emergence in Western culture was catalysed by Professor Lodovico Brunetti's (1813–1899) exhibition of a cremator and cremated remains at the World's Fair in Vienna in 1873,[50] an event which attracted much attention especially in medical and public health circles, and may have been seen by the adolescent Freud, who was a keen visitor to the fair.[51] Emanuel's ashes were subsequently interred in a Jewish section of Manchester's Southern Cemetery on 16 November, with Reform Rabbi Jacob Phillips conducting the burial service.[52] The subsequently erected matzevah, however, was devoid of any religious motifs or inscriptions and more generally reflected Emanuel's achieved secular Anglicised Judaism.

In due course, Marie, Bertha, Pauline, and Sam's remains would also be cremated, as would Freud's and others in his immediate family circle.[53] Emanuel's cremation thus stands as the first such practice in the immediate family and here may be regarded as signifying an important step towards a more secular, progressive modernism.

Image 8.6 Emanuel and Marie Freud's matzevah (gravestone), Manchester's Southern Cemetery

Source: author's collection

For his part, Freud regarded 'a grave in the Central Cemetery [in Vienna as] the scariest thing I can think of',[54] the cemetery being a place he very rarely visited. He attended his father's interment there on 25 October 1896 and viewed the matzevah erected on the grave the following year, but by 1930 when his mother died Freud – in delicate health himself – did not attend her funeral there. While it is a moot point whether Freud would have had his remains buried there if he had stayed in Vienna,[55] on 31 January 1919 he had expressed in his first will his wish to be cremated, 'if it is convenient and cheap'.[56] And ultimately, this is what would happen. As an avowed 'out-and-out unbeliever',[57] Freud eschewed religious rituals wherever possible, and his choice of cremation and urn burial also follows in this well-established trajectory in his life.[58] That said, this was ground Emanuel had already firmly broken, very possibly for reasons not dissimilar to those of his younger brother, and Freud's decision to be cremated in London 25 years later inevitably stands in the shadow of his favourite older brother's obsequies.

In his will, dated 23 June 1914, Emanuel's estate in England and Wales was valued at £3,245 gross for probate purposes.[59] Making provision for his wife through a trust, Emanuel left his remaining assets to Samuel, Bertha, and Pauline, with John totally unmentioned. Marie, Bertha, and Pauline returned to live closer to Manchester in the winter of 1914, purchasing a small house at 35 Lansdowne Road, West Didsbury. Sam was most likely responsible for finding this property. It was just around the corner from 31 Elm Road and he probably moved back in with his mother and two sisters at this time. This would be the family home for the next 25 years.

Freud first heard of Emanuel's death on 10 November and writing to Ferenczi the following day remarked that 'He was, to be sure, 81 years old, but the information says: railway accident. I think he would not have withstood the war; he was very full of life and got [to be] exactly as old as our father'.[60] Freud seems to be hinting at the possibility that Emanuel's death was not wholly accidental, that it may have been a suicide due to the war between his country of birth and his adopted country. There is no independent evidence to support such a suspicion.

Reflections

This final period of Emanuel's life was marked with his temporary restoration to Europe, the source of his previous brief but periodic 'refreshment' forays, whence he might again feel 'at home', no longer the émigré, closer to his now deceased father and mother, and to his siblings and wider family members.

Though life in Berlin seems to have been congenial, it largely failed to produce regular close contacts with Freud or the other members of the Freud family 325 miles away (as the crow flies) in Vienna. The exception was Mitzi and her family, who lived a few streets away from Emanuel's flat in Savigny Platz, regularly met during 1908 and 1909.

While more personal contact continued to be something Emanuel wanted, Freud now seemed more reluctant to see him, procrastinating and cancelling proposed trips. They met just once in Hanover in September 1911, in the wake of Philipp's death, their subsequent final meeting, in Vienna in May 1913, involving Emanuel and Sam arriving there unannounced. Perhaps Emanuel had given up waiting for Freud: a case of 'If the mountain won't come to you . . .'.

Freud increasingly felt unable to spare the time to see his brother, claiming that he was driven to work, time out from which, as he told Ferenczi, 'I don't like to think about'.[61] However, during Easter 1913 Freud did not choose work over seeing Emanuel, instead he chose to holiday with Anna in Italy. That which Freud did not want to think about, was perhaps something other than the financial opportunity cost of taking time off to see his brother. With Emanuel remaining keen to support sibling relationships, Freud for his part was drawing away, struggling I suggest with thoughts of his brother's aging and the inevitable approach of his death, something which would in turn leave Freud as the actual oldest son (and the oldest male, the patriarch) in the family. Then, when Emanuel did die, the war ensured there was no possibility of attending a funeral or mourning with his surviving British family and Freud was left wondering about his brother's end. Freud's complicated grief over the loss of Emanuel seems likely to have informed his key text 'Mourning and melancholia', which was verbally delivered to the Vienna Psycho-Analytical Society on 30 December 1914, ten weeks after Emanuel's death, and then composed as a first written draft in February 1915.[62]

Notes

1 Emanuel Freud to Sigmund Freud, 29 May 1909, LoC ref: mss39990, box 2, folder 21.
2 Emanuel Freud to Sigmund Freud, 25 October 1908, LoC ref: mss39990, box 2, folder 21.
3 Emanuel Freud to Sigmund Freud, 13 February 1909, LoC ref: mss39990, box 2, folder 21.
4 Emanuel Freud to Sigmund Freud, 28 December 1909, LoC ref: mss39990, box 2, folder 21.
5 Emanuel Freud to Sigmund Freud, 29 May 1909, LoC ref: mss39990, box 2.
6 Emanuel Freud to Sigmund Freud, 29 May 1909, 6 October 1909 and 24 October 1909, LoC ref: mss39990, box 2; Emanuel renewed his passport on 4 December 1908 in the midst of this trip (TNA ref: FO 611/20 'Index of names of passport holders, 1904–1908').
7 Freud to Karl Abraham, 23 May 1909, *Freud-Abraham*, p. 91.
8 Also noted in various sources as 'Lisbeth Seidler', her death certificate records her as 'Lina Seidler' (*née* Firkewirth), as does the *Kleine Volks-Zeitung*, 12 January 1933, p. 7 and the *Neues Wiener Tagblatt*, 12 January 1933, p. 7; see also *The Guardian*, 12 January 1933, p. 4; *Fitchburg Sentinel*, 11 November 1933, p. 4; *Daily Advertiser* (Wagga Wagga) 23 March 1933, p. 8; and the *Kärntner Volkszeitung*, 11 February 1933, p. 10.
9 Freud initially noted Frau Seidler's name and address in his pocket notebook in May 1909 (see LoC mss39990, box 50A), with discussion of the séance in October that year appearing *Freud-Ferenczi*, 1, pp. 75–78. This led Ernest Jones and other biographers to conclude Freud was present in person at the séance (see e.g., *Life & Work*, 2, p. 72 and 3, pp. 411–412; Ronald W Clark *Freud: The Man and the Cause*, London: Jonathan Cape and Weidenfeld & Nicholson, 1980, p. 276). A careful reading of the correspondence, however, fails to positively corroborate Freud's physical presence at the séance, a point also noted by Michael Schröter ('The beginnings of a troubled friendship', *International Forum of Psychoanalysis*, 1996, 5, 2, page 138, footnote 7). Whether Freud was physically present or merely psychologically represented at the séance remains a moot point. See also C Tögel *Freud Diarium*, Giessen: Psychosozial-Verlag, 2023, p. 518; T Rabeyron & R Evrard 'Historical and contemporary perspectives on occultism in the Freud-Ferenczi correspondence', *Recherches en Psychanalyse*, 2012, 1, 13, pp. 98–112; Claudie Massicotte 'Psychical transmissions: Freud, spiritualism, and the occult', *Psychoanalytic Dialogues*, 2014, 24, pp. 88–102; Yiukee Chan *Experience into Psychoanalytic Ideas: A Psychobiographical Study of Ferenczi's Introjection*, unpublished PhD thesis, University of Essex, 2016, especially pp. 148–166.
10 Sándor Ferenczi to Freud, 3 July 1912, *Freud-Ferenczi*, 1, p. 388.
11 Eva Brabant *et al* in *Freud-Ferenczi*, 1, p. 78.
12 *Manchester Courier*, 25 October 1909, p. 7.
13 1911 English census, TNA ref: RG 14/22868.
14 Emanuel Freud to Sigmund Freud, 28 December 1909, LoC ref: mss39990, box 2; 1911 English census, TNA ref: RG 14/22868.
15 Manchester Electoral Register, Citizens' Rolls, 1910–11 through to 1914–15.
16 Emanuel Freud to Sigmund Freud, 28 December 1909, LoC ref: mss39990, box 2.
17 Ibid.
18 Paul Roazen *Freud: Political and Social Thought*, London: Hogarth Press, 1969, especially pp. 218–232 and 244–246.

19 Thoughts of his own death became increasingly prevalent for Freud from the 1920s, see for example Freud to Ernest Jones, 28 February 1922, *Freud-Jones*, p. 511.
20 Freud to Ludwig Binswanger, 10 September 1911, in *Freud-Binswanger*, p. 73.
21 Freud to the family, 17 September 1911, LoC ref: mss39990, box 10, folder 14; Oliver Freud to Freud, 18 September 1911, in *Freud-Freud*, pp. 48 and 49, note 13.
22 In his pocket notebook Freud simply recorded '25 Sept. Hannover . . . Geld wechseln', i.e. change money. My thanks to Christfried Tögel for drawing this entry to my attention.
23 Freud to E Jones, 28 April 1912, *Freud-Jones*, p. 137.
24 Freud to E Jones, 22 July 1912, E Jones to Freud, 30 July 1912, *Freud-Jones*, pp. 144–145.
25 Freud to K Abraham, 11 August 1912, in H C Abraham & E L Freud (eds) *A Psycho-Analytic Dialogue: The Letters of Sigmund Freud and Karl Abraham 1907–1926*, London: Hogarth, 1965, p. 122 and Freud to E Jones, 11 August 1912, *Freud-Jones*, p. 151.
26 For the initial correspondence on this plan see E Jones to Freud, 30 July 1912, Freud to E Jones, 1 August 1912, and E Jones to Freud, 7 August 1912, *Freud-Jones*, p. 146, 147 and 149 respectively; Freud to S Ferenczi, 12 August 1912, *Freud-Ferenczi*, 1, p. 404; see also *Life & Work*, 2, pp. 172–188; Phyllis Grosskurth *The Secret Ring: Freud's Inner Circle and the Politics of Psychoanalysis*, London: Jonathan Cape, 1991.
27 E Jones to Freud, 7 August 1912 and 23 August 1912 and Freud to E Jones, 11 August 1912, *Freud-Jones*, pp. 149 and 153 and 151 respectively.
28 Freud to S Ferenczi, 22 August 1912, *Freud-Ferenczi*, 1, p. 406; see also Freud to S Ferenczi, 12 August 1912 and 20 August 1912, *Freud-Ferenczi*, 1, pp. 403 and 405 respectively, and pp. 394–395, note 9.
29 Freud to S Ferenczi, 30 December 1912, *Freud-Ferenczi*, 1, p. 457.
30 Martin Freud *Glory Reflected: Sigmund Freud – Man and Father*, London: Angus and Robertson, 1957, pp. 12–13. Here, Martin dated this visit to 1913, an error given Freud's letter to him of 2 August 1912 about this holiday (LoC ref: mss39990, box 10, folder 22).
31 Ibid., p. 13.
32 Freud to Martin 2 August 1912, LoC ref: mss39990, box 10, folder 22.
33 Freud to Anna Freud, 2 February 1913, *Freud-Freud*, p. 66.
34 Freud to S Ferenczi, 10 February 1913, *Freud-Ferenczi*, 1, p. 469.
35 Freud to Anna Freud, 10 March 1913, *Freud-Freud*, p. 68.
36 Sam Freud to Freud, 15 January 1928, Rylands Library ref: SSF/1/2/51.
37 Harry Freud in interview with Kurt Eissler, 5 September 1952, LoC ref: 39990, box 115, f. 17.
38 Emanuel Freud to Freud, 1 January 1914, LoC ref: mss39990, box 2.
39 Emanuel Freud to Freud, 24 March 1914, LoC ref: mss39990, box 2.
40 Ibid.
41 Emanuel had perhaps seen the *Daily News* (London) review of Tuckey's book which noted that 'An exposition of the psychology of Professor Freud, by Dr Constance Long, forms a most valuable appendix to this book' (26 February 1914, p. 4).
42 Freud to Ernest Jones, 19 March 1914 and Ernest Jones to Freud, 25 March 1914, *Freud-Jones*, pp. 269–271.
43 Emanuel Freud to Freud, 5 April 1914, LoC ref: mss39990, box 2.
44 Emanuel Freud to Freud, 29 June 1914, LoC ref: mss39990, box 2.
45 Freud to Anna Freud, 16 July 1914, *Freud-Freud*, p. 83.
46 Freud to Anna Freud, 22 July 1914, *Freud-Freud*, p. 85.
47 GRO death record: Wigan Registrar's District, October–December 1914, vol. 8c, p. 2; *The Guardian*, 19 October 1914, p. 12; *Wigan Observer and District Advertiser*, 20

October 1914, p. 2 and 24 October 1914, p. 8; *Liverpool Daily Post*, 19 October 1914, p. 12; *Southport Guardian*, 21 October 1914; *Southport Visiter* [sic], 20 October 1914; *Ormskirk Advertiser*, 22 October 1914. The passenger who saw Emanuel fall is merely noted as 'Mrs Brennell' in press reports; the additional identification here comes from the 1911 English census, which lists just one woman of this name in the area.
48 *The Guardian*, 20 October 1914, p. 12.
49 For a discussion of this see Edward D Joseph 'Cremation, fire, and oral aggression', *Psychoanalytic Quarterly*, 1960, 29, pp. 98–104.
50 William Eassie *Cremation of the Dead: Its History and Bearings upon Public Health*, London: Smith Elder & Co, 1875, pp. 80–81.
51 Before Emanuel's death, Freud appears to mention cremation just once, in a joke about Crown Princess Louise, in *Jokes and their Relation to the Unconscious, SE*, 1905, 8, p. 123.
52 Section A, Grave 59, position 1, Southern Cemetery, Manchester Reform Synagogue, Register of Deaths 1857–1959, Manchester Central Library, ref: GB127.M779/Box 76, and Manchester Corporation Register of Burials, Southern Cemetery, 1914, p. 305.
53 The first of these would be Freud's daughter Sophie, who died on 25 January 1920 from the effects of the Spanish flu. See *Freud-Ferenczi*, 2, pp. 5–7, and *Freud-Pfister*, pp. 74–75 for details.
54 Freud to M Bernays, 16 August 1882, *Die Brautbriefe*, 1, p. 291.
55 Christfried Tögel 'Über Sigmund Freuds erste und über seine *beinahe* letzte Unterkunft in Wien', 2019, available online at: www.freud-biographik.de/kleine-texte-zur-freud-biographik/.
56 In the original German: 'Wenn es bequem und billig geht: Verbrennung' (Freud's will dated 31 January 1919, LoC ref: mss39990, box 50A); Christfried Tögel, email to the author, 28 October 2023; see also Paul Roazen 'Freud's last will', *Journal of the American Academy of Psychoanalysis and Dynamic Psychiatry*, 1990, 18, pp. 383–391.
57 Freud to Charles Singer, 31 October 1938, *Freud Letters*, p. 448.
58 Christfried Tögel 'Freud and religion', *Balkan Journal of Philosophy*, 2010, 2, 2, p. 144.
59 National Probate Register, 1914, p. 234. The Bank of England inflation calculator suggests this figure is the equivalent of £296,920 in November 2022.
60 Freud to S Ferenczi, 11 November 1914, in *Freud-Ferenczi*, 2, p. 26.
61 Freud to S Ferenczi, 10 February 1913, *Freud-Ferenczi*, 1, p. 469. In time, as will be seen shortly, Emanuel's son Sam would all too often cite 'work' as preventing him meeting with Freud.
62 James Strachey 'Editor's note', to Sigmund Freud's 'Mourning and melancholia', *SE*, 1917 [1915], 14, p. 329.

Chapter 9

Freud's British nephews
Sam and John

Introduction

We noted earlier the family dynamic through which Freud's elder brothers, and Emanuel in particular, stepped aside to give priority to their father's new wife and family, Freud assuming the mantle of the visible eldest son. An unasked-for promotion, it probably contributed to Freud's continuing emotional ties and indebtedness to Emanuel and in due course to his son Sam. The pattern of replacement continued in Emanuel's family, with his eldest son, John, being marginalised in favour of his younger son Sam.

Both nephews were significant for Freud, his early competitive play with John forming a key template for later relationships, while with Sam, who was reserved to the point of inhibition, his practical helpfulness to Freud was an important support in the immediate post-war period. Sam's loyal followership was accepted, yet all this still left him a pale and somewhat tantalising substitute for his displaced older brother. Freud's wishes for a more vital relationship with him were stymied. The present chapter concludes the main history of the Manchester Freuds by tracing the later histories of Sam and John (and his subsequent life in London), told here for the first time, and discusses their relevance for Freud.

'*I know so little about you*': Sam and Freud

Following his father's death, Samuel continued the family business at 61 Bloom Street, though over the next decade – driven probably by economic factors – he reduced his share of the leasehold, such that the business was only occupying the first and second floors of the building by 1925.[1] Having been in occasional correspondence with Freud since his youth (and having met him in person in 1875 in Manchester and in 1900 and 1913 in Vienna), he now continued his father's role of chief correspondent for the Freud family in Britain with his uncle. While only part of their correspondence survives (69 letters – or parts thereof – from Sigmund to Sam dating between 1911 and 1938 and a further 58 mainly drafts of pieces that travelled in the opposite direction dating from 1914 to 1936), the material offers a vivid insight into Freud's emotional attachments to his extended family, and day-to-day concerns particularly during the difficult times following the First World War. The correspondence was conducted in English.[2]

Following the Armistice on 11 November 1918, communications became easier between Britain and Vienna, though the economic blockade and travel restrictions substantially continued until after the signing of the peace treaty on 28 June 1919. Foodstuffs were in very short supply as were many other day-to-day commodities during the war as well as afterwards, when their availability was aggravated by hyperinflation in Austria.

It was a miserable time for Freud and his family in Vienna. From at least July 1917, he was noting the lack of food in his correspondence with colleagues, the situation becoming a 'hunger emergency' by March 1918.[3] A year on, as the malnutrition worsened despite the Armistice, Freud observed that 'the lack of meat and chronic hunger contributes to the amelioration of affect in me'.[4] He now began to broadcast the seriousness of the situation in Vienna and in October joined in with the Internationalen Psychoanalytischen Vereinigung appeal for aid to children in famine-stricken countries.[5]

Having renewed contact with Sam in May 1919, Freud wrote to him in October that year describing the severe food shortages (having not been so explicit before). Freud revealed that, although he had 'a big name and plenty of work', he was unable to cover the family's day-to-day outgoings and was therefore 'eating up my reserves'. Accepting Sam's offer to send food parcels, Freud asked for 'fat corned beef, cocoa, tea, English cakes and what not'.[6] Feeling 'deeply pained' to hear his uncle's news, Sam's initial attempts to organise parcels were frustrated by carriers declining them and the centralisation and pooling of relief for Vienna.[7] By 18 November 1919, Sam was able to get his first packet despatched to Vienna and others followed (one or more a week at times), though these did not begin to turn up at Berggasse 19 until about early February 1920.[8] Sam also began sending supplies to Freud's sister Pauline Winternitz (1864–1942) and probably some of his others relatives in Vienna.[9] Some went missing in transit or had contents 'pilfered', but new arrangements to send parcels through the Secretary of Vienna Relief in London and with Sohenker & Co improved the reliability of deliveries. Aside from foodstuffs, Freud just made one request for a personal item, asking Sam to select 'a soft Shetland cloth – pepper and salt or mouse grey or tête-de-nègre in colour' for a spring and autumn suit.[10] In the meantime, Freud had managed to procure some further supplies through friends and psychoanalytic 'pupils' hand delivering them from Holland and Switzerland.[11] Max Eitingon was particularly active in organising food parcels for Freud and his family during this period.[12]

One year on from his initial wish-list, Freud wrote that Martha would really like 'milk, extract of meat, coffee, oats, and some spices [such] as: white pepper, cinnamon', before continuing on his own behalf that 'I am very fond of cheese, which can scarcely be had here . . . marmalade is very good, but corned beef is quite common here'.[13] Freud was clearly very grateful for the care and practical support Sam showed in this period of crisis. Sam for his part rose to the organisational and tangible challenge. However, by the end of November 1920 Freud suggested they 'pause [sending further food parcels] for a while [as] Martha [was] taking exception at the prices'.[14] Food shipments did not resume thereafter, although at the beginning of February 1922 Freud would ask Sam to send him a pair of strong 'best quality' boots.[15] With the cessation of food parcels between Manchester and Vienna, communication between Freud and Sam became more sporadic (declining from a combined total of 28 letters in 1920 to a mere seven the following year).

Hunger was not the only difficulty Freud and his family faced in Vienna. With hyperinflation there eroding Freud's savings,[16] he made it clear to Sam that it was only through taking on foreign – and mostly English speaking, British or American – patients, who were able to pay his fees in sterling or other hard currencies, that he gradually managed to work his way back to a sounder financial position. The first of these overseas pupils to arrive was the British paediatrician, psychiatrist, and psychoanalyst David Forsyth (1877–1941), who saw Freud six times a week from 6 October to 18 November 1919.[17] On 15 October 1920 Freud informed Sam that 'I have somewhat recovered by the treatment of foreign patients and am in possession of a deposit of good money at The Hague'.[18] Just over a year later, on 4 December 1921, Freud further noted that he was:

> deeply in work with 6 Americans, 3 Englishmen, 1 Swiss, listening and talking 9 hours a day and so I have gone on for these two months. As I am earning foreign money, I am exepted [sic] from the miseries of our town. I have even succeeded in regaining a part of the amount of money lost by the war and as long as I can continue working, I am sure to be free of financial cares. I am glad to say none of the family is still dependent on the scarce and irregular subsidies from Eli [Bernays].[19]

To safeguard his new post-war earnings, Freud now maintained accounts with several banks including the Dutch Jewish firms of Lissa & Kann in The Hague and Lippmann, Rosenthal & Co in Amsterdam, while by 1925 he was also directing deposits of royalties to Anna Freud's account with the Anglo-Austrian Bank in London, a prudent course of action given the political instability and post-war hyperinflation.[20] Through them he arranged several transfers to Sam in reimbursement for the various goods he sent them (and was insistent that Sam both inform him of the costs involved and accept payment), though he also routed money to Sam through other channels, having James Strachey pay him a cheque for £28 on one occasion.[21]

The 15 months between October 1919 and December 1920 constituted the most intense period of the correspondence between Sam and Freud, with 36 of their surviving letters (19 from Freud and 17 from Sam) clustering during this short time. This is no surprise. The defeat of Austro-Hungarian Empire in the war, its subsequent dismemberment, the economic blockade, and the hyperinflation caused profound difficulties for many in Vienna. For Freud, the food shortages there were – after a time – significantly offset by the very practical help he received from Sam and other friends and colleagues, for which he was very grateful. At the same time, Freud rebuilt his private practice and was able to work his way out of financial ruin at a time when others of his age and class might legitimately be looking towards retirement.

Freud's *original* economic success, that moved him from his poor working-class origins, was – as it was in the aftermath of the Great War – particularly facilitated by working long hours in his practice. Hard work and monetary success among Jews, however, were commonly disparaged as a sign of avarice, a deadly sin, within the prevailing zeitgeist. No stranger to such anti-Semitic tropes, Freud would for example tell Sándor Ferenczi how the Wolf Man's initially saw him in the transference as 'a Jewish swindler'.[22] Not to be put off by such restrictive ideas, Freud tended to actively reclaim business and economic rewards as something of a virtue.[23] Indeed, as we have seen earlier, being able to provide economically for his family was one of Freud's key personal values, a plank of his identity and self-esteem, something he acknowledged repeatedly to colleagues and relatives. He thus told Ferenczi in that same letter from February 1910 that he was 'only a machine for making money',[24] a phrase he recycled to his niece Lilly Freud-Marlé, depicting himself as 'a mere money-acquisition-machine'.[25] Elsewhere, in his correspondence with Jung he noted his 'money-making complex',[26] while to Karl Abraham he wrote how his 'mental constitution urgently requires me to earn and spend money on my family in fulfilment of my father complex',[27] and in yet another letter to Ferenczi he declared he was 'fulfilling my primary function, i.e., to earn money, as intensively as possible'.[28] Given this commitment to achieving financial security and to looking after the family, reimbursing Sam for the various goods he was supplying was thus very characteristic of Freud, and of Freud-the-family-man in particular. Amid the flux of post-war Austrian identity renegotiation, it was perhaps especially important.

Aside from his capacity to earn and to pay his way as sources of esteem, Freud's routine interactions with Sam and his Manchester relatives offered him further emotional support. Some of this, which touched on his recognition, Freud seems to have been wary about. He was, as he factually acknowledged to Sam in October 1919, 'a big name'. Revisiting this 12 months later, Freud wondered whether Sam's mother and sisters were 'aware that my name in the world at large and in England too is far more respectable than my riches?'.[29] Sam was quick to inform his uncle that 'we are always eagerly watching for your name in the papers we read', before rehearsing recent sightings in the *Daily News*, *Punch*, and *John O'London*.[30] In his response, Freud sought to distance himself from the idea he might be seeking either positive strokes or celebrity:

> I am anxious you could misconstrue my question about my renown in England, I wanted to know how much of the noise had reached your quiet home. Popularity in itself is utterly indifferent to me, must at the best be considered a danger for more serious achievement.[31]

Sam, however, indicated that their frequent sightings of references to Freud in print confirmed his uncle's widespread public recognition, whilst privately 'We are always greedily searching the papers for news about you & eagerly & delightedly devour all we can find'.[32] Freud allowed the matter to lapse, though it re-emerged 12 months on, at the end of November 1921, after a period of several months silence. This time, Sam nudged his uncle for news, adding 'We often talk of you and think how proud and delighted Pa [Emanuel] would have been to read in the English papers all those references to Freudian theories, etc. A newly coined adjective!'[33] Quick to reply, Freud wondered 'Do you think he would have enjoyed my actual popularity? It's a burden to me'.[34] It was not a question Sam took up, although (without any apparent sense of irony) he offered Freud his congratulations on his appearance in *Who's Who*.[35]

Sharing family news (sometimes slowly and with hesitation), was at the core of Freud's communications with Sam, with births and marriages typically noted and celebrated, yet health concerns – both physical and psychological – and death represented a strong and perhaps stronger counterpoint. Some such casual comments were passed without much ruffling of the surface, such as Freud's description of his niece Martha (aka Tom: 1892–1930), daughter of his sister Maria ('Mitzi'; 1861–1942) and her husband Moritz Freud (1857–1920), as 'gifted, yet half-crazy' when she became engaged to the Hebrew scholar Jankew 'Jakob' Seidmann (1892–1929) in November 1920.[36]

Other events in the family produced greater emotional resonance, being deeply upsetting for Freud, Sam, and other family members. When Freud's daughter Sophie died from influenza and grippe-pneumonia on 25 January 1920 in Hamburg (a victim of the deadly Spanish flu pandemic), Freud quickly shared the news with Sam,[37] confiding that 'We feel rather depressed as you may imagine. Martha is deeply shaken by our loss'.[38] One year later, on 21 January 1921 Freud wrote to Sam 'I did not wish you a happy new year. I was so horribly disappointed the last time that I lost all confidence. It is just a few days before the anniversary'.[39] It was a loss, the pain of which Freud would continue to feel, the pain being – as he told Ludwig Binswanger in 1929 – 'the only way of perpetuating a love that we do not want to abandon'.[40]

There was further traumatic news the following year. Freud's niece, Caecilie Graf, finding herself pregnant and unmarried, attempted suicide with an overdose of veronal. Hospitalised, she developed pneumonia and died on 18 August 1922. It was, incidentally, Amalia Freud's 87th birthday. Writing to Sam at some length, Freud depicted Caecilie as 'a sweet girl . . . passionate, yet obstinate and very secluded'.[41] Noting a catalogue of stressors and negative life-events she had experienced (from her brother Hermann's death from war wounds on 19 June 1917, through her dropping out of studying chemistry, a failed business venture, her difficult relationship with her boyfriend, and a poor relationship with her mother), Freud wrote that he was *still* unsure what the exact motive behind her suicide was.[42] Sam was 'thunderstruck' at the news when he got Freud's letter, responding that 'it is really awful to think of the tragedy', before going on to inform his uncle that 'You will understand that we do not tell mother [who was probably suffering from 'senile decay' at this point] any disquieting news'.[43] Sam's coda here is interesting, both in the limit it sets on the sharing of news (or alternatively on its occasional repression) and on Sam's belief that Freud would understand this.

Freud placed considerable emphasis on honesty, though this was not without qualification. During his self-analysis he would note, for example, in his letter to Wilhelm Fliess of 15 October 1897 that 'Being totally honest with oneself is a good exercise'.[44] Similarly, in the clinical context, the rule of free association – wherein the analysand is asked to say everything that comes to mind without selection or omission – gradually became the fundamental rule structuring the analytic situation.[45] In his personal life Freud showed a considerable 'ability to meet the truth', as Anna Freud would later remark.[46] Taking this up in the context of his doctors and colleagues unhelpful delicacy in addressing his need for urgent and radical medical treatment, Gay writes: 'In Freud's eyes, no one had the right to lie to him, not even from the most compassionate of motives. To tell the truth, however appalling, was the greatest kindness'.[47] However, in his published writings while Freud was more candid than many in his self-disclosures, particularly in *The Interpretation of Dreams* in reporting his own dreams, associations and interpretations, he acknowledged 'I have been unable to resist the temptation of taking the edge off some of my indiscretions by omissions and substitutions'.[48] Where this occurred, Freud stated, the resultant material was less satisfactory. This has led others into re-examining Freud's dreams in varyingly motivated attempts to address the interpretative shortcomings Freud himself acknowledged.[49] What is less often considered in relation to the value of honesty (as distinct from disclosure), is the countervailing role privacy played for Freud in self-experience. Some of this may be seen in the present family context, where Freud – though silent on Sam's censoring of 'disquieting news' to his own mother – was probably in broad agreement with his nephew's decision.[50]

Sophie's younger child, Heinz (otherwise known as Heinele), became a much-loved grandson, 'a charming naughty devil of a boy'.[51] When he also died from acute tuberculosis on 19 June 1923, it was a particularly painful loss for Freud, leaving him painfully depressed, with – as he said himself – an 'aversion to life'.[52] Heinz was four years old and was being cared for by Freud's daughter Mathilde and her husband Robert Hollitscher (1875–1959) when he died. Freud recalled him to Sam as 'the cleverest, sweetest child I have ever met. We were very fond of him, all of us'.[53]

Having broken the news of Heinz's death to Sam, Freud continued in the same letter to inform him that 'Two months ago I had a growth removed from the soft palate which might have degenerated but had not yet. Remember that I am an old man now'.[54] Freud's juxtapositioning of the news of Heinz's death against his minimal report of own condition and surgery in the letter was telling, the association being reinforced by his parting injunction that Sam recognise that he was '*an old man*'. With mouth problems and thoughts of oral cancer going back to 1917,[55] Freud had more recently noticed a lesion on the right side of his palate. After several months of hesitation, he had it investigated and then underwent surgery for it on 20 April 1923. With his first ill-chosen doctors initially minimising what was in fact cancer but was variously passed off as a leukoplakia or epitelioma, Freud too initially disavowed the life-threatening seriousness of his condition. Reluctant to see his beloved cigar smoking as an aetiological factor and to face surrendering

Image 9.1 Freud with Heinz and Ernst, 1923
Source: Chronicle/Alamy

the habit, the underlying spectre of death must have exerted a still more powerful influence on his psyche at this time.[56] Freud, in partial identification with Heinz, was evidently struggling to contemplate his own decline and the prospect of death. Sam opened his reply by declaring he 'was really somewhat taken aback by your letter, not having the slightest idea that you had been unwell',[57] before going on to hope he would be fully recovered soon.

Freud's recovery from the operation was slow as he told Sam on 24 September (though only doing so *after* a long catalogue of other family news). 'I have not', he wrote, 'yet overcome the effects of my last operation in the mouth, have pains and difficulty in swallowing and am not yet sure of the future'.[58] Further and more radical oral surgery followed on 4 and 12 October, news of which Freud conveyed rather more promptly and directly to Sam, writing that the operation 'is said to have succeeded well but will take some weeks more before swallowing and speaking are all right'.[59]

In Manchester, there was more painful news. Marie Freud, having been suffering from increasing senility and cardiac problems, died at home on 21 October 1923.[60] She was 87 years old. Sam wrote to his uncle that 'Poor dear mother passed away early this morning. She was unconscious for some little time and her end was the most peaceful imaginable',[61] to which he added a warm postscript on getting

Freud's 20 October letter, hoping he would be feeling better. Cremated in Manchester Crematorium on 23 October, Marie's ashes were interred after some considerable delay next to those of Emanuel in a Jewish section of the Southern Cemetery on 7 November, Reform Rabbi Jacob Phillips again conducting the burial service.[62]

Freud received Sam's note on 24 October when he, as he frankly put it, 'returned home from the Sanatorium . . . very much broken and enfeebled',[63] following his latest cancer surgery. Nevertheless, turning to the death of his sister-in-law, Freud made two precise points to Sam about Marie: 'how happy she was as a wife and how her children venerated her'.[64] Concluding his letter, Freud intimated how thoughts of those in Manchester buoyed him up somewhat, declaring 'If I recover and become movable, to see all three of yours [sic] would be an enjoyment I would try to attain'.[65] (When his own mother died seven years later, on 12 September 1930, aged 95, Sam was one of the people Freud broke the news to that same day).[66]

Freud's repeated surgery in October was successful in excising the cancer, though recovery was prolonged and very uncomfortable. Over the ensuing years, however, although the full-blown cancer would not reappear until 1936, Freud would develop recurring leukoplakias which would require over 30 surgical interventions to manage. During the period from October to December 1923 talking and eating were particularly difficult for Freud, both helped and complicated in part by a prosthesis he now had to wear and have regularly adjusted.[67]

It was not until the beginning of January 1924 that Freud was able to resume his clinical work. Writing to Sam on 9 January that year, Freud declared 'I am glad to let you know that I am rapidly recovering and was able to take up my work with this new year. My speech may be impaired but both my family and my patients say it is quite intelligible'.[68] Here, Freud seems hesitant about both his objective functioning and the reassurance offered. When Freud subsequently attended a meeting of the *Wiener Psychoanalytische Vereinigung* (WPV; the Vienna Psychoanalytical Association), one of the members present, Isidor Sadger (1867–1942), recalled how he and others were discomforted both by Freud's acquired speech impairment and his appearance. While Freud looked pale, his face deeply sunken and very sad, Sadger noted 'The impression made by the Professor's speech was simply horrible . . . Everyone looked down, embarrassed, their eyes lowered'.[69] Almost two years later, Freud was clearly attuned to the ways in which those around him, and his analysands in particular, might evade the reality of his actual impairments. Freud thus wrote somewhat wryly to Sam on 19 December 1925: 'Yet I have continued to do some work, I give 5–6 hours treatment daily and my patients or pupils feign not to notice my defects. I write a paper from time to time'.[70]

In the summer of 1925, Freud's eldest son Martin (1889–1967) paid an overnight visit to Sam and the family in Manchester. Writing to Sam afterwards, Freud noted Martin had 'told me much about you but not enough',[71] highlighting their desire for and yet struggles with communication in the family. Freud then updated Sam on his mother's 90th birthday, which they had celebrated on 18 August with a surprise party at the Austrian spa town of Bad Ischl where she was on holiday. Though Freud – who spent the summer at *Villa Schüler* in Semmering in apparently delicate health – was unable to go to the event, most of the rest of the immediate family were there, including Freud's sister Anna Freud Bernays who had travelled over with several of her children from New York. Amalia was, Freud wrote, 'mentally all right', though her hearing was impaired, and she was 'subject to attacks of heart failure'. Echoing Sam's earlier strategy with his own mother, Freud then told his nephew that:

> We had made a secret of all the losses in the family: my daughter Sophie, her second son Heinele, [Mitzi's son] Teddy in Berlin [who drowned in Eberswalde on 10 July 1923], Eli Bernays [who died in New York on 12 October 1923], and your parents. (She knows the death of Caecilie [Mausi]).[72]

The catalogue of loss here for Freud and the extended family was substantial and – if his text was strictly correct, which it is not – the withholding of news of deaths in the family from his mother, Amalia, went back at least 11 years, to that of Emanuel in October 1914. It seems very unlikely that Amalia would not have been told at some point by somebody of these deaths, especially given the weekly Sunday family meals at her home. And in fact, we know from surviving correspondence that Freud himself had broken the news of Sophie's death to Amalia by letter on 26 January 1920.[73] Whether Freud meant to imply to Sam that his own (and others) withholding of distressing news of deaths from Amalia was of such long standing and so all-encompassing is unclear. In the context of his letter to Sam, written when he was unwell himself (and weeks away from further investigations for cancer),[74] it would be unsurprising if the shadow of the many losses suffered fell heavily on him, and understandable too that the family might collectively avoid the topic with the nonagenarian Amalia on her birthday. Clarification of such possible discretion or more radical censorship within the family, and in this case specifically towards Amalia, was not explored in the surviving correspondence with Sam.

Freud's niece, Judith Bernays Heller (1885–1977), noted the *reciprocal* of this process with Amalia, in which she herself would selectively filter out specific information, limiting who consciously knew what. Heller observed how Amalia:

> successfully used her increasing deafness in order to avoid hearing what she did not want to hear – principally the report of any event that might require her to bestow an extra measure of sympathy or consolation upon some member of the family.[75]

While Heller here describes this from the perspective of individual psychology, Ana-Maria Rizzuto highlights the *relational* process implicit in such narcissistic behaviour, noting that Amalia 'demanded to be protected from any knowledge that might cause *her* any pain or remove her from centre stage'.[76] Although the status of this 'demand' may be debated (whether it was perceived as a need, demand or desire), it was unconsciously taken up by Freud and others in their efforts at creating and maintaining 'secrets', ostensibly as a caring protective measure.

For Sam, telling or more specifically withholding supposedly distressing news was an issue he and his sisters had in relation to his own mother, but more generally self-censorship and inhibition seem to have held Sam in a pervasive, less conscious grip. Somatic issues were regularly alluded to and enquired into, although Sam *rarely* specified what the health concerns in his own immediate family were and *never* asked for his uncle's medical opinion. For example, in 1922 Sam wrote 'mother is rather weaker than she has been and although now and again she seems a shade better, she is at times extremely weak. Pauline is very far from being well. Bertha and I [are] all right in health'.[77] Freud's health and that of the family in Vienna also became a source of concern for Sam and his sisters, about which Sam could initiate conversation with his uncle. These concerns, just as we saw during the food crisis in 1919 and 1920, became structuring nuclei in which Sam was engaged. In their absence, Sam struggled to initiate open communication and letters became more infrequent. This in turn became a source of self-criticism, as – for example – on 9 February 1923 when he wrote 'I feel somewhat ashamed of myself for neglecting to write – lack of news is my only excuse'.[78] This supposed 'lack of news' and a sense of stagnation became regular refrains in Sam's irregular letters. He wrote to Freud on 12 September 1923 declaring 'There is nothing new to tell about ourselves';[79] and again on 31 December that year 'There is nothing special to write about';[80] similarly, on 20 April 1924 he wrote 'If I had any news you may be sure I would have written you before now. There is no change with us';[81] while on 4 April 1925 it was a similar refrain, 'There is nothing new to tell about ourselves. Pauline keeps the same, no improvement. Bertha has been unwell, but is now decidedly better. . . . Business [is] very flat indeed'.[82] The effect of all of this was inevitably stultifying.

Freud encouraged Sam to be more forthcoming. On 19 December 1925 however, feeling increasingly frail, he was at his most direct with his nephew, writing:

> Is it so long since I last wrote you? It may be time is flying rapidly and I lack the incentive to chatter easily with you as I know so little about you and the whereabouts of your life. Even Martin when he saw you at Manchester did not bring me satisfactory information. However, I am ready to tell you all that may interest you about myself and our people, not all of it glad or glorious news, nothing particularly sad.[83]

Framing his uncle's remarks as a 'dressing down', Sam initially highlighted the brevity of Martin's overnight stay as if this might be a defence. 'What could he [Martin] tell you', Sam wrote, 'other than what I have already told you myself in previous letters – only written down in 3 or 4 lines'.[84] Continuing, Sam wrote that while he 'cannot weave a romance around a plain fact or statement',[85] he would try to give a more detailed account of events there. What followed was a familiar inventory of his own and his sisters' states of health and the depressed prices in the cotton trade, together with less familiar assurances they were all proud of Freud and they basked in his reflected glory. It was, Sam suggested in closing, the longest letter he had ever written (three pages) and might thus test Freud's patience as he waded through it. Freud's challenge to his nephew had been met with Sam's default narratives, albeit at somewhat greater length. Any hopes, if hopes there were, for a qualitative shift in the communication were disappointed. Freud's actual response to the letter is unrecorded.

Five years before, in September 1920, Freud had hoped to visit Sam and his other relatives in Manchester, following the International Psychoanalytical Association (IPA) Congress at The Hague. This plan had fallen through due to a delay in the arrival of Anna Freud's visa and news of the death of Freud's brother-in-law, Moritz Freud, in Berlin from heart disease on 7 September 1920.[86] As a last-minute alternative, Freud invited Sam to join them at the Hotel Paulez in The Hague, though Sam declined this as being 'impossible',[87] later writing that, 'it was mainly for "home" reasons I could not get away',[88] adding that his mother had been unwell some time previously. In retrospect, Freud deeply regretted not having made the journey to visit Sam and the family in Manchester, noting he had been also expected in Cambridge where there was developing interest in psychoanalysis.[89]

Freud's wish to see the family in Manchester remained undiminished and was to an extent stoked by thoughts of his own mortality.[90] With the latter clearly in mind, on 1 February 1926 he invited Sam and Bertha to his upcoming 70th birthday (Pauline being too unwell to travel, he thought). Their presence, Freud movingly declared to Sam, 'would give me the highest gratification I can imagine at that occasion. I pray you will consider my proposal – you need not answer at once'.[91] Sam sat on the invitation for almost two months before finally telling Freud that he did not feel able to come:

> Apart from home affairs – Bertha has been far from well the last few weeks – there are one or two matters which make it necessary that I should be here on the spot or at least not more than a few hours journey away from home.[92]

It was a similar refrain to Sam's 1920 apologia declining Freud's invitation to visit him in The Hague. On this occasion he sent Freud a fountain pen for his birthday and a congratulatory telegram on the day itself. Though grateful for the gift and Sam, Bertha, and Pauline's birthday wishes, they were poor substitutes for actually seeing them face-to-face. 'My dear ones', Freud would afterwards write, 'I have missed you sadly, it was perhaps the last opportunity to see you once more'.[93]

These were not issues which Sam took up directly, at least in the surviving correspondence. He was, however, moved the following year to muse on the stagnation that continued to pervade his communication:

> I wonder by what combination of happenings, we have not heard from each other for such a long while. I cannot justify my silence by saying I have no news to send. That's not good enough – but I am sure it is the only reason and I am also sure I am not satisfied with it.[94]

The pattern of this, unhappily, did not change and the surviving correspondence diminished over the next decade, most probably because Freud's hopes for greater intimacy and reciprocity with Sam were stymied and their correspondence was increasingly stale.

That said, economic and political events occasionally peeped through in the exchange of letters. Freud thus surprised Sam in December 1928 with the apparent suggestion that an *Anschluss* with Germany might offer Vienna salvation from its increasing problems. It was a minority view in Austria Sam thought.[95] By the time Hitler came to power in Germany in 1933, any residual appeal this idea held had long evaporated. Writing to Sam at the end of July that year, Freud told him that Oliver and Ernst had to flee Berlin and that the latter was staying in London and making preparations to settle there. Acknowledging the uncertainty of the political situation in Austria, Freud nevertheless declared that he was 'determined to stick it out here to the last. Perhaps it may not come out too bad'.[96] Freud of course was very wrong about this, though he did stick it out until his own escape was almost impossible. And for four of his sisters it would be impossible.

Five years later, on Saturday 4 June 1938, Freud wrote several notes, among which was a postcard to Sam, sent to his Bloom Street address. It was a simple though poignant message: 'Leaving Vienna for good today. Next address: 39 Elsworthy Road, London, NW3. Any chance of our meeting after so many years?'.[97] Departing by train at 3.25 pm that same afternoon, Freud travelled via Paris and the Dunkirk-to-Dover ferry to London, arriving there on Monday 6 June. Three days later, Sam travelled down from Manchester and met Freud at 39 Elsworthy Road – one of his first visitors in his new home.[98] It had been a much-anticipated meeting and Freud's housekeeper Paula Fichtl – who opened the door when Sam arrived – recalled that it was 'a moving reunion between "Uncle Sigi" and his sixty-eight-year-old nephew'.[99] Although Freud lived for a further 15 months in London, this would be the last time they would meet. Freud would note in his *Kürzeste Chronik* a further ten letters back and forth between Sam and himself over this time, none of which appear to have survived.[100] The last of these was Sam, Pauli, and Bertha's greetings to Freud on his 83rd birthday, which he punctually received on 6 May 1939.

During all this time, Sam continued to manage E Freud & Son, preserving the business name unchanged for three decades after Emanuel's death, and sustaining operations in Bloom Street until 1941.[101] Then, in his 80s, Sam moved premises a short distance to 2 and 4 Beaver Street,[102] from whence he finally retired during the course of the Second World War.

Sam, Pauline and Bertha continued to live together at 35 Lansdowne Road until their ends. In 1940 the first of the trio died. Becoming increasingly senile, Bertha fell down the stairs at home on 3 December 1940 and died at the end of the month on 30 December 1940 at Withington Hospital, the ex-Chorlton Workhouse,[103] aged 81. Her body was cremated and, after a six-week delay (perhaps occasioned by the recent German blitz on the city that killed an estimated 684 people), her ashes were buried in the Jewish section of the Southern Cemetery on 14 February 1941. Rabbi Percy Selvin Goldberg, of the Reform Synagogue, oversaw their interment. Three years later, on 26 January 1944, Pauline died, aged 87, from senile confusion and senility at Park House, the ex-Crumpsall Workhouse.[104] Fritz Hartwig noted she was 'stone deaf' at the end.[105] Her body was cremated and her ashes interred next to Bertha in the Southern Cemetery, with Rabbi Goldberg again conducting the service. Their deaths briefly brought Sam into renewed contact with the wider Freud clan, with Harry Freud renewing written contact with him.[106]

In October 1944, when Lilly Freud-Marlé came to seek out the last surviving Manchester Freuds and met Poppy, she also encountered Sam during her visit to the city. Poppy thought Sam could be reluctant to meet her. 'Sam has gotten old and weird', she warned Lilly, 'He is over eighty years old; he doesn't want anyone in his home, not even you. But I'll call him, maybe he'll leave his cell after all, and we could meet him in a little tearoom'.[107] Accepting Poppy's invitation to her surprise, the trio met in a café in Manchester city centre, Lilly describing Sam as 'small, delicate, and very well groomed, with a round bucket hat and umbrella', a heavy gold Albert attached to his pocket watch decorating his waistcoat, completing what struck her as 'a perfect picture of a nineteenth-century man'.[108] Over tea, Sam nostalgically recounted past visits to family members in Berlin and Vienna and theirs to Manchester, while gently parrying Lilly's enquiries about any family photographs he might have. Seeing Sam to his bus home, both he and Poppy competitively gossiped about the other to Lilly, before Sam's final departure, taking with him a requested kiss on his cheek from Lilly. Poppy declared him 'charming' and suggested Lilly had seen him at his best. It was Poppy who acquiesced to Lilly's desire to see family photos, of which she had a large box, among which was one of 'the young, nineteen-year-old Sigmund, sent from Vienna to Manchester with a dedication to his half-brother [*presumably* Philipp]. At that time, he still signed himself with Sigismund, his real first name'.[109] Although by no means a wholly reliable historian, Lilly's account of her meeting offers a unique first-hand account of Sam which reveals the traits of his character clearly further hardening in old age.

Less than a year after this meeting, on 2 September 1945, Sam died from the effects of cardiac muscle failure and arteriosclerosis in a nursing home at 390 Wilbraham Road, Chorlton-cum-Hardy. His body was cremated in the Manchester Crematorium two days later,[110] though it would be another five months before the ashes were interred on 13 February 1946 alongside those of Bertha and Pauline and close to their parents' graves in the Southern Cemetery. Sam died intestate, with his estate valued at a not insignificant £6,044, which his cousin Pauline Marie Hartwig inherited.[111]

The (dis)appearance of John Freud

The fate of John Freud has been the subject of considerable speculation, several Freud scholars labelling it a mystery,[112] with a small minority filling in the lacuna with lurid speculations of his having been murdered, an act supposedly committed or commissioned by Sigmund Freud.[113] With John, as noted earlier, gaps in the archive and hints of material being withheld have contributed to this sorry picture.[114] Here we may include Ernst Freud's comments, that his father's correspondence with John has: 'obstinately refused to come to light',[115] as a prime example. Another source that catalysed such speculation were brief comments made by Fritz Hartwig in the 1950s. Following his death on 18 January 1958, Eric Arnold donated the surviving Freud correspondence to the John Rylands Library, which included Fritz Hartwig's brief recollections. Hartwig made the comment that John 'left his parents at an early age and nobody has ever heard or seen anything of him since'.[116] This and much of the other speculation on John is rather less than accurate.

John is recorded living at home on the 1861 and 1871 editions of the English census. By the time of the latter, on 2 April 1871, John had left school and was working as an office boy. Freud met him during his visit to Manchester in July to September 1875, where he was still apparently living at home with his parents.[117] At the time, Freud described his assimilation, his education and his foreign language skills approvingly to Silberstein.[118]

Sometime over the following five years John moved into independent accommodation, being one of two lodgers in George Statham's household at 13 Hyde Road, Ardwick, by 1881.[119] The census return describes John as being born in Bohemia, Austria, 25-year-old, unmarried, and working as a warehouseman, evidently with Emanuel. John had not moved very far from his parents and was at this time living on the same road as his uncle Philipp and his family. In the Spring of 1886, with Emanuel's business in the doldrums, John left the family firm and found another post. Writing to Rosa about John's move, Emanuel regretted having been unable to keep him with him but thought his new job was a good one. At the same time he portrayed John as looking 'remarkably well, being in robust health and good spirits on which bad times have no effect. He is well informed and can express himself in a way that makes social intercourse with him a genuine pleasure though I say it myself'.[120]

Over the next five years this parting of the ways became solidified and John moved increasingly away from his family, both relationally and geographically. As he did so, he began to shed the remaining vestiges of his middle-European Jewish identity and adopt a more English persona. In doing so, traces of him in the archives blur. Contemporary digitisation of primary source material however, has made it possible to document John Freud's later years with a reasonable degree of probability. In 1891 he thus seems to reappear boarding with the Butler family at 15 Burton Crescent, St Pancras, in London.[121] Described as a 36-year-old merchant's clerk, this John Freud however was noted as born in Manchester. Of the four markers of his identity on the census, three thus correspond very closely to Emanuel Freud's son: he has the correct name, is within five months of John's actual age, and was working in a similar trade. The one discrepancy to a positive identification is his place of birth, Manchester, rather than the already varying birthplaces recorded on the three previous iterations of the English census: (1) Austria, (2) Moravia, Austria, and (3) Bohemia, Austria as he is listed on the 1861, 1871, and 1881 censuses respectively. Manchester however corresponds to where he lived for over 20 of his previous years, making it arguably his 'native' city and indeed as previously noted Freud had remarked in 1875 that John was then 'an Englishman in every respect',[122] suggesting he had assimilated into British culture. That said, returning John as 'from Manchester' would be an even simpler mistake to make if the census was completed by the head of the household. Furthermore, an examination of registered births in the Manchester area failed to reveal any other men named John Freud (or close variants thereof) during the decades either side of his projected birthdate, while Manchester census returns also fail to reveal another man of an approximating name. More circumstantial evidence comes from a consideration of the other boarders at 15 Burton Crescent when the 1891 census was taken: two of the other six were employed in the traditional Freud family's business sphere, the textile trade, namely, 21-year-old Isidor Meyer, a tailor's cutter from Germany, and 24-year-old Thomas Sneath, a tailor's salesman from Peterborough.

Further corroborative evidence that *this* John Freud was Emanuel's son comes from John's grandson Peter Greenop's later life recollections of his grandfather. Though John was reticent about his past to his own family, his grandson remembered him as having a command of several languages including French and German (Freud having specifically remarked on his fluency in modern languages in 1875) and as working at various times as a tour guide with Thomas Cook.[123] While the latter company briefly featured on Freud's 1908 London itinerary, Freud despondently noted that John was 'away on a journey' at that time, an action wholly characteristic of a professional tour guide.[124]

As Michael Molnar suggested, something had gone wrong in Emanuel Freud's family.[125] In this context, John's disappearance may be seen as less of a mystery and more of an attempt to establish himself outside of the *huis clos* of the family set up. John Freud was a man trying to make a break from his past, perhaps particularly with his controlling father, and as such some degree of reinvention of his identity may be expected, a trend that would continue over the next few years. Peter Greenop suggested John's estrangement from his family related to financial matters, a breakdown he attributed to an unspoken-of action by his grandfather.[126] If this is correct, it may go some way to explaining the earlier noted exclusion of John from Emanuel's will.

At 15 Burton Crescent the Butler family had 22-year-old Mrs Annie Newport (née Sheather: 1868–1934), who they employed as a domestic servant, living with them in April 1891. Annie had married Metropolitan Police Constable Alfred Newport (1863–1889) in September 1885, when she was just 17, though he died two months before their only child, Agnes Annie 'Kate' (1889–1941) was born. Annie and John Freud developed a relationship, probably during the period he was also boarding at 15 Burton Crescent. In about July 1891 Annie became pregnant and she (presumably with John) moved to live in Pimlico. From this time onwards, Annie and John presented themselves as a married couple, a fiction they appear to have used for social purposes.[127]

On 13 April 1892 Annie gave birth to a daughter, Ethel Rose (1892–1959), in a lodging house at 85 Tachbrook Street. By the time Annie registered the birth six weeks later, she was living a block away at 44 Lillington Street. Ethel's birth certificate describes her father, John, as a commercial clerk and ascribes the now modified surname 'Frued' to all the family members listed.[128] A year later, on 5 May 1893, she was baptised in St Saviour's Church, Pimlico, where the family – having moved yet again – were then resident very nearby at 10 Moreton Terrace. Again, the family surname was registered as 'Frued'.[129] It was a joint ceremony that day, with Annie's nephews Louisa and Henry Sheather also being baptised. St Saviour's was part of the High Church or Anglo-Catholic Church of England congregation and it may be that the relatively long lapse of time between Ethel's birth and baptism contained some hesitation for John about making such a symbolic step, shifting him further from his specifically Jewish family origins.

Ethel would be John and Annie's only child. She most probably had her early education at the local National School in Pimlico, which Kate attended. Ethel grew up – as her family would recall – to have a somewhat nervous disposition. Perhaps more significantly, she suffered throughout her adulthood from chronic ulcerative colitis, which appeared to have a hereditary link. Her granddaughter Jill would also develop this. As a condition, studies suggest about 12 per cent of people with ulcerative colitis have a family history of it. It is especially prevalent among people of Ashkenazi Jewish descent.[130] In retrospect, it is tempting and indeed plausible to conclude that this or a related condition contributed to the chronic health complaints within Emanuel's family. Certainly, Freud suffered from chronic gastro-intestinal problems for much of his adult life, which at times he referred to as colitis.[131]

In 1899 the family moved from Pimlico north to Chalk Farm, living initially at 55 Chalk Farm Road. Kate and Ethel were admitted to Haverstock Hill School in April and July that year respectively, the family surname being now recorded by the school as 'Froud'.[132] They then turn up in 1911 (no trace of them being found on the 1901 census) living in Kentish Town, at 87 Bartholomew Road, where John was now described in the census as a 54-year-old shorthand typist from Manchester, while Annie was a school caretaker, Kate a school chemistry maid, and Ethel a typist.[133] John's projected date of birth was thus 1856 or early 1857, making him one year younger than John Freud's actual age, although making him a year older than he had represented himself on the 1891 census. He and the rest of the family were continuing to style themselves as 'Froud', while John and Annie were described, fictitiously, as having been married for 23 years. Ten years later, when the 1921 census was taken on 19 June, John varied his age yet again, declaring he was 66 years and 5 months old, suggesting a birthdate of January 1855, and gave his occupation as a self-employed stenographer.[134]

The family had moved to live in Brecknock Road, Islington, by 1918, where they initially rented number 96, before moving a short way down the road to number 70 by 1928.[135] In contrast to his siblings in Manchester, John's step-daughter and daughter both married and had families of their own. Kate went first, marrying law clerk Frederick William Wakeling (1888–1921) on 7 August 1915.[136] They would have two children. Three years later, on 21 December 1918, Ethel was married to pianist Joseph Norton Greenop (1891–1961).[137] John and Annie continued living on Brecknock Road until Annie's death in June 1934, following which John moved to live with his widowed step-daughter Kate at 42 Dalmeny Road in Tufnell Park. It was there, on 19 January 1936, that John Freud died from senile myocardial degeneration. Ethel registered his death, recording his surname as 'Froud', his occupation as a tourist agent's guide and his age as 85 years.[138] He was buried with Annie in Highgate Cemetery in Camden.[139] In his will, John left all his assets, valued at £791, to Ethel.[140]

The identification of the present John Freud as Emanuel's hitherto missing son is based on very strong, although not incontrovertible evidence. Some further support for the identification comes from genealogical DNA testing conducted by the present John Freud's great-granddaughter, Lucy Polkinghorne. This highlighted that she has a percentage of DNA commonly found in the Galician Jewish population, though no sample has as yet been cross-matched with Joseph Freud's acknowledged descendants.[141]

Leaving aside this possibility of DNA corroboration (which may provide indicative support using autosomal DNA testing, though current generations on either side would be distant relatives), we are left with the question why did John disappear? The Manchester Freuds, and Emanuel's family in particular, lived an

Image 9.2 John Froud's grave marker, Highgate Cemetery, London
Source: author's collection

enmeshed shut-in lifestyle, with health anxieties being prevalent especially around the females in the family. It seems likely that the early deaths of four of Emanuel's children, including Henrietta, Emily, and Matilda while they were in Manchester, contributed to this sorry state of affairs. The remaining children struggled to separate and establish independent lives. (Philipp's family was more successful in this respect, though the relative estrangement that afflicted his relationship with Freud leached into the rest of his immediate family's relationships with Freud to varying degrees.) While John's departure did not fatally rupture his relationship with Freud (with whom there is evidence of continued contact up to 1908), with other members of the family, his whereabouts and life in general seems to have been enigmatic. This was, most probably, a deliberate part of his effort to establish his own independent identity, less encumbered by the vortex of his past. Included with this was an abandonment of any observable allegiance to Judaism. At the same time, however, in doing this John was displaced in the family by his younger brother Sam, substantially repeating his own father's fate vis-à-vis Freud, his younger brother. Beyond this, little more can be said with certainty of John's adult life. In the Freud archives and literature, he is largely a revenant, a ghostly liminal figure who has been invoked as a foil in mapping out Freud's early relational psychodynamics.

Reflections

The life stories of John and Sam intersect very closely with Freud's biography during key periods, including (with respect to John) his early formative years in Freiberg and his 1875 trip to Britain and (with respect to Sam) the struggle to sustain the idea of the integrated extended family, especially in the wake of Emanuel's death, and the immediate post-war period when food and other necessities were in desperately short supply. Of these episodes, John's relationship with Freud became inscribed into the psychoanalytic literature by Freud writing it into *The Interpretation of Dreams*. What John himself made of being thus written about is unknown, as is whether he gave any consent to Freud to be publicly used in this manner.

The lives and relationships of John and Sam discussed here, highlight the sustained relationships Freud had with both of them over an extended time. Thus, with John it is now clear that while he was estranged from his father and probably his immediate family, the same cannot be said with confidence about his relationship with Freud. Indeed, Freud was very aware of him in London in 1908 and of his activities there, and seems to have anticipated at one stage that he might have been able to see him. John thus remained a significant figure in Freud's mental economy. Professionally, John helped Freud conceptualise early childhood sibling-type relationships and their enduring influence throughout the lifespan, reflections further built upon by subsequent generations of psychoanalysts and psychotherapists. It is particularly unfortunate that no correspondence survives between them. The reconstruction here of John's later life, addresses a long-standing lacuna in the literature on Freud and his family: he is no longer one of the disappeared. More specifically, rediscovering John helps to discount the lurid speculation by Miller and Scagnelli that he had been murdered. The Freud family tree, and in particular the Manchester branch of that, is thus extended beyond what was hitherto known into the present.

In contrast to John, Sam's life remained substantively private over its whole course. Clearly very attached to Freud and an important cheerleader for him in the family in Manchester, Sam was no raconteur with respect to his own life. His letters were painfully inhibited, whilst all the time soliciting news of Freud's activities, and Freud was often left feeling he actually knew very little of Sam. Nevertheless, Sam was a key transferential link for Freud to his older brother's family, offering a certain relational continuity for him following Emanuel's death. Sam gave Freud emotional support and encouragement, as best he could, and was a key figure in organising food parcels and other relief supplies for Freud for a year following the Great War when many in Vienna were starving.

Overall, in this section on Freud and his British family, the sustained importance of working lives, sibling, and wider kinship relationships is clear, as is the effort the Freuds put into maintaining these. With a complex family structure, the extended Freud family in Freiberg separated into two distinct units in 1859, Freud and his immediate family moving to Vienna and his older half-brothers and their entourage setting in Manchester. The family's financial and material enterprise was considerable and ultimately sustained three households and the relationships between them, despite changing circumstances and periods of marked adversity and poverty. Religious and ethnic affiliations supported this long-distance kinship network, ties which for the Manchester Freuds extended into the local Jewish communities and thus supported their business enterprises.[142] In Vienna, Freud's longstanding involvement with the local B'nai B'rith Jewish lodge served a related supportive and cultural function.[143]

The intra-familial relationships, however, were something of a compromise formation, incorporating a positional displacement of Emanuel as the eldest son in favour of the younger Freud, with the children of Jacob's first marriage being further relocated to a British provincial city while the parties to his marriage to Amalia went to the capital of an empire. This pattern of displacement of the first-born son continued in Emanuel's family, with the younger Sam replacing the elder John, who in turn largely disappears. Women within the system, and particularly within the Manchester families, were often silent, appearing – when they did – as suffering from non-specified maladies, varieties of hysteria perhaps in a controlling and patriarchal system. Certainly, Emanuel's household appeared enmeshed, John being the only child managing to achieve a sort of independence, though that was at some cost. For his part, Philipp only developed his relationship with Bloomah when he and Emanuel separated. The deaths of three of Emanuel's children between 1866 and 1868 is one factor that contributed significantly to this level of inhibition and stasis within that family.

Freud's relationships with the family in Manchester promoted his emotional and intellectual attachments to Britain and the English language. His visit to Manchester in 1875 exerted a particularly catalytic effect on his Anglophile stance, which was reinforced by his 1908 trip, though by that time or soon after he was beginning to experience very mixed feelings with respect to seeing Emanuel. These seemed to stem from Freud's sense of Emanuel aging and the accompanying premonitions of mortality. These issues of incipient loss, depression and death would come to the fore again during the 1920s with respect to other bereavements and Freud's own battles with cancer,[144] issues which he would explore in part during his correspondence with Sam. And they reappear in a very palpable fashion in 1938 and 1939 as Freud – by then terminally ill – and his immediate family followed Emanuel and Philipp in seeking a new life in Britain, to which story we now turn.

Notes

1 Manchester Electoral Registers, 1915 to 1925.
2 The original correspondence is housed at the John Rylands Library, University of Manchester (ref: GB 133 SSF). It was collated in 1996 by Thomas Roberts in *Vienna and Manchester: The Correspondence of Sigmund Freud and Sam Freud 1911–1938*, though has remained so far unpublished in English. Several copies exist, one being in the Freud Museum London. Published editions have appeared in French (see Claude Vincent (ed) *Lettres de Famille de Sigmund Freud et des Freud de Manchester 1911–1938*, Paris: PUF, 1996) and Spanish (see Thomas Roberts (ed) *Viena y Manchester: Correspondencia entre Sigmund Freud y su sobrino Sam Freud (1911–1938)*, translated by Pedro Navarro Serrano, Madrid: Síntesis, 2000).
3 Freud to Lou Andreas-Salome, 13 July 1917, *Freud Letters*, p. 325; Freud to Sándor Ferenczi, 3 March 1918, *Freud-Ferenczi*, 2, p. 270.
4 Freud to Sándor Ferenczi, 28 March 1919, *Freud-Ferenczi*, 2, p. 339.
5 'Aufruf für die Kinder der vom Hunger heimgesuchten Länder', *Internationale Zeitschrift für Ärztliche Psychoanalyse*, 1919, 5, 4, pp. 333–334; cf. Christfried Tögel 'Freud als Unterzeichner von Aufrufen', 2019, available online at: www.freud-biographik.de.
6 Freud to Sam Freud, 27 October 1919, Rylands Library ref: SSF/1/1/4.
7 Sam Freud to Freud, 4 November 1919, Rylands Library ref: SSF/1/2/2.
8 Nothing having been received by 26 January 1920, Freud acknowledged that 'Another of your parcels in good condition arrived' on 9 February: Freud to Sam Freud 9 February 1920, Rylands Library ref: SSF/1/1/9.
9 Sam Freud to Pauline Regine Winternitz, 31 December 1919, LoC ref: mss39990, box 13, folder 46.
10 Freud to Sam Freud, 22 February 1920, Rylands Library ref: SSF/1/1/11; Freud suggestion of salt-and-pepper coloured fabric for his suit may be an echo of his associations to the 'grey horse' dream in which he noted 'the pepper-and-salt colour of the suit of my colleague P was wearing when I had last met him in the country', see Freud *The Interpretation of Dreams*, *SE*, 1900 [1899], 4, p. 231.
11 Freud to Sam Freud 24 November 1919, Rylands Library ref: SSF/1/1/5.
12 Freud to Max Eitingon, 2 December 1919, *Freud Letters*, p. 331.
13 Freud to Sam Freud, 15 October 1920, Rylands Library ref: SSF/1/1/19.
14 Freud to Sam Freud, 28 November 1920, Rylands Library ref: SSF/1/1/22.
15 Freud to Sam Freud, 5 February 1922, Rylands Library ref: SSF/1/1/27.
16 At one point, Freud wrote to Sam that 'all of us have lost 19/20 of what we possessed in cash': see Freud to Sam Freud, 27 October 1919, Rylands Library ref: SSF/1/1/4.
17 Maria Pierri *Sigmund Freud and the Forsyth Case: Coincidences and Thought-Transmission in Psychoanalysis*, Abingdon: Routledge, 2023.
18 Freud to Sam Freud, 15 October 1920, Rylands Library ref: SSF/1/1/19.
19 Freud to Sam Freud, 4 December 1921, Rylands Library ref: SSF/1/1/26.

20 See for example Sam Freud to Lissa & Kann Bank, 15 May 1922, Rylands Library ref: SSF/1/2/26, Freud to Sam Freud, 22 July 1920, Rylands Library ref: SSF/1/1/16, and Freud to George Allen & Co 10 May 1926, UOR SC, ref: A&U A/112. See also D Cohen *The Escape of Sigmund Freud*, New York: Overlook Press, 2012, p. 93.
21 Strachey was in analysis with Freud at the time and the cheque was part of his fee liability. See James Strachey to Sam Freud, 30 November 1920, Rylands Library ref: SSF/1/1/23.
22 Freud to S Ferenczi, 13 Ferenczi 1910, *Freud-Ferenczi*, 1, p. 138; see also John Forrester *Dispatches from the Freud Wars*, Cambridge, MA: Harvard University Press, 1997, p. 209.
23 Freud would at the same time link money to anality. See for example his 'Character and anal erotism', *SE*, 1908, 9, pp. 168 and 174.
24 Freud to S Ferenczi, 13 Ferenczi 1910, *Freud-Ferenczi*, 1, p. 138.
25 Freud to Lilly Freud Marlé, 14 March 1911, LoC ref: mss39990, box 11, folder 12; quoted in P Gay *Freud: A Life for Our Times*, London: Max, 2006, p. 418 and *Freud-Jones*, p. 160.
26 Freud to C Jung, 22 January 1911, *Freud-Jung*, p. 231.
27 Freud to Karl Abraham, 18 December 1916, *Freud-Abraham*, p. 340.
28 Freud to S Ferenczi, 10 February 1913, *Freud-Ferenczi*, 1, p. 468.
29 Freud to Sam Freud, 15 October 1920, Rylands Library ref: SSF/1/1/19.
30 Sam Freud to Freud, 30 October 1920, Rylands Library ref: SSF/1/2/16.
31 Freud to Sam Freud, 5 November 1920, Rylands Library ref: SSF/1/1/21.
32 Sam Freud to Freud, 16 November 1920, Rylands Library ref: SSF/1/2/17.
33 Sam Freud to Freud, 29 November 1921, Rylands Library ref: SSF/1/2/22.
34 Freud to Sam Freud, 4 December 1921, Rylands Library ref: SSF/1/1/26.
35 Sam Freud to Freud, 29 December 1921, Rylands Library ref: SSF/1/2/23.
36 Freud to Sam Freud, 28 November 1920, Rylands Library ref: SSF/1/1/22. Tom was an artist and children's book illustrator. Her subsequent marriage to Jankew Seidmann ended when the latter committed suicide in 1929. The impact of this resulted in Tom being institutionalised and she too committed suicide on 7 February 1930. See also Freud to Sam Freud, 6 December 1929, Rylands Library ref: SSF/1/1/65; Martha's engagement to Seidmann was noted by Freud in his letter to Sam of 28 November 1920; for a discussion of Tom see Byrony Davies 'The life and work of Tom Seidmann-Freud', available online at: www.freud.org.uk/2018/11/01/the-life-and-work-of-tom-seidmann-freud (accessed 11 April 2020); and for a discussion of Freud and his relations with Mitzi see Christfried Tögel 'Freuds Berliner Schwester Maria (Mitzi) und ihre Familie', *Luzifer-Amor: Zeitschrift zur Geschichte der Psychoanalyse*, 2004, 17, 33, pp. 33–50 and Christfried Tögel & Michael Schröter 'Briefe an Maria (Mitzi) Freud und ihre Familie', *Luzifer-Amor: Zeitschrift zur Geschichte der Psychoanalyse*, 2004, 17, 33, pp. 51–72.
37 Freud to Sam Freud, 26 January 1920, Rylands Library ref: SSF/1/1/8; see also *Freud-Ferenczi*, 2, pp. 5–7, and *Freud-Pfister*, pp. 74–75.
38 Freud to Sam Freud, 15 February 1920, Rylands Library ref: SSF/1/1/10.
39 Freud to Sam Freud, 21 January 1921, Rylands Library ref: SSF/1/1/57.
40 Freud to Ludwig Binswanger, 12 April 1929, in *Freud-Binswanger*, p. 196.
41 Freud to Sam Freud, 20 August 1922, Rylands Library ref: SSF/1/1/32. Caecilie (or Mausi as she was known in the family) was the daughter of Freud's sister Rosa and her husband Heinrich Graf. For a discussion of Caecilie's suicide see P Gay *Freud: A Life for Our Times*, London: Max, 2006, p. 418, *Freud-Rank*, p. 141, and *Freud-Jones*, pp. 499–501.
42 For a brief discussion of Freud's views on suicide see for example Élisabeth Roudinesco *Freud in his Time and Ours*, Cambridge, MA: Harvard University Press, 2016, p. 204.

43 Sam Freud to Freud, 26 August 1922, Rylands Library ref: SSF/1/2/27.
44 Freud to W Fliess, 15 October 1897, *Freud-Fliess*, p. 272.
45 For an accessible discussion of this see J Laplanche & J-B Pontalis *The Language of Psycho-Analysis*, London: Hogarth, 1973, pp. 178–179.
46 A Freud to E Jones, 4 January 1956, BPAS Archives ref: P04-C-C-06.
47 P Gay *Freud: A Life for our Times*, London: Max, 2006, p. 425.
48 S Freud *The Interpretation of Dreams, SE*, 1900 [1899], p. xxiv; see also the 1913 George Allen & Co, London, edition, p. vi.
49 See for example Max Schur 'Some additional "day residues" of the "specimen dream of psychoanalysis', 1966, in M Kanzer & J Glenn (eds) *Freud and his Self-Analysis*, New York: Jason Aronson, 1979, pp. 87–116; Max Schur 'The background of Freud's "disturbance" on the Acropolis', *American Imago*, 1969, 26, pp. 303–323; Alexander Grinstein *On Sigmund Freud's Dreams*, Detroit: Wayne State University Press, 1968; Didier Anzieu *Freud's Self-Analysis*, London: Hogarth, 1986; Barbara Mautner 'Freud's Irma dream: A psychoanalytic interpretation', *IJPA*, 1991, 72, pp. 275–286; Sarah Ackerman 'I may allow myself to do this: Conflcit in Freud's writing of *The Interpretation of Dreams*', *JAMA*, 2019, 67, 5, pp. 767–787.
50 Earlier examples in Freud's adolescence may be seen in his keeping his 1873 hopes of a trip to Britain temporarily secret from his mother and similarly asking Eduard Silberstein to refrain from mentioning a rumoured Cholera outbreak to her (see *Freud-Silberstein*, pp. 21 and 24).
51 Freud to Sam Freud, 4 December 1921, Rylands Library ref: SSF/1/1/26.
52 Freud to S Ferenczi, 18 July 1923, *Freud-Ferenczi*, 3, p. 109.
53 Freud to Sam Freud, 26 June 1923, Rylands Library ref: SSF/1/1/36. Heinrich Rudolph Halberstadt had been born on 8 December 1918. For further discussion of the loss of Heinz see Peter Gay *Freud: A Life for our Time*, London: Max, 2006, pp. 421–422.
54 Freud to Sam Freud, 26 June 1923, Rylands Library ref: SSF/1/1/36.
55 Freud to S Ferenczi, 6 November 1917, *Freud-Ferenczi*, 2, p. 245.
56 Freud's health and cancer treatments are most extensively discussed by Max Schur (see his *Freud: Living and Dying*, London: Hogarth Press, 1972), but see also Peter Gay *Freud: A Life for our Time*, London: Max, 2006, pp. 418–428; Élisabeth Roudinesco *Freud in His Time and Ours*, Cambridge, MA: Harvard University Press, 2016, pp. 252–255; and Joel Whitebook *Freud: An Intellectual Biography*, Cambridge: Cambridge University Press, 2017, p pp. 350–361, among many other commentators.
57 Sam Freud to Freud, 9 July 1923, Rylands Library ref: SSF/1/2/31.
58 Freud to Sam Freud, 24 September 1923, Rylands Library ref: SSF/1/1/38.
59 Freud to Sam Freud, 20 October 1923, Rylands Library ref: SSF/1/1/39. This letter, unlike previous letters in this correspondence, is in fact typed, perhaps by Anna Freud, indicating Freud's debilitated state.
60 GRO death record: Chorlton Registrar's District, October–December 1923, vol. 8c, p. 706.
61 Sam Freud to Freud, 22 October 1923, Rylands Library ref: SSF/1/2/33.
62 Section A, Grave 60, Southern Cemetery, Manchester Reform Synagogue, Register of Deaths 1857–1959, Manchester Central Library, ref: GB127.M779/Box 76.
63 Freud to Sam Freud, 25 October 1923 (also typewritten), Rylands Library ref: SSF/1/1/40.
64 Ibid.
65 Ibid.
66 Freud to Sam Freud, 12 September 1930, Rylands Library ref: SSF/1/1/67.
67 See also André Haynal 'Freud, his illness, and ourselves', *American Journal of Psychoanalysis*, 2008, 68, pp. 103–116; Xavier Riaud 'Treatment of Sigmund Freud's maxillary jawbone cancer by Hans Pichler and Varaztad Kazanjian (1856–1939)', *Journal of Trauma and Treatment*, 2015, 4, 1, pp. 1–4.

68 Freud to Sam Freud, 9 January 1924, Rylands Library ref: SSF/1/1/42.
69 Isidor Sadger *Remembering Freud*, edited by Alan Dundes, Madison, WI: University of Wisconsin Press, 2005, p. 124.
70 Freud to Sam Freud, 19 December 1925, Rylands Library ref: SSF/1/1/49–50.
71 Freud to Sam Freud, 21 August 1925, Rylands Library ref: SSF/1/1/48. For Sam's reply see his letter of 26 August 1925, ref: SSF/1/2/41.
72 Ibid.; relatedly, Freud regarded Amalia as neither able to grasp the inflation during the latter period of the war nor allow Dolfi the independence to manage their household finances. In these circumstances, Freud arranged with Alexander to give the necessary funds to Dolfi for her household kitty, keeping the arrangement secret from Amalia: see Freud to Alexander Freud, 5 April 1918, *Freud Letters*, p. 326.
73 Freud to Amalia Freud, 26 January 1920, *Freud Letters*, p. 332.
74 For a discussion of Freud's health during this period see Max Schur *Freud: Living and Dying*, London: Hogarth Press, 1972, pp. 377–393 and *passim*.
75 J B Heller 'Freud's mother and father', *Commentary*, May 1956, 21, 5, p. 421.
76 Ana-Maria Rizzuto *Why Did Freud Reject God? A Psychodynamic Interpretation*, New Haven: Yale University Press, 1998, p. 201.
77 Sam Freud to Freud, 26 August 1922, Rylands Library ref: SSF/1/2/27.
78 Sam Freud to Freud, 9 February 1923, Rylands Library ref: SSF/1/2/29.
79 Sam Freud to Freud, 12 September 1923, Rylands Library ref: SSF/1/2/32.
80 Sam Freud to Freud, 31 December 1923, Rylands Library ref: SSF/1/2/36.
81 Sam Freud to Freud, 20 April 1924, Rylands Library ref: SSF/1/2/37.
82 Sam Freud to Freud, 4 April 1925, Rylands Library ref: SSF/1/2/40.
83 Freud to Sam Freud, 19 December 1925, Rylands Library ref: SSF/1/1/50.
84 Sam Freud to Freud, 29 December 1925, Rylands Library ref: SSF/1/2/43.
85 Ibid.
86 Freud to Sam Freud, 2 October 1920, Rylands Library ref: SSF/1/1/18.
87 Sam Freud to Freud [telegram], 20 September 1920, Rylands Library ref: SSF/1/2/14.
88 Sam Freud to Freud, 10 October 1920, Rylands Library ref: SSF/1/2/15.
89 Freud to Sam Freud, 15 October 1920, Rylands Library ref: SSF/1/1/19; see also John Forrester & Laura Cameron *Freud in Cambridge*, Cambridge: Cambridge University Press, 2017, pp. 97 and 191–192.
90 Freud to Sam Freud, 28 November 1920, Rylands Library ref: SSF/1/1/22; see also Freud to Ernest Jones, 28 February 1922, *Freud-Jones*, p. 511.
91 Freud to Sam Freud, 1 February 1926, Rylands Library ref: SSF/1/1/51.
92 Sam Freud to Freud, 30 March 1926, Rylands Library ref: SSF/1/2/44.
93 Freud to Sam Freud, 16 May 1926, Rylands Library ref: SSF/1/1/52.
94 Sam Freud to Freud, 1 August 1927, Rylands Library ref: SSF/1/2/49.
95 Freud to Sam Freud, 6 December 1928, Rylands Library ref: SSF/1/1/60 and Sam Freud to Freud, 18 December 1928, Rylands Library ref: SSF/1/2/53.
96 Freud to Sam Freud, 31 July 1933, Rylands Library ref: SSF/1/1/72; see also Freud to Ferenczi, 2 April 1933, *Freud-Ferenczi*, 3, p. 449 and Freud to Ernest Jones, 7 April 1933, *Freud-Jones*, p. 716.
97 Freud to Sam Freud, 4 June 1938, Rylands Library ref: SSF/1/1/74; this was one of a series on change of address notes Freud wrote to friends, another to Arnold Zweig being in the Freud Museum, London, collection.
98 S Freud 'Kürzeste Chronik', entry for 9 June 1938, LoC ref: mss39990, box OV 10, reel 5; also M Molnar (ed) *The Diary of Sigmund Freud 1929–1939: A Record of the Final Decade*, London: Hogarth, 1992, p. 240.
99 Detlef Berthelsen *Alltag bei Familie Freud: Die Erinnerungen der Paula Fichtl*, München: Deutscher Tasachenbuch Verlag, 1989, p. 81.
100 Freud's *Kürzeste Chronik*, LoC ref: mss39990, box OV 10; reel 5.

101 *Kelly's Manchester and Salford Street Directory*, 1940, p. 1,050.
102 *Manchester Street Directory*, 1942.
103 GRO death record: Manchester Registrar's District, January–March 1941, vol. 8d, p. 378. Bertha's place of death is recorded as '20 Nell Lane, Withington', a superficially ordinary street address utilised to soften the stigma of association with the historic local workhouse (see also www.workhouses.org.uk/addresses/c.shtml).
104 GRO death record: Manchester Registrar's District, January–March 1944, vol. 8d, p. 493. Here again the location of death was simply recorded as '223 Crescent Road, Crumpsall', rather than Park House of Crumpsall Workhouse (see www.workhouses.org.uk/Manchester).
105 Fritz Franz Oswald Hartwig recollections of the Freud family in Manchester, undated (post 1951), LoC ref: mss39990, box 2.
106 Sam Freud to Harry Freud, 29 February 1944, LoC ref: mss39990, box 13, folder 45.
107 Lilly Freud-Marlé *Mein Onkel Sigmund Freud: Erinnerungen an eine grosse Familie*, edited by Christfried Tögel & Magdalena Frank, Berlin: Aufbau-Verlag, 2006, p. 272.
108 Ibid.
109 Ibid., pp. 273–274. This photograph is not among the handful of family images that form part of the Freud Papers in the John Rylands Library, Manchester. It and much, if not all, of the box of images that Lilly notes as having been in Poppy's possession appears to have been lost.
110 *Manchester Evening News*, 3 September 1945, p. 7.
111 National Probate Calendar, 1945, p. 354, and related letters of administration. The Bank of England inflation calculator suggests this figure is the equivalent of £206,858 in November 2022.
112 See for example Max Schur 'The background of Freud's "disturbance" on the Acropolis', *American Imago*, 1969, 26, 4, p. 313, Ronald W Clark *Freud: The Man and the Cause*, London: Jonathan Cape and Weidenfeld & Nicholson, 1980, p. 394 and Marianne Krüll *Freud and his Father*, London: Hutchinson, 1986, p. 129.
113 Eric Miller *Passion for Murder: The Homicidal Deeds of Dr Sigmund Freud*, San Diego: Future Directions, 1984, and Paul Scagnelli *Deadly Dr Freud: The Murder of Emanuel Freud and the Disappearance of John Freud*, Durham, NC: Pinewood Publishing, 1994; Alan Gall 'The deadly Doctor Freud – A tale from the archive', *The Journal: The Institute of Science & Technology*, Spring 2008, pp. 28–29.
114 See also Peter Gay *Freud: A Life for Our Time*, London: Max, 2006, pp. 784–785.
115 Ernst L Freud 'Preface', in *Freud Letters*, p. vii.
116 Fritz Franz Oswald Hartwig recollections of the Freud family in Manchester, undated (post 1951), LoC ref: mss39990, box 2. A variety of dates, each purporting to be the last sighting of John, are recorded in the Freud archives and literature, some of which are reviewed by Scagnelli, *op cit*.
117 Freud to E Silberstein, 3 August 1875, *Freud-Silberstein*, p. 123.
118 Freud to E Silberstein, 3 August 1875 and 9 September 1875, *Freud-Silberstein*, pp. 123 and 127.
119 1881 English census, TNA ref: RG 11/3895/62/2.
120 Emanuel Freud to Rosa Freud, no date but probably *c*.March 1886, LoC ref: mss81404, box 1.
121 1891 English census, TNA ref: RG 12/122/8/9.
122 Freud to E Silberstein, 9 September 1875, *Freud-Silberstein*, p. 127.
123 Lucy Polkington, interview with the author, 3 February 2021.
124 Freud visited the Oxford Street branch of Thomas Cook & Son during his visit to London in September 1908. Though this was most probably for tickets, one wonders whether John's sometime association with the company was also a prompt for this stop on Freud's itinerary and his notebook entry. The company archives have no surviving

125 Michael Molnar *Looking Through Freud's Photos*, London: Karnac, 2015, p. 83.

126 Lucy Polkington, interview with the author, 3 February 2021.

127 No registration of a marriage has been found on the General Register Office indexes and (tellingly) in April 1911 they were explicitly claiming to have been married for 23 years, i.e. from 1888, when Annie would have been still married to Alfred Newport.

128 GRO birth record: St George Hanover Square Registrar's District, April–June 1892, vol. 1a, p. 478. According to the 1891 English census, the boarding house at 85 Tachbrook Street was then run by Clementina Clarke (*c*.1830–1919).

129 St Saviour's Church, Pimlico, Parish Register, City of Westminster Archives Centre, ref: SSP/PR/1/3, p. 62.

130 See for example Ryan E Childers *et al* 'Family history of inflammatory bowel disease among patients with ulcerative colitis: A systemic review and meta-analysis', *Journal of Crohn's and Colitis*, 2014, 8, pp. 1480–1497, and Yiming Wu *et al* 'Identifying high-impact variants and genes in exomes of Ashkenazi Jewish inflammatory bowel disease patients', *Nature Communications*, 2023, 14, 2256.

131 See for example *Life & Work*, 2, especially pp. 4, 92, 101, 436–437; Jones dismissively suggests these were 'psychosomatic' in nature (p. 4).

132 Haverstock Hill School admission register, London Metropolitan Archives ref: LCC/EO/DIV02/HAV/AD/003.

133 1911 English census, TNA ref: RG 14/715.

134 1921 English census, TNA ref: RG 15/00844/0403.

135 The ratepayer at 96 Brecknock Road was Frederick Joseph Wray (*London Street Directory*, 1918 and 1928 editions).

136 GRO marriage certificate: St Pancras Registrar's District, July–September 1915, vol. 1b, p. 26.

137 GRO marriage certificate: Islington Registrar's District, October–December 1918, vol. 1b, p. 708.

138 GRO death certificate ref: Islington Registrar's District, January–March 1936, vol. 1b, p. 200. A careful digital examination of UK death registers failed to show up any other men having this or similar names.

139 The Highgate Cemetery register notes John Froud was buried in grave number 42230, in square 148, on 22 January 1936. The grave also contained Frederick William Wakeling (buried on 7 September 1921), Annie Froud (buried 2 July 1934), and later Annie Agnes Kate Wakeling (buried on 15 January 1941). The grave is marked with a small stone memorial flower holder, inscribed on three sides to Frederick Wakeling, Annie Froud, and John Froud.

140 National Probate Register, 1936, p. 464. The Bank of England inflation calculator suggests this figure is the equivalent of £44,331 in November 2022.

141 Lucy Polkinghorne to the author, 29 May 2018, on ancestry.co.uk.

142 Leonore Davidoff *Thicker Than Water: Siblings and Their Relations 1780–1920*, Oxford: Oxford University Press, 2012, p. 54.

143 See for example Freud 'Address to the Society of B'nai B'rith', *SE*, 1926, 20, 271–274.

144 See for example Freud to Ernest Jones, 28 February 1922, *Freud-Jones*, p. 511.

Chapter 10

Berggasse in London, NW3, 1938–1939

Introduction

With the rise of National Socialism in Germany, conditions there for Jews worsened under its anti-Semitic ideology, the situation becoming markedly more difficult from January 1933 onwards following Hitler's appointment as Chancellor. Over the next few years the persecution of the Jews followed a typical course, from harassment and exclusion from business and the professions, to expulsion, and finally to extermination. Two of Freud's sons, Oliver, an engineer, and Ernst, an architect, were living in Berlin at the time when Hitler came to power and both fled the country, moving with their families to France and Britain respectively.[1] As the majority of German psychoanalysts were also Jewish and/or of the political left, deprived to the opportunity to work and subject to intimidation, the profession was decimated, most analysts emigrating between 1933 and 1936. The *Deutsche Psychoanalytische Gesellschaft* (the German Psychoanalytical Society) was thus reduced from 56 members in 1932 to a rump of 14 in December 1935.[2] It was a situation that would be repeated across continental Europe as the tide of National Socialism spread.

In Austria in the 1930s, the *Wiener Psychoanalytische Vereinigung* (WPV) was swollen for a time with the influx of analysts fleeing Germany, but its members faced increasing difficulties with the rise of Austro-fascism. The situation was not made easier by the WPV instructing analysts to forego political activities in an effort to escape persecution, a position endorsed by Ernest Jones at the IPA Congress in Lucerne in 1934. Making their own decisions, however, Jewish and left-wing analysts began to relocate to what were thought to be safer countries. Following the *Anschluss* on Saturday 12 March 1938, amid burgeoning anti-Semitic violence, this trickle of emigration became a flood as life became far more difficult for Jews in Vienna.[3] Many of the more radical European analysts made their way to the USA, though not all would manage to escape.

In was in this context that Freud and his immediate family would decide to finally leave Vienna for the perceived safety of London.[4] Briefly telling the events of their escape, this chapter will go on to reveal the story of Freud's third and final time in Britain, where this time he would stay. Settling in London (rather than the family's more traditional environs of Manchester) for the last 476 twilight days of his life, Freud would here persevere in the familiar rhythms of work and family life till the end, until – as he said himself – it made no sense any more.

A negotiated exit

The new regime quickly began to impact on Freud and his family. On 15 March a party of Nazi *Sturmabteilung* (SA), or brownshirts, muscled their way into both the offices of the *Internationaler Psychoanalytischer Verlag* (the International Psychoanalytic Press) at Berggasse 7, where its manager, Freud's son Martin, was detained, and into Freud's home at Berggasse 19 . Freud was recovering at the time from recent surgery for his oral cancer. They searched both premises, interrogated the Freuds, and eventually decamped with a sizeable amount of their cash and their confiscated passports. Martin had the worst of it, being held at gun point for much of the day. Fortunately, he managed to flush some of the potentially compromising financial papers he held down the toilet. Ernest Jones, with previous encouragement from Dorothy Burlingham (1891–1979) and Marie Bonaparte (1882–1962), had flown to Vienna that same day, where he landed at 4.00 pm, and arrived at the *Verlag's* offices while Martin Freud was still being detained there. Jones's arguments that the *Verlag* was an international non-political scientific body cut no ice with the SA men. And his request to be allowed to contact the British Embassy similarly failed to gain traction. Being released after a short time, Jones went down the road to Berggasse 19 and lent what moral support he could there to the Freud family, their much shorter raid being by then over.[5]

Before setting out for Vienna, Jones had approached Lord Halifax, the Lord Privy Seal, regarding his concerns for Freud's safety. As a result, the Foreign Office requested W Henry B Mack (1894–1974), the chargé d'affaires at the British Embassy in Vienna, assist Jones. Although downgraded to a consulate at this point due to the *Anschluss*, British diplomatic staff in Vienna did a lot to help over the next week and Jones later singled out Mack and the Consul, Captain John William Taylor (1895–1974), for particular thanks.[6]

Diplomatic pressure was being brought to bear from other directions too. The United States consul general in Vienna, John Cooper Wiley (1893–1967), had already met with Freud on 10 and 14 March, and his wife Monique (1906–1972) had visited on 13 March, conveying offers of assistance from the US embassy.[7] Later, at 1.00 pm on 15 March with the first raid in progress, Wiley himself alerted the US Secretary of State in Washington about Freud's dangerous situation, as a result of which communique President Franklin D Roosevelt instructed Wiley and the US ambassadors in Berlin and Paris to assist. Roosevelt had been informed that Parisian friends – presumably Marie Bonaparte – would welcome the Freud family there and this was then proposed through the US channels as an interim solution. Alongside Wiley, the US Ambassador to France, William Bullitt, sought to recruit the help of the German Ambassador in Paris in extricating Freud and his family from Austria. He also lent Wiley his political muscle and promised financial support too. Bullitt had known Freud personally since the mid-1920s and they had been attempting to collaborate on a psychological study of Woodrow Wilson since 1930.[8]

In Paris, as we have already seen, Marie Bonaparte was alert to the Freuds danger and no doubt lent her diplomatic weight with the Greek and French governments to the mounting efforts to ensure Freud's safety. She went to Vienna herself on 17 March and would stay until 10 April, mostly with the Freuds, chaperoning them as much as she could from Nazi excesses. She would return on at least two further occasions (17–19 April and 29 April-4 May), continuing to press the various embassies for help and assisting the Freuds with their packing, smuggling gold coins and two key pieces from Freud's collection out of his apartment and the country in her diplomatic luggage,[9] gathering reminiscences from Freud, and helping preserve parts of his archives which he was inclined to destroy at the time. Martin viewed her presence as making this period bearable, while Freud saw her role in his family's escape from Vienna as decisive.[10]

Previous to the first SA raid, the board of the WPV had met on 13 March at Berggasse 19 and all the members present declared their intentions to emigrate as soon as possible given the clear and present danger the Nazis posed. Freud joined the meeting following these declarations and Anna briefed him both on the members' individual decisions and their agreement that the WPV's home would be wherever Freud would settle. Welcoming the board's decision, Freud significantly situated the plan in a scriptural context. 'After the destruction of the Temple in Jerusalem by Titus', Freud declared, 'Rabbi Jochanan ben Sakkai asked for permission to open a school at Jabneh for the study of the Torah. We are going to do the same'.[11] Freud thus associated both the group's present persecution with that of the ancient past and psychoanalytic scholarship with that of the Torah study in a yeshiva. Freud later drew this idea out further in *Moses and Monotheism*, where he would quote the same historical reference to highlight the ways in which sacred texts and scholarship promoted both group cohesion, particularly in a diasporic context, and intellectuality in the face of forced material renunciation.[12] Clearly, mourning was an important part of this process.

While the account of the WPV meeting on 13 March suggests Freud and his family were determined to leave Austria, *where* they might move to was apparently up in the air for a time. Anna suggested Holland was a probable option.[13] By contrast, Ernest Jones later claimed – probably with his usual hyperbole – that he had actually persuaded a reluctant Freud to emigrate, though it may have been as much London as a destination that he nudged him towards. Jones thus described himself countering the numerous impediments Freud highlighted and crucially drawing an analogy between Freud and Charles Lightoller (1874–1952), the Second Officer on the *Titanic*, who declared he never left his ship, but that the ship left him.[14] Freud of course would not have needed much encouragement to imagine a new life in Britain: it was something he had thought about since his childhood in Freiberg and, aside from philosophical, literary, and scientific affinities, and his command of English, as the home of Emanuel, Philipp, and their half of the family he had close family ties to the country. Be that as it may, Martin also suggested he sensed his father was reluctant to leave, doing so after Jones returned to London to lobby for British residence and work permits for Freud and his entourage. It was only consequent to the events of 22 March that Martin felt his father became convinced of the necessity to leave Vienna. That day, Martin turned up at his parents' apartment at 1 pm as usual, only to find 'SS men in smart uniforms' there searching the premises and he saw Anna being taken away by them for questioning. Marie Bonaparte was unable to either prevent Anna's arrest or get herself arrested so she could accompany her. In the end, after an extremely anxious day and efforts by Otto Pötzl (1877–1962), Hans Pichler (1877–1949), and John Wiley, the Nazis left Freud's apartment and Anna returned at around 7.00 pm, much to everyone's relief.[15] The need to leave was now overwhelmingly obvious, particularly to safeguard Anna and the younger members of the family.

Over the following weeks concrete preparations for leaving Vienna began to fall into place. Jones quickly secured residence and work permits for Freud and his family from the British Home Office, helped in negotiating these with the Home Secretary, Sir Samuel Hoare (1880–1959), whom he knew through his ice skating club, by both his brother-in-law, Wilfred Trotter, and the president of the Royal Society, Sir William Bragg (1862–1942).[16] The far more difficult negotiations were with the new Nazi regime in Vienna, to secure exit permits and agree on what 'fines' and 'taxes' would be levied. As the Freuds engaged in these negotiations, helped by their diplomatic allies, they were also fortunate in having friends or at least some sympathisers within the Viennese National Socialist establishment. Three such may be mentioned here. Hans Pichler, who was Freud's oral surgeon since 1923, was a long-standing member of the National Party of Greater Germany and someone Martin described as a Nazi. Pichler wrote letters during the raids on both 15 and 22 March 1938 certifying Freud was his patient and that he was in a very delicate state of health,[17] which it was believed reduced his prospects of being arrested, and he also intervened repeatedly to mitigate the harassment Freud and the family faced.[18] Otto Pötzl, the Professor of Psychiatry in the University of Vienna and a sometime member of the WPV, was also affiliated with the Nazis, yet helped the Freuds from behind the scenes. The final member of this trio is perhaps the most enigmatic and certainly the most influential. Anton Sauerwald (1903–1970) was appointed a *Nazi-Kommissar* and had responsibility for liquidating Jewish businesses and extracting fines and taxes from Jews, especially as they sought to emigrate. Initially vehemently anti-Semitic, Sauerwald's attitude towards Freud soon moderated, perhaps influenced by his having studied chemistry under one of Freud's early Jewish friends, Professor Josef Herzig (1853–1924), at the University of Vienna, or by his reading some of Freud's books, or by Freud's personality. Whatever the case, Sauerwald would assist the Freuds' emigration in many ways, including turning a blind eye to some of his overseas bank accounts, easing the bureaucratic processes, helping with packing, and much more.[19] Hans von Demel (1886–1951), the curator of the Kunsthistorisches Museum in Vienna, also helped, valuing Freud's collection of antiquities on 21 May at 30,000 reichsmarks, thus both allowing their export and reducing the Nazi tax bill on them. It was, seemingly, a significant undervaluation. With this, the *Reichsfluchtsteuer*, a concocted Reich emigration tax levied at 25 per cent of a person's assets (125,318 reichsmarks in Freud's case), was calculated on 25 May at 31,329 reichsmarks, a manageable figure.[20] Or at least it might have been if the *Verlag* had not been liquidated, its stock pulped, and much of Freud's capital had not been already seized by the Nazis. Bonaparte stepped in again at this crucial juncture and settled the debt, following which – on 2 June – Freud obtained his *Unbedenklichkeitserklärung* ('Declaration of no impediment'), certifying the Nazi authorities demands had been met and he might leave the country.

While all this was going on, Ernst Freud – who had been settled in London since having to flee Berlin in 1933 – had been hunting for a property there for his parents. In mid-May he managed to secure a house, 39 Elsworthy Road, on a short-term lease, its owner, film producer Richard Butler Wainwright (1895–1985), being abroad.[21] It was conveniently close to Ernst's own home at 32 St John's Wood Terrace and would provide the Freuds with temporary accommodation while Ernst continued to look for a more permanent home for them.

Back in Vienna, just as Marie Bonaparte and Anna were trying to preserve some of Freud's paper archive for posterity, the psychoanalyst and educationalist August Aichhorn (1878–1949) was anxious to preserve a record of the visual culture of Freud's working and living space. With the Freuds' agreement, he commissioned the Viennese Jewish photographer Edmund Engelman (1907–2000) to make a photographic record of Freud's apartment in Berggasse 19. Beginning on a 'wet May morning', Engelman took 106 images of the rooms and their contents in secret across four days. He also photographed Freud, Martha, and Anna.[22]

With taxes paid and the necessary travel documents obtained, the Freuds began their exodus from Vienna. Minna Bernays went first on 5 May, collected by Dorothy Burlingham from the nursing home where she had been laid up with various health problems in addition to post-operative recovery from cataract surgery. Martin and Mathilde, with her husband Robert Hollitscher followed, departing on 14 and 24 May respectively, each taking two days to get to London.[23] Alexander and his family left on 17 May, initially for Switzerland. Later, they would follow Freud to London, where they would arrive on 4 September 1938, in supposedly very straitened circumstances as a result of Nazi expropriations. These latter claims, as we shall see, may have been somewhat exaggerated.

Finally, on Saturday 4 June 1938, Freud would leave Vienna, accompanied by Martha, Anna, their red chow Lün, Paula Fichtl, and Josefine Stross (1901–1995), a paediatrician who had to stand in as Freud's doctor as his personal physician Max Schur (1897–1969) had been hospitalised at the last minute with appendicitis. Reputedly taking 19 pieces of luggage,[24] the Freuds went in taxis that afternoon to Vienna's Westbahnhof station to wait for the Orient Express, which would initially take them to Paris.

While there, Freud had recourse to a wheelchair, due, Ernst Waldinger (1896–1970) said, to 'the strain, and because his heart was weakened'.[25] Waldinger and his wife, Freud's niece Beatrice Rose (née Winternitz: 1896–1969), were the only family members present to see the Freuds off, though Heinz Kohut (1913–1981) was also there watching from a distance and recalled seeing Freud thus ensconced as he waited for the train.[26] A very rarely mentioned accessory, while Jacob had needed a wheelchair towards the end of his life,[27] Freud's own use of one – given his strong independent streak – was probably largely confined to times when his health and mobility were particularly compromised. Increasingly frail from 1931 onwards, Freud acknowledged finding stairs and inclines more difficult to manage. Further heart problems in the late summer of 1933,[28] left Freud very debilitated. Roy Grinker (1900–1993) noted that his 'physical liveliness was gone. He walked very slowly and the abounding energy in his movements had disappeared. The next summer he moved only around the porch of his villa'.[29] Not long after Grinker initially observed these changes, Freud told Arnold Zweig (1887–1968) that 'I cannot climb my stairs, am therefore under house arrest. I think this time I have established my right to a sudden fatal heart attack, not a bad prospect'.[30] Ernest Jones recalled Freud using a 'bath-chair' in May 1934 to get to part of the garden in his summer residence in Grinzing where access was steep.[31] When Hanns Sachs (1881–1947) visited him there two years later, Freud's physical decline from the previously 'indefatigable walker' also struck him. It was only on a 'good day' that Freud could slowly walk up the ascending garden path, while 'at other times he moved in a wheel chair while I walked at his side'.[32] On the present journey, on Freud's arrival in Paris, some of the newspapers noted a collapsible bath-chair among his baggage and the *Yorkshire Post* commented he 'cannot walk far without assistance and . . . he used to be wheeled through the streets of Vienna'.[33] Whether it was Anna or someone else in the household who would push Freud on these occasions was not stated. Such sightings were extremely rare, a status that Freud most likely curated, not wishing to display his sometime reliance on such an external prosthesis, the counterpart of the less visible and extremely painful oral prosthesis Freud had to contend with since his cancer surgery in 1923.

Boarding the Orient Express for its 3.25 pm departure that afternoon, Freud's journey attracted attention from the press and particularly Reuter's news agency which circulated the story.[34] Crossing the border at 3.45 am, the train got into Gare de l'Est in Paris at 10.12 am on Sunday 5 June. Ernst, Alexander's son Harry, Marie Bonaparte, and William Bullitt met them at the station.[35] Bonaparte had an ambulance ready for Freud should it be needed, but he preferred instead to go in one of the two cars she had brought, a Rolls Royce and a Bentley, to her home in Saint-Cloud. There, Freud and his party spent the day relaxing, hugely relieved to have escaped the dangers of Vienna. And Bonaparte returned the gold coins, the statue of Athena, and the antique Chinese jade screen to Freud that she had recently smuggled out of Freud's home, adding several Greek terracotta figures she procured for him as comforts.[36]

That evening, Freud took the 9.50 pm boat train to Dunkirk. Before their departure, Ernst told a *News Chronicle* reporter: 'You can say that my father is delighted at the idea of going to settle down in London. He is looking forward to being able to continue his work in a country he has always loved'.[37] At Dunkirk, the carriages were hauled directly onto the boat for the night crossing and they docked at Dover at 6.15 am the following morning. Lün was taken into quarantine at this point, being placed at Kevin Quinn's kennels in North Kensington for six months.[38] After 25 minutes, with the carriages coupled up to a new locomotive, the train set off on the last leg of its journey to London.

While Freud's emigration superficially complied with the draconian regulations of the National Socialist regime, he would remain a person of interest to the Nazis. As such, he was one of over 2,300 people in Britain placed on a Gestapo list of people to be automatically arrested following Operation Sealion, the planned invasion of the United Kingdom.[39] Others on it included Noel Coward, Stefan Zweig (1881–1942), Vera Brittain, H G Wells, Virginia Woolf, Chaim Weizmann, Alexander Korda, and Aldous Huxley. There were two other psychoanalysts on the list, Paula Heimann (1899–1982) and Hans Thorner (1905–1991), both of whom had to flee Berlin in 1933.

Back in Austria, most of its 190,000 Jewish population did not have Freud's elite connections and struggled to find sanctuary in other countries, many of which were closing their borders to refugees. Britain would reluctantly host some 30,000 Austrian refugees, 90 per cent of whom were Jewish, by the time war was declared.[40] Viennese Jewry faced an intensification of anti-Semitic hatred, with murders and deportation to Dachau and other concentration camps becoming commonplace. While the absolute horror of the Shoah remained over the horizon, it was nevertheless an increasingly terrifying milieu, one in which Freud's younger sisters – Dolfi, Rosa, Pauli, and Mitzi – remained. They would all be murdered.

Arrival at Victoria Station

Arriving at Victoria Station at about 9 am on Monday 6 June, Freud's train halted at an out of the way platform in order to avoid the waiting press and interested onlookers. Having been greeted by the railway and station executives, Freud and Martha were taken by Ernest Jones in his car at a stately 20 miles per hour on a slightly circuitous route – past Buckingham Palace, around Piccadilly Circus, and along Regent Street – to their new home at 39 Elsworthy Road. Freud's daughter, Mathilde, was there to welcome them in.[41] She and Robert Hollitscher would keep house for the Freuds while they lived here for the next several months, following which the Hollitschers would get an apartment of their own very nearby at 2 Maresfield Gardens.

Back at Victoria Station, Martin Freud had arrived at the platform barrier just in time to see his father being driven away by Jones. Together with Anna and Ernst, he collected the myriad pieces of luggage and they made their way by taxi to Elsworthy Road.

Martin would tell a Press Association reporter, probably at Victoria, that while Freud had 'no plans' as yet, 'what he wants most is peace and quiet for the remainder of his days'.[42] He was clear that they were still hoping to retrieve at least some of their belongings from Vienna. Understandably complimentary about Britain,

Martin told reporters that his sister Anna hoped to get permission to practice psychoanalysis there and his brother Ernst – who was working as an architect – was due to submit his application for naturalisation.[43] For his own part, Martin was frank about having no immediate ideas about how he might earn a living now that the *Verlag* was liquidated, but hoped the British government might grant him residency. Reflecting something of this imposed transience, Martin would live at the Mount Royal Hotel (*now* the Thistle Hotel) in Marble Arch for much of 1938 and '39.

A *Daily Sketch* columnist reported that, in an interview that evening, Freud had told him 'I and my family were treated by the authorities well and politely. I was never in confinement or under house arrest'.[44] Alongside Martin and Ernst, Anna reinforced this message emphatically, declaring that 'everybody has been most kind', including 'the police in Vienna' and that they 'were among the very few Jews who were treated decently. We were all free to come and go as we pleased'.[45] Clearly bending the truth here, the family's circumspection was evidently intended to minimise the risk of further prejudicing the Nazi regime against them, which could have endangered relatives and friends they had left behind and may well have resulted in the confiscation of their own personal possessions in Vienna which they were hoping against hope would be shipped.

39 Elsworthy Road

Coming fully furnished, 39 Elsworthy Road was a pretty house, with a bright green door. Freud particularly enjoyed his study there, which opened onto a veranda and had views over the flower-filled garden and out onto Primrose Hill, with Regent's Park beyond. There were downsides to the house too, with Freud finding the stairs unmanageable. 'It is difficult for us', he wrote to Jeanne Lampl-De Groot (1895–1987), 'to live vertically instead of horizontally'.[46] Freud and Martha thus had their bedroom and dining-room on the ground floor too. To get upstairs, where the rooms were 'particularly beautiful', Freud needed to be carried up and down in a sedan chair (or '*tragsessel*' as he described it).[47] He was not, however, initially taken upstairs to see Minna, who – having arrived at Elsworthy Road before Freud – was very ill and bed-bound in her room on the top floor.

In his first letter from the new house, written to Max Eitingon, having related the story of their escape, Freud went on to note that 'The triumphant feeling of liberation is too strongly mixed with the work of mourning, for one still loved the prison from which one was released very much'.[48] Continuing in the same vein to Eitingon, Freud dryly remarked he was sometimes tempted to exclaim 'Heil Hitler!' as an ironic thank you to the Nazis for pushing him into a delightful new setting, though a shadow was cast over any pleasure by unease at the foreign environment in Britain,[49] by Minna's illness, and apprehensiveness about his own weakened heart. In correspondence with others later in the month, this shadow deepened, Freud noting how the ongoing distressing news and appeals for help from Vienna magnified his and the family's feelings of helplessness, while Martha voiced the

Image 10.1 Mathilde Hollitscher, Sigmund Freud, and Ernest Jones, on the doorstep of 39 Elsworthy Road on 6 June 1938
Source: Sueddeutsche Zeitung Photo/Alamy

more specific fears about the precarity of Freud's sisters lives there.[50] Further letters followed, many of which were in response to the flood of correspondence that was soon pouring in from friends, colleagues, and well-wishers. Freud was back in harness, not least as a writer and correspondent, with which his mood and productivity picked up. The warm reception he received in Britain clearly helped, this fanning his Anglophilia and helping to renew his energy. He thus told one reporter, 'I love England, and here I intend to finish my work'.[51] This was also evident on 22 June 1938 when he wrote to his younger brother Alexander (who was still in Switzerland), telling him in a wry and less apprehensive tone about their new country:

> This England . . . is – in spite of everything that strikes one as foreign, peculiar and difficult, and of this there is quite enough – a blessed, a happy country inhabited by well-meaning, hospitable people. Our reception was cordial beyond words. We were wafted up on the wings of a mass psychosis. (I feel compelled to express myself poetically). After the third day the post delivered letters correctly to 'Dr Freud, London' or 'Overlooking Regent's Park'. . . As

for the letters – I have been working like a writing-coolie for two whole weeks trying to sift the chaff from the wheat and (forgive the lame comparison) answer the latter. There were letters from friends, a surprising number from complete strangers who simply wanted to express their delight at our having escaped to safety and who expect nothing in return. In addition, of course, [there have been] hordes of autograph hunters, cranks, lunatics, and pious men who send tracts and texts from the Gospels which promise salvation, attempts to convert the unbeliever and shed light on the future of Israel.[52]

It was in part, Freud suggested rather disingenuously, his first experience of being famous. He had for years been the object of attention of autograph hunters and others attracted by his fame.[53] However, some of the attention he was now receiving, as he alluded to Alexander, had theological overtones. Aside from this being a reflection of a more religious age and of degrees of anti-Semitism, some of Freud's interlocutors' attempts at theological engagement with him stemmed from his renewed work on the third section of what would be his last major work, *Moses and Monotheism*.

Image 10.2 Freud engaged with his manuscript of *Moses and Monotheism* at his desk in 39 Elsworthy Road in summer 1938

Source: Chronicle/Alamy

He had struggled with this work since 1934, with various rewrites, and had published the first two parts in *Imago* in 1937. By his own account, part of the block inhibiting completion of the book was his fear that it would alienate the Catholic church in Austria, which previously Freud had (wrongly) regarded as offering a modicum of protection to himself and to psychoanalysis. Facing expulsion, this block had crumbled and his new refuge in England proved liberating. Describing this catalyst to his re-emerging productivity, he wrote in the second prefatory note to part three of the book:

> I was met with the friendliest reception in lovely, free, magnanimous England. Here I now live, a welcome guest; I can breathe a sigh of relief now that the weight has been taken off me and that I am more able to speak and write – I had almost said 'and think' – as I wish or as I must.[54]

Freud had thus begun to toy with the manuscript during his last weeks in Vienna and the British newspapers reported his work in progress with interest following his arrival. Now, in Elsworthy Road, he had taken up his pen to continue his work on the manuscript on 21 June.

This was accomplished in the face of considerable opposition to the project, particularly from Jews who were critical of Freud's arguments that Moses was originally an Egyptian and that he was murdered by his Jewish followers, but also from theists more generally who objected to his general thesis that 'religious phenomena are only to be understood on the pattern of the individual neurotic symptoms familiar to us'.[55] Freud encountered this criticism not only from correspondents, but also face-to-face from visitors. One of the first such people to come to his house, on 11 June, was the Jewish scholar Abraham Shalom Yahuda (1877–1951), who was living at 25 Elsworthy Road. While Yahuda failed to dissuade Freud from his work, the two now neighbours would regularly meet over the next several weeks.[56] Freud reported to Arnold Zweig on 28 June that he was enjoying his renewed writing. To what extent the community opposition to it contributed to this is unclear, though Freud questioned whether anyone could 'really believe that my arid treatise would destroy the belief of a single person brought up by heredity and training in the faith, even if it were to come his way?'.[57] In any event, after less than four weeks of relatively intensive writing, Freud noted in his *Kürzeste Chronik* on 17 July 1938 that *Moses* was finished. One copy of the complete manuscript was sent to Allert de Lange in Amsterdam, who would bring out the German language edition, while another copy went to Ernest Jones, whose wife Katherine (née Jokl: 1892–1983) was eager to translate it into English for its publication in Britain and the United States.[58]

From the day of his arrival in Britain, Freud had a steady stream of visitors wanting to meet him. We noted Sam's much anticipated and emotional visit on 9 June earlier. Alongside a host of members of the British psychoanalytic community who came by that first month, other guests included Bronislaw Malinowski (1884–1942), Chaim Weizmann (1874–1952), Prince Hubertus Lowenstein

(1906–1984), H G Wells (1866–1946), and on 22 June Marie Bonaparte arrived for three days. She was followed the day after by a delegation from the Royal Society, chaperoning its historic charter book into which Freud formally added his signature. He had been a Foreign Member of the Society since 1936 and his continuing frail health precluded him going to the Society's headquarters in Burlington House to perform the ceremony.

The following month was marginally quieter, after the initial rush of guests. Two visitors are particularly worth noting here: Melanie Klein, who came on about 17 July and Salvador Dalí, two days later, on the nineteenth. Freud had met Klein twice in Vienna in the early 1920s and he received a welcome letter from her the day after he arrived in Elsworthy Road asking if she might visit. Thanking her by letter on 11 June, Freud expressed his hope they would meet soon, the actual meeting being subsequently arranged between Klein and Anna. In her 1954 recollections of the visit, Klein noted they 'talked about many things *except work*', the latter lacuna keeping them away from the controversies over theory and technique that had emerged, particularly between Klein and Anna Freud. Instead, Klein vividly recalled Freud telling her that he had finished writing *Moses and Monotheism* that very day, alluding to the papers on his desk: 'Now it's finished. There it's lying'. Relatedly, Klein noted some of the tribal differences between the English national character and that of the Continental European. It was a topic Klein thought Freud showed an interest in, harking back at one level perhaps to Freud's initial sense of unease at Britain's foreignness to him. Like most of Freud's visitors at this period, Klein clearly greatly admired him and had no qualms about describing him as a genius. Following this meeting, she would see him on just one further occasion, probably at Maresfield Gardens, during a meeting with Anna: as the two women walked through one of the rooms in the house, Freud was there playing cards with others. Without a word, he got up from his seat and bowed, a characteristic – Klein thought – of his attitude.[59]

Stefan Zweig recalled Freud as increasingly evincing 'the shadow of death' on his face during this period. 'It hollowed his cheeks', Zweig wrote, 'it chiselled the temples out of his brow, it twisted his mouth, it checked the words on his lips'.[60] Nevertheless, Zweig introduced Salvador Dalí to Freud and he accompanied the surrealist painter to Elsworthy Road on 19 July, along with Dalí's wife, Gala, and his then patron, the English poet Edward James (1907–1984).[61] James had a double interest in the meeting, being firstly invested in art and its psychology and secondly having a wish to go into analysis with Freud. Nothing came of the latter hope, Freud having quickly identified his lack of ardour. James did bring with him Dalí's 1937 painting *Metamorphosis of Narcissus* to show Freud and Dalí brought a magazine in which he had written an article on paranoia. Previous to the visit, Dalí – who had been trying to meet Freud for years by this point without success – had an epiphany into Freud's 'morphological secret', namely that 'Freud's cranium is a snail!' This artistic idea, achieved over dinner (no doubt prompted by Dalí's escargot hors d'oeuvre), was followed by the thought that Freud's 'brain is in the form of a spiral – to be extracted with a needle!'[62] Much as he may have wanted to extract Freud's brain or ideas and devour them, the actual meeting with Freud proved frustrating – for Dalí at least. Freud would thank Stefan Zweig the following day, and declared that Dalí – 'That young Spaniard, with his candid fanatical eyes and his undeniable technical mastery' – had led him to revise his hitherto poor view of the surrealists.[63] He was intrigued by Dalí's painting and the creative process behind it.

For his part, Dalí had hoped they would have discussed his own ideas and his article on paranoia more. Instead, as he later concretely wrote, 'we devoured each other with our eyes'.[64] Communication was probably not helped by Freud's recurrent problems with catarrh, which left him partially deaf that day. They did however discuss art and Freud, according to Dalí, said to him that 'In classic paintings, I look for the sub-conscious – in a surrealist painting, for the conscious', which the painter hyperbolically interpreted as 'the pronouncement of a death sentence on surrealism as a doctrine'.[65] It was amidst this atmosphere that Dalí sketched Freud in Elsworthy Road, stylistically riffing on his earlier snail fantasy to produce a rather top-down snail-like view of Freud's head. Zweig was reluctant to show Freud the resultant drawing, feeling that 'clairvoyantly Dalí had already incorporated death in the picture'.[66]

Thoughts of his proximity to death, however, would not have been news to the 82-year-old Freud, or indeed to anybody who had a personal acquaintance with him. Having been first formally diagnosed with cancer of the jaw in April 1923, he and his doctors had fought a running battle with the disease since then, with 33 surgical procedures, hundreds of appointments, and daily adjustments to the surgical prosthesis he had to wear despite the marked discomfort it caused. During these 15 years, Freud's physical care was principally in the hands of his personal physicians, beginning briefly with Felix Deutsch (1884–1964) and then Max Schur from 1929, with Hans Pichler undertaking most of the major operations he would undergo, following the initial botched surgical interventions by Marcus Hajek (1861–1941) that occurred in 1923.[67] With Freud's move to London, Pichler recommended he consult the oral surgeon George Gerhard Exner (1902–1965), who had trained under him. Following his own surgery, Schur had managed to leave Vienna with his family six days after Freud and spent several days convalescing in Paris before finally arriving in London on 15 June 1938. He then resumed supervision of Freud's day-to-day healthcare almost immediately. Back in 1929, Schur had agreed two ground-rules with Freud: that he tell him the truth and that he would not let him suffer unnecessarily during his terminal care.[68] The second of these rules has been typically understood as a euthanasia pact. These rules would be crucial in managing Freud's care over the next fifteen months.

Looking towards his inevitable end, Freud also sought to do what he could to get his affairs in order. On 17 July, having finished the German manuscript for *Moses and Monotheism* that day, he composed his last will and testament. Subsequently drafted by Stanley de Leon solicitors, Anna then made several amendments including inserting her name as an executor (alongside Ernst and Martin) and as the designated recipient of Freud's psychology library and collection of antiquities.

Eleven days later, on 28 July, Freud signed the finalised document, which was witnessed by Kathleen Corduff (1909–), a nurse who was employed to perhaps look after Minna, and Kate Jeffcoat, a domestic then working for the Freuds at 39 Elsworthy Road.[69] That same day Freud agrees to purchase 20 Maresfield Gardens, though it would be another eight weeks before they could move in due to the legal formalities and necessary renovations.

During the period the will was being drafted, Freud began writing another scientific work, *An Outline of Psycho-Analysis*, on 22 July 1938. In it, he offered a carefully articulated up-to-date summary of his views on psychoanalysis, intended for an analytic audience rather than the general public. The 66-page manuscript is variously described as having been either left unfinished or in draft form.[70] It was a state that perhaps reflected Freud's increasing sense of working against the clock, when dotting the i's and crossing the t's might be left to others. And people *were* stepping forward to assist Freud and psychoanalytic publishing. Hanns Sachs had proposed earlier that month relaunching the journal *Imago* as an English-language periodical in the United States. Freud was initially hesitant about the idea as he was hoping to revive his German-language journal of the same name, albeit merged with his other defunct journal, the *Internationale Zeitschrift für Psychoanalyse*. Following discussions with Anna and Ernest Jones however, Freud agreed to its US publication under the revised title *American Imago* and took on the nominal editorship, with Sachs as the managing editor.[71] The new journal would, they hoped, exercise a moderating influence on the Americans, particularly regarding the toxic issue of lay analysis in the United States. At the same time, Freud and Anna's ambitions to preserve German-language psychoanalysis, despite the Nazi's assault on it, also took several steps forward, this time with the help of the author, translator, and publisher John Rodker (1894–1955). By early August, Rodker was making moves towards founding the Imago Publishing Company (IPC), to continue German-language psychoanalytic publishing. Martin Freud served as an associate director for a time. As part of this new venture, Rodker brought out the *Internationale Zeitschrift für Psychoanalyse und Imago*, combining Freud's two defunct *Verlag* journals in one. Freud's *Outline* would first appear in this new journal in 1940. Rodker also slowly set about publishing Freud's *Gesammelte Werke*. Despite financial support from Marie Bonaparte and others, it was an underfunded nostalgic enterprise and struggled to secure an immediate market at a time when the Continental German speaking audience for psychoanalysis had been decimated by the rise of National Socialism and English was becoming the *lingua franca* of psychoanalysis.[72]

Freud and his circle were attempting to bring something of the everyday cultural and emotional lives they had to leave behind in Vienna to their new domicile in London, a process of salvage, preservation, and mourning that was particularly acute during 1938 and 1939. The IPC may be seen as one such venture. Closer to home, on 8 August 1938 they were reunited with the furniture, books, and Freud's collection of antiquities from Berggasse after an anxious two month wait. With less than a month to go before the lease on Elsworthy Road expired, however, most of these precious possessions probably remained in store pending the family's move into Maresfield Gardens. August also saw Freud briefly reunited with Poppy, from Manchester, one of the continuing stream of visitors (the Wolf Man was another later that month). Poppy and Freud had been exchanging letters that summer and – as with Sam's earlier visit – this must have been an emotional meeting. Though the content of their meeting has not been preserved, other efforts at the time to capture something of the present remain. Thus, on 20 July a family friend, Willy Lévy (later known as Peter Lambda: 1911–1995), began to sculpt a bust of Freud and a month later, on 21 August, another Hungarian artist, the photographer Marcel Sternberger (1899–1956), took several portrait photographs of Freud at Stefan Zweig's request. Both sittings produced results that would be widely celebrated. These achievements in London however were in contrast to the suffering and losses in Vienna, from whence the news was unremittingly grim: this cast a continuing shadow over Freud and his family, feelings which were compounded by their inability to really help.[73]

As Freud's time in Elsworthy Road ebbed away, Max Schur's concerns over his health deepened. At the end of August 1938, after weeks of indecision between the doctors involved, Schur observed what he believed was the beginning of a papilloma high in Freud's mouth at the site of previous surgery. Schur, Exner, and radiologist John Francis Carter Braine (1893–1953) agreed surgery was now indicated, but before that could happen Freud and his family had to vacate their temporary home.

The Hotel Esplanade, 2 Warrington Crescent

With the expiry of the lease on 39 Elsworthy Road, Freud needed some other temporary accommodation until 20 Maresfield Gardens was ready for him to move into. Ernst again found a solution by booking at least his parents and Anna into the Hotel Esplanade, at 2 Warrington Crescent, Maida Vale. Minna, who remained very unwell, was cared for in a nursing home as an interim arrangement.

The Hotel Esplanade was a newly opened small hotel, owned by a Russian Jew, a widow Marie Lilly Davidowa (née Rabinovitch: 1895–1972). Smiley Blanton (1882–1966) described it as mainly catering to émigrés, a view borne out by the residents' names on the following year's 1939 Register. Davidowa would later fall foul of the law for running a brothel just around the corner at 24b Clifton Gardens, in which enterprise she was assisted by two other Russian Jews, the Esplanade's manager Leon Schapiro (1878–1955), who she later married, and Schapiro's then wife Debora (née Rauchwerger: 1880–1967).[74] Whether the brothel was in operation at the time of Freud's stay in the hotel is unknown.

Moving in on 2 September 1938, Freud was able to continue work there with at least one analytic patient, Smiley Blanton (of whom more later), that same day. Blanton reported his wife's fears that Freud might be exposed to English cooking, which they thought was awful. Agreeing with Blanton's cultural stereotype, Freud reassured him that he would be well provided for as the Esplanade had a French

Image 10.3 Freud and W Ernst Halberstadt at the Esplanade Hotel in September 1938
Source: Chronicle/Alamy

chef.[75] Freud also continued working on *An Outline of Psycho-Analysis* here for a few days, after which he would not return to the manuscript.[76]

Having initially anticipated the surgery would be performed by Exner on 7 September, Freud announced on the sixth that it had been postponed until the eighth.[77] This was occasioned by Schur and Anna Freud having asked Professor Pichler if he would come to London to operate on Freud. Pichler agreed and flew over from Vienna on 7 September. Examining Freud that same day, he confirmed Schur's diagnosis.

The following morning Freud underwent the surgery with Pichler in the London Clinic. The lengthy two-and-a-quarter hour operation entailed a lengthy incision through Freud's lip and along his nose to get access to the tumour and its removal with a diathermy needle. The initial results appeared positive and a preliminary biopsy suggested the tumour had been pre-cancerous. Freud's immediate recovery seemed positive: he was able to read a little that same day and slept well that night. Having seen Freud again the following morning, Pichler was satisfied with his patient's progress and flew back to Vienna later that morning.[78] It was a view that others shared. Ernst Freud, for example, suggested to the press that it was a minor operation and that 'My father is very well and is already smoking'.[79] Despite such initial reports, Freud would spend 20 days in the London Clinic, twice as long as he had previously anticipated, being discharged when his new home had been set up.

20 Maresfield Gardens

The house at Maresfield Gardens, designed by the Balham architect Albert Hastilow, had been built in about 1920, in the Queen Ann revivalist style. A large red-brick property, with eight bedrooms, three reception rooms, and two bathrooms, with a mature garden, it had been the family home of Beryl Anne (*née* Blenkinsop: 1914-) and her husband David Stuart Duncan (1902–1980), a chartered accountant and grandson of the polymath Herbert Spencer's secretary and assistant David Duncan (1839–1923), the author of *The Life and Letters of Herbert Spencer*, which had been published in 1908 by Methuen. The Duncans short marriage ended in divorce and the house was consequently sold to Freud on 28 July.[80] The £6,500 sale price was partly funded with the aid of a £4,000 loan from Barclays Bank, which was repaid in just five years.[81] The family had come a long way economically since Freud's early working-class childhood in Freiberg.

Ernst was busy that August and September adapting 20 Maresfield Gardens to the family's needs, particularly by knocking through two ground floor rooms into one to make a large office cum consulting room for his father, reminiscent of the atmosphere of Berggasse though with a far lighter modernist colour palette, and installing a lift to allow Freud and Minna to access upstairs.[82] While Freud was still recuperating in the London Clinic, Martha, Anna, and Paula Fichtl moved into the house on 16 September 1938 and set about unpacking and arranging their furniture and possessions that had arrived from Vienna in a manner that evoked Berggasse.

This evocation and indeed recreation of the family's lost environs in Vienna extended to their new neighbourhood in Hampstead and its surrounds, with other family members, friends and other Viennese and German refugees settling there also. Ernst and Lucie were just over a mile away at 41 St John's Wood Terrace and in about 1940 temporarily moved much closer to a flat at 2 Maresfield Gardens.[83] Alexander Freud, having arrived in Britain in September 1938, was based for a while in a flat in Oxford Street before moving further afield, to Hove, in Sussex, where he lived at 21 Wick Hall, Furze Hill. Ernst's son Lucian (1922–2011) recalled him fondly, saying 'there was a feeling of good living and opulence [about Alexander]; he took me to lunch at the Hungarian restaurant Csardas in Soho'.[84] Hove was some distance from London and Alexander wanted a place closer to his brother. In the summer of 1939, he purchased 4 Maresfield Gardens as an investment property and Ernst drew up plans to sub-divide the property into flats.[85] Martin, having lived initially as we have seen at the Mount Royal Hotel in Marble Arch, moved during the summer of 1939 to a flat just two miles away at Holly Terrace, West Hill, Highgate. Others were much closer. Dorothy Burlingham had acquired a flat at 2 Maresfield Gardens in 1938, as did Mathilde and her husband Robert Hollitscher. Having cared for Freud and the family in Elsworthy Road, Mathilde now opened a very fashionable boutique, Robell, at 44 Baker Street, towards the end of September 1938, doing so in partnership with a pair of Jewish émigré dress designers from Innsbruck, Ernst and Anna Stiassny.[86] Robert, who had been a silk merchant in Vienna, lent his assistance and Ernst redesigned the shop itself.[87] With 20 Maresfield Gardens as its epicentre, the neighbourhood became what Ernst's biographer Volker Welker aptly described as the new Berggassen quarter.[88] It was not only the wider Freud family that clustered in the Berggassen quarter, so did a significant number of psychoanalysts subsequently, attracted no doubt by the proximity of a growing number of like-minded colleagues, themselves attracted by the iconic Freudian neighbourhood.

Freud himself arrived in the house on 27 September, having been discharged from the London Clinic that day, the press reporting that he had made a good recovery.[89] Privately, he would write to Jeanne Lampl-de Groot that he was making a 'Slow recovery from the surgery, which was the worst since 1923. . . I still can't eat and smoke properly, find it difficult to speak, [but] the pain is receding'.[90] Ernest Jones would declare that Freud 'never really fully recovered from the effects of this severe operation and became more and more frail'.[91] While categorically Jones's view may be correct, it rather overlooks how determined Freud was to experience what was to be his final year and to work through as much of it as he possibly could. For an 82-year-old, with very serious debilitating health problems, and constant pain and discomfort, Freud still managed to use his time creatively.

The new lift was installed by Ernst at the expense of a guest bedroom, the accommodation being further strained by two nurses – hired to look after the bedbound Minna – who used the first floor living room and bathroom. Minna had come back from the nursing home on 2 October, her health still precarious, with cardiac problems, cystitis, and previously pneumonia. It was Martha who found these compromises to her own domestic domain especially irksome, Freud suggested, with problems with the windows, the central heating, the lighting, and the lift adding to the small niggles.[92] The latter problems were not made easier by difficulties obtaining workmen to attend to them.

Getting to work in Maresfield Gardens, Freud was occupied both with patients (as will be discussed later) and as an author. On 20 October 1938, he thus began writing another expository paper, to which he gave the English title 'Some elementary lessons in psycho-analysis'. The last of his psychoanalytic works, this seven-page manuscript in some respects mirrors the *Outline*. It was left unfinished, in what Ilse Grubrich-Simitis described as 'the final stroke beneath his monumental lifework as an author in the fatigue of approaching death'.[93] While that paper would be only published posthumously, two other very brief contributions, written in October and November 1938, on anti-Semitism, would quickly emerge. The first of these, 'A comment of anti-Semitism', was written for a special English issue of Arthur Koestler's magazine *Die Zukunft*, a Parisian magazine aimed at German émigrés, while the second, 'Anti-Semitism in England', appeared in *Time and Tide*, in a special issue on the subject.⁹⁴ In both pieces Freud neatly avoids the ingratiator's dilemma by giving the burden of arguments against anti-Semitism to non-Jewish speakers. The first article is perhaps the most remarkable, most of the paper being a précis of an article, the name of whose author Freud claimed to have forgotten, a lapse he ascribed to being 'a very old man and my memory is no more what it was'. A reader, he suggested, might be able to supply the name of the nameless author. While Marion Richmond would decades later suggest the précised text came from Mark Twain,⁹⁵ Freud's latent question to his readers seems less about retrieving the original author's name and more about energising bystanders into thought and action.

That was something Freud, as a writer, could try to do, despite feeling otherwise painfully helpless. The news from Europe was 'abominable' as he told Eitingon,⁹⁶ the violence and destruction wrought by the Nazis on *Kristallnacht* on 9–10 November heightening Freud's fears, particularly for his sisters in Vienna. He and Alexander had left them 160,000 Schilling for their day-to-day living expenses, though he confided to Marie Bonaparte on 12 November that this may have been already confiscated. At the same time Freud mooted moving his sisters to Nice or its environs, with which plan he hoped the redoubtable Bonaparte might be able to assist.⁹⁷ All attempts to rescue them over the months ahead failed.

While Freud did not tidy up either the *Outline* or 'Some elementary lessons in psycho-analysis' for publication, he did spend considerable time working on the German proofs of *Moses*, despite continuing encouragement from visitors and correspondents to abandon the supposedly heretical project. Freud was considerably invested in this book at multiple levels. The figure of Moses had exerted a long-term fascination on him, going back in his professional writings to his initially anonymously published 1914 paper 'The Moses of Michelangelo', though the cultural and personal origins clearly emerged far earlier from his family's Judaism. While wrestling with this, as he had wrestled with his observant brother Philipp (who died just a year before the serious activation of Freud's preoccupation with and initial research into Moses), Freud in the book now contested the received religious narrative. He thus asserted that Moses had been an aristocratic Egyptian, that his championing of a monotheistic Judaism had its origins in Akhenaten's worship of Aten, and that he was killed by the Israelites. Current events in Nazi Germany were a further spur to Freud's thinking, the excursion into the historical past being both a relief from helpless anxieties about the destruction of his work in Germany (with his own books being burned and psychoanalysts persecuted and forced into exile) and an expression of a hope for his doctrine's survival, just as the monotheism of Moses survived persecution, exile, and trauma.⁹⁸ This complex inevitably left its marks on the book, evident in its uneven structure and somewhat repetitive content. Now free in Britain, Freud's released creativity allowed him to complete the work and ultimately nurse it through to publication. The ambition to achieve this was an important motivation for Freud during 1938 and 1939. The final investment in *Moses* was an economic one: given the major financial losses Freud had incurred in escaping from the Nazis, he was desperate to monetise this final book as much as he could.

Having signed a publishing contract with Allert de Lange for a German language edition, Freud with Martin's help initially sold the US rights for an undisclosed amount to Alfred A Knopf, negotiating the details with the pioneering Blanche Knopf (1894–1966) in July 1938. Cassell approached Freud about publishing the book in Britain, offering a substantial £500 advance on potential royalties and Martin used this as leverage with the Hogarth Press – the established British psychoanalytic publisher, who worked in association with the Institute of Psychoanalysis – to secure an advantageous contract. Hogarth thus agreed on 27 July to bring the book out in Britain and across the Empire, granting Freud a slightly smaller though still healthy £450 advance on royalties.[99] It was the largest advance they had paid for any of Freud's works and they did so with the belief that the book would appeal to a far wider market than his primarily psychoanalytic writings. Blanche Knopf clearly shared this belief and both publishers had contracted without having seen the full manuscript. The Institute of Psychoanalysis underwrote 50 per cent of the Hogarth Press advance.[100] Following the completion of the manuscript on 17 July back in Elsworthy Road, Freud had sent a copy to Allert de Lange for publication in German and another copy towards the end of August to Katherine Jones, who was to translate it with Ernest Jones's assistance for the Hogarth Press and Alfred Knopf.

The British and American firms agreed at a meeting in London on 19 August 1938 to a coordinated approach to the publication, sharing the £50 translation fees, and for Hogarth to take the lead on setting the text and supplying Knopf with corrected proofs from which they could print the US edition.[101] Neither publisher had actually seen the full manuscript by this stage. Blanche Knopf was the first to do so and then alarm bells started to ring. Following a careful reading of the German typescript, she wrote to Leonard Woolf (1880–1969) on 11 October that she was 'extremely disturbed': the manuscript was, she declared, 'extremely disorganised', with 'excessive repetition' which, if it were 'eliminated, an already very short book would be made considerably shorter, to its great disadvantage and to your and our loss'.[102] Commenting on this for Leonard Woolf, Ernest Jones acknowledged that Knopf's criticism had some justification and that 'there is no doubt that the book is rather badly strung together, not having been written as a whole'.[103] This was, as Woolf replied, 'very disturbing' news, particularly from a commercial point of view. James Strachey now read the manuscript at Jones's invitation and was perhaps slightly more successful in allaying Woolf's fears. While the book was 'a little eccentric' in Strachey's opinion, there was less repetition than he expected and each iteration served to bring out 'fresh aspects of the material'; taken as a whole, the book was 'exceedingly interesting'.[104] He declined however to comment on the book as a commercial proposition.

In parallel with these behind-the-scenes discussions, Freud resumed work on the manuscript during November 1938. He was, as Jones reported, 'working again at the troublesome third part and has made some improvements as well as omitting some repetitions'.[105] Not having seen these, Blanche Knopf then sent Woolf and Jones a three-page list of proposed changes, aimed at making the narrative more coherent for general readers, to reduce repetition, and to expand on certain sections, such as Freud's discussion of the narcissism of minor differences, and to recap on some of the arguments previously brought up in *Totem and Taboo*.[106] Jones responded on 22 November that two pages with duplicated material had been cut and replaced with a new paragraph, and that the separate essays had been more clearly distinguished. Describing the book as a scientific rather than a popular text, thus contradicting the publishers' clear expectations, Jones combatively went on to imply some of the deficits Knopf identified lay not with the book but with potential readers: they might thus be advised to 'remedy the deficiency in their reading'. Jones then added that he had submitted Knopf's suggestions to Freud (presumably during a recent visit to Maresfield Gardens) and his reaction was 'entirely negative', which Jones contextualised by noting that Freud was very unwell and thought he was finished with this book. Concluding on a more reassuring note, Jones remarked that his wife was making good progress with the translation and 'the final result will be a very polished one'.[107] With this, the question of further substantial changes to the book ceased.

The translation of the *Moses* manuscript into English by the Joneses took longer than Blanche Knopf and Freud had anticipated. Both were initially under the impression that it was to be delivered on 1 November, just over two months after Katherine Jones had received it. This unlikely date, however, was one that neither Katherine nor Ernest Jones appeared to have been party to. When that date arrived, Freud protested to Jones about the delay on behalf of Knopf and still more so on his own account. He added plaintively – though with considerable realism – that 'a few months mean more to me than to someone else, when I cling to the understandable wish that I myself may still [live to] see the book finished'.[108] Though Jones sought to rebut the claim that the translation was taking longer than agreed and successfully retained the commission in the face of Freud's wish to procure another translator to expedite the work, Freud suggested to Eitingon that Jones was delaying the translation, that he appeared to want to sabotage the book, and that the friendliness he exhibited on their arrival on 6 June seemed exhausted.[109] For his own part, Freud took until 26 December 1938 to correct the German proofs for Allert de Lange, incorporating into them at least some of the modifications that were now to be part of the English text.

The German edition appeared in late March 1939 under the lengthy title *Der Mann Moses und die monotheistische Religion: Drei Abhandlungen*, Freud receiving the first two advance copies from Allert de Lange on the thirteenth. He would gift more than 28 books from this edition to members of his family, friends, and collaborators in the next few months, his partial list of such presentation copies beginning with Anna and then Marie Bonaparte. They received those first two advance copies that same day. Seeing the publication was, Freud told Hanns Sachs, 'A very worthy end'.[110] By mid-June it was reported that 1,800 books from this edition has been sold, much to Freud's satisfaction.[111]

The English editions, the translation of which had been completed by early February 1939, were typeset by the Hogarth Press, and Knopf received copies of the corrected proofs on 27 March.[112] During the setting process the question of the book's title came up. The Hogarth Press and Knopf both favoured the simple and emphatic *Moses* rather than *Moses and Monotheism*, the English title Freud had specified. Leonard Woolf took this up with Freud on 15 March, arguing that the shorter title would be much better from a publishing perspective and that the inclusion of the word 'monotheism' would frighten-off potential readers in England.[113] Freud, however, was set on the longer title. *Moses and Monotheism* was thus published in Britain by the Hogarth Press on 25 May 1939 and in the United States by Knopf four weeks later, on 19 June 1939.[114] It is unclear how many author copies the Hogarth Press supplied, but Blanche Knopf despatched 10 advanced copies to Freud on 26 May. Over twelve of these English language editions were presented by Freud, mainly to friends and collaborators, including H G Wells, Havelock Ellis, and his radiologist, Neville Finzi (1881–1968). Two went to relatives in Manchester: one to Sam and a Knopf edition to Poppy. Sam's sisters, Pauli and Bertha, still in the shadows, did not it appears receive their own personal copies from their uncle. Though the book's press reviews were distinctly mixed as Freud had anticipated, with his heightened media profile in Britain and a moderate advertising campaign, the Hogarth Press first impression of 3,000 copies sold well

Image 10.4 Freud's BBC recording at 20 Maresfield Gardens, 7 December 1938
Source: © Freud Museum, London

and by April 1940 – amid wartime paper shortages – a second impression was being negotiated with the printers.[115] This next impression would be incorporated into the *International Psycho-Analytical Library* series as Volume 33. With the American reviews rather more critical than those in Britain, it would not be until January 1947 that the Knopf edition went into a second printing.

While the publication of *Moses and Monotheism* was the undoubted intellectual highlight of 1938–39, Freud's calendar was peppered with other red-letter days. Lün's release from her six-month quarantine on 6 December 1938 was particularly celebrated, with the press carrying photographs of her with Anna and Marie Bonaparte.[116] The following morning Freud was recorded speaking by Howard Lynton Fletcher (1903–1983), from the BBC, for the Corporation's historical library. As a script, Freud wrote a brief two-and-a half-minute summary of his professional life in English, concluding this with a line in German.[117] Fletcher encouraged Freud to speak at greater length and proposed he might read the opening section of one of his books, a suggestion Freud declined on the day. On 12 January 1939, the BBC confirmed that the editing of the recording was recently completed and enquired both whether Freud had any stipulations about its future and how many records Anna and others in the family might want.[118] At the end of June 1939, a further enquiry from the BBC invited Freud to discuss *Moses and Monotheism* with Ivo Geikie-Cobb (1887–1953), a neurologist who broadcast for them under the pseudonym Anthony Weymouth. Geikie-Cobb was planning a programme on the book for the Corporation's Empire (overseas) programming. Whether anything came of this request is unclear and probably unlikely given Freud's failing health. Other requests were easier to meet, such as the various organisations that wanted to add Freud to their boards or membership rosters in some honorary capacity. Freud thus accepted positions with the Austrian Circle for Arts and Science, the Austrian Centre in London,[119] the Jewish Health Research and Planning Institute, the Maccabi World Union, and the Austrian PEN group in London.

Just as there had been at Elsworthy Road, there was a steady stream of visitors to Freud at Maresfield Gardens. Most were prominent members of the analytic community, such as Heinz Hartmann (1894–1970), Hanns Sachs, Jeanne Lampl-de Groot and her husband Hans Lampl (1889–1958), Ruth Mack Brunswick (1897–1946), Elizabeth Severn (1879–1959), and of course Marie Bonaparte, and Jones. Others were literary, artistic, or intellectual figures, such as David Baumgardt (1890–1963), Arnold Zweig, Isaiah Berlin (1909–1997), and the cabaret singer Yvette Guilbert (1865–1944), the latter attending Freud's last birthday celebration on 6 May 1939, much to his delight. Marie Bonaparte's daughter Eugénie filmed the celebration held in the garden of Freud's new home.[120]

Three visitors may be specifically mentioned here. The first two, Leonard and Virginia Woolf (1882–1941), visited Freud for tea on Saturday afternoon, 28 January. Although they had been publishing his work since 1924, this was the Woolfs first and only meeting with Freud. It was not an easy tea party. Leonard and Virginia described it as an 'interview', Virginia adding they were like patients sitting together in Freud's study. They probably talked about the *Moses* book, certainly about the rise of Hitler and the Nazis. One lighter source of some amusement to the Woolfs if not to Freud was Leonard's story about a man recently charged with stealing books, including one of Freud's: the presiding judge apparently expressed the wish that he could be sentenced to read all of Freud's writings as a punishment. Woolf's *later* account of this in his autobiography seems to have been something of a confabulation, mixing one of several reports of trials of individuals charged with stealing books from Foyle's in London's Charing Cross Road with a story that appeared in *The Bookseller* about the Freudian-inspired Danish author Aksel Sandemose (1899–1965) who, having lost a lengthy libel case in Norway, was supposedly condemned by the court to read twenty volumes by Freud.[121]

Not someone who was easily impressed, Leonard Woolf thought Freud had an aura of true greatness. 'There was something about him', Leonard recalled, 'as of a half-extinct volcano, something sombre, suppressed, reserved. He gave me the feeling ... of great gentleness, but behind the gentleness, great strength'.[122] To Virginia's eyes, the 82-year-old Freud appeared a 'screwed up shrunk very old man: with a monkey's light eyes, paralysed spasmodic movements, inarticulate: but alert'.[123] Nevertheless, she too felt she was in the presence of someone with 'immense potential', even though Freud was like 'an old fire now flickering'. Anna and Martin were there as well and helped ease the conversation somewhat, no doubt made more difficult by Freud's ill health, pain, and oral prosthesis. Yet Virginia Woolf divined a certain neediness in the younger Freuds as the conversation touched on their own writing and a possible hope for patronage from the Bloomsbury couple. There was, she declared acerbically: 'A certain strain: all refugees are like gulls with their beaks out for possible crumbs. Martin & his novel; she on her book. The strain on us too of being benefactors'.[124] It was probably towards the end of the tea that Freud, who Leonard saw as extraordinarily courteous, presented Virginia with a flower: a narcissus.

The third visitor was keen to be a benefactor. H G Wells and Freud seem to have first met in 1933 and Wells had called on him in Elsworthy Road on 19 June 1938, shortly after his arrival in the country. Following the move to Maresfield Gardens, Wells visited on 29 November and then on 24 July 1939, being probably accompanied in July by his lover, the suspected spy Baroness Maria Budberg (1892–1974). On both visits the idea of Freud becoming a naturalised British citizen came up, Wells writing to Freud in advance of the 24 July meeting to say he had been pressing others to secure a special act of parliament to grant Freud exemption from the normal five-year residency requirement.[125] In his reply, Freud told Wells that 'since I first came over to England as a boy of eighteen years, it became an intense wish phantasy of mine to settle in this country and become an Englishman'. Continuing, Freud seems to locate the origins of this wish even earlier, 'But an *infantile* phantasy needs a bit of examination before it can be admitted to reality'.[126] Having thus initially located the origins of his wish to be an Englishman in his 1875 visit, Freud then shifts these back to an infantile period, presumably to 1859 when Philipp, Emanuel and his family emigrated to Britain, leaving the young Sigismund bereft of half his extended family. The reality constraint Freud brought to bear on Wells and his own wish was his rapidly failing health. The timescale for securing an Act of Parliament was outside of the time Freud – with good reason – thought he had left. On their last meeting it seems likely that Wells' wish continued to be discussed. The matter was not raised in parliament.

As Freud had here intimated, his health since moving to Maresfield Gardens was poor. Recovery from the surgery of 8 September 1938 was slow. By 3 November Freud told Eitingon he was still experiencing 'local pain, facial paresis, disturbance in speaking, drinking and smoking, all of which are the understandable consequences of prolonged illness and pain-bound mood'.[127] Some of the pain Freud was experiencing was due to bone necrosis following the last operation and a few splinters of bone were expected to emerge. Two chips emerged in December, in part with Max Schur's assistance. While waiting for the second of these, Freud dryly told Eitingon how he was 'waiting like a hungry dog for a bone. Which has been promised to me, only it is supposed to be one of my own'.[128] That brought a little relief for Freud – though his headaches continued – over what was a white Christmas in London, though the scenic impression was offset by frozen pipes and an uncertain heating system in Maresfield Gardens.

In mid-January 1939, Schur observed a new swelling high up in Freud's mouth which he suspected was an epithelioma. Consulting with colleagues, Exner and Wilfred Trotter were doubtful. It was perhaps this occasion that Schur sought out Freud's Viennese dentist, Moritz Tischler (1886–1962). When Tischler examined Freud he was convinced it was a malignant neoplasm, which he later described being the size of a walnut.[129] Antoine Lacassagne (1884–1971), from the Institut Curie in Paris, was then called in and examined Freud in London on 26 February. He was similarly concerned. Following the results of a biopsy the next day, the diagnosis of a malignant epithelioma was confirmed. Surgery was ruled out and on 9 March Freud was instead started on a daily course of radiotherapy with Neville Finzi in his offices at 107 Harley Street. This was supplemented with radium irradiation, beginning on 15 March. The treatment was, as Freud joked darkly with Hanns Sachs, 'at least gentler than cutting off my head, which would have been the other alternative'.[130] Practically, it offered several more weeks or months of life and held out the possibility that Freud could continue his analytic practice at the same time.[131] The side effects were very unpleasant, but by April there appeared a distinct improvement in the size and appearance of the cancer and a reduction in Freud's pain.

With Freud in what appeared to be a slight remission, Schur took the opportunity to visit New York where he wanted to settle, having to go at this juncture to satisfy visa regulations and to begin the process of securing US medical licensure. During his absence, from 21 April to 8 July, a Viennese physician Bernard Samet (1897–1980) took over Freud's day-to-day medical care with assistance from others. Samet had gained his MD degree in Vienna in 1922, though at this time he was still studying for his British medical qualifications, which he would eventually receive in July 1941. During the remainder of April 1939 and into early May the reports of Freud's health appeared encouraging. On 15 May however, Exner confirmed the resurgence of the cancer.[132] The radium and x-ray irradiation treatment was resumed aggressively, taking up two hours a day. This would lead to a reduction in size of the immediate tumour, though subsequently the cancer would metastasise. Freud had felt since Schur's departure that his doctors were trying to encourage false optimism. On 16 June, he confided in Marie Bonaparte that Finzi's therapeutic optimism was 'luring me half against my will into continuing to hope and in the meantime into continuing to suffer', which was in the context of Freud's subjective experience that 'the radium has once again begun to eat away at something, causing pain and toxic manifestations, and my world is what it was previously: a small island of pain floating on an ocean of indifference'.[133]

When Schur got back to Britain on 8 July, he found Freud much worse. He had lost weight, the skin on his right cheek was discoloured and much of his beard on that side had gone, there seemed to be further carcinomatous ulceration, and there was a very unpleasant smell, which in due course it was agreed was coming from skin and bone necrosis. Clearly now into palliative care, Freud's physical state was going rapidly downhill. Before considering that, we shall turn briefly to look at Freud's psychoanalytic practice which had been continuing – whether sensibly or not – in the face of so much adversity.

Freud's last patients

Freud's clinical practice was severely disrupted by the move to London, his age, and his declining health. New patients were in particularly short supply there. He would write to Max Eitingon on 3 November 1938 that his professional practice took up just 'two hours a day [and] the giant city [London] has not yet delivered any new patients',[134] while to Jeanne Lampl-de Groot he wrote shortly afterwards that, while Anna was very busy, though mostly with old cases, 'no new ones have erred their way to me either'.[135] Freud attributed the lack of patients to being – as Michael Molnar puts it – 'old and liable to die soon'.[136] Nevertheless, Freud was able to continue working with several analysands who left Vienna at the same time, including briefly with Dorothy Burlingham, and more substantively with an American psychologist, Sophie Ritholz (1904–1979), he had seen since September 1937, and a wealthy Dutchman, Herman Claus, whose difficult analysis had also begun in 1937. Claus would later move for further analysis to Grete Bibring (1899–1977), who was already analysing his wife Marie.[137]

In one of the few accounts written by Freud's analysands from this period of his practice, that by Sophie Ritholz is particularly evocative. She had maintained contact by letter while Freud was settling into his new home and probably recommenced her analysis on 3 October 1938, alongside two other patients, less than a week after Freud's release from the London Clinic where he had surgery on his tumour. Noting his return to work the following day to Marie Bonaparte, Freud acknowledged 'it is not going easily'.[138] For Ritholz, her analysis would continue until July 1939. On 5 April 1956, some 17 years later, she recalled 20 Maresfield Gardens during this time as:

> a cheerful, happy household, as it appeared to me, despite the undercurrent of tragedy after the Professor's ailment had become worse . . . one would hear the

tinkle of spoons on teacups, a light clatter of dishes being washed, and cheerful voices engaged in conversation. . . . But underneath it all was the reality of the Professor's affliction, his fortitude and infinite patience – sitting there so often, far too often, with a hot water bag pressed to his face, but totally absorbed in the session, in expounding, in listening.[139]

While somewhat rose-tinted no doubt, the picture Ritholz paints of the household and of Freud's determination to work coheres with other accounts.

Some ex-patient colleagues also returned, generally for brief periods of analysis. At least two of these travelled from the United States. The first of these was Ruth Mack Brunswick, who came on 29 July 1938 and worked with Freud until 24 August, albeit with an interruption to attend the 15th IPA Congress which was held in Paris at the beginning of that month. She would also see Sergei Pankejeff (better known as the Wolf Man: 1886–1979), whose treatment she took over in 1926. She was in poor health and addicted to opiates. Freud thought she looked 'bad' and Mack Brunswick felt she was depressed, Freud graphically adding that she 'gnashes uninterruptedly'.[140] Just prior to her departure to the USA, Freud wrote how this episode of 'follow-up analysis . . . will probably do her good', though tempered this by remarking, 'How incomplete my earlier analyses were!'.[141] Never a 'therapeutic enthusiast', Freud here echoes ideas about the limits of analysis which he had explored in his 1937 paper 'Analysis terminable and interminable'.[142]

The second American analyst to return for brief treatment was the previously mentioned Smiley Blanton, who saw Freud for eight sessions between 30 August and 7 September 1938, initially at 39 Elsworthy Road and then, from 2 September, at the Hotel Esplanade.[143] Blanton had consulted Freud previously in 1929–30, with further spells of analysis in August 1935 and 1937. Hearing of Freud's escape from Vienna, he made the trans-Atlantic crossing again, driven in part by his relief at the Professor's safety. Much of Blanton's report of this short period of analysis is taken up with questions of inclusion and exclusion, of Freud's and his own. Feeling marginal, for example, within the New York Psychoanalytic Society, Blanton was interested in founding his own analytic group in Nashville and gaining recognition as a training analyst. Wanting Freud's imprimatur of his suitability, Blanton instead was encouraged to seek a university professorship towards which Freud thought his name would carry more weight. It was a type of transference, a wish for anointment and transformation, that Freud was familiar with.

Freud listed two other analysands by surname in the Frank Smython's 'Featherweight' notebook that he used in London to help keep track of his caseload: 'Gilchrist' and 'Lipton'. Their identities remain speculative.[144] As Christmas 1938 approached, Freud's clinical practice seems to have grown to four hours a day.[145] Over the next seven months of 1939, Freud would continue seeing his patients. By 31 July 1939, however, he recognised himself that he was too ill to continue and ended his practice.

Whether Freud was well enough to work during the preceding few months is a moot point. He certainly regarded work, the 'free play of the imagination', and the capacity to earn money to support his family as an important part of his identity and had previously voiced his ambition to 'die in harness'.[146] It was something he came very close to, while his business determination, like that of his older brothers before him, was remarkable. Considering the fee remittances from these last analysands offers an insight into that achievement during this period. Freud operated a sliding scale of fees, ranging from three to six guineas in 1938–39, with three of the six people whose fees are known (Ruth Mack Brunswick's are not recorded) paying three guineas per session. From August 1938 through to the end of July 1939, Freud would earn something in excess of £2,689 (equivalent to £144,871 in November 2023) for his clinical work.[147] It was income that was evidently needed, given the extensive demands on his purse.

Freud's last war

In July, despite his worsening condition, Freud was still able to maintain something of his previous routine seeing patients, reading, and a little correspondence. He would be in the garden whenever possible, often lounging in a swing-couch which had been erected there. With Schur, he worked on oral hygiene, nutrition, and mild pain relief such as aspirin, Pyramidon, and the topical application of Orthoform. This did little to alleviate the severe and debilitating pain Freud was increasingly suffering, but he was reluctant to accept morphine or other strong analgesics, believing they would also dull his thinking. The discomfort was increasingly disturbing his normally good sleep. Speaking now took enormous effort.[148] Towards

Image 10.5 Freud walking in the garden at 20 Maresfield Gardens, 1939
Source: © Freud Museum, London

the end of the month Freud suffered from cardiac asthma as a result of left ventricular failure one night. While Schur was able to help him, the treatment inhibited his already failing appetite.

For visitors during these months, their meetings with Freud became final farewells. In August alone, these included Marie Bonaparte, Harry Freud, Ruth Mack Brunswick, Eva Freud (1924–1944), and Dorothy Burlingham amongst others. Having been regularly travelling from France to see Freud in 1939, Bonaparte had brought the Parisian antiquarian Emmanuel Ségrédakis (1890–1948) to see him on 1 August and saw Freud for the last time shortly afterwards. When Alexander's son Harry saw Freud on 12 August before returning to America, he expressed the hope that they would meet again at Christmas. Smiling sadly, Freud replied 'You won't see me here when you return'. Harry departed for New York that same day aboard the SS *Mauretania*.[149] Later in the month, Ruth Mack Brunswick and Dorothy Burlingham said their final goodbyes on 23 and 25 August respectively, before also leaving for New York, Mack Brunswick on the SS *Normandie* and Burlingham on the SS *Nieuw Amsterdam*.[150] Burlingham wanted to be back in New York for the birth of her granddaughter. And Oliver's daughter, Eva Freud, left on 25 August also, after a month-long visit, returning to her parents in France.

As August went on, Freud was increasingly tired, weak, losing weight (presumably a result of cancer cachexia), and tormented with pain. An invalid couch was now set up for him in his study,[151] where he could be close to his collections and see the garden which was then in bloom. He would still read and was engaging in correspondence until the 21st, when he wrote what would be his last letters. The discolouration of his cheek, a result of skin necrosis, became worse. So did the smell, which could not be controlled. It was, Schur realised, a result of necrosis of the bone, which was untreatable at the time. Whatever family and visitors thought of the smell is unrecorded, though some sense of its severity was no doubt being conveyed by the often-repeated story of Freud's much-loved pet chow. When Lün was brought into the room, she no longer ran up to Freud as usual and could not be encouraged to do so, but would instead cower in a distant corner.

In late August or early September, the darkening skin on Freud's cheek became gangrenous and in due course decomposed to such an extent that a perforation was created between the surface skin and the oral cavity. While this hole did allow the easier application of Orthoform, thus reducing Freud's pain, the stench became even worse. With this attracting flies to the wound, mosquito-netting was put around Freud's bed to keep them at bay.

By now Freud, though still reading the newspapers, was increasingly detached from external events in the world. His final entry in the *Kürzeste Chronik*, written towards the end of August, was '*Kriegspanik*' or war panic. He would of course have seen barrage balloons over London on his arrival in June the previous year, as well as the start of efforts to sandbag key buildings and the introduction of other air raid precautions. Now, on 3 September 1939, Britain and France declared war on Germany, following the Nazi invasion of Poland. Air raid sirens sounded in London that same day, though German bombing of the city would not begin for another year. While it was a similar picture for British ground forces (with initial disastrous engagements in Norway in April 1940 and in France a month later), there was no such phoney war at sea. The SS *Athenia*, a transatlantic passenger liner with over 1,400 passengers and crew (including 500 Jewish refugees) aboard, was torpedoed and sunk on the first day of hostilities, resulting in 117 deaths. By the war's end the death toll probably exceeded 50 million, most of whom were civilians. In Maresfield Gardens, Freud's bed was moved to a fictionally 'safer' area, presumably away from the windows. Freud watched with some interest as efforts were made to protect his papers and antiquities. Schur, who reported this, had moved into the house at Maresfield Gardens from his home one mile away at 41 Springfield Road, Marylebone, on 1 September so he might be immediately on-hand when needed. As in the First World War, the by then clearly hollow phrase 'the war to end all wars' (initially coined by Freud's friend H G Wells) was trotted out by the media. When Schur asked Freud what he thought of it, Freud's laconic response was: 'My last war'.[152]

Aside from newspapers, Freud read Balzac's 1831 novel *La Peau de Chagrin* that September. In it, its hero Raphaël makes a Faustian pact to secure his wishes, yet each wish granted shrinks the skin mentioned in the book's title, leading ultimately to a shortening of his life. Desire and death combine in the last chapter when Raphaël is visited by his love Pauline. It was the last book Freud would read and on finishing it on 20 September he told Schur 'This was the proper book for me to read: it deals with shrinking and starvation'.[153]

The following day, 21 September, Freud reminded Schur of the second ground-rule they had agreed a decade previously, namely that Schur should not let him suffer unnecessarily during his terminal care. Indicating to Schur that the time had now come, Freud declared 'Now it's nothing but torture and makes no sense any more'.[154] Freud wanted to bring his life of suffering to an end. Schur informed Anna of her father's decision, as he had asked.

Here, matters become more complicated and contentious. What follows is the received narrative, after which several alternative histories will be discussed. Freud was clearly in severe pain the next morning, Friday 22 September, and it was at this point, perhaps around 8 am, that Schur administered an initial twenty or thirty milligram injection of morphine.[155] Schur's various accounts equivocate between these doses, evidently with anxiety that the larger dose could be construed as a potentially fatal one, thus leaving him open to a serious criminal charge of assisting a patient to die. Schur and many subsequent commentators seem to have believed the thirty-milligram dose would be fatal. Morphine, however, at such concentrations would rarely prove fatal. Where death does occur, it is usually within the first hour at peak dose (with the drug's chemical effects only lasting in the body two-to-four hours on average), and is typically due to respiratory depression.[156] The dose Schur administered allowed Freud to sleep peacefully. Schur apparently gave Freud a second morphine injection some 12 hours later according to his printed account, while his manuscript notes add that he gave a third injection sometime the following day.[157] Freud did not regain consciousness following the initial injection and died close to midnight on Saturday 23 September 1939, with – as was and still is socially customary – most of his immediate family gathered in the house. It was, as many have pointed out, the first day of Yom Kippur, the holiest day in the Jewish calendar, the day of Atonement.

Of those who were apparently present when Freud died, it was only Ernst's wife, Lucie (née Brasch: 1896–1989), who left a detailed and contemporaneous account of the events to which we have access. In a private letter to the architect – and co-designer of Freud's famous desk chair – Felix Augenfeld (1893–1984), she thus described the scene, writing:

> It was only on Friday morning [22 September], when it became imperative for the first time to give him morphine and the doctor told us that he would not regain consciousness again and that he, the doctor, could not allow him to do so, did Annerl [Anna Freud] cry for the first time. Death was a release, not as bitter as the theatre of the closure preceding this hour. All of his children and Robert [Hollitscher, Mathilde's husband] and I and Dr Schur and Dr Stross sat with him from Friday morning until Saturday around midnight. We sent Mama and Aunt upstairs after they fell asleep in their chairs on Friday night. Only Annerl and I didn't lie down at all. He slept for forty hours breathing peacefully. His heart wanted to continue beating. Finally it stopped, just before midnight.
>
> We carried the bed upstairs again and his room with your chair, in which I sat sometimes during the nights, is like it was before. Only terribly empty.[158]

Lucie's helpful timeline of the events suggests Schur administered a morphine injection at about 8 am on Friday 22 September, following which Freud was unconscious for the next 40 hours until he died shortly before midnight on Saturday 23 September. While her account that *all* Freud's children were present is slightly inaccurate (Oliver was still in France at the time), and some likely people in the house as passed over in silence,[159] other key elements can be corroborated.

Ernest Jones made a single entry in his private diary for 23 September: 'Freud died before midnight'.[160] In 1957 he confirmed this time in his biography of Freud.[161] Marie Bonaparte would make a similar diary entry, suggesting the time of death was 11.45 pm.[162] Contemporary newspaper reports of the event, by and large, also corroborate the time of Freud's death and indicate some of those present. The *Weekly Dispatch*, in one of the first British reports published on Sunday 24 September, noted 'Freud . . . died at midnight at his home at Maresfield Gardens, Hampstead, London. His son, Dr Ernst Freud, was at his bedside'.[163] The following day, the *Daily Herald* reported that 'Herr Martin Freud the Professor's elder son, said yesterday [i.e., on Sunday, 24 September] that his father had passed away quietly and peacefully when the clock struck midnight on Saturday. He had fallen into a coma from which he never recovered'.[164] The same paper reported Martin characteristically declaring that his father's 'spirit was unbroken by his illness and even by events which necessitated his migration from his Vienna home at the age of 82. The splendid hospitality which he received in Britain made his last months as peaceful as could be'. That same day, *The Times* published a long obituary, stating Freud died 'on Saturday night', though incorrectly situating the event at 'his son's home in Hampstead',[165] a confusion other press reports shared, arising perhaps due to press awareness of Ernst having redesigned 20 Maresfield Gardens or to Martin and Ernst having seemingly been among those who broke the news of their father's death early on the twenty-fourth. The *Daily Record* noted Freud's 'two sons and two daughters' were present at his bedside when he died.[166] Ernst's presence is further corroborated by Freud's death certificate, which was signed by George Exner and noted the causes of death as pulmonary oedema and carcinoma of right maxilla.[167] Exner was probably called in to formally certify Freud's death as neither Schur nor Stross were able to do so, as they were not on the British Medical Register at this time. He was also of course the surgeon that Pichler had handed Freud's care over to and had thus overseen most of that over the previous 15 months. Ernst registered his father's death on Monday 25 September in Hampstead.

Some later accounts, emerging decades after the event, curiously claim Freud died at 3 am on Saturday 23 September. The first appearance of this time found was in the 1960 German edition of *Briefe 1873–1939*, edited by Ernst Freud, and repeated again in its English translation the following year.[168] It next appeared in Milton Jucovy's 1965 report of Max Schur's lecture 'The problem of death in Freud's writings and life' and was repeated in Schur's posthumous volume *Freud: Living and Dying*, from whence it proliferated without serious check in the Freud literature.[169] This timing does appear to be an error, as (aside from the corroborated 'close to midnight' time previously discussed) had Freud died at 3 am on 23 September news of the event would in all likelihood have been widely disseminated that same day. No such stories emerged in the media and no telegrams or letters of condolence were dated that day. These all began on Sunday 24 September. That day, Virginia Woolf thus noted in her diary 'Freud is dead, the stop press says'.[170] BBC radio carried the story that day, apparently repeating the full details of Freud's life and work on every news broadcast, to the frustration of some listeners.[171] Included in the Corporation's schedule, whether that day or later in the week is unclear, was a five-minute tribute by the Scientific Secretary of the British Psychoanalytical Society, Edward Glover (1888–1972), which was also printed in *The Listener*.[172] The initial story was picked up by overseas radio stations, as well as the national and international press. Many papers carried comments made that Sunday by H G Wells, suggesting Freud was disappointed not to have acquired British citizenship before he died, and by Ernest Jones, who noted the Professor's esteem for England.[173] In the United States and elsewhere many newspapers carried the story on Sunday as part of their front-page news, often using material circulated by the United Press and Associated Press news syndicates.

Rather more lurid claims began to emerge in the 1980s, initially from Detlef Berthelsen's 1987 account of Paula Fichtl's reminiscences of her life in the Freud household. In this controversial and at times clearly erroneous memoir, Berthelsen claims Schur left Maresfield Gardens on 23 September, while Freud was still alive, and Stross took over the medical supervision of Freud in his last few hours, including being ready to give a further morphine injection if needed.[174] Berthelsen, however, did not state that Stross actually administered this. Michael Molnar later reported Stross saying that she had delivered the final injection to Freud before he died and that Schur had indeed left the house while Freud was still breathing. Stross made her remarks as a very elderly woman at a social event at the Freud Museum in London, sometime in the late 1980s or early 1990s. Molnar's own perspicacious account, written two decades or more after Stross's comments, contextualises these with reference to both her demonstrably failing and indeed confabulating memory and a politics of possession with respect to Freud and his historical legacy.[175] Both of these accounts, in combination, have been the subject of some discussion, by amongst others Roy Lacoursiere in 2008 and Dany Nobus in 2015 and subsequently.[176] While both the Fichtl and Stross claims are epistemically problematic, particularly in the light of the lengthy passage of time between Freud's death and the emergence of the claims, and the known errors and confabulations in both accounts, this in itself is insufficient to discount them.

The publication of the *Freud Diarium* brings further twists to this story, with the claims that Schur did leave on 23 September, that when Freud became restless during the afternoon, Anna told Stross about the pact her father had with Schur, and that Stross subsequently administered a further injection to Freud. This final injection supposedly consisted of 300 milligrams of morphine, following which Freud slipped into a coma and died shortly before midnight.[177] The source for this entry in the *Diarium* remains anonymous at the present time, though it may be the subject of a future publication by another scholar.[178] Tantalisingly, we must await that event before further evaluation of what happened in the hours leading up to Freud's death on 23 September 1939. The present evidence suggests that Freud may well have died a natural death, made more comfortable by Schur (and possibly Stross) with the morphine injections, whether these were twenty or thirty milligrams or possibly more. Should further evidence be forthcoming clearly documenting a final far higher dose being administered intravenously by Stross, with death following in the subsequent hour or so, then an interpretation of this as physician assisted suicide or euthanasia would have more plausibility.

Three days after Freud's death, on the morning of 26 September, mourners gathered at Golders Green Crematorium to bid a private farewell to the Professor. In line with the new wartime regulations, everyone carried a gas mask. One newspaper estimated there were 150 people present, though Joseph Leftwich later recalled there were 'only a handful of people there', some having come long distances, including Stefan Zweig and Abraham Yahuda who had travelled from Bath.[179] Who precisely was there was not recorded, though Freud's immediate family were the chief mourners. Minna remained too ill to attend.[180] And Ernst's son Lucian did not go. Whether any of the Manchester Freuds managed to get to the funeral is unknown, though a wreath of roses and carnations did come from Sam, Bertha, and Pauline and a further arrangement of dahlias came from Poppy.[181] Flowers also came from Ernest and Katherine Jones, Schur and his wife Helene, Stross, the Lampls, Sophie Ritholz, Sylvia Payne, Barbara Low, and fifteen others. Freud had expressed a wish two decades previously to be cremated, should it prove an easier and cheaper option than a conventional burial.[182] It also followed the precedent set by his older brother 25 years before. In his will from 1919, Freud had wanted a very inexpensive simple service, without eulogies, and with any announcement to be after the event.[183] Here, 20 years later, Freud would not quite get his way. Ernst had asked Harrods to arrange the funeral, which was a private non-religious cremation. Orations were given in English by Ernest Jones and in German by Stefan Zweig and Peter Neumann, the latter representing the Committee of Austrians in England.[184] It was Jones's English text that the domestic press predominantly took up, with his acknowledgement of the support Britain gave Freud and Freud's esteem for the country being trumpeted.[185]

Freud's ashes were later deposited in an antique South Italian bell krater, which was placed in what became known as Freud Corner in the columbarium at Golders Green Crematorium.[186] The krater, from the fourth century BCE, which is decorated with Dionysian scenes, was previously a part of Freud's own collection, having been gifted to him by Marie Bonaparte in 1931. Martha's ashes would be added to those of Freud following her death on 2 November 1951.

Image 10.6 Freud's funerary urn in the columbarium at Golders Green Crematorium

Source: Dadamax

The Austrian Centre subsequently organised a memorial meeting in the Queen Mary Hall at the YWCA in Great Russell Street, Bloomsbury. Beginning at 4 pm on Thursday 12 October 1939, some 500 people including the former Austrian ambassador to Britain Sir George Franckenstein (1878–1953), Ernst Kris (1900–1957), and H G Wells, along with 'eminent psychologists and authors', gathered to remember Freud. Stefan Zweig had also been scheduled to speak but being under travel restrictions as an enemy alien sent his apologies, claiming 'illness'.[187] Half a dozen quiet speeches, some in German, some in English, were given, with a string quartet playing a short Beethoven adagio during a mid-point interlude.[188]

In his will, Freud made provision for Martha, Minna, his children and grandchildren, the gross value of his personal estate amounting to £22,850 and £15,979 net when probate was granted on 1 December.[189] As of 2023, the net value would equate to £864,231 today. With the proceeds from his literary copyrights bequeathed to his grandchildren, Minna was left an annuity of £300, with the residuary estate being left in trust for Martha and after her death in equal shares to their children, with Sophie's son Ernst to receive her share. The only specific bequests Freud made related to his much-loved collection of antiquities and psychological and psychoanalytic books. These went to Anna. The immediate cash value of the residuary estate given these various demands on it was relatively modest. The copyrights by contrast would prove valuable over the decades ahead and with control of them distributed among the grandchildren, it would make future negotiations (for example in developing the *Standard Edition* and the publication of Freud's correspondence) a sometimes-thorny issue amid competing priorities.[190]

In the immediate aftermath of Freud's death and funeral, the family, friends, and colleagues turned in their own ways to other matters, to cope and to live. Martha had adjusted well to life in Britain, but widowhood was a profound existential experience. She expressed something of this to Paul Federn (and others) in November when she wrote:

> I cannot even complain, for I have been granted more than a lifetime in which I have been allowed to look after him, to shield him from the troubles of everyday life. That my life had now lost sense and content is only natural'.[191]

Like her older sister, Minna was grief stricken at Freud's death. Her health continued to be poor and less than a year-and-a-half later, on 12 February 1941, she died as a result of coronary disease in the Hospital of St John & St Elizabeth, in St John's Wood. Like Philipp, Minna was an exception in the family having maintained her filiation with Judaism. She was buried in Hoop Lane Jewish Cemetery on 16 February. Today, the text on the matzevah marking her grave is so weathered as to be virtually illegible. Her estate would amount to just £193.[192]

Martin's first novel, *Parole d'Honneur*, had been published by Gollancz in September before Freud died and its first – mostly favourable – press reviews began to appear from 25 September. Drawing heavily on his own life, the novel followed the adventures of Baron Neustätten, an Austrian artillery officer, on the Austro-Italian front, romantic interludes, experiences as a prisoner-of-war, and later traumatic memories of the war and hints of anti-Semitism.[193] One episode in the book sees the 'common soldiers of the enemy army, little clerks and shopkeepers from Blackpool, Southport, and Preston' respond generously to the Baron's singing 'It's a long way to Tipperary' while a prisoner,[194] a passage no doubt influenced by the family shadows of Emanuel and Sam. Martin also appeared in the press, the day after Freud's funeral, due to his attempts to form an Austrian Legion to fight against Hitler.[195] Despite his clear *bona fides*, he was subsequently interned from 21 June 1940 until 17 September that year in Huyton Internment Camp, near Liverpool, as an enemy alien. On his release he joined the Pioneer Corps and would post-war run a tobacconist's shop at 12 Great Russell Street in Bloomsbury.[196] Ernst would continue his practice as an architect, though with the onset of war his business dwindled and he economised by sub-letting his house and moving with his wife temporarily into a flat at 2 Maresfield Gardens. For her part, Anna, accompanied by Paula Fichtl, went to stay with her long-time friend Loe Kann Jones (1882–1944) for a few days in Jones's country house in Hambledon, Surrey.[197] She would soon go on to make a distinguished contribution running the Hampstead War Nurseries and then in child analysis. Fichtl also would be interned as an enemy alien on the Isle of Man from the end of May 1940 to 25 March 1941, after which she continued working for Anna for many years in Maresfield Gardens.[198]

Alexander, having wanted to settle in London close to Freud when he was alive, now applied and was granted permission in August 1940 to emigrate to Canada with his wife Sophie (née Schreiber: 1878–1970) and her widowed older sister Jennie Anspach (née Schreiber: 1875-*aft*.1940). While it has been suggested he was something of an Anglophobe (based apparently on his criticism of English politics on the eve of the First World War),[199] the decision to emigrate was probably more connected with a desire to be closer to Harry, who had settled in New York in December 1938 and had applied for naturalisation. Indeed, Lucian suggested Alexander had attempted to get a visa for the USA.[200] As part of Alexander's application to settle in Canada, he had transferred $40,000 there, which he proposed to draw on to fund his family's retirement. They embarked on 17 September 1940 for the risky Atlantic crossing (with 57 ships being sunk that month alone by U-boats) and settled in Toronto, where Alexander would die in April 1943. How exactly Alexander had raised the funds for the move to Canada and indeed his earlier purchase of 4 Maresfield Gardens is unclear; it certainly seems dissonant with earlier reports about having lost all his money to the Nazis. Perhaps those reports reflected a strategy of under-reporting his assets to limit the depredations faced in escaping Austria. When he died, aside from his Canadian assets, Alexander left a further £2,250 in England alone.[201]

Max Schur, his wife Helene (1909–1998), and their two young children Peter (1933–) and Eva (1935–), sailed from Southampton for New York aboard the SS *President Harding* on 7 October 1939 to begin the next chapter of their lives there.[202] Josefine Stross went on to secure her British medical qualifications (the Scottish conjoint diplomas), enabling her to join the Medical Register on 5 February 1940. She subsequently had a distinguished career as a paediatrician as well as contributing to the Hampstead War Nurseries and later the Hampstead Child Therapy Course, from which she retired in July 1983. She also worked as personal physician to Anna Freud and Dorothy Burlingham.

Of Freud's sisters, the four who had remained in Vienna would die at the hands of the Nazis. Having lived in increasingly cramped and squalid conditions in the city, they scraped by with the help of a little money Harry sent for their support from the United States. Communication stopped however when that country entered the war. In 1942 the sisters were transported to the Theresienstadt camp-ghetto in Czechoslovakia. There are conflicting accounts of their subsequent movements, though not of their fates. Most suggest that Mitzi, Pauli, and Rosa were moved on from Theresienstadt to Treblinka, in Poland, on 23 September 1942, where all three were apparently murdered in the gas chambers shortly after their arrival. Others indicate Mitzi and Pauli died in the camp at Maly Trostinets, near Minsk. Sources agree that Dolfi was left in Theresienstadt, where she died from malnutrition on or about 29 September 1942.[203]

Reflections

Having long contemplated living in Britain, Freud was 82 years old and dying by the time he began that imagined life in London. On arrival there, Freud's youthful dreams of success – strengthened through his 1875 and 1908 visits to Lancashire and London – were in some respects realised, as evident in the enthusiastic popular reception he received and the flow of people wanting to see him. Vienna however did not relinquish its hold on Freud easily. Ambivalently attached to that familiar city, he only left in the end as a refugee, and then seemingly more out of concern for his children and grandchildren when the Nazis became a clear and present danger. Mourning in such circumstances for that which had been surrendered was difficult, a process made even more so by the continuing emotional ties to family and friends who were left behind. In this context, it was hardly surprising that Freud's London homes became reflections of Berggasse for him and the family.

Unlike Emanuel, John, and Sam, Freud did not become an assimilated Englishman. His age and time were against such a transformation. Citizenship too eluded him, though H G Wells and others were keen to claim this for him. Ernest Jones similarly sought to appropriate Freud to the British Psychoanalytical Society and the domestic psychoanalytic scene, yet Freud was too unwell to personally attend any Society events. He did however send them his good wishes, was a member, and eschewed re-constituting the WPV in London as a quasi-government in exile (in line with its members vote to do so wherever Freud may settle), thus assimilating to the domestic authority structure of his British hosts. His presence in London nevertheless decisively changed the psychoanalytic centre of gravity from continental Europe to Britain, a shift given further flesh by the influx of other psychoanalytic refugees into the country from Vienna and elsewhere in Europe. The United

States too benefitted very significantly, taking in far greater numbers of refugee psychoanalysts than Britain, with both more radical and distinguished members of the movement settling there.[204] But Freud and Anna settling in London was a real trump card (at least for a while) for British psychoanalysis vis-à-vis its status in relation to its IPA sister societies.

For Freud, his escape from the straitjacket that was Nazi Vienna released a final burst of creativity for him while in Britain. This flowering, particularly during his first few months in London, saw Freud complete *Moses and Monotheism* and draft two other notable pieces, *An Outline of Psycho-Analysis* and 'Some elementary lessons in psycho-analysis'. The peak of this period came to an end in September 1938 with Freud's surgery, from which he made a slow and partial recovery. While able to proofread and edit *Moses* during the final few months of 1938, Freud's writing the following year was restricted to letters – of which he would manage to write 306 – by a painful resurgence of the cancer which he had battled for so long. The scene of Freud's peak literary creativity in London was thus 39 Elsworthy Road, which was also the location of several other iconic events, including his reception of the delegation from the Royal Society, and the initial influx of visitors including Malinowski, Chaim Weizmann, Prince Hubertus, H G Wells, Klein, Stefan Zweig, and Dalí. These events have at times been erroneously transposed in the popular imagination to 20 Maresfield Gardens.

Analysands still came throughout the first seven months of 1939, when it must have been clear to them all that Freud was dying. How much Freud took up this reality with them in sessions is unknown, though he certainly mentioned his surgery to Smiley Blanton. Aware of the limited therapeutic benefits of at least some of his earlier analyses, Freud can hardly have thought these final sessions were ideal. Yet the allure of Freud as a psychoanalytic object was clearly a potent force, totemic in nature, one that was not easy to relinquish. More superficially, proximity to Freud could carry a certain value, as though that in itself were enough to render one a member of the chosen. Some might now say Freud should have ceased his clinical practice sooner than he actually did. Perhaps that is so, but his analysands during this late period were competent adults who were themselves often working professionally in the field. And Freud had no one in his orbit to tell him that it was time to stop.

Other visitors also came and went, their motivations mixed: for some Freud was perhaps a mentor, a celebrity, a charismatic transferential figure, a guru, an inspiring genius, a wise man, a dangerous apostate. For many, he was a gentle and much-loved figure. He was a dying aged man also, realistic about his dwindling prospects, and living as much as he could until the end. This quality deeply impressed Max Schur and others, who often regarded it as indicative of the greatness of his character. It was perhaps this model or imago that influenced another British psychoanalyst, Donald Winnicott (1896–1971), years later to contemplate his own death with the prayer: 'Oh God! May I be alive when I die'.[205]

The exact circumstances of Freud's death have attracted some interest and controversy in scholarly and cultural circles. Despite claims to the contrary, it seems clear that Freud died shortly before midnight on 23 September 1939 surrounded by the majority of his family. His final two days were eased with morphine administered by Max Schur and possibly supplemented by Josefine Stross. The currently available sources do not support a chronology consistent with Freud's death being a result of morphine induced respiratory depression. Instead, his death appears to have been a far more prosaic affair, the direct result of his cancer and heart condition.

Notes

1 The British Home Office was initially hesitant about granting Ernst a visa, particularly in the light of the poor economic conditions: see TNA ref: HO 382/194. For a full discussion of Ernst's career as an architect, see Volker M Welter *Ernst L Freud, Architect: The Case of the Modern Bourgeois Home*, New York: Berghahn Books, 2012.
2 For studies of these events see Ludger M Hermanns 'The history of psychanalysis in Germany up to 1950 and its relationship to the IPA', in Peter Loewenberg & Nellie L Thompson (eds) *100 Years of the IPA*, London: IPA/Karnac, 2011, pp. 47–61; Stephen Frosh 'Psychoanalysis, Nazism and "Jewish science"', *IJPA*, 2003, 84, pp. 1315–1332; and Brecht *et al* (eds) *'Here Life. Goes on in a Most Peculiar Way . . .': Psychoanalysis before and after 1933*, Hamburg: Kellner Verlag, 1985.
3 Karen Brecht (see previous note) notes that at the end of this process, 'of the 102 analysts and candidates in Vienna, only two were left' (p. 144).
4 For further discussion of this period of Freud's life see Pater Gay *Freud: A Life for Our Time*, London: Max, 2006, pp. 611–629 and David Cohen *The Escape of Sigmund Freud*, New York: Overlook Press, 2009.
5 Martin Freud *Glory Reflected*, London: Angus & Robertson, 1957, pp. 206–211; *Life & Work*, 3, pp. 233–234; Mark Edmundson *The Death of Sigmund Freud: Fascism, Psychoanalysis and the Rise of Fundamentalism*, London: Bloomsbury, 2007, pp. 57–72.
6 TNA ref: FO 371/22321/2890; Mack later served as the post-war Ambassador to Austria, while Taylor, who had served as a Captain in the Gordon Highlanders in the Great War, became the British Ambassador to Mexico 1950–1954; see also Timothy Schmalz *Anglo-Austrian Diplomatic Backchannels from the Juliputsch to the Anschluss, 1934–38*, PhD thesis, University of Cambridge, 2021.
7 C Tögel *Freud Diarium*, Giessen: Psychosozial-Verlag, 2023, p. 1037; Sophie Ritholz manuscript, Sigmund Freud Archives, 5 April 1956, LoC ref: mss39990, box 125, ff.9.
8 This controversial work would eventually appear as Sigmund Freud & William C Bullitt *Thomas Woodrow Wilson: A Psychological Study*, London: Weidenfeld & Nicholson, 1967; see also James L Franklin 'Wilson on the couch: How Sigmund Freud and William C Bullitt, an American diplomat, came to analyze the American president', 2022, available online at: https://hekint.org/2022/12/27/.
9 The Chinese jade screen and the Roman figure of the Greek goddess Athena are illustrated in Julia Hoffbrand *Leaving Today: The Freuds in Exile 1938*, London: Freud Museum, 2018, p. 53.
10 Martin Freud *Glory Reflected*, London: Angus & Robertson, 1957, p. 214; Sophie Ritholz manuscript made for the Sigmund Freud Archives, 5 April 1956, LoC ref: mss39990, box 125, f. 12.
11 Richard M Sterba *Reminiscences of a Viennese Psychoanalyst*, Detroit: Wayne State University Press, 1982, pp. 159–160.
12 S Freud *Moses and Monotheism*, *SE*, 1939, 23, p. 115.
13 Anna Freud to Max Eitingon, 13 March 1938, *Freud-Eitingon*, p. 902.
14 *Life & Work*, 1, p. 323, and 3, pp. 234–235; for indications of Freud's lingering personal reluctance to emigrate see also Freud to Arnold Zweig, 21 March 1938, *Freud-Zweig*, p. 158 and Freud to E Jones, 13 May 1938, *Freud-Jones*, p. 764.

15 Martin Freud *Glory Reflected*, London: Angus & Robertson, 1957, pp. 211–213; M Molnar (ed) *The Diary of Sigmund Freud 1929–1939: A Record of the Final Decade*, London: Hogarth, 1992, p. 232; C Tögel *Freud Diarium*, Giessen: Psychosozial-Verlag, 2023, pp. 1039–1040; and Max Schur *Freud: Living and Dying*, London: Hogarth Press, 1972, p. 498.
16 *Life & Work*, 3, p. 237.
17 Hans Pichler, 15 March 1938 and 22 March 1938, LoC mss39990, box 38.
18 Martin Freud *Glory Reflected*, London: Angus & Robertson, 1957, p. 215; see also Max Schur *Freud: Living and Dying*, London: Hogarth Press, 1972, p. 497.
19 For more recent detailed accounts of Sauerwald see David Cohen *The Escape of Sigmund Freud*, New York: Overlook Press, 2012, *passim* but especially pp. 164–194 and Mark Edmundson *The Death of Sigmund Freud: Fascism, Psychoanalysis and the Rise of Fundamentalism*, London: Bloomsbury, 2007, *passim*.
20 These were the equivalent of €178,000 and €44,500 in 2020 respectively. This and related documents are reproduced in Julia Hoffbrand *Leaving Today: The Freuds in Exile 1938*, London: Freud Museum, 2018, pp. 44–49.
21 A recently surfaced photograph of the house, showing porters carrying in a large trunk, includes a William Willett estate agent's 'For sale' sign outside the house, indicating further perhaps why it was available as a short-term let. However, whether the photograph was taken on the Freuds arrival in June or later in August 1938 when their main possessions arrived from Vienna is unclear. See Swann Auction Galleries, sale 2634, 27 April 2023, lot 84, available online at: http://tinyurl.com/msvz8raw.
22 Edmund Engelman *Sigmund Freud Berggasse 19, Vienna*, Vienna: Verlag Christian Brandstätter, 1998, p. 100; Engelman apparently began making the photographic record on 24 May 1938, see C Tögel *Freud Diarium*, Giessen: Psychosozial-Verlag, 2023, p. 1045. While Engelman suggested the portraits might be suitable passport photos, the Freuds had received their passports on 12 May. Martha later used this photograph on her British Alien's Registration Certificate, see Julia Hoffbrand *Leaving Today: The Freuds in Exile 1938*, London: Freud Museum, 2018, p. 81.
23 Freud to Max Eitingon, 7 June 1938, *Freud-Eitingon*, p. 901; *Life & Work*, 3, p. 241.
24 *Daily Express*, 6 June 1938, p. 1.
25 Ernst Waldinger 'Aus Freuds letzten Lebensjahren', *Aufbau*, 25 May 1956, p. 22; Waldinger terms it a '*Krankensessel*' or hospital chair.
26 Charles Strozier '1 Glimpses of a Life: Heinz Kohut (1913–1981)', *Progress in Self-Psychology*, 1985, 1, p. 6; Freud's use of a wheelchair at the Westbahnhof was also noted in Helen W Puner's sometimes derided *Freud: His Life and his Mind*, New York: Dell, 1959, p. 272.
27 Freud to Martha Freud, 9 June 1896, LoC ref: mss39990, box 9.
28 Freud's earlier angina pectoris symptoms in February 1926 resulted in a rest cure and seems to have drawn a line under subsequent significant walking. See Felix Deutsch 'Reflections on Freud's one hundredth birthday', 1956, in Hendrik M Ruitenbeek (ed) *Freud as We Knew Him*, Detroit: Wayne State University Press, 1973, p. 301 and Max Schur *Freud: Living and Dying*, London: Hogarth Press, 1972, p. 390.
29 Roy R Grinker 'Reminiscences of a personal contact with Freud', 1940, in Hendrik M Ruitenbeek (ed) *Freud as we Knew Him*, Detroit: Wayne State University Press, 1973, p. 181.
30 Freud to Arnold Zweig, 25 October 1933, *Freud-Zweig*, p. 54.
31 *Life & Work*, 3, p. 202; between 1934 and 1937 Freud and his family spent their summers in Grinzing (Vienna 19), at Strassergasse 47.
32 Hanns Sachs *Freud: Master and Friend*, London: Imago Publishing Company, 1945, p. 171.
33 *Yorkshire Post and Leeds Intelligencer*, 6 June 1938, p. 8; see also *Daily Express*, 6 June 1938, pp. 1–2.

34 *Leicester Daily Mercury*, 4 June 1938, p. 9.
35 See the *Illustrated London News*, 11 June 1938, p. 28, for a picture of Freud here with Marie Bonaparte and William Bullitt.
36 Freud to Max Eitingon, 7 June 1938, *Freud-Eitingon*, p. 902.
37 *Daily News* (London), 6 June 1938, p. 1.
38 Freud to Max Eitingon, 7 June 1938, *Freud-Eitingon*, p. 901.
39 *Die Sonderfahndungsliste GB [Gestapo Invasion Arrest List]*, 1940, p. 62.
40 For a discussion of British government policy towards Jewish refugees during this period, see: Louise London *Whitehall and the Jews, 1933–1948: British Immigration Policy, Jewish Refugees and the Holocaust*, Cambridge: Cambridge University Press, 2001.
41 *Daily Herald* (London), 6 June 1938., p. 1; *Halifax Evening Courier*, 6 June 1938, p. 2.
42 *Evening Standard* (London), 6 June 1938, p. 3.
43 While Jones had already secured Anna's right to work, she wrote to the British Home Secretary on 6 June about their arrival, and the Home Office confirmed on 8 June that 'The Home Secretary is very glad to accord to Professor Freud and his collaborators permission to work in this country in accordance with the arrangements which have already been made with Dr Ernest Jones' (reproduced in Julia Hoffbrand *Leaving Today: The Freuds in Exile 1938*, London: Freud Museum, 2018, p. 50). Ernst's naturalisation, supported by Marie Bonaparte, Ernest Jones, John Rickman, and others, was granted on 30 August 1939 and he swore his oath of allegiance on 4 September 1939, see TNA ref: HO 334/228/1216 and HO 382/194.
44 *Daily Sketch* (London), 7 June 1938.
45 *Manchester Daily Dispatch*, 7 June 1938; *Manchester Daily Express*, 7 June 1938; *Daily Herald*, 7 June 1938, p. 7; *Daily Express*, 7 June 1938, p. 9.
46 Freud to Jeanne Lampl-de Groot, 13 June 1938, *Freud-Lampl-de Groot*, p. 92.
47 Freud to Max Eitingon, 7 June 1938, *Freud-Eitingon*, p. 902.
48 Ibid., p. 903.
49 Similarly, writing to Lampl-de Groot, Freud confided that: 'Naturally everything is still unaccustomed and as if unreal, a clear sense of alienation' (Freud to Jeanne Lampl-de Groot, 13 June 1938, *Freud-Lampl-de Groot*, p. 92).
50 Freud to Arnold Zweig, 28 June 1938, *Freud-Zweig*, p. 163; Freud to Hermann and Mrs Nunberg, 24 June 1938, Swann Auction Galleries, 3 April 2003, lot 49; Freud to Josephine A Jackson, 18 July 1938, Swann Auction Galleries, 25 September 2008, lot 74; Martha Freud to Freud's sisters, 22 June 1938, LoC ref: mss39990, box 13; also quoted in R W Clark *Freud: The Man and the Cause*, London: Jonathan Cape and Weidenfeld & Nicholson, 1980, p. 515. Later, on 30 August 1938 Freud told Smiley Blanton that he was getting letters on a daily basis from Jewish friends in Austria asking for assistance, yet 'we are quite helpless to do anything for them' (S Blanton *Diary of My Analysis with Sigmund Freud*, New York: Hawthorn Books, 1971, p. 102).
51 *Reynolds's Newspaper*, 12 June 1938, p. 11.
52 Freud to Alexander Freud, 22 June 1938, *Freud Letters*, p. 443.
53 For a late example of this see Freud to A A Brill, 26 January 1930 (LoC ref: mss39990, box 20, folder 12), where he remarks that he is suffering from the by-products of fame including requests for photos and autographs.
54 S Freud *Moses and Monotheism, SE*, 1939, 23, p. 57.
55 Ibid., p. 58.
56 Joseph Leftwich in interview with K R Eissler, 10 July 1956, LoC mss39990, box 118.
57 Freud to Arnold Zweig, 28 June 1938, *Freud-Zweig*, p. 163.
58 A little discussed figure in the history of psychoanalysis, for a brief biographical account of Katherine Jones see D Joyce Jackson 'Contributions to the history of psychology XXXVII: Katherine Jones (1892–1983)', *Psychological Reports*, 1985, 57, pp. 75–83.

59 Melanie Klein in interview with Kurt Eissler, 28 July 1953, LoC ref: mss39990, box 117; Phyllis Grosskurth, having been unable to access many of the then closed Freud papers in the Library of Congress, mistakenly assumed no meeting took place, thus adding to a more polarised view of the Freud-Klein controversies (see her *Melanie Klein: Her World and her Work*, London: Hodder & Stoughton, 1985, p. 241).
60 Stefan Zweig *The World of Yesterday: An Autobiography*, London: Cassell & Co, 1943, p. 318.
61 For further discussion of this encounter see: Salvador Dalí *The Secret Life of Salvador Dalí*, New York: Dial Press, 1942, p. 24 and Sharon Romm & Joseph W Slap 'Sigmund Freud and Salvador Dali: Personal moments', *American Imago*, 1983, 40, 4, pp. 337–347.
62 Salvador Dalí *The Secret Life of Salvador Dalí*, New York: Dial Press, 1942, p. 23.
63 Freud to Stefan Zweig, 20 July 1938, in *Life & Work*, 3, p. 251; *Freud Letters*, p. 445.
64 Salvador Dalí *The Secret Life of Salvador Dalí*, New York: Dial Press, 1942, p. 25.
65 Ibid., p. 397.
66 Stefan Zweig *The World of Yesterday: An Autobiography*, London: Cassell & Co, 1943, p. 318.
67 For reviews of Freud's cancer and its treatment see: *Life & Work*, 3, pp. 497–521; Max Schur *Freud: Living and Dying*, London: Hogarth Press, 1972; Sharon Romm *The Unwelcome Intruder: Freud's Struggle with Cancer*, New York: Praeger, 1983; Nicholas Lazaridis 'Sigmund Freud's oral cancer', *British Journal of Oral and Maxillofacial Surgery*, 2003, 41, pp. 78–83; Roy Lacoursiere 'Freud's death: Historical truth and biographical fictions', *American Imago*, 2008, 65, 1, pp. 107–128; and James L Franklin 'My dear neoplasm: Sigmund Freud's oral cancer', *Hektoen International*, 2022, available online at: https://hekint.org/2022/10/28/my-dear-neoplasm-sigmund-freuds-oral-cancer.
68 Max Schur *Freud: Living and Dying*, London: Hogarth Press, 1972, p. 408.
69 The draft will was sold by Christie's, London, in their 20th century books and manuscripts auction, 2 December 2004, lot 106; National Probate Register, 1939, p. 490.
70 Ilse Grubrich-Simitis *Back to Freud's Texts: Making Silent Documents Speak*, New Haven: Yale University Press, 1996, pp. 217–226.
71 Hanns Sachs *Freud: Master and Friend*, London: Imago Publishing Company, 1945, pp. 180–181; S Freud to Hanns Sachs, 11 July 1938, LoC ref: mss39990, box 40.
72 Rémy Amouroux 'A serious venture: John Rodker (1894–1955) and the Imago Publishing Company (1939–60)', *IJPA*, 2011, 92, pp. 1437–1454; M Bonaparte 'John Rodker 1894–1955', *IJPA*, 1956, 37, pp. 199–201.
73 Freud to Ludwig Binswanger, 19 July 1938, in *Freud-Binswanger*, p. 215.
74 Davidowa and her co-defendants were fined £200 plus costs on conviction. See the *Bayswater Chronicle*, 2 February 1945, p. 4.
75 Smiley Blanton *Diary of My Analysis with Sigmund Freud*, New York: Hawthorn Books, 1971, p. 107.
76 Ilse Grubrich-Simitis *Back to Freud's Texts: Making Silent Documents Speak*, New Haven: Yale University Press, 1996, p. 219.
77 Smiley Blanton *Diary of My Analysis with Sigmund Freud*, New York: Hawthorn Books, 1971, p. 113.
78 Max Schur *Freud: Living and Dying*, London: Hogarth Press, 1972, p. 509.
79 *Western Morning Press*, 9 September 1938, p. 7; *Edinburgh Evening News*, 9 September 1938, p. 4.
80 Neil Cumming, the grand-nephew of David S Duncan, personal communication, 10 December 2023; M Molnar (ed) *The Diary of Sigmund Freud 1929–1939: A Record of the Final Decade*, London: Hogarth, 1992, p. 244.
81 Andrew Nagorski *Saving Freud: A Life in Vienna and an Escape to Freedom*, London: Icon Books, 2022, p. 263; Anna Freud purchased the freehold on 16 April 1943 (see

TNA ref: HO 405/13317). Adrian Stephen would gossip at the time that the house was a gift to Freud from Marie Bonaparte (Anne O Bell *The Diary of Virginia Woolf, Volume 5: 1936–41*, Harmondsworth: Penguin, 1985, p. 202).
82 Volker M Welter *Ernst L Freud, Architect: The Case of the Modern Bourgeois Home*, New York: Berghahn Books, 2012, pp. 150–154.
83 Volker M Welter *Ernst L Freud, Architect: The Case of the Modern Bourgeois Home*, New York: Berghahn Books, 2012, pp. 133 and 139.
84 William Feaver *The Lives of Lucian Freud: Youth 1922–1968*, London: Bloomsbury, 2022, p. 59.
85 Volker M Welter *Ernst L Freud, Architect: The Case of the Modern Bourgeois Home*, New York: Berghahn Books, 2012, p. 139; 1939 Register, TNA ref: RG 101/2510b.
86 *Liverpool Echo*, 20 September 1938, p. 6; M Molnar (ed) *The Diary of Sigmund Freud 1929–1939: A Record of the Final Decade*, London: Hogarth, 1992, p. 51.
87 *Jewish Chronicle*, 6 January 1939.
88 Volker M Welter *Ernst L Freud, Architect: The Case of the Modern Bourgeois Home*, New York: Berghahn Books, 2012, pp. 139–160.
89 *Daily News*, 27 September 1938, p. 3.
90 Freud to Jeanne Lampl-De Groot, 8 October 1938, *Freud-Lampl-de Groot*, p. 95; for a later view see Freud to Max Eitingon, 3 November 1938, *Freud-Eitingon*, p. 907.
91 *Life & Work*, 3, p. 247.
92 Freud to Jeanne Lampl-De Groot, 8 October 1938, *Freud-Lampl-de Groot*, pp. 95–96.
93 Ilse Grubrich-Simitis *Back to Freud's Texts: Making Silent Documents Speak*, New Haven: Yale University Press, 1996, p. 228.
94 Freud 'Ein Wort zum Antisemitismus/A comment on anti-Semitism', *Die Zukunft*, 25 November 1938 (*SE*, 23, pp. 287–293) and 'Anti-Semitism in England', *Time and Tide*, 26 November 1938, p. 1649 (*SE*, 23, p. 301).
95 Marion B Richmond 'The lost source in Freud's "Comment on anti-Semitism": Mark Twain', *JAPA*, 1980, 28, pp. 563–578.
96 Freud to Max Eitingon, 19 December 1938, *Freud-Eitingon*, p. 913.
97 Freud to Marie Bonaparte, 12 November 1938, *Freud Letters*, p. 451.
98 Ilse Grubrich-Simitis *Back to Freud's Texts: Making Silent Documents Speak*, New Haven: Yale University Press, 1996, pp. 191–203 and *passim*.
99 Leonard Woolf to Ernest Jones, 27 July 1938, UOR SC ref: CW 530/6/1.
100 See for example Sylvia Payne to Leonard Woolf, 28 June 38 and Ernest Jones to Leonard Woolf, 18 July 38, UOR SC ref: CW 530/6/1.
101 'Notes of interview with Mrs Knopf, RW Postgate, and Martin Freud re Freud: *Moses* on 19/8/38', UOR SC ref: CW 530/6.
102 Blanche Knopf to Leonard Woolf, 11 October 1938, UOR SC ref: CW 530/6.
103 Ernest Jones to Leonard Woolf, 20 October 1938, UOR SC ref: CW 530/6.
104 James Strachey 'Notes upon Freud's "*Moses*"', 6 November 1938, UOR SC ref: CW 530/6.
105 Ernest Jones to Leonard Woolf, 9 November 1938, UOR SC ref: CW 530/6.
106 Blanche Knopf to Leonard Woolf, 11 November 1938 and 'Notes regarding suggested changes in Dr Freud's manuscript', 11 November 1938, UOR SC ref: CW 530/6.
107 Ernest Jones to Blanche Knopf, 22 November 1938, UOR SC ref: CW 530/6.
108 Freud to Ernest Jones, 1 November 1938, *Freud-Jones*, p. 764; see also Max Schur *Freud: Living and Dying*, London: Hogarth Press, 1972, pp. 511–512 for an alternative translation.
109 Freud to Max Eitingon, 3 November 1938, *Freud-Eitingon*, p. 908.
110 S Freud to Hanns Sachs, 12–14 March 1939, LoC ref: mss39990, box 40; '*Der Mann Moses und die monotheistische Religion*: List of persons sent copies, undated', LoC mss39990, box 49; see also Max Schur *Freud: Living and Dying*, London: Hogarth Press, 1972, pp. 521–522.

111 S Freud to Marie Bonaparte, 16 June 1939, quoted in Max Schur *Freud: Living and Dying*, London: Hogarth Press, 1972, p. 524.
112 Blanche Knopf to Norah Nicholls, 27 March 1939, UOR SC ref: CW 530/6.
113 Leonard Woolf to Sigmund Freud, 15 March 1939, March 1939, UOR SC ref: CW 530/6.
114 Hogarth Press to Ellis Roberts, 23 May 1939 and Blanche Knopf to Sigmund Freud, 26 May 1939, UOR SC ref: CW 530/6.
115 'Freud: *Moses*', 10 February 1939, and Hogarth Press to Lowe & Brydone Ltd, 15 April 1940, UOR SC ref: CW 530/6/1.
116 *Daily News* (London), 7 December 1938, p. 3; *Daily Herald*, 7 December 1938, p. 20.
117 For Freud's script see LoC ref: mss39990, box OV 11; reel 5; the line in German was 'Im Alter von zweiundachtzig Jahren verließ ich als Folge der deutschen Invasion mein Heim in Wien und kam nach England, wo ich mein Leben in Freiheit zu enden hoffe' ('At the age of eighty-two, as a result of the German invasion, I left my home in Vienna and came to England, where I hope to end my life in freedom').
118 See H L Fletcher to Anna Freud, 16 November 1938, H L Fletcher to Sigmund Freud, 6 December 1938, and T H Eckersley to Sigmund Freud, 12 January 1939, LoC ref: mss39990, box 19. Several modern sources claim the recording was initially broadcast as part of a BBC radio series titled *Celebrities on Radio* on 27 December 1938. This seems an erroneous claim. No such broadcast or series is listed in the *Radio Times* and indeed Eckersley's letter of 12 January 1939 notes no broadcast permissions had been agreed.
119 Marietta Bearman et al (eds) *Out of Austria: The Austrian Centre in London in World War II*, London: Bloomsbury, 2020, p. 9.
120 The film may be seen at: www.loc.gov/item/2018601155.
121 *The Bookseller*, 26 January 1939, p. 13; Freud to Leonard Woolf, 31 January 1939, Freeman's Hindman, Philadelphia, *Auction of Books and Manuscripts*, 25 June 2024, lot 269.
122 Leonard Woolf *Downhill All the Way: An Autobiography of the Years 1919–1939*, London: Hogarth, 1967, p. 169.
123 Anne O Bell *The Diary of Virginia Woolf, Volume 5: 1936–41*, Harmondsworth: Penguin, 1985, p. 202.
124 Ibid.
125 H G Wells to S. Freud, 14 July 1939, LoC ref: mss39990, box 43.
126 S Freud to H G Wells, 16 July 1939, in *Freud Letters*, p. 455. On 9 May 1939 Marie Bonaparte wrote to the British Home Secretary asking him to expedite Ernst Freud's application for a certificate of naturalisation in order to please Freud. In doing so, she made clear that, as Sigmund and his party had just one year's residence by that point (five years being required), they were not as yet seeking naturalisation for themselves (see TNA ref: HO 382/194); emphasis added.
127 Freud to Max Eitingon, 3 November 1938, *Freud-Eitingon*, p. 907.
128 Freud to Max Eitingon, 19 December 1938, *Freud-Eitingon*, p. 914; Max Schur *Freud: Living and Dying*, London: Hogarth Press, 1972, p. 513.
129 Tischler did not state the date of this (or indeed any) consultation, though did note Schur had called him in, that a subsequent biopsy confirmed his initial diagnosis, and that surgery was not possible. This episode seems to best-fit Tischer's recollections. See Moritz Tischler interview with KR Eissler, Summer 1953, LoC ref: mss39990, box 133.
130 S Freud to Hanns Sachs, 12–14 March 1939, LoC ref: mss39990, box 40.
131 Freud to Max Eitingon, 5 March 1939, *Freud-Eitingon*, p. 921.
132 M Tischler interview with KR Eissler, Summer 1953, LoC ref: mss39990, box 133; C Tögel *Freud Diarium*, Giessen: Psychosozial-Verlag, 2023, p. 1081; *Life & Work*, 3, p. 521.

133 S Freud to Marie Bonaparte, 16 June 1939, quoted in Max Schur *Freud: Living and Dying*, London: Hogarth Press, 1972, p. 524.
134 Freud to Max Eitingon, 3 November 1938, *Freud-Eitingon*, p. 907.
135 Freud to Jeanne Lampl-de Groot, 20 November 1938, *Freud-Lampl-de Groot*, p. 97.
136 M Molnar (ed) *The Diary of Sigmund Freud 1929–1939: A Record of the Final Decade*, London: Hogarth, 1992, p. 263.
137 C Tögel *Freud Diarium*, Giessen: Psychosozial-Verlag, 2023, p. 1056; Tögel (email to the author, 5 November 2023); Freud to Anna Freud, 1 August 1938, *Freud-Freud*, pp. 401 and 404.
138 Freud to Marie Bonaparte, 4 October 1938, quoted in Max Schur *Freud: Living and Dying*, London: Hogarth Press, 1972, p. 511. By contrast, Ritholz recalled the analysis beginning on approximately 15 August 1938, which was impossible as Freud was not discharged home until 27 August 1938 from the London Clinic. She similarly suggested the analysis extended into August 1939, with the last session two or three days after the Molotov-Ribbentrop Pact (23 August 1939) although her last fees record was for £15 15s in July 1939, probably for five sessions, pointing to its probable conclusion that month.
139 Sophie Ritholz manuscript made for the Sigmund Freud Archives, 5 April 1956, LoC ref: mss39990, box 125, ff. 11–12.
140 Freud to Anna Freud, 30 July 1938 and 1 August 1938, *Freud-Freud*, pp. 399 and 401; see also Paul Roazen *Freud and his Followers*, London: Allen Lane, 1976, pp. 415–430.
141 Freud to Jeanne Lampl-de Groot, 22 August 1938, *Freud-Lampl-de Groot*, p. 94.
142 S Freud 'Analysis terminable and interminable', *SE*, 1937, pp. 209–253.
143 Smiley Blanton *Diary of My Analysis with Sigmund Freud*, New York: Hawthorn Books, 1971.
144 Chris Tögel suggests Lipton may have been the future US analyst Samuel David Lipton (1915–1984) (*Freud Diarium*, 2023, p. 1072), while Gilchrist may have been William Gilchrist (1895–1969), who was later associated with Anna Freud (email to the author, 5 November 2023). However, as that Samuel D Lipton only graduated from medical school in the USA in 1939, his being in analysis in London during the first half of that same year seems unlikely. An alternative Gilchrist may be William S L Gilchrist (1907–1985), an Irish-born psychiatrist who was working at the Ewell Mental Hospital, in Epsom, Surrey, in 1938–39.
145 Freud to Max Eitingon, 19 December 1938, *Freud-Eitingon*, p. 914.
146 Freud to Oscar Pfister, 6 March 1910, *Freud-Pfister*, p. 35; see also Freud to W Fliess, 21 September 1899, *Freud-Fliess*, p. 374.
147 Here estimated using the Bank of England's online inflation calculator, available online at: www.bankofengland.co.uk/monetary-policy/inflation/inflation-calculator; other metrics yield higher figures, see for example: www.measuringworth.com/ukcompare. For purposes of comparison, Anna Freud's declared income was £1,313 in 1942–43, £2,184 in 1943–44, £1,752 in 1944–45, and approximately £1,400 for 1945–46 (see TNA ref: HO 405/13317/10.
148 Hanns Sachs *Freud: Master and Friend*, London: Imago Publishing Company, 1945, p. 186.
149 Harry Freud 'My uncle Sigmund', 1956, in Hendrik M Ruitenbeek (ed) *Freud as We Knew Him*, Detroit: Wayne State University Press, 1973, p. 313; SS *Mauretania*, 12 August 1939 passenger list, TNA ref: BT 27/1550.
150 See the SS *Normandie*, 23 August 1939 passenger list, TNA ref: BT 27/1549, and the SS *Nieuw Amsterdam*, 25 August 1939 passenger list, TNA ref: BT 27/1550.
151 Brett Kahr 'Freud's death bed', 2019, available online at: www.freud.org.uk/2019/09/10/freuds-death-bed/

152 Max Schur *Freud: Living and Dying*, London: Hogarth Press, 1972, p. 527.
153 Ibid., p. 528.
154 Ibid., p. 529.
155 Schur expressed the dose in centigrams, which are here given in contemporary milligrams; one centigram equals ten milligrams.
156 My thanks to Drs Gordon Bates, Steve Brinksman and Vanessa Manley for advising on these points; see also the related discussion in David W Kissane 'Freud's palliative care and natural death', *Archives of Internal Medicine*, 2000, 160, p. 117, and Alastair D Macleod 'Was Sigmund Freud's death hastened?', *Internal Medical Journal*, 2017, 47, pp. 966–969.
157 Max Schur *Freud: Living and Dying*, London: Hogarth Press, 1972, p. 529; as yet undigitised, Schur's papers including various versions of his 1954 paper 'An introduction to the medical history of Sigmund Freud', and drafts of and research files supporting his posthumous book *Freud: Living and Dying* are in the US Library of Congress, under reference mss62040. The differing versions of Schur's reporting of the present events have been helpfully discussed elsewhere in Roy Lacoursiere 'Freud's death: Historical truth and biographical fictions', *American Imago*, 2008, 65, 1, pp. 107–128, and more recently by Dany Nobus in his 'Yom Kippur 1939: The last day of Freud's life and its immediate aftermath', 2015 Freud Memorial Lecture, Freud Museum, London, available online at: https://thefreudmuseum.podbean.com/category/dany-nobus, and his forthcoming book *Freud in the Margins: Rethinking the History of Psychoanalysis*, New York: Columbia University Press, particularly the chapter 'Yom Kippur 1939: Freud, Schur and the rupture of the lethal pact'.
158 Lucie Freud to Felix Augenfeld ('Grockchen'), 2 October 1939, LoC ref: mss39990, box 12; *Freud-Freud*, pp. 407–408.
159 The 1939 Register, compiled on 29 September that year, notes that the Freuds had at least two live-in staff there on that date, both of whom were Austrian refugees: a parlour maid Salome Wagner (1904–1988) and a cook (and ex-music teacher) Hermine Heinisch (1897-). While they may have joined the household in the few days since Freud's death, this seems unlikely and one, other, or both may be presumed to have been there during Freud's final days.
160 Ernest Jones *Diary 1939*, BPAS Archives ref: P04-G-A-2, Ewan O'Neill, Archivist, email to the author, 13 November 2023.
161 *Life & Work*, 3, p. 263.
162 Cited in Dany Nobus *Freud in the Margins: Rethinking the History of Psychoanalysis*, New York: Columbia University Press, forthcoming.
163 *Weekly Dispatch* (London), 24 September 1939, p. 1; several other papers repeat this time, see for example *Nottingham Journal*, 25 Sept 1939, p. 6, the *Belfast Telegraph*, 25 September 1939, p. 5, *The Christian Register* (Boston), 5 October 1939, p. 567, and it also given by Ernst Simmel in his 'Sigmund Freud: The man and his work', *Psychoanalytic Quarterly*, 1940, 9, p. 163. American newspapers, often drawing in Associated Press and other news syndicates, where they note a time of death, corroborate it as being 'just before midnight'.
164 *Daily Herald*, 25 September 1939, p. 6 (following up on a page one announcement).
165 *The Times*, 25 September 1939, p. 10.
166 *Daily Record*, 25 September 1939, p. 7.
167 For Freud's death certificate see Hampstead Registrar's District, July–September 1939, volume 1a, page 618, at the GRO; see also Freud Museum London archives ref: SF/06/01/071.
168 Ernst L Freud *Briefe 1873–1939*, Frankfurt: S Fischer Verlag, 1960, p. 500 and in *Letters of Sigmund Freud 1873–1939*, London: Hogarth, 1961, p. 456.
169 Milton E Jucovy 'Meetings of the New York Psychoanalytic Society', *Psychoanalytic Quarterly*, 1965, 34, p. 147; Max Schur *Freud: Living and Dying*, London: Hogarth Press, 1972, p. 529; it then appears in the Freud biographies by Ronald Clark, Peter

Gay, Detlef Berthelsen, Joseph Berke, Mark Edmundson, Élisabeth Roudinesco, Matt ffytche, and Andrew Nagorski among others.
170 Anne O Bell *The Diary of Virginia Woolf, Volume 5: 1936–41*, Harmondsworth: Penguin, 1985, p. 238.
171 *Birmingham Daily Post*, 27 September 1939, p. 9; see also Celia Bertin *Marie Bonaparte: A Life*, London: Quartet Books, 1983, pp. 208–209.
172 Edward Glover 'Sigmund Freud (May 6, 1856-Sept 23, 1939): A broadcast tribute', *The Listener*, 28 September 1939, p. 605.
173 *Northern Whig*, 25 September 1939, p. 4.
174 Detlef Berthelsen *Alltag bei Familie Freud: Die Erinnerungen der Paula Fichtl*, München: Deutscher Tasachenbuch Verlag, 1989, p. 90.
175 Michael Molnar 'Death in the library' (2013) and his emails to the author, 31 October and 3 November 2023.
176 Roy Lacoursiere 'Freud's death: Historical truth and biographical fictions', *American Imago*, 2008, 65, 1, pp. 107–128; Dany Nobus 'Yom Kippur 1939: The last day of Freud's life and its immediate aftermath', 2015 Freud Memorial Lecture, Freud Museum, London, available online at: https://thefreudmuseum.podbean.com/category/dany-nobus, and his forthcoming book *Freud in the Margins: Rethinking the History of Psychoanalysis*, New York: Columbia University Press, particularly the chapter 'Yom Kippur 1939: Freud, Schur and the rupture of the lethal pact'.
177 C Tögel *Freud Diarium*, Giessen: Psychosozial-Verlag, 2023, p. 1087.
178 Christfried Tögel email to the author, 4 February 2024.
179 Joseph Leftwich in interview with K R Eissler, 10 July 1956, LoC mss39990, box 118.
180 The 150 estimate was reported in the *Continental Daily Mail*, 28 September 1939. Those known to have been present included most of the relatives, Marie Bonaparte, Michael Burlingham, Paula Fichtl, Ernest Jones (and most probably his wife Katherine), Josef Leftwich, Peter Neumann, Tinky Valenstein, H G Wells, Abraham Yahuda, and Stefan Zweig (my thanks to Chris Tögel for contributing to this list). Whether Max Schur and his wife were there is unstated. While it was his forty-second birthday that day, there is no evidence that Schur did not attend the event. Ernest Jones incorrectly notes in *Life & Work* (3, p. 263) that the Lampls attended the funeral.
181 For lists of the flowers received see LoC ref: mss39990, box 48, condolence letters, folder 1.
182 Freud's will, dated 31 January 1919, LoC ref: mss39990, box 50A.
183 Ibid.
184 *The Times*, 27 September 1939; *Western Daily Press*, 27 September 1939, p. 4; *Life & Work*, 3, pp. 263–265 (which reprints Jones's oration only); Élisabeth Roudinesco *Freud in His Time and Ours*, Cambridge, MA: Harvard University Press, 2016, p. 414. Stefan Zweig's oration, titled 'Worte am Sarge Sigmund Freuds', he had subsequently printed as a pamphlet, a copy of which is in the Freud Museum, London (ref: SF/06/01/072). See also Werner Michler 'Intellectual hero, most beloved master: Stefan Zweig and Sigmund Freud in British exile', in Elana Shapira & Daniela Finzi (eds) *Freud and the Émigré*, London: Palgrave Macmillan, 2020, pp. 77–94.
185 See for example the *Halifax Evening Courier*, 26 September 1939, p. 2; *Birmingham Mail*, 26 September 1939, p. 8; and *Edinburgh Evening News*, 26 September 1939, p. 3.
186 For a brief discussion see Michael Turner 'Nostalgia & Dionysus: The mystery of Sigmund Freud's final resting place', in Janine Burke (ed) *Sigmund Freud's Collection: An Archaeology of the Mind*, Sydney: MUMA, 2008, pp. 42–45; see also Helen W Puner's *Freud: His Life and his Mind*, New York: Dell, 1959, p. 274.
187 Joseph Leftwich in interview with K R Eissler, 10 July 1956, LoC mss39990, box 118.
188 See for example the *Express and Echo*, 11 October 1939, p. 6; *Dundee Evening Telegraph*, 10 October 1939, p. 3; *Liverpool Daily Post*, 12 October p. 4; *Yorkshire Post and Leeds Intelligencer*, 13 October 1939, p. 6.

189 Sigmund Freud, will and grant of probate, National Probate Register, 1939, p. 490. Whether this represented the totality of Freud's estate, including any assets in overseas banks, is unclear. Certainly, other commentators have suggested more inflated figures. David Cohen, for example, claimed Freud had left an estate valued at $109,000 (see his *The Escape of Sigmund Freud*, New York: Overlook Press, 2012, p. 228).
190 See also Paul Roazen 'Freud's last will', *Journal of the American Academy of Psychoanalysis and Dynamic Psychiatry*, 1990, 18, pp. 383–391.
191 Martha Freud to Paul Federn, 5 November 1939, quoted in Michael Molnar (ed) *The Diary of Sigmund Freud 1929–1939: A Record of the Final Decade*, London: Hogarth, 1992, p. 264; Martha Freud to Ludwig Binswanger, 7 November 1939, in *Freud-Binswanger*, p. 221.
192 National Probate Register, 1941, p. 383. In Hoop Lane Cemetery Minna's grave is in the West London Synagogue portion and can be found in section C, row 41, plot 16.
193 *Daily News* (London), 27 September 1939, p. 8.
194 *Aberdeen Evening Express*, 25 September 1939, p. 4.
195 *Daily News* (London), 27 September 1939, p. 10.
196 Alistair Ross *Sigmund Freud: A Reference Guide to his Life and Works*, Lanham, MD: Rowman & Littlefield, 2022, p. 100.
197 1939 Register, for Fire Thorn, Guildford, TNA ref: RG 101/1954g.
198 See https://imuseum.im/search/collections/people/mnh-agent-99309.html and Detlef Berthelsen *Alltag bei Familie Freud: Die Erinnerungen der Paula Fichtl*, München: Deutscher Tasachenbuch Verlag, 1989.
199 Peter Gay 'Freud et la guerre', *Vingtième Siècle, Revue d'Histoire*, 1994, 41, p. 88; Élisabeth Roudinesco *Freud in His Time and Ours*, Cambridge, MA: Harvard University Press, 2016, p. 402.
200 William Feaver *The Lives of Lucian Freud: Youth 1922–1968*, London: Bloomsbury, 2022, p. 59.
201 Alexander, Sophie, and her sister were granted permission to immigrate to Canada through a Canadian Order in Council, dated 13 August 1940. See Immigrants approved in Orders in Council, 31 July 1940, Library & Archives Canada ref: RG 2, A-1-a, Order in Council no. 3777 dated 13 August 1940, vol. 1683, p. 2; *The Gazette* (Montreal), 23 April 1943, p. 12; WWII Internees (Aliens) Index Cards, TNA ref: HO 396/224; National Probate Register, 1944, p. 342.
202 Passenger list, SS *President Harding*, TNA ref: BT 27/1552.
203 Alfred Gottwaldt 'Sigmund Freud's sisters and death: Notes on their fate in deportation and mass-murder', *Psyche*, 2004, 58, pp. 533–543; David Cohen *The Escape of Sigmund Freud*, New York: Overlook Press, 2012, pp. 232–233; www.yadvashem.org; www.freud-museum.at/en/subsites-gallery/articles/the-murder-of-the-sisters; www.holocausthistoricalsociety.org.uk/contents/jewishbiographies/sigmundfreussdandhissisters.html. There is some variation in the places the sisters were reportedly murdered. Élisabeth Roudinesco, for example, suggests Mitzi and Pauli died in Maly Trostinec, on or after 23 September 1942, while Rosa died in Treblinka, having been taken there on either 29 September 1942 or 1 March 1943. See her *Freud in his Time and Ours*, Cambridge, MA: Harvard University Press, 2016, pp. 415–416 and 507–508.
204 The Freud Museum, Vienna, has a good digitised online exhibition on this (drawing on lists of refugees from the BPAS archives). See www.freud-museum.at/en/subsites-organized-escape/articles/online-exhibition-organized-escape-survival-in-exile.
205 Quoted in Clare Winnicott 'DWW: A reflection', 1978, in Clare Winnicott *et al* (eds) *D W Winnicott: Psycho-Analytic Explorations*, London: Karnac, 1989, p. 4.

Chapter 11

Epilogue

In the difficult days of October 1919, Freud had looked to Britain and the English language as means of economic recovery and a refuge of last resort. Pragmatically, he had recently employed a language tutor to help him improve his spoken English, building on his longstanding accomplishments in that language which he had gained in no small part from Emanuel and his British kin. Increasing his verbal skills still further would better equip him to both treat English-speaking patients who were just then beginning to start knocking on his door and allow him to emigrate to Britain should his savings run out. Writing to Max Eitingon about this, Freud added an important personal note, that 'My two brothers already rest in English soil; perhaps I shall also find room there'.[1] Britain is here made familiar, the home of his brothers, their final resting place, a melancholic image, yet in Freud's almost poetic couplet it appears also one of reunion. Freud's brothers, Emanuel and Philipp, and their families, in an inevitable union with Britain, exerted a considerable influence on Freud as he grew up and indeed throughout his life, yet the lives of these British Freuds and of Freud himself in Britain have, until now, remained very largely undiscovered territory.

In beginning to map this territory in some detail, we begin to see the interrelated emotional connections between Freud, his older brothers, their families, and Britain. Tending these relationships entailed a continuing exchange of news, expressions of warmth, encouragement and solidarity, and challenge where needed, as well as very tangible material and economic support. All of this was hugely important for Freud personally, who looked up to his older brothers, just as it was for others in the family, the Manchester Freuds in their turn looking to their younger brother as the one who seemed to be making-good across the decades on a stupendous scale.

Freud's brothers represented differing imagos, each important in their own way. Both offered Freud a model of enterprise as businessmen, something Freud himself became (though this is not often emphasised), running his own successful private practice, and – again like Emanuel and Philipp – managing to extricate himself from financial crises through hard work. Emanuel appears as an assimilated English businessman, a secular Jew, outgoing, assertive, pragmatic and ultimately economically successful, supporting Freud's career ambitions, and representing

DOI: 10.4324/9781032652023-12

an alternative father-figure. Philipp, or Shraga to give him his Hebrew (or rather Aramaic) name, in contrast to his brothers, overtly retained his more orthodox Jewish identity, a feature which perhaps contributed to his cooler though nonetheless important relationship with Freud. This coolness extended to Philipp's *family* too, an 'estrangement' as Freud frankly put it to Poppy which he 'often regretted'.[2] Yet Freud spent much of his life balancing his cultural Jewishness with his atheism and scientific ambitions. He further balanced the individual lives of many family, friends, colleagues, and patients, with the institutional development of psychoanalysis at a time of unprecedented, and in the case of the Great War, cataclysmic change. This dynamic is evident in his relations with Emanuel and Philipp, with Philipp's orthodoxy probably contributing to Freud's own later engagement with Judaism, particularly in *Moses and Monotheism*.

The new clarity with respect to the lives and influence of Emanuel and Philipp extends to John and Sam as well, both of whom also had important places in Freud's emotional life. While John's paradigmatic role was noted in *The Interpretation of Dreams* as having 'a determining influence on all my subsequent relations with contemporaries',[3] it is only now that his own later life has been retrieved somewhat from private obscurity. Contrary to published reports, which typically have John disappearing as a young man,[4] his whereabouts were clearly known to Freud – and presumably others in the family – in 1908. We may wonder whether his career as a Thomas Cook tour guide was an inspiration for Freud's own travels, just as Emanuel and Philipp's emigrant travels and the Jewish diaspora may have been.[5] For his part, although Sam led a very emotionally restricted life, he attempted – like his father – to tend the relationship between the Manchester and Vienna branches of the family. Seldom seeming to venture beyond the confines of home and office, Sam lacked Emanuel's more ebullient personality, though did inherit something of his father's Freudian rigidity or determination. His correspondence with Freud tended to be rather unidirectional, inviting Freud to share his news but offering little day-to-day gossip and still less about his own or his immediate family's emotional lives in return. Clearly a painful situation for Freud who longed to know Sam better and retain touch with his British kin, his encouragement failed to entice Sam into the open and over time their correspondence dwindled and the relationship rather stagnated. That said, Sam importantly came into the limelight for a couple of years after the Great War, materially helping Freud and his Austrian relatives with vital food parcels at a time when there were serious food shortages for most Viennese. More symbolically, Sam's encounter with Freud in Elsworthy Road in June 1938 was an important reunion of the previously geographically bifurcated family and an emotional welcome of Freud to Britain, the adopted land of his older brothers, his nephews, and nieces.

What is painfully less clear throughout this book are the stories of the Freud women in Manchester, with the partial exception of Poppy who left more traces, both of her social and business lives, bolstered by a few surviving letters to Freud. She, as Freud would acknowledge, persevered in her occasional correspondence with her uncle, despite his sometimes-limited response. Poppy comes across as an active, creative, able, and dynamic woman. It would be nice to know her better.

The lives of the other Manchester Freud women are rather spectral by contrast. Aside from their thin representation in the archives, the Freud women in Manchester often appear inscribed in the surviving texts of male family members (Emanuel and Sam principally) as symptomatic, with chronic or at least recurrent poor physical health, albeit of an often vague or ill-defined nature. Hints coming through the shared history suggest lung disease, gastrointestinal issues consistent perhaps with ulcerative colitis, and depression or melancholia as prevalent among them, but also as wider biopsychosocial complexes within the extended family. Freud's suggestion that there was a 'neuropathological taint' in the family captured part of this, though without adequately addressing bodily illness or environmental and socio-cultural vertices.

These same narratives also depicted Emanuel's adult daughters as suffering from financial deficits, having inadequate dowries to attract suitable husbands, arguments which further restricted their lives to the domestic sphere. Such arguments however appear unconvincing rationalisations, with Sam too never leading a life independent of the family, John having to virtually estrange himself in breaking free, and Philipp only marrying when he was 37, having seemingly secured his window of opportunity by remaining behind at 96 Shudehill when Emanuel and his family moved to live in the south Manchester suburbs. Their lives were thus substantially enmeshed and for the Freud women their only visible respite from this *huis clos* were trips to the coast, spas, or other tranquil parts of the county, trips often justified by their supposed health benefits.

In this sense, they were not wholly dissimilar to the more vocal Amalia, with her lengthy summer visits to spas at Rožnau and later Baden and Aussee. And she was of course often joined on these trips by her quieter daughters, other women from the Freud clan, and female friends. Whatever their actual health status was, donning the sick-role conferred certain secondary gains or limited privileges on the Freud women. Among other things, it rather perversely increased their power from its low baseline and expressed a degree of veiled resistance to the prevailing constricting habitus. For their part, Emanuel and Philipp would also periodically escape its stifling confines, taking trips to the Continent for what they termed 'refreshment'. Whether this was a euphemism is unknown. Certainly, the glimpse we get of the brothers 1883 trip to Leipzig and Dresden with Freud seems innocuous enough.

With his women patients, Freud would explore the social and emotional restrictions that contributed to their neuroses and attempt where possible to reach a better compromise solution.[6] For instance, in his 1917 *Introductory Lectures on Psycho-Analysis*, Freud argued so-called flights into illness are accompanied by primary and secondary gains, and illustrated the latter with what he saw as 'the commonest example', namely a woman ill-treated by her husband. She might thus develop and use her subsequent neurotic symptoms as leverage in the relationship. The prognosis for treatment, if it was even attempted, in such cases was poor, Freud remarked, and with a degree of perspicacity for the time commented that: 'we must allow that in some cases . . . flight is fully justified, and a physician who has recognised how the situation lies will silently and solicitously withdraw'.[7] Just as his self-analysis provided some understanding of such neurotic states, his reflections on the women in his family circle undoubtedly fed his insights into these interpersonal and intrapsychic situations. However, aside from his unsuccessful efforts to nudge Sam into a freer engagement with him, Freud adopted a rather laissez-faire attitude towards his female relatives in Manchester and their ostensibly emotionally crippled lives. To have done otherwise would have probably meant stepping considerably outside of contemporary social and familial conventions, including challenging Emanuel as the head of the family when he was alive and disrupting their important relationship with no certain gain. It was a road not travelled. Closer to home for Freud, the welfare of his elderly sisters who remained in Vienna following the *Anschluss* and his own escape to London clearly troubled him and the wider family considerably and they did what they could to liberate them, without any success.[8] It was a species of survivor guilt not uncommon among Jews who had managed to escape the Nazi genocide.

Freud's very close family connections to Britain reveal the roots of his own strong Anglophile leanings and better contextualise his thoughts of settling in Britain and his hopes that Britain would prove fertile ground for psychoanalysis. This biographical foundation strongly augments his better-known admiration for British science and literature and what he formatively understood as Britain's culture of intellectual freedom.[9] Yet, following his 1875 visit to Manchester, Freud did not set foot again in Britain for over three decades, declining many invitations during the intervening years. His rivalry with his elder brothers probably contributed to this. With the passage of time, perceiving Emanuel aging seemed particularly difficult for Freud, with no doubt thoughts of his mortality evoking painful memories of past bereavements beginning with the death of baby Julius and later his father Jacob. As a mid-life issue it also pointed forward to Freud's own changing position in the family and the prospect of his own death at some future point. Guilt feelings at having displaced Emanuel as the eldest son were no doubt also part of this complex, with the ravages of aging Emanuel displayed and the prospect of his death further compounding these.

The history of filial passions evident in Freud's relationships with his British family, as well as with his wider family and friends, contributed to forms of idealisation and distancing within the early psychoanalytic community. The after-effects of this continue to persist, for example within the family romances common to those in psychoanalysis: who was analysed by whom and how ones analytic genealogy or pedigree may be traced back to Freud or to another of the early pioneers.[10] Charles Rycroft interestingly discussed a version of this tendency in his fine paper 'On the ablation of parental images, or the illusion of having created oneself', in which he explores how some in psychoanalysis dismiss their actual parents and replace them with supposedly better psychoanalytic versions. Such people may choose their own analysts and substitute analytic ancestors, turning around the supposed narcissistic humiliation of their lack of choice in who their actual parents were.[11]

While Freud's paradigmatic discussion of the Oedipus complex depicts it heuristically within a basic nuclear family, Freud's own family was anything but that. With Freud as the first child of his father's second family, Emanuel functioned not just as his oldest brother but also as a sometimes idealised sometimes preferred father figure, just as Freud's childhood nannie occupied the position of his early second mother. And some have suggested Philipp held the split off and projected sexual and bad parts of Freud's father, a brother Freud went on to maintain a lifelong distance from. With his religious sensibility and physical peculiarities, Philipp was a vulnerable, conspicuous easy mark for such hostility, projections, and enactment, not just from Freud but also from others across the piste.

Horizontal and vertical relationships in Freud's family setup were confusing if not confused. Substitutions within his family system exacerbated this, with younger brothers replacing or assuming priority over older brothers. Sibling relationships in this context can intertwine with Oedipal relationships, with an emphasis on inclusion and exclusion or marginalisation, and in Freud's case a multiplication of parental figures was promoted by the significant age disparity between him and his older brothers, vertical and horizontal distinctions being partly elided. That such structures were clearly not as immutable as might be believed, that they might be changed, could cause both reverberations throughout the prevailing hegemonic or orthodox ways of being and at the same time open up prospects for freer revised relationships.

Freud's involvement with his siblings promoted questions about identity and character. Some of this emerges in surprising form, in his consideration of the ways in which physiognomy might reflect not just supposed ethnic or racial characteristics, but might also embody traces of canalised cathexes, or patterns of object relations, of mental, intellectual and emotional commitments. Might a book, in this sense, be read from its cover? Or more broadly, how might one read or experience art? Or what were the implications to be discerned in Freud's scrutiny of Emanuel's aging face? Freud would reapproach some of these questions in the clinic in his mature shift from symptom to character analysis, which Wilhelm Reich developed substantially albeit controversially. The surprising physiognomical thread in Freud's thinking however, deserves further study.

Freud's final move to London in 1938 came when both Emanuel and Philip were dead, yet they had made the country a familiar territory for their younger brother. As with other immigrants, the Vienna Freuds however did not immediately embrace the native mores, seeking instead to preserve or recreate something of that which they had been exiled from by the Nazis. Berggasse was thus recreated in London, NW3, with family and friends trying to settle in the same neighbourhoods, while the interior spaces in Maresfield Gardens came to reflect something of Freud's Vienna apartment. It was not identical however and Ernst Freud in redesigning the house made it brighter and further augmented this through the introduction of a radically lighter colour palette in the decoration. Reluctant earlier to embrace such an aesthetic, Freud was delighted with his new surroundings. They certainly showed off his collection of antiquities to greater effect.

Other things too were brought a little more into the light as a consequence of Freud's move to London. The flurry of press interest underscored for Freud something of his international recognition: he felt famous for the first time, or at least so he declared. The glimpse of his wheelchair was a more unusual sight for Freud's public and has been left in the shadows by almost everybody ever since. It exists, in that sense, as a counterpoint to the opening characterisation here of Freud's working-class origins in Freiberg and Vienna, both images of Freud which sit uneasily with the hegemonic image of the Professor. Yet both extend the Freudian journey. Freud had travelled far in his life from his first visit to Manchester and the Lancashire coast as a young man in 1875. Once an idealistic, hopeful, eager student, his return 63 years later was as the world-famous Viennese professor, founder of psychoanalysis. Yet he was still a man seeking refuge, struggling with cancer, and whose life had been profoundly shaped by his English family. These stories are crucial in offering a new understanding of Freud and his contributions to modernity.

Notes

1 Freud to Max Eitingon, 12 October 1919, *Life & Work*, 3, p. 5.
2 Freud to Pauline Hartwig, 23 September 1937, Rylands Library ref: SSF/1/5/2.
3 Freud *The Interpretation of Dreams*, *SE*, 1900 [1899], 5, p. 424.
4 See for example R W Clark *Freud: The Man and the Cause*, London: Jonathan Cape and Weidenfeld & Nicholson, 1980, p. 394; M Krüll *Freud and his Father*, London: Hutchinson, 1987, p. 129; W Boehlich, *Freud-Silberstein*, p. 124 n.4.
5 For Freud's later oedipal and economic views on his motivations to travel see his paper 'A disturbance of memory on the Acropolis', *SE*, 1936, 22, pp. 237–248.
6 See for example L Appignanesi & J Forrester *Freud's Women*, London: Weidenfeld & Nicholson, 1992.
7 S Freud *Introductory Lectures on Psycho-Analysis*, *SE*, 1916–17, 16, p. 382. For the later and related concept of the sick-role see Talcott Parsons *The Social System*, Glencoe, IL: The Free Press, 1951.
8 Élisabeth Roudinesco *Freud in his Time and Ours*, Cambridge, MA: Harvard University Press, 2016, pp. 415–416 and 507 note 4.
9 S Freud to E Silberstein, 9 September 1875, *Freud-Silberstein*, pp. 125–128.
10 For an accessible discussion of this see Ernst Falzeder *Psychoanalytic Filiations: Mapping the Psychoanalytic Movement*, London: Karnac, 2015, especially pp. 51–102.
11 Charles Rycroft 'On the ablation of parental images, or the illusion of having created oneself', in Peter Fuller (ed) *Psychoanalysis and Beyond*, London: Hogarth, 1985, pp. 214–232.

Sources and References

Note: In addition to the following principal manuscript and printed sources, numerous newspaper reports, Street Directories, Rate Books, and other such sources are cited only in the notes for reasons of space.

Manuscript sources

British Psychoanalytical Society Archives
Ernest Jones Papers (P04)

Freud Museum, London
Sigmund Freud Papers

Library of Congress, Washington, DC
Rosa Freud Graf Papers (MSS81404)

- Box 1: Emanuel Freud correspondence, 1885–86

Sigmund Freud Papers (MSS39990), especially:

- Box 2: Emanuel Freud correspondence
- Boxes 3–8: Martha Bernays correspondence
- Box 10: Freud family correspondence
- Box 11: Rosa Freud and Lilly Freud Marlé correspondence
- Box 12: Emanuel Freud to Eli Bernays correspondence, 1892
- Box 12: Eli Bernays and Pauline Hartwig correspondence
- Box 13: Freud papers and correspondence, including Philipp, Marie, and Sam Freud
- Box 50A: Freuds pocket notebooks
- Box 115: Kurt Eissler interview with Harry Freud
- Box 117: Kurt Eissler interview with Melanie Klein
- Box 118: Kurt Eissler interview with Joseph Leftwich
- Box 122: Kurt Eissler interview with George S Viereck
- Box 131: Kurt Eissler interview with Oscar Philipp

- Box 131: Kurt Eissler interview with Moritz Tischler
- Box OV 10: Freud's Kürzeste Chronik

Max Schur Papers (MSS62040)

The National Archives, London
Aliens Registrations Cards (Metropolitan Police only)

- Ernest Freud (1892-): MEPO 35/29/4
- Lucie Freud (1896-): MEPO 35/29/5

Board of Trade company papers

- Freud & Co Ltd (1910–1915): BT 31/13111/107894, company number 107894
- Miss Freud Ltd: BT 31/29221/208206 and BT 34/5048/208206

Naturalisation papers (Home Office)

- Anna Freud: HO 334/163/18733, HO 396/23/288 (exemption from internment), and HO 405/13317
- Ernst Freud: HO 334/228/1216 and HO 382/194
- Emanuel Freud: 29 Jan 1877: HO 45/9428/61301 and HO 334/7/2149
- Fritz Hartwig: HO 144/11720, f. 210, HO 144/15676 and HO 334/130/2418
- Jean Martin Freud: HO 334/184/29447

Passport holders, Index of names of (Foreign Office)

- Emanuel Freud: FO 611/13, 14 and 20

World War II Internees (Aliens) Index Cards

- Alexander and Sophie Freud: HO 396/224

University of Manchester, Department of Special Collections, John Rylands Library
Freud family Papers (GB 133 SSF)

- SSF/1/1: Letters and related material from Sigmund to Sam Freud
- SSF/1/2: Letters and related material from Sam to Sigmund Freud
- SSF/1/3: Letters from Anna to Sam Freud
- SSF/1/4: Letters from Sam to Anna Freud
- SSF/1/5: Letters from Sigmund Freud to Pauline Hartwig
- SSF/1/6: Other family letters
- SSF/2/1: Photographs and newspaper cuttings relating to Sigmund Freud and family
- SSF/2/2: Envelope of photographs of Sigmund Freud and family

University of Reading, Special Collections
George Allen & Unwin Ltd Archive

- Allen & Unwin Authors Ledger, 1924–1932: A&U A/112
- Correspondence re *Moses and Monotheism* and its translation by Katherine Jones, 1938–74: CW 530/1

Printed sources (including theses)

Abraham, Karl (1923) 'Contributions to the theory of the anal character', *IJPA*, 4, pp. 400–418.
Aleinikov, Sergey V (2017) '12 Green Street', available online at: freudproject.ru/?p=7948.
Amouroux, Rémy (2011) 'A serious venture: John Rodker (1894–1955) and the Imago Publishing Company (1939–60)', *IJPA*, 92, pp. 1437–1454.
Anon (1851) *Official Catalogue of the Great Exhibition of the Works of Industry of All Nations*, London: Spricers Brothers and W Clowes & Sons.
Anzieu, Didier (1986) *Freud's Self-Analysis*, London: Hogarth.
Appignanesi, Lisa & Forrester, John (1992) *Freud's Women*, London: Weidenfeld & Nicholson.
Augusta, Georg (2015a) 'Die familie Nathansohn', *Zeitschrift für psychoanalytische Theorie und Praxis*, 30, 3–4, pp. 431–453.
Augusta, Georg (2015b) '"Dann kamen die langen, harten Jahre": Zur Situation der Familie Freud nach ihrer Ankunft in Wien im Jahr 1859' ("Long and difficult years followed": The situation of Freud's family after their arrival in Vienna in 1859'), *Luzifer-Amor*, 28, pp. 108–129.
Bearman, Marietta, Brinson, Charmian, Dove, Richard, Grenville, Anthony, & Taylor, Jennifer (eds) (2020) *Out of Austria: The Austrian Centre in London in World War II*, London: Bloomsbury.
Bell, David (1999) *Psychoanalysis and Culture: A Kleinian Perspective*, London: Duckworth.
Bergstein, Mary (2006) 'Freud's Moses of Michelangelo: Vasari, photography, and art historical practice', *The Art Bulletin*, 88, 1, pp. 158–176.
Bergstein, Mary (2010) 'Freud's Egyptian photographs: Scenes from a library', *Visual Resources*, 26, 3, pp. 274–288.
Berke, Joseph H (2015) *The Hidden Freud: His Hassidic Roots*, London: Karnac.
Bernays, Anna Freud (1940) 'My brother, Sigmund Freud', *The American Mercury*, 51, pp. 335–342.
Bernfeld, Siegfried (1946) 'An unknown autobiographical fragment by Freud', *American Imago*, 4, pp. 3–19.
Bernfeld, Siegfried & Bernfeld, Suzanne C (1944) 'Freud's early childhood', in Hendrik M Ruitenbeek (ed) *Freud as we Knew Him*, Detroit, MI: Wayne State University Press, 1973, pp. 188–196.
Bernfeld, Suzanne C (1951) 'Freud and archeology', *American Imago*, 8, 2, pp. 107–128.
Berthelsen, Detlef (1989) *Alltag bei Familie Freud: Die Erinnerungen der Paula Fichtl*, München: Deutscher Tasachenbuch Verlag.
Bertin, Celia (1983) *Marie Bonaparte: A Life*, London: Quartet Books.
Bion, Wilfred R (1970) *Attention and Interpretation: A Scientific Approach to Insight in Psycho-Analysis and Groups*, London: Tavistock.
Bird, John C (2015) *Control of Enemy Alien Civilians in Great Britain 1914–1918*, Abingdon: Routledge.
Blum, Harold P (2015) 'Reconstructing Freud's prototype reconstructions', *International Forum of Psychoanalysis*, 24, pp. 47–57.
Boehlich, Walter (ed) (1990) *The Letters of Sigmund Freud to Eduard Silberstein 1871–1881*, Cambridge, MA: Belknap Press.
Bögels, Gertie (ed) (2023) *The Letters of Sigmund Freud and Jeanne Lampl-de Groot, 1921–1939*, London: Routledge.
Bonaparte, Marie (1956) 'John Rodker 1894–1955', *IJPA*, 37, pp. 199–201.
Bonomi, Carlo (2015) *The Cut and the Building of Psychoanalysis, Volume 1: Sigmund Freud and Emma Eckstein*, Hove: Routledge.
Borch-Jacobsen, Mikkel & Shamdasani, Sonu (2012) *The Freud Files: An Inquiry into the History of Psychoanalysis*, Cambridge: Cambridge University Press.

Bowlby, Rachel (2006) 'The Cronus complex: Psychoanalytic myths of the future for boys and girls', in Vanda Zajko & Miriam Leonard (eds) *Laughing with Medusa: Classical Myth and Feminist Thought*, Oxford: Oxford University Press, pp. 21–44.

Boyarin, Daniel (1997) *Unheroic Conduct: The Rise of Heterosexuality and the Invention of the Jewish Man*, Berkeley: University of California Press.

Brecht, Karen, Friedrich, Volker, Hermanns, Ludger M, Kaminer, Isidor J, & Juelich, Dierk H (eds) (1985) *'Here Life. Goes on in a Most Peculiar Way . . .': Psychoanalysis before and after 1933*, Hamburg: Kellner Verlag.

Breines, Paul (1990) *Tough Jews: Political Fantasies and the Moral Dilemma of American Jewry*, New York: Basic Books.

Browne, Thomas ([1658] 1893) *Hydriotaphia, Urn Burial*, London: Charles Whittingham & Co, Chiswick Press.

Buriánek, Václav (2015) 'Paradise lost and trauma mastered: New findings on little Sigmund', *International Forum of Psychoanalysis*, 24, 1, pp. 22–28.

Chan, Yiukee (2016) *Experience into Psychoanalytic Ideas: A Psychobiographical Study of Ferenczi's Introjection*, unpublished PhD thesis, University of Essex.

Childers, Ryan E et al (2014) 'Family history of inflammatory bowel disease among patients with ulcerative colitis: A systemic review and meta-analysis', *Journal of Crohn's and Colitis*, 2014, 8, pp. 1480–1497.

Clark, Ronald W (1980) *Freud: The Man and the Cause*, London: Jonathan Cape and Weidenfeld & Nicholson.

Cohen, David (2012) *The Escape of Sigmund Freud*, New York: Overlook Press.

Collins, Alan F (1999) 'The enduring appeal of physiognomy: Physical appearance as a sign of temperament, character, and intelligence', *History of Psychology*, 2, pp. 251–276.

Dalí, Salvador (1942) *The Secret Life of Salvador Dalí*, New York: Dial Press.

Davidoff, Leonore (2012) *Thicker Than Water: Siblings and Their Relations 1780–1920*, Oxford: Oxford University Press.

Davies, J Keith & Fichtner, Gerhard (2006) *Freud's Library: A Comprehensive Catalogue*, London & Tübingen: Freud Museum and Edition Diskord.

de Mijolla, Alain (ed) (2005) *International Dictionary of Psychoanalysis*, 3 volumes, Farmington Hills, MI: Thomson Gale.

de Mijolla, Alain & Ohayon, Annick (2015) 'De l'histoire personnelle à l'histoire de la psychanalyse: une trajectoire', *Nouvelle Revue de Psychosociologie*, 2, pp. 247–262.

Deutsch, Felix (1956) 'Reflections on Freud's one hundredth birthday', in Hendrik M Ruitenbeek (ed) *Freud as we Knew Him*, Detroit: Wayne State University Press, 1973, pp. 297–305.

Eassie, William (1875) *Cremation of the Dead: Its History and Bearings Upon Public Health*, London: Smith Elder & Co.

Edmundson, Mark (2007) *The Death of Sigmund Freud: Fascism, Psychoanalysis and the Rise of Fundamentalism*, London: Bloomsbury.

Ellenberger, Henri F (1970) *The Discovery of the Unconscious: The History and Evolution of Dynamic Psychiatry*, New York: Basic Books.

Engelman, Edmund (1998) *Sigmund Freud Berggasse 19, Vienna*, Vienna: Verlag Christian Brandstätter.

Engels, Friedrich (1892) *The Condition of the Working-Class in England in 1844*, London: Swan Sonnenschein & Co.

Ezriel, Henry (1973) 'Psychoanalytic group therapy', in L R Wolberg & E K Schwartz (eds) *Group Therapy 1973: An Overview*, New York: International Medical Books, pp. 183–210.

Falzeder, Ernst (ed) (2002) *The Correspondence of Sigmund Freud and Karl Abraham*, London: Karnac.

Falzeder, Ernst (2012) '"A fat wad of dirty pieces of paper": Freud on America, Freud in America, Freud and America', in John Burnham (ed) *After Freud Left: A Century of Psychoanalysis in America*, Chicago: University of Chicago Press, pp. 85–109.

Falzeder, Ernst (2015) *Psychoanalytic Filiations: Mapping the Psychoanalytic Movement*, London: Karnac.
Falzeder, Ernst, Brabant, Eva & Giampiere-Deutsch, Patrizia (eds) (1992–2000) *The Correspondence of Sigmund Freud and Sándor Ferenczi*, 3 volumes, Cambridge, MA: Belknap Press.
Fanon, Frantz (2001 [1961]) *The Wretched of the Earth*, London: Penguin.
Feaver, William (2022) *The Lives of Lucian Freud: Youth 1922–1968*, London: Bloomsbury.
Fichtner, Gerhard (ed) (2003) *The Sigmund Freud-Ludwig Binswanger Correspondence 1908–1938*, New York: Other Press.
Fichtner, Gerhard, Grubrich-Simitis, Ilse & Hirschmüller, Albrecht (eds) (2011–2021) *Die Brautbriefe, 1882–1886*, 5 volumes, Frankfurt am Main: S. Fischer.
Fischer, Thomas & Tögel, Christfried (2024) 'Der Briefwechsel zwischen Emma Jung und Sigmund Freud', *Luzifer-Amor*, 73, pp. 173–210.
Forrester, John (1997) *Despatches from the Freud Wars: Psychoanalysis and Its Passions*, Cambridge, MA: Harvard University Press.
Franklin, James L (2022a) 'My dear neoplasm: Sigmund Freud's oral cancer', *Hektoen International*, available online at: https://hekint.org/2022/10/28/.
Franklin, James L (2022b) 'Wilson on the couch: How Sigmund Freud and William C Bullitt, an American diplomat, came to analyze the American president', *Hektoen International*, available online at: https://hekint.org/2022/12/27/.
Freud, Anna (1968 [1936]) *The Ego and the Mechanisms of Defence*, London: Hogarth.
Freud, Ernst L (ed) (1960) *Briefe 1873–1939*, Frankfurt: S Fischer Verlag.
Freud, Ernst L (ed) (1961) *Letters of Sigmund Freud 1873–1939*, London: Hogarth.
Freud, Ernst L (1969) 'Some early unpublished letters of Freud', *IJPA*, 50, pp. 419–427.
Freud, Ernst, Freud, Lucie & Grubrich-Simitis, Ilse (1985) *Sigmund Freud: His Life in Pictures and Words*, New York: Norton.
Freud, Harry (1956) 'My uncle Sigmund', in Hendrik M Ruitenbeek (ed) *Freud as We Knew Him*, Detroit: Wayne State University Press, 1973, pp. 312–313.
Freud, Martin (1957) *Glory Reflected: Sigmund Freud – Man and Father*, London: Angus and Robertson.
Freud, Sigmund (1884) 'A new histological method for the study of nerve-tracts in the brain and spinal chord', *Brain*, 1 April 1884, 7, 1, pp. 86–88.
Freud, Sigmund (1899) 'Screen memories', *SE*, 3, pp. 299–322.
Freud, Sigmund (1900 [1899]) *The Interpretation of Dreams*, *SE*, 4–5.
Freud, Sigmund (1901) *The Psychopathology of Everyday Life*, *SE*, 6.
Freud, Sigmund (1905) *Jokes and their Relation to the Unconscious*, *SE*, 8.
Freud, Sigmund (1908) 'Character and anal erotism', *SE*, 9, pp. 167–176.
Freud, Sigmund (1909) *Selected Papers on Hysteria, and Other Psychoneuroses*, translated by A A Brill, New York: The Journal of Nervous and Mental Disease Publishing Company.
Freud, Sigmund (1913a) *Selected Papers on Hysteria, and Other Psychoneuroses*, 2nd edition, translated by A A Brill, New York: JNMD Publishing Co.
Freud, Sigmund (1913b) *Totem and Taboo*, *SE*, 13, pp. vii–162.
Freud, Sigmund (1914a) *On the History of the Psycho-Analytic Movement*, *SE*, 14, pp. 1–66.
Freud, Sigmund (1914b) 'The Moses of Michelangelo', *SE*, 13, pp. 209–238.
Freud, Sigmund (1916–17) *Introductory Lectures on Psycho-Analysis*, *SE*, 15–16.
Freud, Sigmund (1921) *Group Psychology and the Analysis of the Ego*, *SE*, 18, pp. 65–143.
Freud, Sigmund (1930) *Civilization and Its Discontents*, *SE*, 21, pp. 57–145.
Freud, Sigmund (1936) 'A disturbance of memory on the Acropolis', *SE*, 22, pp. 237–248.
Freud, Sigmund (1937) 'Analysis terminable and interminable', *SE*, 23, pp. 209–253.
Freud, Sigmund (1939) *Moses and Monotheism*, *SE*, 23, pp. 1–137.
Freud, Sigmund (1940a) *An Outline of Psycho-Analysis*, *SE*, 23, pp. 139–207.
Freud, Sigmund (1940b) 'Some elementary lessons in psycho-analysis', *SE*, 23, 23, pp. 279–286.

Freud, Sigmund (1953–1974) *The Standard Edition of the Complete Psychological Works of Sigmund Freud*, 24 volumes, edited by James Strachey, London: Hogarth Press.
Freud, Sigmund (2002) *Unser Herz zeigt nach dem Süden: Reisebriefe 1895–1923* [Our Heart Points to the South: Travel Letters 1895–1923], edited by Christfried Tögel in collaboration with Michael Molnar, Berlin: Aufbau-Verlag.
Freud, Sigmund & Bullitt, William C (1967) *Thomas Woodrow Wilson: A Psychological Study*, London: Weidenfeld & Nicholson.
Freud-Marlé, Lilly (2006) *Mein Onkel Sigmund Freud: Erinnerungen an eine grosse Familie*, edited by Christfried Tögel & Magdalena Frank, Berlin: Aufbau-Verlag.
Frosh, Stephen (2003) 'Psychoanalysis, Nazism and "Jewish science"', *IJPA*, 84, pp. 1315–1332.
Gall, Alan (2008) 'The deadly Doctor Freud – A tale from the archive', *The Journal: The Institute of Science & Technology*, Spring 2008, pp. 28–29.
Gandolfi, Laura (2010) 'Freud in Trieste: Journey to an ambiguous city', *P&H*, 12, 2, pp. 129–151.
Gay, Peter (1987) *A Godless Jew: Freud, Atheism and the Making of Psychoanalysis*, New Haven: Yale University Press.
Gay, Peter (1994) 'Freud et la guerre', *Vingtième Siècle, Revue d'Histoire*, 41, pp. 86–92.
Gay, Peter (2006) *Freud: A Life for our Times*, London: Max.
Gicklhorn, Renée (1969) 'The Freiberg period of the Freud family', *Journal of the History of Medicine and Allied Sciences*, 24, 1, pp. 37–43.
Gicklhorn, Renée (1976) *Sigmund Freud und der Onkeltraum: Dichtung und Wahrheit*, Horn, NÖ: Ferdinand Berger & Söhne.
Ginsburg, Lawrence & Ginsburg, Sybil (1992) 'Paradise in the life of Sigmund Freud: An understanding of its imagery and paradoxes', *IRPA*, 19, pp. 285–308.
Goetz, Christopher G (1991) 'Visual art in the neurologic career of Jean-Martin Charcot', *Archives of Neurology*, April, 48, pp. 421–425.
Goldberg, P Selvin (1957) *The Manchester Congregation of British Jews 1857–1957*, Manchester: MCBJ.
Goodnick, Benjamin (1994) 'A childhood letter of Sigmund Freud', *Psychoanalytic Psychology*, 11, 4, pp. 537–543.
Gottwaldt, Alfred (2004) 'Sigmund Freud's sisters and death: Notes on their fate in deportation and mass-murder', *Psyche*, 58, pp. 533–543.
Gresser, Moshe (1994) *Dual Allegiance: Freud as a Modern Jew*, Albany, NY: SUNY Press.
Grinker, Roy R (1940) 'Reminiscences of a personal contact with Freud', in Hendrik M Ruitenbeek (ed) *Freud as we Knew Him*, Detroit: Wayne State University Press, 1973, pp. 180–185.
Grinstein, Alexander (1980) *Sigmund Freud's Dreams*, New York: International Universities Press.
Grinstein, Alexander (1990) *Freud at the Crossroads*, Madison, CT: International Universities Press.
Grosskurth, Phyllis (1985) *Melanie Klein: Her World and her Work*, London: Hodder & Stoughton.
Grubrich-Simitis, Ilse (1996) *Back to Freud's Texts: Making Silent Documents Speak*, New Haven: Yale University Press.
Hartley, Lucy (2001) *Physiognomy and the Meaning of Expression in Nineteenth-Century Culture*, Cambridge: Cambridge University Press.
Heller, Judith Bernays (1956) 'Freud's mother and father', *Commentary*, May, 21, 5, pp. 418–421.
Hermanns, Ludger M (2011) 'The history of psychanalysis in Germany up to 1950 and its relationship to the IPA', in Peter Loewenberg & Nellie L Thompson (eds) *100 Years of the IPA: The Centenary History of the International Psychoanalytical Association 1910–2010*, London: IPA/Karnac, pp. 47–61.

Hill, Christopher (1972) *The World Turned Upside Down: Radical Ideas during the English Revolution*, London: Maurice Temple Smith.
Hoffbrand, Julia (2018) *Leaving Today: The Freuds in Exile 1938*, London: Freud Museum.
Hoffman, Anne G (2009) 'Archival bodies', *American Imago*, 66, pp. 5–40.
Holland, Norman N (1960) 'Freud on Shakespeare', *PMLA*, 75, 3, pp. 163–173.
Hylton, Stuart (2016) *A History of Manchester*, Stroud: Phillimore.
Hyman, Stanley E (1962) 'On *The Interpretation of Dreams*', in Perry Meisel (ed) *Freud: A Collection of Critical Essays*, Englewood Cliffs, NJ: Prentice-Hall, 1981, pp. 121–144.
Jackson, D Joyce (1985) 'Contributions to the history of psychology XXXVII: Katherine Jones (1892–1983)', *Psychological Reports*, 57, pp. 75–83.
Johnston, Thomas E (1965) *Freud and Political Thought*, New York: Citadel Press.
Jones, Ernest (1940) '[Obituary] Wilfred Trotter', *IJPA*, 21, p. 114.
Jones, Ernest (1953–1957) *Sigmund Freud: Life and Work*, 3 volumes, London: Hogarth.
Jones, Ernest (1959) *Free Associations: Memories of a Psycho-Analyst*, London: Hogarth.
Joseph, Edward D (1960) 'Cremation, fire, and oral aggression', *Psychoanalytic Quarterly*, 29, pp. 98–104.
Jucovy, Milton E (1965) 'Meetings of the New York Psychoanalytic Society', *Psychoanalytic Quarterly*, 34, pp. 144–147.
Kahr, Brett (2019) 'Freud's death bed', available online at: www.freud.org.uk/2019/09/10/freuds-death-bed/
Kidd, Alan (1996) *Manchester*, Keele: Keele University Press.
Kirby, Dean (2022) *Fredrich Engels and Angel Meadow: The Origin and Development of Victorian Manchester's 'Hell upon Earth' Slum*, PhD thesis, Manchester Metropolitan University.
Klein, Melanie (1980 [1932]) *The Psychoanalysis of Children*, London: Hogarth.
Knafo, Danielle (1992) 'The significance of the Oedipal in dreams of Sigmund Freud and C G Jung', *IRPA*, 19, pp. 351–358.
Kuhn, Philip (2002) '"Romancing with a wealth of detail": Narratives of Ernest Jones's 1906 trial for indecent assault', *Studies in Gender and Sexuality*, 3, pp. 344–378.
Kuhn, Philip (2015) 'In "The dark regions of the mind" – a reading for the indecent assault in Ernest Jones's 1908 dismissal from the West End Hospital for Nervous Diseases', *P&H*, 17, 1, pp. 7–57.
Kuhn, Philip (2017) *Psychoanalysis in Britain 1893–1913: Histories and Historiography*, Lanham, MD: Lexington Books.
Lacoursiere, Roy (2008) 'Freud's death: Historical truth and biographical fictions', *American Imago*, 65, 1, pp. 107–128.
Laible, Eva (1993) 'Through privation to knowledge: Unknown documents from Freud's university years', *IJPA*, 74, pp. 775–790.
Laplanche, Jean & Pontalis, Jean-Bertrand (1973) *The Language of Psychoanalysis*, London: Hogarth.
Larsen, Kim (1999) '[Review of] Questions for Freud: The Secret History of Psychoanalysis', *Scandinavian Psychoanalytic Review*, 22, 2, pp. 311–314.
Lavater, Johann K (1775–78) *Physiognomische Fragmente zur Beförderung der Menschenkenntnis und Menschenliebe*, Leipzig: Winterthur.
Lazaridis, Nicholas (2003) ,Sigmund Freud's oral cancer', *British Journal of Oral and Maxillofacial Surgery*, 41, pp. 78–83.
Lewis, Emanuel & Casement, Patrick (1986) 'The inhibition of mourning by pregnancy: A case study', *Psychoanalytic Psychotherapy*, 2, 1, pp. 45–52.
Lieberman, E James & Richter, Gregory C (eds) (2012) *The Letters of Sigmund Freud and Otto Rank: Inside Psychoanalysis*, Baltimore: Johns Hopkins University Press.
Lippman, Robert (2009) 'Freud's botanical monograph screen memory revisited', *Psychoanalytic Review*, 96, 4, pp. 579–595.

Livshin, Rosalyn D (2015) *Nonconformity in the Manchester Jewish Community: The Case of Political Radicalism, 1889–1939*, PhD thesis, University of Manchester.

London, Louise (2001) *Whitehall and the Jews, 1933–1948: British Immigration Policy, Jewish Refugees and the Holocaust*, Cambridge: Cambridge University Press.

Looney, J Thomas (1920) *Shakespeare Identified*, London: Cecil Palmer.

Lotto, David (2001) 'Freud's struggle with misogyny: Homosexuality and guilt in the dream of Irma's injection', *JAPA*, 49, pp. 1289–1313.

Macleod, Alastair D (2017) 'Was Sigmund Freud's death hastened?', *Internal Medical Journal*, 47, pp. 966–969.

Macmillan, Malcolm & Swales, Peter J (2003) 'Observations from the refuse heap: Freud, Michelangelo's Moses, and psychoanalysis', *American Imago*, 60, 1, pp. 41–104.

Marcus, Laura (2014) 'Oedipus express: Psychoanalysis and the railways', in *Dreams of Modernity: Psychoanalysis, Literature, Cinema*, Cambridge: Cambridge University Press, pp. 41–58.

Marcus, Steven (2017) *Engels, Manchester, and the Working Class*, Abingdon: Routledge.

Margolis, Deborah P (1989) 'Freud and his mother', *Modern Psychoanalysis*, 14, pp. 37–56.

Marx, Karl (1852) *The Eighteenth Brumaire of Louis Bonaparte*, in Karl Marx & Friedrich Engels (eds) *Collected Works*, vol. 11, London: Lawrence & Wishart, 2010, pp. 99–197.

Massicotte, Claudie (2014) 'Psychical transmissions: Freud, spiritualism, and the occult', *Psychoanalytic Dialogues*, 24, pp. 88–102.

Masson, Jeffrey M (ed) (1985) *The Complete Letters of Sigmund Freud to Wilhelm Fliess 1887–1904*, Cambridge, MA: Belknap Press.

Mathieu, Marianne & Philipp, Michael (eds) (2022) *Face au Soleil: Un Astre dans les Arts*, Vanves: Éditions Hazan.

Mayer, Andreas (2015) 'Thinking in cases: On the afterlife of Galton's composite photographs in psychoanalysis', *Annual of Psychoanalysis*, 38, pp. 71–86.

McGrath, William J (1974) 'Freud as Hannibal: The politics of the brother band', *Central European History*, 7, 1, pp. 31–57.

McGuire, William (ed) (1974) *The Freud/Jung Letters The Correspondence between Sigmund Freud and CG Jung*, Princeton, NJ: Princeton University Press.

Meghnagi, David (2011) 'From the dreams of a generation to the theory of dreams: Freud's Roman dreams', *IJPA*, 92, pp. 675–694.

Meltzer, Donald (1992) *The Claustrum*, Perthshire: Clunie Press.

Meng, Heinrich & Freud, Ernst L (eds) (1963) *Psychoanalysis and Faith: The Letters of Sigmund Freud & Oskar Pfister*, New York: Basic Books.

Meyer-Palmedo, Ingeborg (ed) (2014) *Correspondence 1904–1938 Sigmund Freud and Anna Freud*, Cambridge: Polity Press.

Micale, Mark S (1993) 'Henry F Ellenberger and the origins of European psychiatric historiography', in *Beyond the Unconscious: Essays of Henri F Ellenberger in the History of Psychiatry*, Princeton, NJ: Princeton University Press.

Michler, Werner (2020) 'Intellectual hero, most beloved master: Stefan Zweig and Sigmund Freud in British exile', in Elana Shapira & Daniela Finzi (eds) *Freud and the Émigré: Austrian Émigrés, Exiles and the Legacy of Psychoanalysis in Britain*, London: Palgrave Macmillan, pp. 77–94.

Miller, Eric (1984) *Passion for Murder: The Homicidal Deeds of Dr Sigmund Freud*, San Diego: Future Directions.

Miller, Ian S (2020) 'Spinoza: Multiple identities at the origins of psychoanalytic psychology', *International Forum of Psychoanalysis*, 29, pp. 207–214.

Molnar, Michael (ed) (1992) *The Diary of Sigmund Freud 1929–1939: A Record of the Final Decade*, London: Hogarth.

Molnar, Michael (1998) 'Sigmund Freud's notes on faces and men: National Portrait Gallery, September 13, 1908', in M S Roth (ed) *Freud: Conflict and Culture*, New York: Knopf, pp. 41–50.

Molnar, Michael (2012) 'Freud in the national portrait gallery', *American Imago*, 69, 1, pp. 107–133.
Molnar, Michael (2013) 'Death in the library', unpublished.
Molnar, Michael (2015) *Looking Through Freud's Photos*, London: Karnac.
Murken, Barbara (1981) 'Tom Seidmann-Freud: Leben und Werk', *Die Schiefertafel*, December 1981, 4, 3, pp. 163–201.
Murken, Barbara (2004) '". . . die Welt ist so uneben . . ." Tom Seidmann-Freud (1892–1930): Leben und Werk einer grossen Bilderbuch-Künstlerin', *Luzifer-Amor*, 17, 33, pp. 73–103.
Nathan, David (1991) 'Failure of an elderly gentleman: Shaw and the Jews', *Shaw*, 11, pp. 219–238.
Nobus, Dany (2015) 'Yom Kippur 1939: The last day of Freud's life and its immediate aftermath', Freud Memorial Lecture, Freud Museum, London, available online at: https://thefreudmuseum.podbean.com/category/dany-nobus.
Nobus, Dany (forthcoming) 'Yom Kippur 1939: Freud, Schur and the rupture of the lethal pact', in *Freud in the Margins: Rethinking the History of Psychoanalysis*, New York: Columbia University Press.
Nunberg, Herman & Federn, Ernst (1962) *Minutes of the Vienna Psychoanalytic Society*, vol. 1 (1906–1908), New York: International Universities Press.
O'Donoghue, Diane (2019) *On Dangerous Ground: Freud's Visual Cultures of the Unconscious*, London: Bloomsbury Academic.
Panayi, Panikos (1995) *German Immigrants in Britain during the Nineteenth Century 1815–1914*, Oxford: Berg.
Panayi, Panikos (2014) *The Enemy in our Midst: Germans in Britain during the First World War*, London: Bloomsbury.
Parsons, Talcott (1951) *The Social System*, Glencoe, IL: The Free Press.
Paskauskas, Richard Andrew (1993) *The Complete Correspondence of Sigmund Freud and Ernest Jones 1908–1939*, Cambridge, MA: Belknap Press.
Pearl, Sharrona (2009) 'Through a mediated mirror: The photographic physiognomy of Dr Hugh Welch Diamond', *History of Photography*, 33, pp. 288–305.
Pierri, Maria (2023) *Sigmund Freud and the Forsyth Case: Coincidences and Thought-Transmission in Psychoanalysis*, Abingdon: Routledge.
Prawer, Siegbert S (2009) *A Cultural Citizen of the World: Sigmund Freud's Knowledge and Use of British and American Writings*, London: Legenda.
Puner, Helen W (1959) *Freud: His Life and His Mind*, New York: Dell.
Rabeyron, Thomas & Evrard, Renaud (2012) 'Historical and contemporary perspectives on occultism in the Freud-Ferenczi correspondence', *Recherches en Psychanalyse*, 1, 13, pp. 98–112.
Rice, Emanuel (1990) *Freud and Moses: The Long Journey Home*, Albany: SUNY Press.
Rieff, Philip (1956) 'The origins of Freud's political psychology', *Journal of the History of Ideas*, 17, 2, pp. 235–249.
Rizzuto, Ana-Maria (1998) *Why Did Freud Reject God? A Psychodynamic Interpretation*, New Haven: Yale University Press.
Roazen, Paul (1969) *Freud: Political and Social Thought*, London: Hogarth Press.
Roazen, Paul (1976) *Freud and his Followers*, London: Allen Lane.
Roazen, Paul (1990) 'Freud's last will', *Journal of the American Academy of Psychoanalysis and Dynamic Psychiatry*, 18, pp. 383–391.
Roazen, Paul (1993) *Meeting Freud's Family*, Amherst, MA: University of Massachusetts Press.
Roazen, Paul (2001) *The Historiography of Psychoanalysis*, New Brunswick, NJ: Transaction Publishers.
Roazen, Paul (2005) *Edoardo Weiss: The House That Freud Built*, Abingdon: Routledge.
Roberts, Thomas (1996) *Vienna and Manchester: The Correspondence of Sigmund Freud and Sam Freud 1911–1938*, unpublished manuscript.

Roberts, Thomas (ed) (2000) *Viena y Manchester: Correspondencia entre Sigmund Freud y su sobrino Sam Freud (1911–1938)*, translated by Pedro Navarro Serrano, Madrid: Síntesis.

Rocah, Barbara S (2002) 'The language of flowers: Freud's adolescent language of love, lust, and longing', *The Psychoanalytic Study of the Child*, 57, 1, pp. 377–399.

Rolnik, Eran J (2012) *Freud in Zion: Psychoanalysis and the Making of Modern Jewish Identity*, London: Karnac.

Romano, Cesare (2018) 'L'enigma di Rebekka Freud', *Psicoterapia e Scienze Umane*, 52, pp. 215–248.

Romm, Sharon (1983) *The Unwelcome Intruder: Freud's Struggle with Cancer*, New York: Praeger.

Rose, Paul (1970) *The Manchester Martyrs: The Story of a Fenian Tragedy*, London: Lawrence & Wishart.

Rosenberg, Warren (2001) *Legacy of Rage, Violence, and Culture*, Amherst, MA: University of Massachusetts Press.

Roudinesco, Élisabeth (2016) *Freud in His Time and Ours*, Cambridge, MA: Harvard University Press.

Rubinstein, William D (2010) *Antisemitism in the English-Speaking World*, New York: Oxford University Press.

Sajner, Josef (1989) 'Die Beziehungen Sigmund Freuds und seiner Familie zu dem mährischen Kurort Rožnau', *Jahrbuch der Psychoanalyse*, 24, pp. 73–96.

Sala, George A (1868) *Notes and Sketches of the Paris Exhibition*, London: Tinsley Brothers.

Sartre, Jean-Paul (1945) *Huis Clos – Piece en un Acte*, London: Horizon.

Scagnelli, Paul (1994) *Deadly Dr Freud: The Murder of Emanuel Freud and the Disappearance of John Freud*, Durham, NC: Pinewood Publishing.

Schmalz, Timothy (2021) *Anglo-Austrian Diplomatic Backchannels from the Juliputsch to the Anschluss, 1934–38*, PhD thesis, University of Cambridge.

Schorske, Carl E (1981) *Fin-de-Siècle Vienna: Politics and Culture*, Cambridge: Cambridge University Press.

Schröter, Michael (1996) 'The beginnings of a troubled friendship', *International Forum of Psychoanalysis*, 5, 2, pp. 33–150.

Schröter, Michael (ed) (2004) *Sigmund Freud-Max Eitingon, Briefwechsel 1906–1939*, Tübingen: edition diskord.

Schröter, Michael & Hermanns, Ludger M (1992) 'Felix Gattel (1870–1904): Freud's first pupil', *IRPA*, 19, pp. 91–104 and 197–208.

Schröter, Michael & Tögel, Christfried (2007) 'The Leipzig episode in Freud's life (1859): A new narrative on the basis of recently discovered documents', *Psychoanalytic Quarterly*, 76, 1, pp. 193–215.

Schur, Max (1966) 'Some additional "day residues" of the "specimen dream of psychoanalysis"', in M Kanzer & J Glenn (eds) *Freud and his Self-Analysis*, New York: Jason Aronson, 1979, pp. 87–116.

Schur, Max (1969) 'The background of Freud's "disturbance" on the Acropolis', *American Imago*, 26, 4, pp. 303–323.

Schur, Max (1972) *Freud: Living and Dying*, London: Hogarth Press.

Shengold, Leonard (1993) *'The Boy Will Come to Nothing': Freud's Ego Ideal and Freud as Ego Ideal*, New Haven: Yale University Press.

Simmel, Ernst (1940) 'Sigmund Freud: The man and his work', *Psychoanalytic Quarterly*, 9, pp. 163–176.

Simmons, Laurence (2006) *Freud's Italian Journey*, Amsterdam: Rodopi.

Stekel, Wilhelm (1926) 'On the history of the analytical movement', *P&H*, 2005, 7, 1, pp. 99–130.

Sterba, Richard M (1982) *Reminiscences of a Viennese Psychoanalyst*, Detroit: Wayne State University Press.

Strozier, Charles (1985) '1 Glimpses of a life: Heinz Kohut (1913–1981)', *Progress in Self-Psychology*, 1, pp. 3–12.
Swales, Peter J (2002) 'Physiognomy, phrenology, craniometry, and questions of character: Pondering Freud's cognitive style', paper given at the Richardson History of Psychiatry Seminar series, The Institute for the History of Psychiatry, New York, 2 January 2002.
Swan, Jim (1974) 'Mater and Nannie: Freud's two mothers and the discovery of the Oedipus complex', *American Imago*, 31, 1, pp. 1–64.
Sylwan, Barbro (2010) 'Freud & Co, marchands de Manchester: À propos de la mort de Philipp Freud et ses effets', in B Sylwan & P Réfabert (eds) *Freud, Fliess, Ferenczi: Des Fantômes qui Hantent la Psychanalyse*, Paris: Herman, pp. 225–245.
Szaluta, Jacques (1983) 'Freud's ego ideals: A study of admired modern historical and political personages', *JAPA*, 31, pp. 157–186.
Tagore, Rabindranath (1912) '60 [On the seashore]', in *Gitanjali*, with an introduction by W B Yeats, London: The India Society, pp. 34–35.
Taylor, Simon, Cooper, Malcolm & Barnwell, P S (2002) *Manchester: The Warehouse Legacy*, London: English Heritage.
Thomson, Mathew (2011) 'The solution to his own enigma: Connecting the life of Montague David Eder (1865–1936), socialist, psychoanalyst, Zionist and modern saint', *Medical History*, 55, pp. 61–84.
Tögel, Christfried (2004) 'Freuds Berliner Schwester Maria (Mitzi) und ihre Familie', *Luzifer-Amor: Zeitschrift zur Geschichte der Psychoanalyse*, 17, 33, pp. 33–50.
Tögel, Christfried (2010) 'Freud and religion', *Balkan Journal of Philosophy*, 2, 2, pp. 143–148.
Tögel, Christfried (2019a) 'Freud als Unterzeichner von Aufrufen', available online at: www.freud-biographik.de
Tögel, Christfried (2019b) 'Über Sigmund Freuds erste und über seine *beinahe* letzte Unterkunft in Wien' ('About Sigmund Freud's first and almost his last accommodation in Vienna'), available online at: www.freud-biographik.de/kleine-texte-zur-freud-biographik/.
Tögel, Christfried (2023) *Freud-Diarium 1856–1939*, in Christfried Tögel (ed) *Sigmund-Freud-Gesamtausgabe*, vol. 22, Giessen: Psychosozial-Verlag.
Tögel, Christfried & Kurz, Thomas (2019) 'Wien – Paris – London. Zum Ablauf der Flucht Sigmund Freuds aus Wien', available online at: www.freud-biographik.de/kleine-texte-zur-freud-biographik.
Tögel, Christfried & Schröter, Michael (2004) 'Briefe an Maria (Mitzi) Freud und ihre Familie', *Luzifer-Amor: Zeitschrift zur Geschichte der Psychoanalyse*, 17, 33, pp. 51–72.
Tögel, Christfried, Tögel, Ginka, Tögel, Ina & Tögel, Infrid (2018) 'Sigmund Freud in Dresden: Anmerkungen zu einem Besuch und zu Freuds ästherischer Auffasang', *Werkblatt Zeitschrift für Psychoanalyse und Gessellschaftskritik*, 80, pp. 1–21.
Trosman, Harry & Wolf, Ernest S (1973) 'The Bernfeld collaboration in the Jones biography of Freud', *IJPA*, 54, pp. 227–233.
Trotter, Wilfred (1940) *Instincts of the Herd in Peace and War*, London: Ernest Benn.
Turner, Michael (2008) 'Nostalgia & Dionysus: The mystery of Sigmund Freud's final resting place', in Janine Burke (ed) *Sigmund Freud's Collection: An Archaeology of the Mind*, Sydney: MUMA, pp. 42–45.
Tytler, Graeme (1982) *Physiognomy in the European Novel: Faces and Fortunes*, Princeton, NJ: Princeton University Press.
Vallin, Jacques (2002) 'Mortality in Europe from 1720 to 1914: Long-term trends and changes in the patterns by age and sex', in Roger S Schofield, David S Reher and Alain Bideau (eds) *The Decline of Mortality in Europe*, Oxford: Clarendon Press, pp. 38–67.
Vincent, Claude (ed) (1996) *Lettres de Famille de Sigmund Freud et des Freud de Manchester 1911–1938*, Paris: PUF.
Vitz, Paul C (1993) *Sigmund Freud's Christian Unconscious*, Leominster: Gracewing.
Weber, Nicholas Fox (2017) *Freud's Trip to Orvieto*, New York: Bellevue Literary Press.

Weiss, Edoardo (1960) *The Structure and Dynamics of the Human Mind*, New York: Grune & Stratton.
Weiss, Edoardo (1991) *Sigmund Freud as a Consultant: Recollections of a Pioneer in Psychoanalysis*, London: Routledge.
Weissberg, Liliane (2010) 'Ariadne's Thread', *MLN*, 125, 3, pp. 661–681.
Welter, Volker M (2012) *Ernst L Freud, Architect: The Case of the Modern Bourgeois Home*, New York: Berghahn Books.
Whitebook, Joel (2017) *Freud: An Intellectual Biography*, Cambridge: Cambridge University Press.
Whitfield, Roy (1988) *Friedrich Engels in Manchester: The Search for a Shadow*, Salford: Working Class Movement Library.
Whyte, Lancelot L (1960) *The Unconscious Before Freud*, New York: Basic Books.
Williams, Bill (1976) *The Making of Manchester Jewry 1740–1875*, Manchester: Manchester University Press.
Williams, Bill (1989) 'East and West: Class and culture in Manchester Jewry, 1850–1920', *Studia Rosenthaliana*, 23, pp. 88–106.
Williams, Bill (2008) *Jewish Manchester: An Illustrated History*, Derby: Breedon Books.
Willoughby, Roger (forthcoming) 'Freud's use of iconography in curating his public profile'.
Winnicott, Clare (1978) 'DWW: A reflection', in Clare Winnicott, Ray Shepherd, & Madeleine Davis (eds) *D W Winnicott: Psycho-Analytic Explorations*, London: Karnac, 1989, pp. 1–18.
Winnicott, Donald Woods (1967) 'The Location of cultural experience', in *Playing and Reality*, Harmondsworth: Penguin, 1985, pp. 112–121.
Wittels, Fritz (1924) *Sigmund Freud: His Personality, his Teaching, and his School*, London: Allen and Unwin.
Wittenberger, Gerhard & Tögel, Christfried (1999) *Die Rundbriefe des 'Geheimen Komitees, Band 1: 1913–1920* [The Circular Letters of the Secret Committee, Volume 1: 1913–1920], Tübingen: Diskord.
Wittenberger, Gerhard & Tögel, Christfried (2000) *Die Rundbriefe des 'Geheimen Komitees, Band 2: 1921* [The Circular Letters of the Secret Committee, Volume 2: 1921], 4 volumes, Tübingen: Diskord.
Wittenberger, Gerhard & Tögel, Christfried (2003) *Die Rundbriefe des 'Geheimen Komitees, Band 3: 1922* [The Circular Letters of the Secret Committee, Volume 3: 1922], Tübingen: Diskord.
Wittenberger, Gerhard & Tögel, Christfried (2006) *Die Rundbriefe des 'Geheimen Komitees, Band 4: 1923–1927* [The Circular Letters of the Secret Committee, Volume 4: 1923–1927], Tübingen: Diskord.
Woolf, Leonard (1967) *Downhill All the Way: An Autobiography of the Years 1919 to 1939*, London: Hogarth Press.
Woolf, Virginia (1998 [1929]) *A Room of One's Own*, edited by M Schiach, Oxford: Oxford University Press.
Wu, Yiming *et al* (2023) 'Identifying high-impact variants and genes in exomes of Ashkenazi Jewish inflammatory bowel disease patients', *Nature Communications*, 14, 2256.
Young-Bruehl, Elisabeth (1994) 'A history of Freud biographies', in Mark S Micale & Roy Porter (eds) *Discovering the History of Psychiatry*, Oxford: Oxford University Press, pp. 157–173.
Zweig, Stefan (1943) *The World of Yesterday: An Autobiography*, London: Cassell & Co.

Index

Abraham, Karl 74, 118, 124, 127, 141
Adams, Leslie 3
Aichhorn, August 167
Alfred A Knopf (publishers) 98, 182, 185
Allert de Lange (publishers) 173, 182–183
Anspach, Jennie 198
anti-Semitism 9, 16, 22, 30, 35, 54–55, 60, 72, 80, 96, 99, 141, 162–163, 166, 169, 172, 180–181, 198
Anzieu, Didier 12, 45, 58, 77
Augusta, Georg 20, 23n18

Barclays Bank 179
Baumgardt, David 185
Belcredi, Richard Graf von 35–36
Bell, David 4n14
Berke, Joseph 46
Berlin, Isaiah 185
Berlyn, Moses 89
Bernays, Edward 76
Bernays, Eli 39n37; bankruptcy 76; death 146; emigrates to USA 76–77; remittances to the Freuds in Vienna 21, 74, 76, 140
Bernays, Judith 76
Bernays, Leah 76–77
Bernays, Minna 167, 179, 197; illness 170, 175, 177, 180, 195
Bernfeld, Siegfried 9, 15
Bernfeld, Suzanne 17
Bibring, Grete 188
Binswanger, Ludwig 94
Blanton, Smiley 177, 189, 200, 203n50
Bonaparte, Marie 181, 183, 188, 193, 196; countering the Nazi threat 164–167; and Freud's sisters 181; meeting in Paris 168; supports Ernst's naturalisation application 203n43, 206n126; supports

Imago 176; visits Freud in London 174, 185, 191
Bragg, William 166
Braine, John F C 177
Breslau 19
Bretholz, Sigmund 19
Brill, Abraham A 81, 127
Brittain, Vera 169
Brücke, Ernst 8
Bryan, Douglas 130
Budberg, Baroness Maria 186
Bueckers Hotel 112, 120n38
Bullitt, William 164–165, 168
Buriánek, Václav 24n35
Burlingham, Dorothy 164, 167, 179, 188, 191, 199
Burt, Cyril 73

Campbell-Bannerman, Henry 81
Charcot, Jean-Martin 8, 60, 73, 75, 81
Clark, Roland 3, 59, 119n26, 209n169
Claus, Herman 188
Claus, Marie 188
Clerk-Maxwell, James 56, 59
Cocker, Frank Barlow 96
Cohen, David 42, 210n189
Cohen, Leopold Louis 90
Copenhagen, SS 117
Corduff, Kathleen 176
Coward, Noel 169

Dalí, Gala 174
Dalí, Salvador 174–175, 200
Darwin, Charles 54, 73, 115
Davidoff, Leonore 2, 29, 31, 36
Davidowa, Marie Lilly 177
Deutsch, Felix 175, 202n28
de Vere, Edward 116

230 Index

Diamond, Hugh Welch 73
Dickens, Charles 38n20, 55
dreams 2, 7, 43, 74, 96, 143; 'bird-beaked figures' 45; 'grey horse' 157n10; 'Hollthurn' 56–59, 63n36, 63n39; 'Non Vixit' 13, 44
Dreschfield, Julius 60
Dresden 65, 67–69, 74, 92, 104, 213
Duncan, Beryl A 179
Duncan, David 179
Duncan, David Stuart 179
duplication, displacement and replacement: dynamic of 15, 17, 22, 61, 67, 99, 138, 156, 214–215; *see also* marginalisation

Eckstein, Emma 15
Eder, Montague David 112, 127, 130
Eitingon, Max 139, 170, 181, 183, 187–188, 211
Ellenberger, Henri 2
Ellis, Havelock 80, 112, 116, 184
Elsworthy Road 149, 167, 169–177, 180, 182, 185–186, 189, 200, 212
Engelman, Edmund 167, 202n22
Engels, Friedrich 30–31
Excelsior Hotel 117
Exner, George G 175, 177–178, 187, 194

family romance 2, 9, 214
Fanon, Frantz 1
Farman, Henri 125
Fear, Jill (John's great granddaughter) 153
Ferenczi, Sándor 130, 134, 141; and Britain 127–128; and the paranormal 124, 135n9; travels and holidays with Freud 106, 124, 127–128
Fichtl, Paula 149, 167, 179, 194–195, 198
Finzi, Neville 184, 187–188
Fletcher, Howard Lynton 185
Fliess, Wilhelm 8, 12–15, 52, 77, 143
Fluss, Emil 19
Fluss, Gisela 15
Ford's Hotel 111–113
Forsyth, David 140
Franckenstein, Sir George 197
Frankel, Burman 93, 101n39
Frankel Maria 89
Frankel, Moses 89
Freiberg 7, 9–10, 12–13, 15–19, 22, 29, 36, 155–156, 165, 179, 216
Freud, Abraham (Jacob's brother) 19, 27n110

Freud, Alexander 8–9, 45, 74, 130, 160n72, 171–172, 179, 181, 191, 198; and Emanuel Freud 77; emigration to Canada 198, 210n201; leaves Austria 167
Freud, Amalia Nathansohn 7, 15, 19, 42, 44, 50, 58, 75, 130, 142, 146, 156; alleged affair with Philipp 15–16, 45; cares for Judith Bernays 76; character 11, 146, 160n72; deafness 146; and Emanuel in Berlin 124; her health 11; marriage 8; middle class origins 11, 42; parents support of 20, 42; precedence in the family 17, 146; spa usage 11, 65, 213
Freud, Anna (Freud's daughter) 35, 55, 110, 143, 148, 167–170, 175, 177, 179, 183, 185–186, 197–199, 203n43, 204n81, 206n126, 215; 1914 visit to Britain 123, 129, 131–132; and Anglo-Austrian Bank 140; caring for Freud 178, 192–193, 195; displaces Emanuel as Freud's 1913 holiday companion 130, 134; emigration 165; income 207n147; and Klein 174; Maresfield Gardens 204n81; permission to practice in Britain 166, 170, 203n43; practice in London 188; and the psychoanalytic establishment 165, 176, 200; purchases the freehold of 20; questioned by the Nazis 166
Freud, Anna (*later* Bernays) (Freud's sister) 9, 12, 19, 31, 55, 146
Freud, Bertha (Emanuel's daughter) 13, 29, 66, 76, 78–79, 123, 132, 134, 148, 195; death 149; health problems 123–124, 147; lack of a dowry 60, 76; timidity 81
Freud, Bloomah (Philipp's wife) 52–53, 93, 98, 100n6, 102n50, 156; background and marriage 89–91; death 97; and the Great War 96
Freud, Emanuel 7, 8, 12, 16; assimilation as an 'Englishman' 55, 65, 79, 128, 211; bereavements 42–43, 45, 47; and bills of exchange 18, 22; in business on his own account 31–32, 46, 66–67, 75–77; in business with Jacob 12, 24n46; in business with Philipp as Freud & Co 32–33; character 52–53, 67–68, 74–75, 105–108, 124, 128–130, 132; children 12–13, 41–43, 45, 47, 130; contemplating retirement

Index 231

78–79; correspondence with Freud 33–34, 39n37; cremation 132; death 132–134; early years 12; emigration to Britain 29–31; family difficulties 47, 65; financial difficulties 32, 41; as Freud's alternative father figure 7, 15, 17, 54, 58, 212, 215; Judaism 31, 36, 41, 46–47, 66, 132; naturalisation 66; politics 81–82, 126; refreshment on the Continent 65, 67–72, 82, 123, 134, 213; servants 33, 45, 86n75; stepping aside as the eldest son 17, 138, 156, 214; in suburbia 45–46, 66; supporting the family in Vienna 21, 65–66, 69–70, 74–76

Freud, Ernst 3, 34, 98, 151, 175, 196; career as an architect 163, 170, 179–180, 198, 201n1; facilitates the Freuds move to London 167–170, 177; flees Berlin 149, 163; gains refuge in Britain 149, 163, 201n1; his father's death 193–194; naturalisation 170, 203n43, 206n126; redesign of Maresfield Gardens 179–180, 194, 215

Freud, Esther (Dolfi) (Freud's sister) 9, 77, 160n72, 169, 199; and Emanuel in Berlin 124

Freud, Eva (Oliver's daughter) 191

Freud family 7–22; and neuropathology 75; servants 11–12, 19, 24n35, 208n159; working class origins and poverty 3, 8–9, 22, 23n18, 52, 74

Freud, Harriet Emily (Emanuel's daughter) 41–45, 47, 61, 155

Freud, Harry (Alexander's son) 150, 168, 191; on Emanuel 130; financially supports Freud's sisters 199; settles in USA 198

Freud, Henrietta (Emanuel's daughter) 41–45, 47, 61, 155

Freud, Jacob 7, 8, 11, 15, 19, 58, 74–75, 76; bankruptcy of 20; and bills of exchange 18, 20–21; in business 8–9; cares for Judith Bernays 76; character 10–11; death 77, 214; denied residence in Leipzig 19; marginality of 10–12, 70; settles in Vienna 20–21, 28n120; visits Manchester 67; as working class 8

Freud, Johann (John) (Emanuel's son) 13–14, 15, 29, 33, 50, 58, 151–157; assimilation in Britain 53, 66, 129, 151–152; career 76, 151–154, 212;

death 154; and *Die Räuber* 43–45; and Judaism 153, 155; leaves home 66–67, 151; in London 112, 151–155; marriage 152; multilingualism 53, 152

Freud, Josef (Freud's uncle) 29; and the counterfeit roubles affair 29, 34–36, 95

Freud, Julius (Freud's brother) 11–15, 17, 214

Freud, Lucian (Ernst's son) 179, 195, 198

Freud, Lucie (Ernst's wife) 179; account of Freud's death 193

Freud, Margarethe (Mitzi's daughter) 117

Freud, Marie (Mitzi) (Freud's sister) 9, 74, 118, 142, 146, 158n36, 169; in Berlin 117, 124, 134; death 199, 210n203

Freud, Marie Rozená (Emanuel's wife) 12, 13, 58, 132, 134; death 144–145; health problems 78, 123–124, 142, 147

Freud, Martha (*later* Tom Seidmann-Freud) (Mitzi's daughter) 117–118, 142, 158n36

Freud, Martha 60, 72, 74–76, 98, 112, 116, 124, 139–140, 169–170; cares for Leah Bernays 76–77; death 196; flees Vienna 167; and the Freud sisters 170–171; on her bereavement 197; at Maresfield Gardens 179–180; religious observance 99; and Sophie's death 142; wedding 76

Freud, Martin (Freud's son) 8, 10–11, 83n10, 165–166, 175; 1912 visit to Britain 123, 128–129, 132, 136n30; 1925 visit to Britain 128–129, 145, 147; detained by the Nazis 164; on Freud's death 193–194; interned 198; leaves Austria 167; in London 169–170, 179, 186; and *Parole d'Honneur* 197–198; and psychoanalytic publishing 164, 176, 182

Freud, Mathilde (*later* Hollitscher) (Freud's daughter) 108–110, 120n30, 128, 143, 180; cares for Freud in London 169, 171, 180; cares for Heinz 143; and Freud's death 193; leaves Austria 167; opens Robell boutique 180; and the Oppenheimer portrait 110

Freud, Matilda (Emanuel's daughter) 33, 42–45, 47, 61, 155

Freud, Moritz (Maurice) 74, 78, 117; as an Anglophile 117–118; death 148; and Freud & Co 93

Freud, Morris H W 83n10, 90; career 98; death 98; emigration to South Africa 93; estrangement from Freud 90, 93, 103n71, 111, 212; meeting with Jacob 91–92, 101n26

Freud, Oliver (Freud's son) 60, 83n10, 126, 163, 191, 193; flees Berlin 149, 163

Freud, Paula (Pauli) (later Winternitz) (Freud's sister) 9, 139, 169, 199, 210n203

Freud, Paulina (Pauline) (Emanuel's daughter) 13–15, 29, 54, 58, 66, 75–76, 78, 79, 123, 132, 134; death 149–150, 195; health problems 75, 80, 85n48, 123–124, 147–148; lack of a dowry 60, 76

Freud, Pauline (Poppy) Maria (*later* Hartwig) (Philipp's daughter) 83n10, 90–91, 94, 96, 99, 103n71, 150, 161n109, 184, 195, 212; career 93, 96–97; death 98; and the Great War 96; marriage 97; meeting with Jacob 91–92, 101n26; sustains a relationship with Freud 98, 111, 177, 212

Freud, Philipp 12, 15–16, 18; and bills of exchange 18, 22; in business 16, 26n68, 89, 92–93, 96; in business with Emanuel as Freud & Co 32–33; character 7–8, 16, 52–53, 99; death 94–96; disparagement of 3, 88, 99; eschews naturalisation 66; European journeys 67–72, 92–94; his religious sensibility 7–8, 31, 36, 91, 99, 101n24, 118, 125, 212; holding the negative 7, 15–16, 45, 215; Jacob visits 91–92; as Joycean hero 88–96, 99; and London 74; marginalisation 16, 67; marriage 89–90; physical features 16, 26n72, 45, 62n6, 215; relationship with Freud 12, 15–16, 22, 45, 50, 93–94, 99, 111, 212; servants 91, 99; in suburbia 90–92

Freud, Regine (Rosa) (*later* Graf) (Freud's sister) 9, 28n116, 78, 159; death 169, 199, 210n203; and Emanuel 60–61, 74–76, 151; neurasthenic tendencies 75

Freud, Sally Kanner 7, 17

Freud, Samuel (Solomon) (Emanuel's son) 32, 33, 53, 66, 138–150, 195; arranges food parcels 139–140, 156; assimilation as an 'Englishman' 129; death 150; education 53; in the family business 66, 76, 78, 85n63, 125–126, 138; independent living 125–126, 134; marked inhibition 130, 138, 142, 147, 156, 212

Freud, Schlomo (Solomon) 32

Freud, Sigmund: 1875 visit to Britain 50–61, 186; 1908 visit to Britain 104–122; 1938 emigration to Britain 149, 163, 165–170; 'A disturbance of memory on the Acropolis' 8, 62n23; and art 69–73, 104, 106, 112–117; bank accounts 140, 166, 179; British naturalisation 186–187, 194, 206n126; cancer 143–145, 159n56, 164, 168, 175, 177–179, 187–188, 190–191; cares for Leah Bernays 76–77; *Civilization and its Discontents* 8; death 192–195, 200–201; and *Die Räuber* 43–44; dogs 167, 169, 185, 191; funeral 196; *The Future of an Illusion* 8; *Group Psychology and the Analysis of the Ego* 126; his Anglophilia 50, 51, 53, 167, 171, 214; *The Interpretation of Dreams* 2, 13–14, 17, 22n1, 35, 44–45, 54, 56, 74, 107, 143, 155, 212; Judaism 22, 61, 72, 99, 133, 141, 156, 173, 181, 185, 196; losses 11–12, 17, 22, 94, 104, 106–110, 118, 132–135, 139, 142–145, 148, 174–175, 214; *Moses and Monotheism* 8, 61, 95, 98–99, 165, 172, 174–175, 184–185, 200, 212; and the Nazis 163–167, 169–170, 181, 186, 200; *On the History of the Psycho-Analytic Movement* 1; *An Outline of Psycho-Analysis* 176, 178, 180–181, 200; and the paranormal 124, 135n9; permission to practice in Britain 166; and physiognomy 71, 73–74, 83n20, 104, 114–116, 215; politics 81–82, 126; poverty, working-class origins and money 3, 8–9, 22, 23n18, 52, 62n23, 74, 140, 141; *The Psychopathology of Everyday Life* 45, 89, 130–131; recognition 60, 94, 104–105, 116, 118, 141–142, 216; relationship with Amalia 19–20, 50, 145–146, 159n50, 160n72; relationship with Emanuel 7, 15, 17, 22, 50–61, 67–68, 74, 76–77, 105–106, 123–124, 130, 134; relationship with Jacob 10–11, 50, 51, 54, 70, 74, 107–108; relationship with John 13–15, 43–45, 53, 150–157; relationship with Philipp

12, 15–16, 22, 45, 50, 93–94, 99, 111, 124–125, 212, 215; relationship with Sam 138–150; 'Screen memories' 14, 54; and the seashore 55–56, 90, 108; self-analysis 2, 7, 14, 22; sisters in Vienna 169, 171, 181, 199, 214; 'Some elementary lessons in psycho-analysis' 180–181, 200; *Totem and Taboo* 8, 61, 94, 126, 130–131, 183; transference to Britain 34, 53–54, 60, 199, 211; two mothers 17; and USA 60–61, 124; wheelchair 167–168, 216
Freud, Sophie (*later* Halberstadt) (Freud's daughter) 129–130, 137n52, 142–143, 146, 197
Freud, Sophie (Alexander's wife) 198, 210n201
Freud, Teddy (Mitzi's son) 117, 146
Freud-Marlé, Lilly (Mitzi's daughter) 78–79, 97–98, 117, 141, 150, 161n109
Frisch, Israel Leib 18

Galton, Francis 73–74
Gay, Peter 9, 11, 143
Gebrüdern Wagschal 18
Geikie-Cobb, Ivo 185
Gentilli, Professor 116, 121n60
Gicklhorn, Renée 24n46
Goldscheid family 33
Goodnick, Benjamin 34, 39n32
Graf, Caecilie (Mausi) (Rosa's daughter) 142, 146, 158n41
Graf, Heinrich 78
Greece and Denmark, Princess Eugénie of 185
Green, André 12
Greenop, Ethel Rose (previously Froud) (John's daughter) 152–154
Greenop, Joseph N 154
Greenop, Peter 152
Gresser, Möshe 46
Grinker, Roy 168
Grinstein, Alexander 39n38, 58
Guilbert, Yvette 185
Guttenberg, Marcus 91

Hajek, Marcus 175
Halberstadt, Heinz (Heinele) (Sophie's son) 143–144, 146, 159n53
Halberstadt, Max 129
Halberstadt, W Ernst (*later* Freud) (Sophie's son) 144, 178, 197

Hamilcar Barca 10–11, 54
Hampstead 179–180, 193, 194; the Berggassen quarter 180
Hampstead Child Therapy Course 199
Hampstead War Nurseries 198–199
Hannibal 10–11, 54
Hart, Bernard 112, 127
Hartmann, Heinz 185
Hartwig, Fritz F O 97, 103n75, 150–151
Hasdrubal 54
Hastilow, Albert 179
Hecks, Leopold 20
Heckscher, Martin 81
Heimann, Paula 169
Heller, Judith Bernays (Freud's niece) 10–11, 76, 146
Herzig, Josef 166
Hill, Christopher 1
Hoare, Samuel 166
Hofmann, Siskind 8
Hogarth Press (publishers) 182–184
Hollitscher, Robert 120n30, 169, 180; cares for Heinz 143; and Freud's death 193; leaves Austria 167
Hotel Bristol 105
Hotel Esplanade 177–179, 189
Hotel National (Vienna) 17, 18, 20, 25n47, 26n68
Hotel Paulez 148
Hotel Russell 112
Hotel Schröder 20
Hotel Stadt Freiberg 67–68
Hrazek, Anna 19, 24n35
Huddersfield, SS 52
Huxley, Aldous 169
Huxley, Thomas Henry 54

James, Edward 174
Jeffcoat, Kate 176
Jones, Ernest 1, 3, 15–16, 35, 88, 96, 99, 105, 112, 120n40, 121n44, 127–128, 130, 163–166, 168–169, 171, 173, 176, 180, 182–183, 185, 193–196, 198, 199, 209n180
Jones, Katherine 195, 203n58; translates *Moses and Monotheism* 173, 182–183
Jones, Loe Kann 198
Joyce, James 89, 99
Jucovy, Milton 194
Judaism 2, 41, 46, 99, 125, 132, 153, 155, 181, 197, 212; Birmingham Hebrew Congregation 90; and cremation 43,

132–133, 145, 149, 150, 195, 196; Manchester Great Synagogue 31, 38n15, 42–43; Manchester Synagogue of British Jews (later named the Manchester Reform Synagogue) 31, 43, 46, 97, 145, 149; Reform tradition 8, 31, 43, 46–47, 97, 98, 132; schlemiel characters 10–11, 54, 107; South Manchester Synagogue 46; tough Jews 10–11, 23n22, 54
Jung, Carl Gustav 15, 52, 106, 108, 110, 116, 130, 141
Jung, Emma 108

Kahlbaum, Siegfried 80
Klein, Melanie 58, 63n45, 174, 200, 204n59
Knopf, Blanche 182–184
Koestler, Arthur 180
Kohut, Heinz 168
Korda, Alexander 169
Kornhauser, Adolf 35
Kris, Ernst 197
Krüll, Marianne 11, 16, 46, 75, 106, 107

Lacassagne, Antoine 187
Laible, Eva 8
Lampl, Hans 185, 195, 209n180
Lampl-de Groot, Jeanne 170, 180, 185, 188, 195, 203n49, 209n180
Lavater, Johann 73
Leftwich, Joseph 195
Leipzig 17–20, 30, 51, 65, 67–68, 83n20, 92, 213
Leisorowitz, Benjamin 20, 27n112
Lévy, Willy (*aka* Peter Lambda) 177
Lockyer, Joseph Norman 54
London Clinic 178–180, 188
Long, Constance 130–131, 136n41
Looney, John Thomas 116
Lotto, David 15
Low, Barbara 195
Lowenstein, Prince Hubertus 173–174, 200
Lün 167, 169, 185, 191
Lyell, Charles 54

Mack Brunswick, Ruth 185, 189–191
Mack, W Henry B 164, 201n6
Malinowski, Bronislaw 173, 200
Manchester *passim*: Ancoats 42, 80; Angel Meadow 31, 33, 47; Ardwick 33, 45, 47, 48n24, 51, 89–90, 151; Chorlton-on-Medlock 45–46, 48n24, 66, 91–92, 97, 149; Deansgate 42, 48n24, 80; Jewry 30–31, 37n5, 38n14; and radicalism 30–31, 37n6; Shudehill 30, 33, 41–43, 45–47, 89, 90, 92, 213
Manchester Hotel 112, 120n38
Maresfield Gardens, No. 2 169, 179, 180, 198
Maresfield Gardens, No. 4 179, 198
Maresfield Gardens, No. 20 98, 174, 176–177, 179, 180, 183–190, 192–194, 200, 215; Anna Freud purchases the freehold 204n81; purchase of 176
marginalisation 1, 3, 11, 16, 17, 54, 70, 138, 189, 215; *see also* duplication, displacement and replacement, dynamic of
Meghnagi, David 108
Meynert, Theodor 73
Micale, Mark 2
Miller, Eric 155–156
Molnar, Michael 17, 39n32, 112, 115, 121n55, 152, 188, 195
mortality 48n24; childhood 42–43, 48n12
Mount Royal Hotel 170, 179
Myers, Maurice 90
Myers, Myer 89–90
Myers, Rebecca 89

Nathansohn, Jacob 11, 20–21, 42
Nathansohn, Sara 11, 20–21, 42
Neumann, Peter 196
Newport, Annie 152–154, 162n139
Nobus, Dany 195, 208n157

Oppenheimer, Max 105, 110, 120n30

Panayi, Panikos 96
Pankhurst, Emmeline 77
Payne, Sylvia 195
Philipp, John 124–125
Philipp, Oscar Isaac 112, 120n40
Phillips, Jacob 90
Phillips, Rabbi Jacob 97, 132, 145
Pichler, Hans 166, 175, 178, 194
Polkinghorne, Lucy (John's great granddaughter) 154
Pötzl, Otto 166

Rank, Otto 118n2, 127
revenants 13–14, 43–44, 45, 58, 155
Rice, Emanuel 46

Richmond, Marion 181
Ritholz, Sophie 188–189, 195, 207n138
Rizzuto, Ana-Maria 146
Rjepa, Franz 19
Rocah, Barbara 15
Rodker, John 176
Rokachová, Babeth Kanner 12
Rokachová, Ferdinand 12
Rolland, Romain 8
Roosevelt, Franklin D 164
Roudinesco, Élisabeth 16, 210n203
Royal Society 105, 166, 174, 200

Sachs, Hanns 168, 183, 185, 187; and *Imago* 176
Samet, Bernard 187
Sandemose, Aksel 186
Sauerwald, Anton 166
Scagnelli, Pauk 155–156, 161n116
Schapiro, Debora 177
Schapiro, Leon 177
Schiller, Friedrich 25n56, 43–44, 56–57, 63n36
Schorske, Carl 2
Schur, Eva 198
Schur, Helene 198
Schur, Max 167, 175, 177, 187–188, 190–195, 198, 200–201, 206n129, 208n157, 209n180
Schur, Peter 198
Schwerdtner, Carl 116
Ségrédakis, Emmanuel 191
Seidler, Lina 124–125
Severn, Elizabeth 185
Shakespeare, William 34, 45, 61, 110, 114–116
Shaw, George Bernard 80
Sheather, Henry 153
Sheather, Louisa 153
Silberstein, Eduard 52–53, 55, 90, 109, 151
Sinclair, Upton 79–80
Smith, Adam 56, 58–59
South Africa 16, 93, 97–98, 111, 113
spas, visits to 11, 24n35, 65, 82, 145, 213
Spencer, Herbert 179
Spielrein, Sabina 15
Stanley de Leon (solicitors) 175
Stekel, Wilhelm 113
Sternberger, Marcel 177
Stiassny, Anna 180
Stiassny, Ernst 180
Strachey, James 63n35, 140, 158n21, 182

Stross, Josephine 167, 193–195, 198–199, 201
Sylwan, Barbro 95

Tagore, Rabindranath 55
Taylor, John William 164, 201n6
Thomas Cook & Son 116–117, 152, 161n124, 212
Thomson, William (*later* Lord Kelvin) 54
Thorner, Hans 169
Tischler, Moritz 187, 206n129
Tögel, Christfried 63n36, 82, 207n144
Trotter, Wilfred 105, 112, 119n2, 166, 187
Tuckey, Charles Lloyd 130
Twain, Mark 181
Tyndall, John 54
Tysmenitz 8, 12, 18, 32

von Demel, Hans
von Moltke, Helmuth 124

Wainwright, Richard B 167
Wakeling, Agnes Annie Kate (John's stepdaughter) 152–153, 162n139
Wakeling, Frederick W 153, 162n139
Waldinger, Beatrice Rose 167–168
Waldinger, Ernst 167–168
Weich, Osias 35
Weiss, Edoardo 110
Weissen Ross Gasthof 20
Weizmann, Chaim 169, 173, 200
Welker, Volker 180
Welldon, James 80
Wells, H G 169, 174, 184, 186–187, 192, 194, 197, 199, 200
Whitebook, Joel 11–12
Whyte, Lancelot 1
Wiley, John C 164, 166
Wiley, Monique 164
Williams, Bill 46, 55
Wilson, Joseph 117
Winnicott, Donald W 55–56, 200
Woolf, Leonard 182, 184, 185–186
Woolf, Virginia 1, 169, 185–186, 194

Yahuda, Abraham S 173, 195
Young-Bruehl, Elisabeth 3

Zeisler & Bretholz 18–19, 22, 27n93
Zweig, Arnold 168, 173, 185
Zweig, Stefan 169, 174–175, 177, 195–197, 200, 209n184

For Product Safety Concerns and Information please contact our EU
representative GPSR@taylorandfrancis.com
Taylor & Francis Verlag GmbH, Kaufingerstraße 24, 80331 München, Germany

www.ingramcontent.com/pod-product-compliance
Lightning Source LLC
Chambersburg PA
CBHW050532300426
44113CB00012B/2054